Covenant & Polity in Biblical Israel

Daniel J. Elazar

Covenant & Polity in Biblical Israel

BIBLICAL FOUNDATIONS & JEWISH EXPRESSIONS

Volume I
of the Covenant Tradition in Politics

Transaction Publishers
New Brunswick (U.S.A.) and London (U.K.)

Preparation of this book for publication was made possible through the Milken Library of Jewish Public Affairs, funded by the Foundations of the Milken Families.

This book is printed on acid-free paper that meets the American National Standard for Permanence of Paper for Printed Library Materials.

Library of Congress Catalog Number: 93-37985
ISBN: 1-56000-151-8
Printed in the United States of America

Library of Congress Cataloging-in-Publication Data

Elazar, Daniel Judah.
    Covenant and polity in Biblical Israel : Biblical foundations and Jewish expressions / Daniel J. Elazar.
        p. cm. — (The Milken library of Jewish public affairs) (The Covenant tradition in politics ; v. 1)
    Includes bibliographical references and index.
    ISBN 1-56000-151-8
    1. Covenants—Biblical teaching.   2. Bible. O.T.—Criticism, interpretation, etc.   3. Politics in the Bible.   4. Covenants—Religious aspects—Judaism.   5. Judaism and politics.   I. Title.   II. Series.   III. Series: Elazar, Daniel Judah. Covenant tradition in politics ; v. 1.
    BL65.P7E43   1994 vol. 1
    320'.01'1 s—dc20   93-37985
    [296.3'877'0901]   CIP
                                                                  r93

To the memory of my father

אברהם בן-יהודה אלעזר תנצב"ה

Albert Elazar

who was born in the Jerusalem of the Ottoman Empire and died in
Jerusalem, the capital of the reborn State of Israel, whose
greatness lay in the way in which he saw all Jews as *bnai
brit* and all humans of good will as at least potential *baalei
brit* and how he strove to bring each group together to fulfill
its fullest potential in the finest Jewish and American
traditions of covenant.

*I will bring you to the wilderness of the peoples and there will
I plead with you face to face. Just as I pleaded with your
fathers in the wilderness of the land of Egypt, so will I plead
with you, saith the Lord God. I will cause you to pass under the
rod [of My authority] and will bring you into the tradition
(bond) of the covenant.*

—Ezekiel 20:35-37

*Speak not of the Law of nature
As if there were a mindless moral nature
Built into matter proper;
For the universe of matter has no moral nature
Choosing neither good nor evil in existence
But forcing man to be the moral teacher.*

*Speak not of the Law of Nature
As if every man by his very nature
Knows what is right and proper;
For man we know, when living just in nature
Is prone to follow paths of least resistance.
To live in barbarous folly or as a simple creature.*

*What then is to be said of Laws of Nature?
Speak, rather, of fundamental law
Built somehow into the world's foundation
By the Architect of All Creation
Who brings man into law beyond his nature
Through covenant between man and his Maker.*

*God enters this world through emanation,
Creating by the spheres both man and nature
In four worlds—the higher and the lower.
Then stepping back from His grand creation
He covenants with both man and nature
Making each free but within limitation
Of His sovereign will and His dominion,
Each with its sphere yet sharing minions.*

*The Sovereign of the Universe established
His order and His law for man and nature
Through covenant in which we stand as partners
Bound to His law yet free in gracious stature
To choose the way that leads to human nurture
Of that part of man reflecting God's own nature.*

Contents

Part III—The Classic Biblical Utopia

Preface

Sometime during the period when I was completing high school and beginning university I discovered the covenantal basis of Judaism and the Jewish people, perhaps the best kept secret of my otherwise rather good Jewish education. During the next several years, my university studies of history brought me face to face with the covenantal basis of Reformed Protestant Christianity and its derivation from the same biblical tradition. It was also at that time that my study of American government led me to understand how the American polity was founded on that Reformed Protestant covenantal tradition in its Puritan expression and in its secularized Lockean form.

By the end of the 1950s, the convergence of these various lines of exploration brought me to a recognition that covenant was a truly seminal concept in Western civilization and stimulated me to begin what has been a decades-long exploration of the covenant tradition in the Western world, especially in its political dimensions. In the interim I have published several books and numerous articles on the subject, have organized two continuing research workshops, in Israel and the United States, and quite a few conferences and seminars in both countries to further the exploration and to learn from others, as I have, to my immense benefit. After two decades of systematic exploration I felt the need for a more comprehensive study of the covenant tradition in Western politics than any I had thus far undertaken.

While I felt, and still feel, inadequate to the task, a decade ago I resolved to begin it. This work is the result. After devoting so many years to it I feel no less inadequate with the product in hand. I am confident that a better scholar could have produced a better result, and that my poor effort is unworthy of the subject it treats. Nevertheless, I submit it to the reading public for what it is.

It goes without saying that the end product is entirely my own. At the same time I wish to express my gratitude to all those who assisted me in this project. My initial education came from a group of Jewish scholar-theologians whose work in the 1950s restored covenant to its rightful place in Jewish thought: Eugene B. Borowitz, Monford Harris, Jacob J. Petuchovoski, and Arnold Jacob Wolf. While I learned from them initially through their writings, all of them subsequently became friends as well as teachers.

I was not so privileged with regard to Andrew J. McLaughlin, whose writings introduced me to the connections between the covenant tradition and the American founding. While I studied at the University of Chicago, the institution at which he taught for so many years, I did so many years after he had passed on. Nevertheless, I consider him my premier mentor in this sphere. Later I discovered that I was indeed following in his tradition of political science and am pleased to acknowledge that fact, since by now I am convinced that our common rootedness in the covenantal view of politics makes that so.

I am equally grateful to my good friend Harold Fisch, whose writings brought me to see from whence emerged these two great expressions of covenant. Professor Fisch also was of great assistance through the Kotler Institute for Judaism and Contemporary Thought, which he founded at Bar-Ilan and which he put at my disposal for the organization of an initial conference on the subject.

As my exploration into covenant expanded, the inadequacy of my knowledge became increasingly apparent to me. In an effort to overcome those inadequacies I organized the Workshop in the Covenant Idea and the Jewish Political Tradition at Bar-Ilan University in 1975 through the Senator N.M. Paterson Chair in Intergovernmental Relations in the Department of Political Studies and the Center for Jewish Community Studies, now part of the Jerusalem Center for Public Affairs. Funding for that workshop came principally from Bar-Ilan University sources, for which I am duly grateful, and from funds provided by the president of the university, Professor Emanuel Rackman, who was also a participant in the workshop. I owe a special debt to Meir Kassirer, coordinator of the workshop, who has been of great assistance over the years and whom I count among my friends.

I am indebted to all my colleagues who participated in and contributed to these workshops, most especially Ella Belfer, Lawrence V. Berman, Gerald Blidstein, Gershon Cohen, Stuart A. Cohen, Yoel Cohen, Eliezer Don-Yehiya, Menachem Elon, Harold Fisch, Gordon M. Freeman, Marc Galanter, Ruth Gil, Shlomo Dov Goitein, Steven Goldstein,

Moshe Greenberg, Ilan Greilsammer, David Hartman, Yosef Lanier, Sam Lehman-Wilzig, Charles S. Liebman, Leah Bornstein Makovsky, Peter Y. Medding, Avraham Melamed, Meir Nitzan, Emanuel Rackman, Yaakov Reuveny, Neal Riemer, Yechiel Rosen, Pinchas Rosenblit, Mordechai Rotenberg, Shmuel Sandler, Eliezer Schweid, Dan V. Segre, Martin Sicker, Bernard Susser, Moshe Weinfeld, and Aaron Wildavsky.

A year later I organized a similar workshop in covenant and politics through the Center for the Study of Federalism at Temple University in the United States. That workshop received its principal support from the National Endowment for the Humanities and also from the American Jewish Committee, the Earhart Foundation, and the United Church of Christ. It brought together several dozen leading scholars in the United States and abroad and had over two hundred corresponding scholars on its list. I owe much to the participants in workshop meetings and conferences, particularly to my close colleague and friend Vincent Ostrom, who built a bridge between my historically oriented investigations and the more rigorous methodologies of contemporary political theory. Other scholars to whom I owe a debt of gratitude include J. Wayne Baker, James D. Bratt, Harold Fisch, Gordon M. Freeman, Vernon L. Greene, J. David Greenstone, Charles Hyneman, John Kincaid, Franklin Littell, Donald S. Lutz, Alexandre Marc, Charles S. McCoy, Stuart D. McLean, John Peacock, W. Stanford Reid, Neil Reimer, Rozann Rothman, Filippo Sabetti, Stephen L. Schechter, Mary Lyndon Shanley, Rowland A. Sherrill, James W. Skillen, John F.A. Taylor, and James B. Torrance.

The Fellows of the Center for the Study of Federalism were also very helpful in this effort, as in all my others of similar character: John Kincaid, first my student, then my colleague and always my friend, undertook responsibility first as coordinator and then as co-director of the Philadelphia Covenant Workshop. The workshop initially brought me into contact with Donald Lutz, who has taught me so much about the American experience. Stephen L. Schechter and Ellis Katz were active members of the workshop inner circle, while Benjamin Schuster, program director of the center at the initial stages of the work, was of invaluable assistance.

Support for the workshop and connected conferences and colloquia came principally from the National Endowment for the Humanities and secondarily from the American Jewish Committee, the International

Association of Centers for Federal Studies, Liberty Fund, the Scaife Foundation, and the United Church of Christ. I am grateful to them all.

My seemingly interminable effort to produce this book has been supported from the beginning by the Earhart Foundation of Ann Arbor, Michigan. I owe them an immeasurable debt of gratitude for enabling me to carry on this work, which has brought me in contact with civilizations and new societies across the length and breadth of the globe and the ideas and actions spawned within them.

In the course of my work I have been assisted by a string of excellent research assistants in Israel, including Ruth Gil, Ellen Friedlander, Kirk Preuss, Rina Edelstein; and in the United States, including Alexis Samryk, Gail Charette, Joseph Marbach, Rasheeda Didi, Steven D'Agguano, and Paul Neal.

Special thanks are due to Clara Feldman, who shared responsibility for the functioning of the Bar-Ilan Workshop, and Sarah Mayer, who worked with me for several years on this project and stimulated me enormously. Mark Ami-El has done yeoman work in preparing the manuscript of this book for publication.

A project of the magnitude of this one requires considerable support from many sources, but no support is more extensive or more critical than that provided by one's own family. My wife Harriet and my children were everything that one could possibly expect in this connection and even more, making it possible for me to live and work in a way most conducive to beginning this undertaking, staying with it, and finally bringing it to a proper conclusion. My love for them is inexpressible as is my gratitude.

Introduction

No one seriously immersed in the Jewish and Christian traditions has escaped the theological impact of the covenant idea. Covenant was once the subject of so many theological treatises that now it sometimes seems as if there is little new to be said about it. On the other hand, covenant is less a theological concept than a theo-political one. The word itself is used so frequently in the English language that it has become a mere commonplace term, if not quite like *freedom* and *democracy,* then certainly like *republic* and *constitution.* Even so, far too little has been written about covenant as a factor in political affairs.

Politically, a covenant involves a coming together (con-gregation) of basically equal humans who consent with one other through a morally binding pact supported by a transcendant power, establishing with the partners a new framework or setting them on the road to a new task that can only be dissolved by mutual agreement of all the parties to it.

The covenants of the Bible are the founding covenants of Western civilization. Perforce, they have to do with God. They have their beginnings in the need to establish clear and binding relationships between God and humans and among humans, relationships that must be understood as being political far more than theological in character, designed to establish lines of authority, distributions of power, bodies politic, and systems of law. It is indeed the genius of the idea and its biblical source that it seeks both to legitimize political life and to direct it into the right paths; to use theo-political relationships to build a bridge between heaven and earth—and there is nothing more earthly than politics even in its highest form—without letting either swallow up the other.

The covenant idea has within it the seeds of modern constitutionalism in that it emphasizes the mutually accepted limitations on the power of all parties to it, a limitation not inherent in nature but involving willed concessions. This idea of limiting power is of first importance in the biblical worldview and for humanity as a whole since it helps explain why an omnipotent God does not exercise His omnipotence in the affairs of humans. In covenanting with humans, God at least partially withdraws from controlling their lives. He offers humans freedom under the terms of the covenant, retaining the covenantal authority to reward or punish the consequences of that freedom at some future date. By the same token, the humans who bind themselves through the covenant accept its limits in Puritan terms, abandoning natural for federal liberty in order to live up to the terms of their covenants. Beyond that, the leaders of the people are limited in their governmental powers to serving the people under the terms of the covenant. Thus the idea of constitutional or limited government is derived from the idea of covenant.

Covenant as a theo-political concept is characterized by a very strong measure of realism. This recognition of the need to limit the exercise of power is one example of this. It also recognizes the distinction between those who are bound by the covenant and those who are not. At the same time it makes provisions for appropriate linkages between those so bound and others who do not see themselves as covenant bound, granted of a different order than covenantal linkages, but designed to keep the peace in the world in the face of the realities of conflicting human interests, needs and demands. In this book we are concerned with the political use of the idea of covenant, the tradition that has adhered to that idea, and the political arrangements that flow from it.

In more secular terms, the task of politics is not simply to construct civil societies compatible with human nature but to help people make the most of their potential by creating conditions and opportunities for leading the best possible lives. As Aristotle observed: people form political associations not only to maintain life but to achieve the good life.

II

Politics has two faces. One is the face of *power*; the other is the face of *justice*. Politics, as the pursuit and organization of power, is concerned (in the words of Harold Lasswell) with "who gets what, when and how." However, politics is equally a matter of justice, or the determination of who *should* get what, when and how—and why. Power is the means by which people organize themselves and shape their environment in order to live. Justice offers the guidelines for using power in order to live well.

Politics cannot be understood without reference to both faces. Without understanding a polity's conception of justice, or who should have power, one cannot understand clearly why certain people or groups get certain rewards, at certain times, in certain ways. On the other hand, one cannot focus properly on the pursuit of justice without also understanding the realities of the distribution of power. Both elements are present in all political questions, mutually influencing each other.

The need to pursue justice through a politics set on the right path is as real in a secular age as in a religious one. The true essence of *realpolitik* is the understanding that just as politics cannot avoid the realities of human relationships and power, it cannot be detached from the pursuit of justice and the paths of morality either. Machiavellian methods are effective only in the short run simply because in the long run, everyone involved in political affairs comes to understand the use of those methods. Those who cannot use them, leave the political arena, turning it over to those who can, who then proceed to transform that arena into a jungle, in which every man's hand is raised against every other man's as each tries to use the political methods that the master suggested to his prince—returning to what seventeenth- and eighteenth-century political theorists referred to as the state of nature with the chaos and insecurity which that entails. Realistically, Machiavellian methods work best in situations where they are unexpected; that is to say, where there already exists a connection between politics and a sense of morally obligatory limitations on political behavior, which, of course, those methods then subvert.

The collapse of a shared moral understanding inevitably leads to a collapse of the rules of the game. We are witness to just such a collapse in many polities in our time, for precisely that reason, a collapse which has brought in its train the present crisis of humankind. It is the discovery of a proper moral base or foundation, and its pursuit in such a way that recognizes the realities of power that is essential for a good politics. That is what the conceptual system rooted in covenant is all about. The rules of the game for some may have emerged originally through an evolutionary process to be accepted by those bound by them as a matter of course. Once disrupted, however, they can only be restored by consent, that is to say, through covenanting.

Through covenant, the two faces of politics, power and justice, are linked to become effective both morally and operationally. In the course of this book, I will suggest that covenant is by far the best source for developing a proper moral understanding and proper moral path in politics, that it is, indeed, the way to achieve a general public commitment to the political institutions required for the good life and to emerge from the Machiavellian jungle as free, morally responsible people. Perhaps such covenants may be civil rather than theo-political in character; that is still a question facing humanity. The idea of a civil covenant is one of the most important contributions of the last previous great revival of the covenant idea, the period from the sixteenth through the eighteenth centuries, the crucible that led to the emergence of modern democracy. The range of its possibilities was tested in the modern epoch and, by itself, found very useful but wanting. So, too, with the theo-political covenants of the past.

The genius of the covenant idea does not rest upon its philosophic explication although such explication has much to contribute for a finer understanding of 'that idea.' While ideas have their own subtle influence on people, their influence grows exponentially if they are embodied in a tradition—in the case of the covenant idea, a political tradition that continues from generation to generation. Such a tradition has both visible and invisible, conscious and subconscious manifestations. Its visible ones are easily traced, but the greatest part of its impact is in its invisible ones, those that are part of the substructure of the society, that constitute its culture, in this case political culture. To the extent that the covenant idea is mediated through certain political traditions, to become part of the political culture, it has become second nature to those peoples influenced by it.

III

What are the components of a political tradition? First of all, it is a mode of thinking and body of thoughts shared by members of a particular body politic, especially those in any way involved in politics. In order to think about political things, they must have a political vocabulary—a set of terms that, individually and in relation to one another, offer ways to delineate and express political meaning. Such terms constitute a political vocabulary that represents the "program" through which people consider political things. The key words in any political vocabulary are what Kadushin has referred to as value concepts, that is to say, terms whose precise definition may be difficult or well nigh impossible, but which are understood to have a common core meaning within a particular culture.[1]

A political tradition begins with the founding of the body politic and revolves around certain fundamental principles and the relations—including the tensions—between them, which already are part of the founding. Every body politic is founded on its own principles of organization, power and authority relationships, and fundamental tensions, explicit or implicit. The latter are those that are "present at the creation" of the body politic and that have to be bridged in order for the body politic to come into existence. Because they are only bridged but not resolved, they are built into the very fabric of the body politic, which must reconcile them anew in every generation as long as the body politic exists in the same form. It is a task of the political tradition to keep those principles, relationships, and tensions alive and operational as the body politic confronts changing situations and circumstances.

The political tradition is kept alive by the chain of political leaders and thinkers who utilize that vocabulary to undertake or explain the political acts that shape and direct the body politic. In the course of time, a tradition becomes embodied in certain basic texts that reflect the political ideas of a particular body politic, its political vocabulary, and celebrate the figures, events, and concepts that most embody the tradition. In that sense, the visible dimensions of a tradition sooner or later come to involve the interaction of texts and behavior in dealing with the internal and external influences on the body politic.

In sum, a tradition is a major integrative force within the body politic. Some polities rely on tradition more than others for integration. Covenanted polities are particularly in need of an appropriate political tradition for their integration. In every case they are covenanted polities because their political tradition rests upon the covenant idea and a covenantal political culture.

This book is an exploration of the original covenant tradition, explicating its ideas through living examples of their application, examining the ways in which that idea and its derivatives penetrated and permeated, shaped, or gave rise to particular political systems, institutions, and behavior. These indeed are the elements of politics that count, through which ideas are made meaningful and real. Thus, it is simultaneously the statement of a thesis, its documentation through case studies, and something of a guide for those who would learn how to conduct political life according to the covenant tradition.

Understanding covenant as a seminal political concept offers us a way to better understand politics as a whole. Indeed, through the covenant idea we can begin to develop a field theory of political science. Let us begin by defining the subject matter of political science, namely, the relationship between power and justice in organized human relationships, particularly those of political society or the polity. The elements of such a field theory include the foundations of political life, which are: biological, psychological, and cultural. All human life, including its political dimension, somehow is anchored in the biological basis of the human species, which, in turn, has various manifestations, psychological and cultural. The former is individual and the latter is collective. Culture is the second nature of humanity, as it were—so much so that the line between biology and culture is indistinct. The two flow into one another to create what the Bible very accurately describes as *derekh* or "way." All things and creatures, including humans, have their own respective ways. In humans, these ways represent syntheses of nature and culture. Both nature and culture exist without the need to be consciously understood, but humans are self-conscious about them, and thus seek to understand and interpret them through ideas, hence the foundation of human understanding in its various branches and disciplines. In our case, we seek political understanding, which, when systematized, leads to political science.

More than anything else, cultures, systems, and humans informed by the covenantal perspective are committed to a way of thinking and conduct that enable them to live free while being bound together in appropriate relationships, to preserve their own integrities while sharing in a common whole, and to pursue both the necessities of human existence and the desiderata of moral response in some reasonable balance. There is a dialectic tension between each of these dualities, which adds the requisite dynamic dimension to covenant-based societies, one that makes such societies covenant-*informed* as well as covenant-based. This dialectic tension is an integral element in covenantal systems, one which provides such systems with the necessary self-corrective mechanisms to keep them in reasonable balance over the long haul, at least so long as covenantal principles continue to inform and shape the polities concerned.

This is not to suggest that all of human life is informed by covenant. As we will discuss below, there are hierarchical and organic ideas and systems that compete with covenantal ones and that have shaped very substantial segments of the human race. Presumably, they, too, can be penetrated to achieve better understanding of human behavior.

At the same time, the extent to which covenantal relationships are spread among humans is an open question. It is possible to understand covenantal relationships as the property of a rather exclusive segment of the human race, those who have achieved that level of equality and social cooperation through some measure of conscious understanding and semi or subconscious behavior. It is also possible to see covenantal behavior as a human psychological necessity and, hence, extremely widespread, even within otherwise hierarchical and organic systems, at least in certain respects. Of course there are positions between these two extremes.

We must approach the subject aware of two realities: (1) that partisans of each worldview, such as the Bible in the matter of covenant or Greek philosophy in the matter of organic development, will claim that it is the most natural and that where it does not exist, it is being artificially prevented from being; and (2) reality suggests that there are hierarchical, organic, and covenantal socio-political arrangements in the world, and combinations of the three. This writer takes a moderate position, holding that there is a somewhat exclusive club of those peoples and polities consisting of that segment of the human race that is truly immersed in the covenantal way of life, that in some ways all human beings have some psychological propensity to contractual relationships, that is to say, transactional ones based upon mutual agreement, which can include a covenantal dimension, and that there are gradations of covenantalism to be found in between.

IV

Since covenants are grounded in moral commitment, they also provide a basis and a means for placing all of us under judgment. That is to say, a proper covenant not only offers humans the right path or way but provides means for the self-same humans to judge and be judged as to how well they stay on that path or maintain that way. Given human propensities to stray from the right path, no human system and especially no political system can afford not to be under judgment.

The covenant relationship is to social and political life what the I-Thou relationship is to personal life. Through covenants humans are enabled to enter into dialogue and are given (or themselves create) a framework for dialogue. The ties of covenant are the concretization of the I-Thou relationship, which, when addressed to God, makes man holy and, when addressed to one's fellows, makes men human. As the Bible itself makes clear, the covenantal bonds transform a mystical union into a real one, making life possible in an all-too-real world and, at the same time, creating the possibilities for a whole new realm of what has been called "normal mysticism," or the fusion of the highest goals of the mystics' quest with the demands of everyday living. The progress of civilization can be traced as corresponding to the periods in human history when the historical vanguard has recognized the covenant idea and sought to concretely apply it to the building of human, social, and political relationships.

We shall see that in its biblical origins, covenant (*brit* in Hebrew) is related to the way or path, that is to say to the bio-cultural basis of behavior, both concretizing and modifying it. The Bible emphasizes their interaction and that it is the task of biology and culture to bound, channel, and modify *derekh*. Modern secularism has come to emphasize path over covenant. It has gone even further to abandon path for nature (as understood by moderns), implying that what is biological is all, and that what is cultural—not to speak of covenantal—while "real" is usually an interference with natural processes unless it is constantly reformed to be brought into harmony with nature as humans understand it at any particular time. Even in considering nature, it has rejected higher nature on behalf of lower. The result, as anyone who understands the teachings of covenant in relation to human experience would have forecast, opens the door to the return of the human race to the Hobbesian state of nature, different only in that it is not simply the war of all against all but the exploitation of all by all—Buber's jungle alongside that of Hobbes. Even as the world community of states moves toward some kind of order, the social fabric of those states is being rent by an unrestrained self-centeredness that is the antithesis of the covenantal way. Restoration of the covenant tradition in an appropriately contemporary way may help serve as a means of rescuing humankind from what is rapidly becoming its most desperate predicament, namely the inability to escape the egoism of the Hobbesian jungle.

V

This study is divided into three volumes. The first, *Covenant and Polity in Biblical Israel: Biblical Foundations and Jewish Expressions*, consists of an in-depth, if necessarily selective, exploration of the biblical sources of the covenant tradition, its development in Scripture, and subsequently in Jewish history and thought. Volume 2, *Commonwealth: The Western Covenantal Tradition from Christian Separation to Protestant Reformation,* examines the Christian adaptation of the biblical tradition, its integration with the traditions of the tribal oath societies of Northern Europe, the perforce limited medieval expressions of that synthesis, and the revival of covenant as the architectonic principle of the Protestant Reformation. It also examines covenant and hierarchy in Islam and other premodern polities. Volume 3, *Constitutionalism: Modern Covenants and the New Science of Politics,* examines the progressive secularization of the covenant idea in the seventeenth and eighteenth centuries and its application through principles of constitutionalism and federalism to the building of new societies in the New World and the efforts to reconstitute old societies in Europe, and concludes with a general analysis of the dynamics of covenant and the possible future role of the covenant tradition in the postmodern world.

This work, despite its scope, cannot trace all the human connections that show the transmission of covenant ideas and ways. Consequently, it seeks to highlight those critical elements that shaped history and civilization, particularly in the Western world. In a sense it is also a history of, first, the *westering* (an American pioneer term for moving westward with the frontier) of covenant and then its universalization in the politics of constitutional democratic republicanism.

Ideally, it is the aim of this work not only to trace the interconnections between ideas, culture, institutions, and behavior, but between peoples and generations as well, to follow the path of the covenant idea and covenantal cultures and behavior in time and space. This is a daunting task requiring dozens of monographic studies not yet undertaken and probably can never be done because of the great gaps in the historical data available. For example, in the history of ancient southwest Asia and adjacent regions, by far the most substantial record we have is the Bible, much of which is not corroborated by any other source in regard to the matters under discussion here.

The scriptural account, while full of fascinating behavioral details that give us great insight into covenantal ideas, culture, institutions, and behavior, useful in fostering our understanding of other covenantal situations in other times and climes, is not comprehensive history but rather a series of moral case studies designed for purposes other than illustrating the issues under consideration here. By and large, biblical accounts are not otherwise documented in other available sources. However, where they are, they are confirmed in almost every case, thereby strengthening confidence in their overall accuracy. Thus, we also can benefit from the documents of other ancient west Asian civilizations discovered since the last century.[2] In recent years archeologists have discovered records from various ancient southwest Asian archives that testify to the existence of vassal treaties in one form or another and modified covenantal elements among peoples adjacent to ancient Israel, but the only record we have of a fully covenantal civilization is that of ancient Israel as portrayed in Scripture.

History in the more conventional sense begins with the Greeks, more or less at the end of the First Jewish Commonwealth in the fifth and sixth centuries B.C.E. Greek histories focus on heroic actions and events. They give us the political and military histories of the Greek Leagues, the most important of which were in Asia Minor, also a part of southwest Asia—a point often ignored or forgotten. But again, their purpose is not to trace connections. There, too, we have only those limited written records. Documentation is lacking and not likely to be found. Not only that but the survival of Greek philosophic works that are emphatically noncovenantal has strongly influenced our understanding of Greek political life.[3]

There is a greater variety of sources from the Hellenistic and Roman periods, when a particular brand of political compacting was developed. Careful study of those materials in light of the prior Greek and biblical sources helps to reveal which cultures were more covenantally oriented and which were not, and helps us begin to trace the macro connections, but we are still at a loss when it comes to the micro. We can continue the macro kind of tracing through medieval Europe. The situation improves considerably with the coming of the Renaissance and the Reformation, which created more awareness of issues of ideas, culture, and behavior. Indeed this was one of the great contributions of both eras to the forging of the modern epoch. They also opened an era of better and more comprehensive record keeping. Indeed, it can be said that those two great historical events brought a sea change to historiography, for the first time making it possible to trace historical connections in a more comprehensive manner.

From that point on the problem is increasingly one of information overload, replacing the fragmented nature of available information in earlier epochs. So, for example, we can trace lines of intellectual influence in the Reformation, that is to say, who studied with whom and where, a very important addition to understanding the flow of ideas and even culture, but more limited on the behavioral side. It has been too easy for historians to treat the great chain of thought as if it were equally a chain of action. That is a pitfall that must be avoided.

Thus, for example, the seventeenth-century European political philosophers were given much more credit for shaping the British colonies in North America and subsequently the United States of America, than they deserved. We now know that, having explored the less philosophically glitzy manifestations of Reformed Protestant, especially Puritan, patterns of thought and behavior as manifested in British North America most especially as a result of the Puritan Great Awakening in England during the first half of the seventeenth century. The recovery of the true character of that line of development over the last forty years or so has not only much enriched our understanding of American beginnings but also has demonstrated what it is possible to do when the records are available for study. But what has been done for American history has not been done for any other.[4]

It seems that the only possibilities for tracing a set of connections from the ancient world to the present lies within those religious, philosophic, and legal writings that refer to prior sources or where prior sources can be identified. Jewish texts, in particular, provide sufficient records to trace intellectual connections rather fully for two thousand years, partially for another five hundred, and then another five hundred to one thousand years before that. The Hebrew multivolume study, *Etz Haim* (the Tree of Life), prepared in our times by Rafael Halperin, traces the line of teaching and *halakhic* authority from the earliest times to the present through the generations.[5] It is an amazing feat that is extremely valuable in the study of the history of Jewish ideas including constitutional matters. It may be possible to do similar tracings in philosophy. In these volumes, while we have to rely upon work already done in most cases, we will do the best we can to trace these patterns with all due awareness of the limitations of our data.

VI

The biblical discussion of the government of ancient Israel stands at the very beginning of Western political life and thought just as the political experience of ancient Israel as recounted in the Bible laid the foundations of the Jewish political tradition in all its aspects. The Bible's concern with teaching humans the right way to live in this world gives the Scriptural political dimension particular importance. The highly social character of biblical concern with achieving the good life leads to its emphasis on the good commonwealth. The biblical account of the history of the Israelites can be seen in that light.[6]

The biblical account of the origins of the Jewish people reflects a blend of kinship and consent that generates a special political culture and a variety of institutions at home in it. A family of tribes becomes a nation by consenting to a common covenant with God and with each other, out of which flow the principles and practices of religious life and political organization that have animated the Jews as a corporate entity ever since.[7]

The record of that experience represents the oldest stratum in Western political thought and, since the record is derived very directly from the Israelites' experience, the latter is in itself an important factor in the development of Western political institutions.[8] If this is more difficult to perceive today than it was in Hobbes's, Spinoza's, and Locke's time, it is because the study of the political experience of ancient Israel has been generally neglected in the centuries since the Reformed Protestant theologians and state builders and the political philosophers of the sixteenth and seventeenth centuries paid serious attention to it in shaping the political views of the moderns who were to reject Scripture as authoritative.[9]

Biblical political ideas are expressed through the description of the institutions, events, and prophesies connected with the government of ancient Israel. Less formally articulated than Greek political thought, the biblical political teaching must be discovered in the same manner that all biblical knowledge must emerge, by careful examination and analysis of the text with careful attention to recurring words and patterns and the reconciliation of apparent contradictions.

The Bible understands that in order to impart moral lessons, empathy must be generated in the reader. Some people are able to learn moral lessons from more abstract writing but most must identify with and feel the human dimension. This is, of course, the rationale for good history or good fiction as against philosophy and social science, which lack that dimension. Empathy is gained by telling a good story; hence, the moral case studies in the Bible consist of a series of very good tales that draw people in to identify with the characters.[10] Understanding the method necessary to approach the subject, it is indeed possible to learn much about the theory and practice of government in ancient Israel both in terms of the way in which the Israelites governed themselves and in terms of their response to the great questions of politics, which they confronted in their unique way, as every people must.

The Bible does not offer us a philosophically systematic presentation of its political theory or of the workings of particular political institutions. Rather, the theory must be derived inductively from the biblical discussion of the political history and hopes of the Israelites and from biblical critiques of institutions not fully described. Contemporary understanding of biblical political ideas and institutions rests in great measure on our expanded understanding of the political institutions in the ancient Near East as a whole, particularly those of the civilizations of the Fertile Crescent.

Despite all that we have learned about the biblical period in the past century from various sources, principally archeological, we still must rely on the Bible for almost all of what we know about human behavior in ancient Israel, especially political behavior. Archeology corroborates aspects of the biblical account but can do no more. Thus, we cannot say with certainty how the Israelites acquired a covenantal political culture, the institutions to accompany it, and the patterns of behavior that made those institutions work, except through what is available in the biblical account.[11]

Given the problematics of the biblical account for historians, this means we can say very little about what came first and what came last, what was divine and what was human, but the Bible does give us a rather complete sense of the covenantal dimension of Israelite life—cultural, ideological, institutional, and behavioral—and makes a very convincing case for the extraordinary degree in which the Israelite polity and the society it shaped was thoroughly covenantal. Moreover, the subsequent behavior of Jews as a people and as individuals very much reinforces what we learn from the Bible. Some powerful agency had worked to form a thoroughly covenantal people and thoroughly covenantal individuals who have persisted in their culture and ways throughout an extraordinary history under the most adverse conditions. The Bible offers us a set of perceptions and examples of how a covenantal people should act. That, too, is evidence that speaks for itself.

Advances in the study of the history and life of the ancient Near East made during the past two generations have enabled us to better understand the Bible in its political dimension as well as in so many others. Modern biblical scholarship has drawn on that knowledge to raise many questions about the authorship of the Bible and compilation of the biblical text. Approaching Scripture for contemporary scholars cannot be a matter of simple faith in the text as received. With that in mind, here we will look at the Bible as a whole—a comprehensive political teaching, however formed, written, edited, or compiled, one which deserves careful, indeed the most careful, consideration.

Notes

1. Max Kadushin, *Organic Thinking* (New York: Jewish Theological Seminary, 1938) and *The Rabbinic Mind* (New York: Jewish Theological Seminary, 1952).
2. Chaim I. Bermant, *Ebla: A Revelation in Archaeology* (New York: Times Books, 1979); Herbert B. Huffmon, "Prophecy in the Mari Latters," and Anson F. Rainey, "The Kingdom of Ugarit," in Edward F. Campbell, Jr. and David Noel Friedman, eds., *The Biblical Archaeologist Reader*, vol. 3 (New York: Doubleday, 1970); Harry M. Orlinsky, *Understanding the Bible Through History and Archaeology* (New York: Ktav, 1972).
3. Leo Strauss and Joseph Cropsey, eds., *History of Political Philosophy* (Chicago: University of Chicago Press, 1987).
4. Andrew McLaughlin, *The Foundations of American Constitutionalism* (Greenwich, CT: Fawcett, 1961); Perry Miller, ed., *The American Puritans* (New York: Doubleday Anchor Books, 1956), and *The New England Mind: The Seventeenth Century* (Cambridge: Harvard University Press, 1963); Donald Lutz, "From Covenant to Constitution," *Publius* 10, no. 4 (Fall 1980), and "The Theory of Consent in the Early State Constitutions," *Publius* 9, no. 2 (Spring 1979).
5. Rafael Halperin, *Etz Haim*, 7 vols. (Tel Aviv: Hekdesh Ruah Ya'akov, 1978).
6. See, for example, Robert Gordis, "Democratic Origins in Ancient Israel—the Biblical Edah," in *The Alexander Marx Jubilee Volume* (New York: Jewish Theological Seminary, 1950); Martin Noth, *The History of Israel* (New York: Harper and Row, 1958); G. E. Mendenhall, "Ancient Oriental and Biblical Law," *Biblical Archeologist* 17, no. 2 (1954): 26-46; C. Umhau Wolf, "Terminology of Israel's Tribal Organization," *Journal of Biblical Literature* 65 (1946); Norman Gottwald, *All the Kingdoms of the Earth* (New York: Harper and Row, 1964); N. H. Snaith, "The Covenant-Love of God," in *The Distinctive Ideas of the Old Testament* (New York: Schocken, 1964), pp. 94-127.
7. See Daniel J. Elazar, "Kinship and Consent in the Jewish Community: Patterns of Continuity in Jewish Communal Life," *Tradition* 14, no. 4 (Fall 1974): 63-79; "Covenant as the Basis of the Jewish Political Tradition," in *Kinship and Consent: The Jewish Political Tradition and Its Contemporary Uses*, ed. Daniel J. Elazar (Ramat Gan: Turtledove, 1981); and Daniel J. Elazar and Stuart A. Cohen, *The Jewish Polity: Jewish Political Organizations from Biblical Times to the Present* (Bloomington: Indiana University Press, 1985).

8. For an overview of the contribution of the Israelite experience in the development of Western political institutions, see, *inter alia*, G. H. Dodge, *The Political Theory of the Huguenots of the Dispersion* (New York, 1947); Harold Fisch, *Jerusalem and Albion* (New York: Schocken, 1964); Christopher Hill, *Intellectual Origins of the English Revolution* (Oxford: Oxford University Press, 1965); Hans Kohn, *The Idea of Nationalism* (New York: Macmillan, 1961); Zacharas P. Thundyil, *Covenant in Anglo-Saxon Thought* (Madras: Macmillan of India, 1972); Eric Voegelin, *Israel and Revelation* (Baton Rouge: Louisiana State University Press, 1957); Michael Walzer, *Exodus and Revolution* (New York: Basic Books, 1985) and *The Revolution of the Saints* (Cambridge: Harvard University Press, 1965).

9. Johannes Althusius, *Politics*, trans. Frederick Carney (Boston: Beacon Press, 1964); Thomas Hobbes, *Leviathan* (Indianapolis: Bobbs-Merrill, 1958), 143; Benedict Spinoza, *Political-Theological Tractate* (Italian translation by C. Sarchi, 1875 [1670]); John Locke, *First and Second Treatises on Government*, ed. Peter Laslett (New York: Mentor, 1965); Daniel J. Elazar and John Kincaid, eds., *The Covenant Connection* (Grenshaw: Carolina Academic Press, 1990).

10. I am indebted to Catherine H. Zuckert for emphasizing this point on the relationship of political philosophy, history, and story telling in her book *Natural Right in the American Imagination* (Lanham, MD: Rowland and Mitchell, 1990).

11. See, for example, Albrecht Alt, *Essays on Old Testament and Religion* (Garden City, NY: Doubleday, 1968), 173-222; H. Tadmor, "'The People and the Kingship in Ancient Israel: The Role of Political Institutions in the Biblical Period," *Journal of World History* 11 (1968): 46-68; Noth, *History of Israel*; W. F. Albright, "Tribal Rule and Charismatic Leaders," in *The Biblical Period from Abraham to Ezra* (New York: Harper Torchbooks, 1968), 35-52; Yehezkel Kaufmann, *The Biblical Account of the Conquest of Palestine* (Jerusalem: Magnes Press, 1953) and *The Book of Joshua: A Commentary* (Jerusalem: Kiryat Sepher, 1963).

Part I

The Idea

1

Covenant as a Political Concept

Covenant and the Purposes of Politics

Human, and hence scholarly, concern with politics focuses on three general themes: (1) the pursuit of political justice to achieve the good political order; (2) the search for understanding of the empirical reality of political power and its exercise; and (3) the development of an appropriate civic environment through political society and political community capable of integrating the first two to produce a good political life. Political science as a discipline was founded and has developed in pursuit of those three concerns. In the course of that pursuit, political scientists have uncovered or identified certain architectonic principles, seminal ideas, and plain political truths that capture the reality of political life or some significant segment of it, and relate that reality to the larger principles of justice and political order and to very practical yet normative civic purposes.

Covenant is one of the major recurring principles of political import that informs and encompasses all three themes—an idea that defines political justice, shapes political behavior, and directs humans toward an appropriately civic synthesis of the two in their effort to manage political power. As such, covenant is an idea whose importance is akin to natural law in defining justice and to natural right in delineating the origins and proper constitution of political society. While somewhat eclipsed in political science since the shift to organic and then positivistic theories of politics, which began in the mid-nineteenth century, it persists as a factor shaping political behavior in those civil societies whose foundations are grounded in the effort to translate that idea into political reality and in others searching for a means to build a democratic order on federalist rather than Jacobin principles. In the present crisis of transition from the modern to the postmodern eras, covenant is resurfacing as a significant political force just as it did in the transition from the late medieval to the modern era, which took place from the sixteenth to the eighteenth centuries.[1]

Like any great idea, covenant and its related terms are often used as slogans. Such use, while in itself often trivializing, testifies to the seminal character of covenant as a concept, since every truly great idea must rest on so simple a core that it can become a slogan. But sloganeering should not obscure the more profound dimensions of covenant, which requires sophisticated analysis and understanding if the concept is to be used properly for political invention and action.

Covenant can be studied in three dimensions: as a form of political conceptualization and mode of political expression; as a source of political ideology; and as a factor shaping political culture, institutions, and behavior. As a form of political conceptualization covenant shapes the way in which people look at the world and understand the nature of politics and civil society. The covenantal worldview is one of the two or three "mother" worldviews shared by humanity. It is by no means far-fetched to assume that basic to every personality, as it is formed by both nature and culture, is a worldview that is either hierarchical, organic, or covenantal in orientation.

The uses of covenant demonstrate how political conceptualization and expression go hand in hand. Thus, during the sixteenth and seventeenth centuries, the Swiss, the Dutch, the Scots, and the English Puritans not only conceived of civil society in covenantal terms, but actually wrote national covenants to which loyal members of the body politic subscribed. Similar covenants were used in the founding of many of the original colonies in British North America. Covenantal thinking was the common mode of political conceptualization and expression during the American Revolution, where it was reflected in any number of constitutional documents.[2] More recently, such examples as the call for a social contract in England to create a new set of relationships between labor and management and the covenant inaugurated on the Boston Common by the city's major religious groups in 1979 to bring racial peace to that city are but two of many examples of the tendency of those within a covenantal culture area to turn to covenantal forms for political conceptualization and mode of political expression.[3]

As a source of political ideology, covenant shapes the world views or perspectives of whole societies, defining their civil character and political relationships, and serving as a touchstone for testing the legitimacy and often even the efficiency of their political institutions and those who must make them work. To take a "dark" case, the Afrikaners of South Africa built the ideology sustaining their tribalism around the covenant one party of them made with God before a battle with the Zulus at the time of the Great Trek. Their national day is called the Day of the Covenant and their national shrine is designed to celebrate that day. Until recently their national leaders invoked that covenant to justify their policies toward nonwhites and implicitly asked to be judged by it.[4]

Perhaps most important of all is the role of covenant as a factor in shaping political culture, institutions, and behavior. This factor is the most difficult to measure and yet is operationally the most significant dimension of covenant. The power of covenant and the covenant principle flows less from its conception and systematic presentation as philosophy (and certainly not from its reduction to the level of ideology) than from the way it informs culture, especially political culture, endowing particular peoples with a particular set of political perceptions, expectations, and norms and shaping the way in which those perceptions, expectations, and norms are given institutional embodiment and behavioral expression. To take one example, there is every reason to believe that the idea of separation of powers, especially among equals as distinct from the separation of powers among different classes of unequals, is a product of covenantal political culture, and that its various institutional expressions reflect that political culture. Where the same institutions have been introduced into political systems serving people with a different political culture, they have worked in opposite ways from those for which they were intended.

This is in no way better reflected than in the differences between the separation of powers system of the United States where the president, Congress, and the Supreme Court interact in creative tension to balance one another, and similar systems in Latin America that are modeled institutionally on the U.S. Constitution but have been imposed upon a radically different political base. Lack of a covenantal political culture in Latin America with its corresponding lack of a sense of consent rather than force as the basis of political life, of limitations on the use of power, sharing among partners to advance the common good while preserving their respective integrities, and abiding by the rules of the game is both a response to and a generator of circumstances which lead to the abuse or the distortion of the institutional framework.

All the evidence points to the existence of certain covenantal peoples whose political cultures are informed by covenantal and related concepts, which in turn influence their political institutions and behavior. Those peoples emerged out of two nuclear concentrations. The first was at the western edge of southwest Asia some three to four thousand years ago, in what was once known as the Fertile Crescent, especially in what is today Israel and in surrounding Jordan, Lebanon, and Syria. The second was in northwestern Europe, especially in Switzerland and in a band stretching from up the Rhine River Valley through western Germany, eastern France, Belgium, the Netherlands, across the North Sea to Scotland and western Scandinavia, and the eastern coast of England. They subsequently settled and shaped various "new worlds" in North America, southern Africa, and Australasia.

Out of these covenantal peoples emerged Judaism and Christianity with their biblical covenantal base, reformed Protestantism with its federal theology, federalism as a political principle and arrangement, the modern corporation, civil societies based upon interlocking voluntary associations, and almost every other element that reflects social organization based upon what has loosely been called "contract" rather than "status." Moreover, these covenantal peoples seem to have internalized a covenantal approach to life, to a greater or a lesser extent. The Swiss, for example, are a federal people through and through (that is to say, they seek a fair bargain that they are then willing to fulfill in the most complete way), whether they are dealing with their political system or with the way in which they serve customers in their resorts. Americans have many of the same qualities, although in a softer and less sharply defined way. Studying the linkages between political culture, institutions, and behavior and the way in which those linkages have occurred in various political communities and societies is a major intellectual challenge.

The Idea of Covenant

A covenant is a morally informed agreement or pact based upon voluntary consent, established by mutual oaths or promises, involving or witnessed by some transcendent higher authority, between peoples or parties having independent status, equal in connection with the purposes of the pact, that provides for joint action or obligation to achieve defined ends (limited or comprehensive) under conditions of mutual respect, which protect the individual integrities of all the parties to it. Every covenant involves consenting (in both senses of thinking together and agreeing) and promising. Most are meant to be of unlimited duration, if not perpetual. Covenants can bind any number of partners for a variety of purposes but in their essence they are political in that their bonds are used principally to establish bodies political and social.

The definition of covenant in law as a binding promise is a straightforward statement of a concept of far-reaching importance in the relations between individual groups and peoples. In modern law, covenant is defined as "a promise or agreement under consideration, or guarantee between two parties, and the seal or symbol of guarantee is that which distinguishes covenant from modern contract." Theo-politically, "a covenant is a promise that is sanctioned by an oath" accompanied by an appeal to the Deity to 'see' or 'watch over' the behavior of the one who has sworn and to punish any violation of the covenant by bringing into action the curses stipulated or implied in the swearing of the oath. For theological or political significance, "the oath was usually accompanied by a ritual or symbolic act."[5]

Thus, two words used as synonyms for *brit* in the Bible are *shevuah* and *alah*. The first means oath and the second is used as a synonym for covenant but has its origins in the word for cursed. This reflects the way in which a covenant embodies mutual oath taking. The oath-taking basis of covenanting is even more pronounced in the medieval Latin term for confederacy, *coniuratio,* with *iuratio* the Latin term for oath. Later, this was translated into the German *Eidgenossenschaft* from *Eid,* the German word for oath.

The covenant idea, with its derivatives and cognates, offers a particular orientation to the great questions of politics in theory and practice. Perhaps the clearest indication of this special orientation is to be found in Thomas Hobbes's translation of the principles of natural law into what he called articles of peace, that is, the articles of the original civil covenant.[6] In its theological form, covenant embodies the idea that relationships between God and humanity are based upon morally sustained compacts of mutual promise and obligation. God's covenant with Noah (Gen. 9), which came after Noah had hearkened fully to God's commands in what was, to say the least, an extremely difficult situation, is the first of many such examples.

In its political form, covenant expresses the idea that people can freely create communities and polities, peoples and publics, and civil society itself through such morally grounded and sustained compacts (whether religious or civil in impetus), establishing thereby enduring partnerships. In its more poetic (but, for the Bible, no less serious) forms, covenant has even been used to describe relations between God and nature, man and nature, and the various elements of nature.[7] In all its forms, the key focus of covenant is on *relationships*. A covenant is the constitutionalization of a relationship. As such, it provides the basis for the institutionalization of that relationship but it would be wrong to confuse the order of precedence.

It is possible that covenant ideas emerged spontaneously in various parts of the world. If, indeed, covenant thinking is rooted in human nature as well as nurture, it is to be expected that some people everywhere would be oriented toward the idea somehow. In the course of this book we will explore some examples of such spontaneous developments outside of what became the covenantal mainstream: Scandinavian oath pacts, Beduin and American Indian tribal confederacies, and the Hungarian national covenant, to mention a few. In fact, it is not sufficient for random individuals or even groups to be disposed to it for an idea to take root and spread. Somehow a culture or civilization must emerge that embodies and reflects that idea.

The first such civilization and the most influential was that of ancient Israel, located on the western edge of southwest Asia, whose people transformed and perfected a device originally developed among the Amorite and Hittite peoples who inhabited the area.[8] The first known uses of covenant were the vassal treaties through which the lesser rulers and their domains through pacts secured by oath before the respective deities involved. These international or intra-imperial pacts laid out the form that covenants have taken ever since, which included five elements: historical prologue indicating the parties involved, a preamble stating the general purposes of the covenant and the principles behind it, a body of conditions and operative clauses, a stipulation of the agreed-upon sanctions to be applied if the covenant were violated, and an oath to make the covenant morally binding. Often a sixth element was included as well, provisions for depositing the covenant document and of periodic public reaffirmation or recovenanting. These first covenants simultaneously established the political purposes and moral bases for covenanting. This is equally true for ancient Hittite vassal treaties, the covenants of biblical Israel, the Scottish national covenant of the seventeenth century, and the Declaration of the Independence of the United States of America, to name but four examples.

Either parallel to or derived from these ancient vassal covenants there emerged domestic political and religious usages of covenant. The two were connected in the Bible to form the classic foundation of the covenant tradition.[9] God's covenant with Israel established the Jewish people and founded it as a body politic while at the same time creating the religious framework that gave that polity its raison d'etre, its norms, and its constitution, as well as the guidelines for developing a political order based upon proper, that is to say, covenantal relationships.

Biblical adaptation of the forms of the vassal covenants involved a transformation of purpose and content so great as to mean a difference in kind, not merely degree. A covenant was used to found a people, making their moral commitment to one another far stronger and enduring than that of a vassal to an imperial overlord. The Bible draws a distinction between "sons of the covenant," *bnai brit* in Hebrew, and "masters of the covenant," or *ba'alei brit*. *Bnai brit* is used where the covenant has created a new entity whose partners are bound together as sons within a family. The covenant that unites and forms the Jewish people in the biblical account makes all Jews *bnai brit* (as the organization of that name indicates). On the other hand, where the term used is *baalei brit*, it is essentially an international treaty. It does not create a new entity, but establishes a relationship of peace and mutual ties between quite separate entities who remain outside of the limited purpose pact.

This new form of covenant was not simply witnessed by heaven, but brought God in as a partner, thus informing it with religious value and implication for the Israelites, who saw no distinction between its religious and political dimensions. The covenant remained a theo-political document with as heavy an emphasis on the political as could be. The strong political dimension reflected God's purpose in choosing one people to be the builders of a holy commonwealth, which could be a model for all others.

It was only later with the rise of Christianity and the beginning of the long exile of the Jews from their lands that covenant took on a more strictly religious character for some, in which the political dimension was downplayed, if not downright ignored by Christian theologians on the one hand, and diminished by Jewish legists on the other. Christianity embraced the covenant idea as one of the foundations, reinterpreting the old biblical covenant establishing a people as a polity as a covenant of grace between God and individual humans granted or mediated by Jesus.[10] Jewish legists simply took the basic covenantal framework of Judaism for granted and concentrated on the fine points of the law as applied to daily living or the expected Messianic redemption.[11]

Within the Jewish world, the political dimension of covenanting received new impetus in the eleventh century to provide a basis for constituting local Jewish communities throughout Europe. That effort ran parallel to the establishment of municipal corporations throughout that continent, which were legitimized by royal charter, usually negotiated between the municipality and the throne.[12] While these efforts found some expression in political thought, it was really not until the Reformation that covenant re-emerged as a central category, first in political theology and then in political philosophy.

It was at this time that the covenant idea emerged as a powerful force in the second major cultural area, that of western and, most particularly, northwestern Europe. What cultural predispositions lay behind the receptivity of the peoples of that culture area to covenant as a concept remain to be uncovered, if they can be. It cannot be an accident that the federal theology emerged simultaneously in the sixteenth century in four separate places in Switzerland (Zurich, Basel, Berne, and Geneva), where confederal political arrangements had been dominant since the late thirteenth century.[13]

Reformed Protestantism turned on the covenant concept and its spokesmen and churches embraced it with relish, finding in it the most appropriate expression of their theological ideas and expectations for church and civil polity alike. The federal theology that they articulated (federal is derived from the Latin *foedus,* which means covenant) stimulated the renewed political application of the covenant idea, which was given expression first by political theologians and then by political philosophers such as Althusius and in the next century was secularized by Hobbes, Locke, and Spinoza.[14] By the late seventeenth century, the concept had come full circle with its political dimension having taken on an independent life of its own.[15]

The connections between covenant and natural law go back to the seventeenth-century philosophic revolution of Hobbes, Locke, and

Spinoza, which transformed ancient natural law into modern natural law or natural right. Partisans of classic political philosophy view this transformation as a betrayal, gutting, or simple falsification of both classical and medieval natural law theories. Leo Strauss has made the strongest case for this view in *Natural Right and History*.[16] In one sense, they are quite correct. However, it is possible to look upon the transformation in another way, namely the covenantalization of political philosophy. That is to say, the recognition of the power of the philosophic tradition in shaping the idealized frameworks of Western man, which had led to an intolerable gap between ideality and reality in everyday life and therefore the necessity to reconstitute the natural law idea within a new system derived from very different premises. That indeed is what Hobbes, Spinoza, and Locke, among others, tried to do. The end result was modern liberal democracy.

Hobbes and Spinoza are the two most important figures in this process. The great student of medieval philosophy, Harry Austryn Wolfson, has made a strong case for the thesis that medieval philosophy began with Philo and ended with Spinoza.[17] We all know that medieval philosophy is, mainly, a synthesis of biblical and Greco-Roman intellectual systems. What Philo did was to take the biblical outlook and integrate it into the Greco-Roman systems, that is, covenant thought into natural law philosophy, to set a pattern followed by the Church Fathers, the great Catholic and Islamic philosophers, and even Jewish and Protestant thinkers prior to the seventeenth century. Spinoza, in essence, reversed the process. He knocked the props out from under the edifice of medieval philosophy in an effort to replace it with a new secular modernism. Whatever his intentions, in his effort to create an entirely new system, what we have come to call modern thought, he opened the door for the resurrection of the primacy of covenantal thinking. While it certainly cannot be said that, in undoing Philo's syntheses, he desired to make biblical thought supreme, he did open the way for the major political product of the Bible, the covenant idea, to flourish once again.

So, too, with Hobbes, another unabashed modern who controlled the expression of his new system only in so far as he believed it politic to do so. Hobbes, like Spinoza, set out to undermine ancient philosophy and replace it with a modern ideational system, but in doing so, he had to directly confront Scripture and so reestablished the possibility of covenantal thought. That indeed was the first consequence of his effort, one that persisted for some two centuries and that again calls to us today.

From northwestern Europe, covenantally grounded civilization spread to the new worlds opened by northwestern European colonization. Such covenantal societies ranged from what is now the United States, settled by the covenanters from the British Isles in the early seventeenth century, to South Africa, settled by people from the religio-culturally covenantal Netherlands in the late seventeenth century, to New Zealand, settled by British in the nineteenth century. Where settlers from those traditions were dominant, new peoples were established by covenant and they in turn created constitutions that concretized the covenantal dimension through a network of political institutions.

In the late eighteenth century, the American Revolution translated the concept of covenant into a powerful instrument of political reform but only after merging it with the more secularized idea of compact. American constitutionalism is a product of that merger.[18]

Covenant, Natural Law, and Constitutionalism

Thus, over the centuries, *covenant, natural law,* and *constitutionalism* became intertwined. When, for example, the Americans formally declared themselves an independent people in the Declaration of Independence—itself a covenant creating a new relationship based on natural law precepts—they then saw constitution-making as a way of further covenanting or compacting together in order to create civil instruments designed to carry out the promises of the Declaration.[19] The resulting state and federal constitutions were seen as compacts embodying the principles of natural law, especially in their bills of rights. The propriety of subsequent legislation was, therefore, to be judged in light of its "constitutionality," or, in other words, its conformity to both natural law and covenants, one step removed.

Normally, then, a covenant precedes a constitution and establishes the people or civil society, which then proceeds to adopt a constitution of government for itself. Thus, a constitution involves the implementation of a prior covenant—an effectuation or translation of a prior covenant into an actual frame or structure of government. The constitution may include a restatement or reaffirmation of the original covenant as does the Massachusetts Constitution of 1780 in its preamble:

The body-politic is formed by a voluntary association of individuals: It is a social compact, by which the whole people covenants with each citizen with the whole people, that all shall be governed by certain laws for the common good.

But that is optional. Covenant relationships have often been compared to marriages in their permanency, promissory trust, mutuality of responsibility, and respect for the integrity of each partner within the community created by wedding (an ancient Anglo-Saxon term for sealing a contract). The analogy also highlights the way in which covenant links *consent* and *kinship*. In the biblical-covenantal view of marriage, two independent and otherwise unrelated persons unite to become "one flesh" and establish a family.

In politics, covenant denotes the voluntary establishment of a people and body politic. Again, the American Declaration is an excellent example. The diverse inhabitants of the thirteen colonies consented, through their new state and general government institutions, to become a people. It was not without reason, therefore, that Abraham Lincoln fondly described the union created by that act as "a regular marriage."[20] The partners do not, of course, always live happily ever after, but they are bound by covenant to struggle toward such an end, a commitment understood and made explicit by Lincoln during the Civil War. At the same time, covenants beget constitutions almost as a matter of course but also influence every dimension of constitutionalism.

Following Aristotle, every political system is delineated along three dimensions: its moral constitution, its socioeconomic constitution, and its frame of government, which taken together link the two faces of politics.[21]

1. The *moral* basis of the constitution refers to the generally accepted ideas about how people in a particular polity should live. It includes the conception of justice that is held to be the guiding standard of the polity, the picture of the good polity in the minds of citizens, plus other opinions about what kinds of political and social actions are right and good.

2. The *socioeconomic* basis of the constitution refers to the ways people actually live. It includes such things as class structure, ethnic composition, type of economy, and the actual distribution of power; in other words, who is important and influential and why.

3. The *frame of government* refers to the institutions and structures of government itself, including the document (or collection of documents) that sets out the institutions of government, establishes their powers and

FIGURE 1.1
Dimensions of the Political System

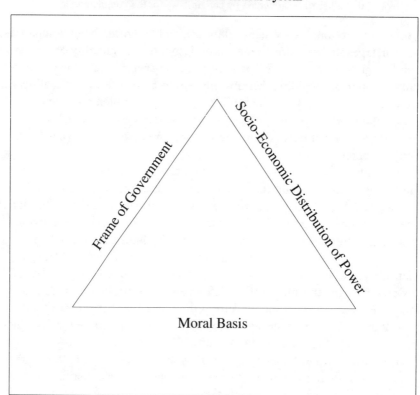

limits of those powers, and indicates who shall govern and how the governors shall be chosen. Figure 1.1 outlines this three-dimensional model.

Unlike many philosophic concepts, covenant addresses all three dimensions of the political system. It delineates the system's moral foundations, offers mechanisms for constructing the institutional system's frame of government, and suggests a behavioral dynamic to shape the system's socioeconomic basis.

Covenant, Compact, and Contract

Covenant is tied in an ambiguous relationship to two related terms, compact and contract. On the one hand, both compacts and contracts are related to, and even may be derived from, covenant, and sometimes the terms are even used interchangeably. On the other hand, there are very real differences between the three that need clarification.

Both *covenants* and *compacts* differ from *contracts* in that the first two are constitutional or public and the last is private in character. As such, covenantal or compactual obligation is broadly reciprocal. Those bound by one or the other are obligated to respond to each other beyond the letter of the law rather than to limit their obligations to the narrowest contractual requirements. Hence, covenants and compacts are inherently designed to be flexible in certain respects as well as firm in others. As expressions of private law, contracts tend to be interpreted as narrowly as possible so as to limit the obligation of the contracting parties to what is explicitly mandated by the contract itself. Contracts normally contain provisions for unilateral abrogation by one party or another under certain conditions (and with penalties where appropriate); compacts and covenants generally require mutual consent to be abrogated, designed as they are to be perpetual or of unlimited duration.

A covenant differs from a compact in that its morally binding dimension takes precedence over its legal dimension. In its heart of hearts, a covenant is an agreement in which a higher moral force, traditionally God, is either a direct party to, or guarantor of the particular relationship. Whereas, when the term compact is used, moral force is only indirectly involved. A compact, based as it is on mutual pledges rather than guarantees by or before a higher authority, rests more heavily on a legal though still ethical grounding for its politics. In other words, compact is a secular phenomenon.

This is historically verifiable by examining the shift in terminology that took place in the seventeenth and eighteenth centuries, reaching a climax in the American and French revolutions and their respective aftermaths. In the United States, the terms *covenant* and *compact* were used almost interchangeably until after 1791. In the British North American colonies the accepted term in the seventeenth century was covenant. Compact was introduced in the mid-eighteenth century as part of the spread of Enlightenment secular thought during the Revolutionary era. Those who saw the hand of God in political affairs in the United States continued to use the term *covenant,* while those who sought a secular grounding for politics turned to the term *compact.* While the distinction is not always used with strict clarity, it does appear consistently.[22]

The issue was further complicated by Rousseau and his followers who talked about the social contract, a highly secularized concept, which, even when applied for public purposes, never develops the same level of moral obligation as either covenant or compact. The Rousseauistic formulation had limited popularity in the United States but became the dominant terminology in revolutionary France, although it did share the field with the other two terms, particularly *compact,* especially in the early years of the Revolution. With the triumph of Jacobin ideas, which themselves are an outgrowth of Rousseaunian thought, the term *social contract* swept the field.[23]

Covenant, then, is the oldest of several terms that deal with the formation of the political order through consent as manifested in a pact or an appropriate level of mutual binding. In the following chapter we will examine this idea of pact and consent in light of the other theories of political order.

Notes

1. See for example, G. H. Dodge, *The Political Theory of the Huguenots of the Dispersion* (New York: Octagon Books, 1947); E. J. Shirley, *Richard Hooker and Contemporary Political Ideas* (Naperville, IL: Allenson, 1949); R. H. Murray, *The Political Consequences of the Reformation* (New York: Russell and Russell, 1960); Christopher Hill, *Intellectual Origins of the English Revolution* (New York: Oxford University Press, 1965); and books listed in the Appendix.
2. H. R. Niebuhr, "The Idea of Covenant and American Democracy," *Church History* 23 (1954): 126–35. Donald Lutz has collected most of the relevant documents in *Documents of Political Foundation Written by Colonial Americans* (Philadelphia: ISHI, 1986) and Charles Hyneman and Donald Lutz, editors, *American Political Writing During the Founding Era, 1760–1805,* 2 vols. (Indianapolis: Liberty Fund, 1983).
3. See "Make the Symbol Appeal Everywhere," *The Boston Globe,* 17 December 1979, p. 14. The *Covenant Letter,* issued periodically by the Center for the Study of Federalism Workshop in Covenant and Politics, regularly documents contemporary uses of covenant.
4. T. R. H. Davenport, *South Africa, A Modern History,* 3d ed. (Johannesburg: Macmillan South Africa, 1989); W. A. de Klerk, *The Puritans in Africa* (London: Rex Collins Ltd., 1975); Leo Marquard, *The Story of South Africa* (London: Faber and Faber Ltd., 1966); and Marquard, *A Federation of Southern Africa* (London: Oxford University Press, 1971).
5. Quotations are from George E. Mendenhall, "Covenant," *Encyclopedia Britannica,* 15th ed., vol. 5 (1975), 226–30.
6. Thomas Hobbes, *Leviathan,* chaps. 14 and 15. See also Vincent Ostrom's discussion of Hobbes's articles of peace in his *Leviathan and Democracy* (forthcoming).
7. Daniel J. Elazar, "Covenant as the Basis of the Jewish Political Tradition," *The Jewish Journal of Sociology* 20, no. 1 (June 1978): 5–37.

8. See, for example, Delbert R. Hillers, *Covenant, the History of a Biblical Idea* (Baltimore: Johns Hopkins Press, 1969).
9. Ibid.
10. Ibid.
11. Gordon Freeman, "Rabbinic Conceptions of Covenant," in Daniel J. Elazar, ed., *Kinship and Consent: The Jewish Political Tradition and its Contemporary Uses* (Ramat Gan: Turtledove Publishing, 1981).
12. Menahem Elon, "Power and Authority in the Medieval Jewish Community" and Gerald Blidstein, "Individual and Community in the Middle Ages" in ibid.
13. B. Bradfield, *The Making of Switzerland* (Zurich: Schweitzer Spiegel Verlag, 1964); Daniel J. Elazar and John Kincaid, eds., *Federal Theology and Politics* (forthcoming). Denis de Rougement, *La Suisse* (Lausanne: La Livre du Mois, 1965); William Martin, *Histoire de la Suisse* (Lausanne: Librairie Payot, 1943); and Walther ab Hohlenstien, *Urschweizer Bundesbrief* (St. Gallen: Ausheferung Durch Das Staatsarchiv, 1956).
14. Thomas Hueglin, "Covenant and Federalism in the Politics of Althusius" in Daniel J. Elazar and John Kincaid, *Covenant, Polity, and Constitutionalism* (Lanham, MD: Center for the Study of Federalism and University Press of America, 1980).
15. See Vincent Ostrom, "Hobbes, Covenant and Constitution," *Publius* 10, no. 4 (Fall 1980): 83–100.
16. Leo Strauss, *Natural Right and History* (Chicago: University of Chicago Press, 1953), chap. 5.
17. Harry Austryn Wolfson, *Philo*, vol. 2 (Cambridge, MA: Harvard University Press, 1947), chap. 14.
18. Edmund S. Morgan, *Puritan Political Ideas, 1558–1794* (New York: Bobbs-Merrill, 1965), and de Klerk, *Puritans in Africa.* See Donald Lutz, "From Covenant to Constitution in American Political Thought," and Rozann Rothman, "The Impact of Covenant and Contract Theories in Conceptions of the U.S. Constitution," *Publius* 10, no. 4 (Fall 1980).
19. Rothman, "Impact of Covenant," and Daniel J. Elazar, "The Declaration of Independence as a Covenant," a working paper of the Workshop in Covenant and Politics, Center for the Study of Federalism.
20. Daniel J. Elazar, "The Constitution, the Union, and the Liberties of the People," in *Publius* 8, no. 3 (Summer 1978): 141–75.
21. Cf. Norton Long, "Aristotle and the Study of Local Government," in *The Polity*, ed. Norton Long (Chicago: Rand McNally, 1962).
22. Cf. Donald Lutz, "From Covenant to Constitution."
23. Simon Schama, *Citizens: A Chronicle of the French Revolution* (New York: Knopf, 1989); Alexis de Tocqueville, *Ancien Regime et la Revolution*, trans. Stuart Gilbert (New York: Doubleday, 1955). See also Jean Jacques Rousseau, *The Social Contract*.

2

Covenant and the Origins of Political Society

Three Models

Since its beginnings, political science has identified three basic ways in which polities come into existence: conquest, organic development, and covenant. This "classification" can be found in most, if not all, works of political philosophy, implicitly if not explicitly. *The Federalist* offers a particularly felicitous formulation in its effort to persuade the people of New York to ratify the United States Constitution of 1787: force, accident, or reflection and choice.[1] These questions of origins are not abstract; the mode of founding of a polity does much to determine the framework for its subsequent political life.

Conquest can be understood to include not only its most direct manifestation, a conqueror (or conquering group) gaining control of a land or a people, but also such subsidiary ways as a revolutionary conquest of an existing state, a coup d'etat, or even an entrepreneur conquering a market and organizing his control through corporate means. Conquest tends to produce hierarchically organized regimes ruled in an authoritarian manner; power pyramids with the conqueror on top, his agents in the middle, and the people underneath the entire structure as portrayed in Figure 2.1. The original expression of this kind of polity was the Pharaonic state of ancient Egypt. It was hardly an accident that those rulers who brought the Pharaonic state to its fullest development had the pyramids built as their tombs. In its constitutionalized form, the power pyramid is transformed into feudalism. Although both the Pharaonic models have been judged illegitimate in contemporary Western society, modern and feudal totalitarian theories, particularly fascism and Nazism, represented an attempt to give the comprehensive state based on hierarchical rule a certain theoretical legitimacy.[2]

FIGURE 2.1
The Power Pyramid

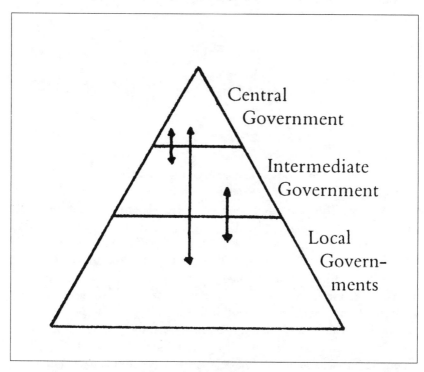

Organic evolution involves the development of political life from families, tribes, and villages into large polities in such a way that institutions, constitutional relationships, and power alignments emerge in response to the interaction between past precedent and changing circumstances with the minimum of deliberate constitutional choice. As a result, in the course of time elites emerge from among the population and political power gravitates into their hands—which Robert Michel has described as "the iron law of oligarchy."[3] Together they form the core of the polity, leaving the others outside of the governing circle. The end result tends to be a polity with a single center of power and a sharp division between center and periphery as portrayed in Figure 2.2.

Classical Greek political thought emphasized the organic evolution of the polity and rejected any other means of polity building as deficient or improper. The organic model is closely related to the concept of natu-

FIGURE 2.2
The Center-Periphery Model

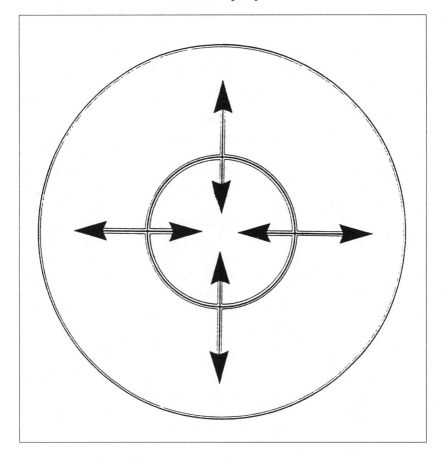

ral law in the political order. Natural law informs the world and, when undisturbed, leads in every polity to the emergence of natural power relationships, necessarily and naturally unequal, which fit the character of its people.

The organic model has proved most attractive to political philosophers precisely because at its best, it seems to reflect true aristocracy of the best and the brightest as the natural order of things. Thus, it has received the most intellectual and academic attention. However, just as conquest tends to produce hierarchically organized regimes ruled in an

authoritarian manner, organic evolution tends to produce oligarchic regimes, which at their best have an aristocratic flavor, and at their worst
are simply the rule of the many by the few. In the first, the goal of politics is to control the top of the pyramid, in the second, the goal is to
control the center of power.[4]

Covenantal foundings emphasize the deliberate coming together of
humans as equals to establish bodies politic in such a way that all reaffirm their fundamental equality and retain their basic rights. Even the
Hobbesian covenant—and Hobbes specifically uses the term—which
establishes a polity in which power is vested in a single sovereign, in
principle maintains this fundamental equality. Polities whose origins are
covenantal reflect the exercise of constitutional choice and broad-based
participation in constitutional design.[5] Polities founded by covenant are
essentially federal in character, in the original meaning of the term,
whether they are federal in structure or not. That is to say, each polity is
a matrix (Figure 2.3) compounded of equal confederates who freely bind
themselves to one another so as to retain their respective integrities even
as they are bound in a common whole. Such polities are republican by
definition and power within them must be diffused among many centers
or the various cells within the matrix.

We find recurring expressions of the covenant model in ancient
Israel, whose people started out as rebels against the Pharaonic model;
among the medieval Swiss rebels against the Holy Roman Empire;
among the Reformation era rebels against the Catholic hierarchy;
among the early modern political compact republicans who were
rebels against either hierarchical or organic theories of the state; and
among modern federalists. Frontiersmen—that is to say, people who
have gone out and settled new areas where there were no preexisting
institutions of government with which they identified and who, therefore, have had to compact with one another to create such institutions for themselves—are generally to be found among the most active
covenanters.

Each of these forms of founding has very real implications for the
character of the regime that emerges from it, in the structure of authority, in the mechanisms of governance, in the distribution of powers—in
general, in the form the regime is likely to take (Table 2.1). Thus, in
regimes founded by conquest and force we expect to find hierarchical
structures of authority dominant, power pyramids in every sense of the

FIGURE 2.3
The Matrix Model

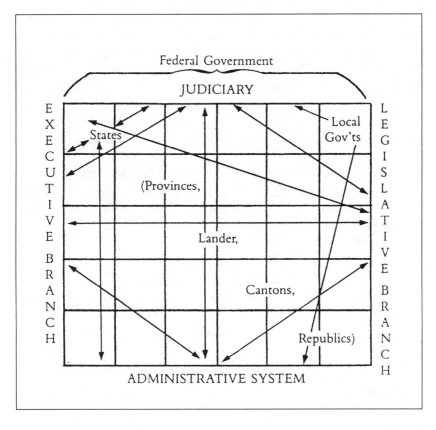

word. In such regimes, administration, which is a matter of a top-down chain of command, takes precedence over politics and constitutionalism. Indeed, the major political arena in such regimes is that of the ruler at the top of the pyramid. In other words it is court politics, limited to a small elite that have secured for themselves places in the court, with the kind of intrigue and jockeying for position associated with the politics of courts. If constitutionalism plays any role at all, the constitution takes the form of a charter granted by the ruler, whose status is at least formally controlled by him (although, as we know from feudal systems, under certain circumstances rulers who seem to be on the top of the pyramid can be forced to grant charters of liberties to subsidiary bodies because there has been a redistribution of force as a result of external factors over which the top of the pyramid has no control).

The apotheosis of such a regime is an army. Indeed, one of the first modern models of the hierarchical state was Prussia, described by Voltaire as "an army transformed into a state." So, too, was Napoleonic France where Napoleon's administrative reorganization of the country fixed its internal structure for the next 170 years regardless of wars, revolutions, coups, and regime changes. The worst manifestation of such regimes are totalitarian dictatorships whereby those at the top of the pyramid attempt, in the name of an ideology, to bring their pyramided powers to bear on every aspect of private as well as public life.

Organic polities that essentially develop by accident and are marked by their center-periphery configuration, while also elite-ruled, organize their mechanisms of government differently. For them politics takes precedence over administration and both over the constitution.

TABLE 2.1
Models of Foundings/Regimes

	Conquest	*Organic*	*Covenant*
Founding:	Force	Accident	Reflection and Choice
Model:	Pyramid	Concentric Circles	Matrix
Structure of Authority:	Hierarchy	Center-Periphery	Frame and cells
Mechanisms of Governance (in rank order):	Administration-top-down bureaucracy	Politics-club-oligarchy	Constitution-written
	Politics-court	Administration-center outward	Politics-open with factions
	Constitution-charter	Constitution-tradition	Administration-divided
Apotheosis:	Army	Westminster system	Federal system
Excess:	Totalitarian	Jacobin state dictatorship	Anarchy

Since the center is by far the most important political arena, their politics is the politics of the club or clubs where the elite gather and maintain continuing relationships with one another regardless of their stand on particular issues, simply because they belong to a common elite or network of elites. Administration is deemed much less important than politics and exists only to the degree that it is necessary, flowing from the center outward. At first the same club members who dominate the regime's politics also undertake much of the necessary administration of functions, but as matters grow more specialized, a separate administrative elite is developed, drawn as much as possible from the same sources as the political elite and maintaining a common old-boy network.

The English system, where studies at Oxford and Cambridge are tickets of admission to either the political or administrative elites, whose members literally speak the same language or at least in the same accents and belong to the same clubs, typifies this kind of regime. Constitutionalism is not unimportant in such regimes; it is not reflected in a single major constitutional document, but in a set of constitutional traditions that may or may not have been set down in writing and transformed into law, as in the English model. The apotheosis of this model is parliamentary government—the Westminster system—while its excess is to be found in Jacobinism where a revolutionary cadre seizes control of the center in the name of the masses and concentrates all power within it in the name of the revolution in order to reconstruct the regime. That cadre and the central elite that it forms never relinquishes control of its own volition, only through another revolution or coup d'etat.

Covenantal regimes, founded on the basis of reflection and choice to establish a matrix of several or many power centers, order the mechanisms of government quite differently. Both the framing institutions and their constituent bodies share authority and power on a fundamentally equal basis. In such regimes the constitution comes first and foremost because it delineates the basis upon which institutions are organized and authority and power are shared and divided. Without the constitution there cannot legitimately be politics or administration. Pursuant to the constitution there develops a politics of open bargaining in which access is guaranteed by the constitution and the constitutional tradition to all citizens who accept the rules of the game. The open competition of parties and factions is encouraged. Administration is subordinate to both constitutional and political standards and is further controlled by being divided between the framing institution and the cells of the matrix.

The apotheosis of this model is a federal democratic republic on the order of the United States or Switzerland. Its excess is anarchy where the framing institutions and cells prove incapable of ordering the exercise of power within the structure. While in real life many polities mix these models within their regimes, the classic examples of political organization tend to be relatively pure representations of one or the other. Both the purer cases and the mixtures teach us about important manifestations of political life.

Biblical Expression of the Three Models

The Bible presents these three models and seeks to account for their origins, implications, and consequences. The Book of Genesis begins with humanity emerging from one common ancestor and then, after the Flood, dividing into three branches or grand families: that of Ham, that of Shem, and that of Japhet (Gen. 10). Ham and the Hamites are located principally in northeast Africa, roughly today's Ethiopia, Sudan, and Egypt, although they cross over into Asia in Canaan and the lower Mesopotamian valley (Sumer) for a brief period. Shem and the Semites are located in southwestern Asia, while Japhet and the Japhetites are located to the north of the Semites in Asia Minor and the Caucasus and westward into southern Europe.

If one reads the biblical text closely, we discover that it presents hierarchical government as originating among the Hamites at two points: in Nimrod's empire in lower Mesopotamia (Gen. 10:1-12), and in Egypt (Gen. 10:13-14). The organic state, on the other hand, originates with Japhet and his descendants, particularly in Yavan, among the Ionians, or Greeks (Gen. 10:2-4). The covenantal polity originates among the Semites, particularly the western Semites, culminating in the covenantal polity of Israel (Gen. 10:21-31).

Both Egyptian and Greek mythologies reinforce this biblical classification. The origins of the biblical world are in creation, while those of the Ionian world, by their description, are through generation and propagation, that is to say, organically. In the first, God, by His will, creates heaven and earth and all things therein, including man and woman with whom He covenants. For the Greeks, the gods are begotten. Gaia, the earth, begets Ouranos, heaven, with whom she then mates to bring forth Kronos and his brothers and sisters, after which there are a series of matings and struggles that create the gods as the Greeks knew them and the world as we know it.[6] The result is a world developed organically but around competition, which is resolved by agreements among elites, as distinct from the world of God's creation in which God and humans are linked by covenant. According to the Egyptian myths, individual gods came down to earth and assumed human form, each to rule his people through a power pyramid as in Pharaonic Egypt.[7]

The myths of the Japhetites, or at least those of them in Ionia, gave birth to philosophy, just as the Semites gave birth to the Bible. Both philosophers and prophets are concerned with the pursuit of justice and righteousness. Hence, they require a just political order for their teachings to be fulfilled. Each sought that political order within the context of the fundamental orientation of their civilization. For the philosophers, that orientation was organic; for the prophets, it was covenantal.

A covenantal politics, then, is directed simultaneously toward linking people and communities as partners in common tasks and allowing them space in which to be free. The very idea of a covenant between God and humankind contains this implication in its most radical form. The omnipotent Deity, by freely covenanting with man, limits His own powers to allow humans space in which to be free, only requiring of them that they live in accordance with the law established as normative by the covenant. This view is reflected in the Midrashic literature. In Genesis Rabbah 38:13 it is specified that Abraham chose God by the way he lived before God spoke to him, while the *Sifrei* makes the same point with regard to the mutual relationship between God and Jacob. In a sense, these Midrashim, developed at the time of the emergence of Christianity, are part of the polemic between Judaism and Pauline Christianity, which emphasizes the unilateral character of God's action as a form of grace.[8]

The Puritans' recognition of this aspect of the covenantal relationship between God and man in sixteenth- and seventeenth-century Britain and America became the basis of their federal theology. John Winthrop, the great Puritan governor of Massachusetts, referred to this relationship as "federal liberty," or the freedom to freely hearken to the law.[9] A century later, when the federal idea was secularized by the descendants of the Puritans, "federal liberty" was redefined in terms of what actions were or were not constitutional.

The ambiguous origins of the Hebrew word *brit* tell us much about this fettered freedom or liberating bondage. Of the two Akkadian words that scholars suggest are related to it, *biritum* means "space between" while *beriti* means "fetter" or "binding agreement." This notion of dividing and then binding together is present in the Hebrew phrase *lichrot brit* (literally: to cut a covenant) and on the ceremony that went with that term, which in earliest form involved the halving of an animal and passing between its two parts to symbolically reunite them.[10] It survives in the Jewish ceremony of *brit millah* (the covenant of circumcision).[11]

Theologians tend to describe the foundations of theistic belief systems as revelations. For the Bible, a more accurate term would be *Divine communication*. According to the Bible, God did not so much reveal himself to his people, that is to say, move from being hidden to being visible, as to enter into direct communication with them. When God speaks to humans, He does so more in the way of a normal communication than a revelation. It is rather matter of fact, as if dialogue between God and man is expected. This is a covenantal posture and outlook. Covenant is not a matter of revelation, which essentially is a unilateral act among radical unequals. The conditions of covenant require communication with both sides participating, in which the radical inequality is modified or suspended at least for purposes of the communication.

In sum, a covenant-based politics looks toward political arrangements established or, more appropriately, compounded, through the linking of separate entities in such a way that each preserves its respective integrity while creating a common and continuing association to serve those purposes, broad or limited, for which it was called into being. These purposes range from keeping the peace through a permanent but very limited alliance of independent entities to the forging of a new polity through the union of previously separate entities to create a new whole. A covenant-based politics is not simply a symbolic matter; it has to do with very concrete demands for power sharing and the development of institutionalized forms and processes for doing so. Whether in its theological form or secularized as the compact theory of the origin of civil society, the covenant principle has manifested itself in different ways, in different times and places, regularly reemerging as one of the fundaments of politics.

Covenants and New Societies

For obvious reasons, covenants and covenanting are especially prevalent in the founding and subsequent building of new societies. "New societies" are, most immediately and simply, those founded "from scratch" as a result of migrations to "virgin" territories (i.e., territories perceived to be essentially uninhabited by the migrants) whose settlers underwent a frontier experience as a major part of the process of settlement. There are in the world today a handful of "new societies," a select company including the United States, Canada, the Republic of South Africa, Australia, New Zealand, and Israel. Each in its own way was founded as a modern society from its very beginning. Among other things, these new societies stand out in sharp contrast to both traditional societies and those that have undergone modernization, whether from a traditional or feudal base, by virtue of that fact. The key to their birth as modern societies from the first lies in the migration of their members to new "frontier" environments since the beginning of the modern epoch in the mid-seventeenth century where their builders could create a social order with a minimum amount of hinderance by the entrenched ways of the past, whether traditional or feudal, or by existing populations needing to be assimilated.[12]

Unlike societies with traditional or feudal backgrounds, which are built upon what are generally accepted as organic linkages between families, communities, or estates whose origins are lost in the proverbial "mists of history," new societies are constructed upon conscious (and usually historically verifiable) contractual or covenantal relationships established between individuals and groups, based on some sense of national vocation that bound their founders together and continues to bind subsequent generations. The founders of the new societies, in creating social and political institutions anew on the frontier, were motivated by a common sense of vocation based on ideologies or commitments they brought with them and forged in the process of nation building; a sense of vocation that continues to serve as a shared mystique (a future-oriented myth) to inspire or justify their efforts or those of their heirs at national development. The actual creation of their civil societies was almost invariably manifested through some kind of constituting act, usually one that was concretized in documentary form. Even if no single pact was involved, the social and political organization of each new society is based on many "little" covenants, compacts, or contracts necessitated by the realities of having to create new settlements and institutions overnight on virgin soil.

While the founders of the new societies obviously brought with them a cultural heritage derived from their societies of origin, their motivation in migrating was almost invariably a revolutionary one. That is to say, they sought to create a better society than the one they had left and, indeed, were motivated to leave because they did not believe it possible to build the society they wanted within the framework of their original homelands. Usually they took what they believed to be the most significant ideas (and institutions) from their homelands and transplanted them, with appropriate adaptations, to their new lands as part of their efforts to build new and better societies.

In the founding of new societies, the organizing principles are more often than not ideological. For the most part, only people committed to a particular ideology, however vaguely articulated, care to participate in what is, after all, a very difficult and dangerous venture. The driving force behind those first formulas was conceptualized by them in specific ideological terms so that membership in the community of pioneers was contingent upon acceptance of the ideology in one of its several versions.

While conflict between proponents of the various specific ideologies was often a fact, almost invariably the pioneers worked out concrete ways of cooperating with one another virtually from the first, containing their conflict within a developing set of ideologically rooted institutions. They were able to do this by judicious, though not always conscious, use of federal principles and techniques. Their strong commitment to the working out of their special ideological principles in practice coupled with the need for unity in the face of the obstacles placed in their way led them to seek federal solutions that allowed them to preserve significant elements of both demands.

As individuals, the pioneers compacted or federated with one another to form settlements, organizations, and institutions (principally religious and political). Then through their settlements and other institutions, they federated with one another to create political or civil societies and polities. As in the case of all such federal structures, the ties linking individuals to institutions and the institutions with one another were essentially voluntary and predicated on the mutual compacting of one with the other. In pre-independence days this was particularly functional, not only as a way of mobilizing energy for the pioneering tasks but as the basis for organizing the incipient commonwealths within the political context set by the colonial authorities.

Thus, federalism—in its modern form the invention of the largest of the new societies, the United States, and in its ancient form the invention of the first of them, Israel—is somehow associated with the particular brand of political and social democracy shared by all the new societies, whether they are federal in structure or not. Federal principles of the constitutional diffusion of power, contractual noncentralization, and negotiated collaboration among the elements of the political system are characteristic even of those polities that are not formally federal.

To a very real extent, the communications gap between new societies and the majority of the world's polities, the old societies, is very great indeed. A brief look at two of the most visibly new societies supports why this is so.

The United States

The United States is the paradigmatic modern new society. Its first settlements were founded in the seventeenth century on a continent that was not only relatively empty of population but whose indigenous inhabitants were not considered by the settlers to be obstacles rather than contributors to the pioneering process. Using covenants such as the charters of the great London trading companies, the Mayflower Compact, the Fundamental Orders of Connecticut, and, ultimately, the Declaration of Independence and the Constitution of 1787, as well as the myriad little compacts that created towns, congregations, and commercial enterprises, those settlers created new social and political institutions to meet their needs "from scratch." They did so by reorganizing, as it were, the cultural "baggage" they brought with them in accordance with a new sense of national purpose (or vocation), which was in turn developed out of a combination of the frontier experiences they passed through and the ideological grounding (essentially religious in origin) they brought with them. The mystique they created has continued to serve as the basis for national consensus and as a major stimulus for national action ever since.

Israel and the Jewish People

Israel falls squarely within the "new society" model, though, like the other new societies, it departs from the American paradigm in those particulars that reflect its own unique historical experience. The settlement of "Palestine" (Eretz Israel in the Bible) by the Zionist pioneers was for them the settlement of new and vacant territories open to the construction of a new society without any locally entrenched encumbrances. Though Palestine in the nineteenth century was not an empty land, not even as empty as North America in the early seventeenth century, for the Zionist pioneers it was effectively empty in that they did not expect to model the society they intended to build upon anything indigenous to the population within it. No matter how much they romanticized certain aspects of the local Arab culture and even affected certain Bedouin modes of dress or behavior, this was never even remotely a possibility for them.

Of course the "old *yishuv*" (the settlements of pious Jews that antedated the Zionist efforts and did not share the same sense of political vocation) was strictly off limits as a model (even though its members would obviously be included within any new Jewish society), since the stated goal of the pioneers was to replace that way of life with a new one that, while in harmony with the highest Jewish ideals, would be fully modern, that is, socialist (or liberal democratic, in some cases). Later, when religiously orthodox Jews entered into the pioneering arena, they, too, showed their modernism by claiming to be social radicals, though within the four ells of traditional Judaism. Moreover, the very essence of Zionism was that Jews could only build their new society by leaving the lands of the diaspora and migrating to a new land, or more accurately by returning to their "old-new land."

The commonwealth that the Zionist pioneers hoped to build was based upon modern ideologies and technologies long since separated from either traditional or feudal principles. Indeed, the Zionists explicitly and consciously intended to build in their own land the kind of society advocated for their countries of origin by those of their European peers sharing the same modern ideologies, whether liberal or socialist. In the process of implanting their settlements and institutions in the new territory, the Zionist pioneers shaped a sense of national vocation that has become, with appropriate modifications, the Israeli mystique. While Zionist theories were based on the ideas of organic nationhood common in nineteenth-century Europe, the organizations and settlements of the pioneers themselves were quite literally based on compacts or covenants linking the dedicated individuals who took upon themselves the burdens of creating a new society. In doing so, they followed a method inevitable in new societies.

Israel's character as a new society is additionally shaped by factors that transcend the immediately modern origins of that sociopolitical phenomenon. As the Jewish state, Israel is really an extension of the Jewish people, the world's oldest "new society" and the first identifiable one in history. While the United States has been called the first new nation and, indeed, is the first new society of the modern world, the first new society recorded in ancient history is that of the Israelites, who, in their migration to Canaan and settlement there under the aegis of the Abrahamic and Sinai covenants, represented the same phenomenon approximately three millennia before the opening of the modern era.

There is now reasonable historical evidence to confirm this, whether the biblical account is exactly accurate or not. Perhaps more important, the Israelite experience as it is described in the Bible is paradigmatic of all subsequent new societies. Indeed, the Bible devotes considerable space to discussing and emphasizing precisely those elements that are here identified as being essential to the definition of new societies in its explanation of the origins of the Jewish people.

Both the covenantal nature of Jewish political organization and the future-oriented mystique of the Jewish people were institutionalized within Jewish society in the course of time, passing through various permutations in the land and in the diaspora as conditions demanded, to reappear in new form in modern Israel as part of the overall thrust of the Zionist pioneering experience. One consequence of this was that even those Jews who came from distinctly premodern environments had, to some degree, internalized a political culture with "new society" characteristics, which, however latent, could be made manifest upon their settlement in the new territory and relocation in the new society.

The understanding of the political and social systems of the new societies is not to be found in the study of modernization but in the recognition of the fact that they are unique. The crucial questions to be confronted, then, are those that revolve around the actualization of a new society: the problems of political cultural continuity and change or how the particular cultural baggage brought by their founders was subsequently modified by the experience of nation building in the new territory; the impact of the new territory and the confrontation with it (what has been called in the United States "the frontier experience"); and the constitutional problems that necessarily accompany the creation of a new society.

Covenant and the Frontier

The decisive external factor in the shaping of each of the new societies has been its frontier experience, the encounter with vast wilderness and the effort to settle and civilize it. This leads to the concentration of social and economic development around a crucial "civilizing" task, which generates its own patterns of settlement and social organization. In some, if not all, of the new societies, the chain reaction set off in the process of conquering the original land frontier has opened up subsequent urban-industrial and, in some cases, metropolitan-technological frontiers as well, whose impact is no less significant and comprehensive than that of the original frontier.

These civil societies are deeply involved in, challenged by, and forced to respond to the pressures and demands generated by the frontier, namely, a high degree of social and economic change in the society as a whole and in at least a certain portion of its component parts in every generation with its consequent pressures for cultural and political adjustment. The degree to which a given civil society is involved in, challenged by, and forced to respond to the pressures and demands generated by the frontier strongly influences the political issues and problems that confront it and are recognized by it, and the means and processes involved in meeting those issues and problems.

At the beginning of the era of the great frontier (roughly from the last half of the era of Renaissance and Reformation), civilization was redefined in juxtaposition against nature external to humans and the principal task confronting civilized man was to tame that nature—the wilderness—and, for that matter, the inhabitants of that wilderness who were perceived to be "natural men." The great struggle of the next several centuries was seen as the struggle between civilization and wilderness in this sense. (Subsumed within it was a struggle among European and American intellectuals regarding which was better, "civilized" or "natural" man.) In the twentieth century, as the land settlement phase of the great frontier came to a close, it became increasingly apparent that civilization must be juxtaposed against man's internal nature as well, which is perpetually in need of taming. Every new person is, potentially, both a civilizing agent and a new wilderness.

This new (truly, rediscovered) understanding of human nature must lead to a redefinition of civilization in normative terms. Civilization is that which produces *good* people, not just cultivated ones. Herein lies the difference between civilization and culture. All humans are bearers of culture—acculturated, in anthropologists' language—but not all are *civilized*, by any means. "Civilized" implies a civil dimension, a dimension of governance, particularly self-governance within civil society. The Jews and the Puritans understood this as a matter of moral self-government. The Greeks and Romans mixed moral and aesthetic norms. The French misinterpreted this entirely, viewing civilization as an aesthetic rather than moral phenomenon. Understanding civilization as a matter of moral self-government suggests that it is a product of the network of covenants that humans enter into.

Notes

1. *The Federalist*, no. 1.
2. Vincent Ostrom, *The Intellectual Crisis in American Public Administration* (University, AL: University of Alabama Press, 1974); Max Weber, *Theory of Social and Economic Organization*, trans. A. M. Henderson and T. Parsons (New York: Oxford University Press, 1947).
3. Cf. Robert Michel, "The Iron Law of Oligarchy," in *Political Parties: A Sociological Study of the Oligarchical Tendency of Modern Democracy*, ed. Robert Michel (New York: Dover, 1959).
4. Ibid.
5. Vincent Ostrom, "A Computational-Conceptual Logic for Federal Systems of Governance," in Daniel J. Elazar, ed., *Constitutional Design and Power-Sharing in the Post-Modern Epoch* (Lanham: University Press of America, 1991), and *The Political Theory of a Compound Republic* (Lincoln: University of Nebraska Press, 1987).
6. James Frazer, *The Golden Bough* (New York: MacMillan Press, 1929).
7. Ibid.
8. See Eugene Milhaly, "A Rabbinic Defense of the Election of Israel," *Hebrew Union College Annual* 35 (1964): 108f.
9. John Winthrop, "A Model of Christian Charity."
10. See Gen. 15:9-21. This important covenant between Abraham and God is traditionally known in Hebrew as the "Brit bein HaBetarim" or "Covenant between the Pieces." Cf. note 2 in this chapter.
11. See Gen. 17:1-14.
12. Cf. Daniel J. Elazar, *Cities of the Prairie* (Lanham, MD: University Press of America, 1970), chap. 2, and *Israel: Building a New Society* (Bloomington: Indiana University Press, 1986), chap. 1; Louis Hartz, *The Founding of New Societies* (New York: Harcourt, Brace and World, 1964); Seymour Martin Lipset, *The First New Nation* (London: Heinemann, 1963).

3

Biblical Origins

Biblical Beginnings

What is common to all political societies rooted in the covenant idea is that they have drawn their inspiration proximately or ultimately from its biblical source. There is some evidence of other contractual societies of a sort and, of course, constitutionalism of various kinds exists outside of the biblical tradition. But, we have not found any developed covenantal tradition that is not derived from the Bible.

There is, for example, the question of whether the Cheyenne Indians were united by a "covenant of the sacred arrows," which, if it were a covenant, clearly would be outside the biblical tradition. But this terminology is found first in writings of Catholic priests who were missionaries to the Cheyenne. The anthropologists who studied that nation do not use the term; only the Catholic priests use it. It may be impossible to reconstruct the original Cheyenne conception of their social order at this late date given these conflicting reports.[1] The same thing can be said for the compact of the seven tribes that created the Hungarian nation. It is pre-Christian but was given a certain Christian tone by the king, and subsequently St. Stephen, so it remains an open question.[2] The possible exceptions are those described in the Norse sagas describing the oath societies of the pre-Christian Scandinavians. In Norway and more particularly in Iceland, covenant-style oath societies were formed. These were destroyed by the Christianization of Scandinavia, with fragments surviving in the local political culture. Otherwise, we have not found any sources that are not diluted and suspect.[3] Indeed, most sources have been filtered through people who have expressed them through the Christian or Jewish covenant traditions, and therefore cannot be separated out with regard to other possible origins.

On the other hand, the various founding covenants of the peoples, churches, or communities known to us as covenantal usually make clear reference to their biblical origins. Hence, we can talk about the biblical source of the covenant idea in much the same way that we talk about Greco-Roman sources of natural law. This is not a claim to monopoly but a claim to being the foremost in the development and application of the concept and the principal channel for its diffusion.

Modern democratic theory and practice are based on two great classical sources: Greek and Hebrew, the former embodied in philosophy and its teachings and the latter in Torah and its teachings. The Greek polis and its philosophers provided the first and classic expressions of the former while the ancient Israelite commonwealth (*edah* in Hebrew— meaning a body of citizens assembled at set times) and the Bible provided the first and classic expressions of the latter. While the two are more often mutually reinforcing than contradictory, there are important differences between them.

At one time, both sources received equal attention at the hands of political theorists and the political leaders who learned from them. This was true as late as the seventeenth and eighteenth centuries when both contributed mightily to the shaping of modern democracy.[4] Since the secularization of modern political thought, the Hebraic elements have been neglected on the assumption that no systematic political theory inheres in what is essentially a theologically based approach to politics and that the political institutions of the Israelite polity are merely particularistic—confined to their time and place—a view introduced by Spinoza in his effort to develop a fully secular political philosophy.[5] This is a gross error that misreads both the sources involved and their value as the basis of a political tradition whose influence may be greater than some systematic political theories.

Reading the Bible

Students of the Bible are all too aware of the problems that have been raised regarding its textual construction, particularly in the Pentateuch. Here we have taken the Torah as an integrated work. However and whenever it was authored, its integral character as a teaching is its most important feature from a political perspective, particularly since, from that perspective, it makes good sense. The student of politics can leave textual probings to others; the impact of the biblical teaching on human civilization comes not from such matters but from the magisterial character of the work as a whole, of which the sequence of covenants is one excellent manifestation. This approach to the Bible has been gaining currency among biblical scholars in the past several decades, in no small measure as a result of the work of Leo Strauss whose methodology for uncovering the coherence of classic works has begun to have an impact in biblical studies as well.[6]

It is necessary to emphasize that those thinkers who confronted Scripture and were influenced by it, did not look at the Bible of the biblical critics but at the Bible as a whole. The biblical critics see in front of them a difficult text—or a collection of texts and traditions— whose difficulty lies in its composition, not in its meaning. They devote their careers to identifying and trying to resolve textual problems in that spirit. The political thinkers to whom we refer assumed that the Bible was a single coherent work. Premoderns, indeed, assumed it to be unequivocally of Divine origin or at the very least Divine inspiration, which was the position adopted by the early moderns. Thus, the problems they encountered in the text were problems of interpretation rather than composition. To them the textual anomalies or ambiguities opened the door for interpretation, elaboration, and reconciliation rather than criticism.[7]

It is in that spirit that we examine the Bible in this book. Looking at Scripture in this way does not suggest that we are unaware of the problems raised by biblical critics in trying to understand how the biblical texts came to us, but that is a different issue. For those who made the biblical canon and those who were influenced by it, the Bible was a single, coherent whole and so it must be for us in this investigation. It is what the Bible says (or does not say) as a single work that lies at the root of biblical covenantalism.

Serious students of political thought must inevitably become aware of the Bible in shaping the political ideas of the Western world up until the first generations of the modern epoch. Every great political philosopher from Philo of Alexandria (first century C.E.) to those of the eighteenth century felt it necessary to come to grips with biblical ideas and to utilize case studies from Scripture. Even they often miss the full character of biblical political thought because its system is different from that which Western philosophy inherited from the Greeks.

The conventional contrast between "systematic" philosophy and "unsystematic" biblically grounded thought misses the mark. Philosophy is, indeed, systematic in character, primarily deductive in structure, beginning with great principles and moving in linear fashion to identify and elucidate subsidiary and subordinate ones. Biblically grounded thought is best understood as *prismatic*, that is to say, reflective of a well-nigh infinite variety of perspectives of the same core of truth that is simultaneously solid and shifting. The Bible, indeed, is the archetypical and ultimate prismatic work, occasionally paralleled and imitated but never matched. Jewish tradition recognizes this as in the Midrashic statement that "the Torah has seventy faces." Prismatic thought is, perforce, multidimensional at all times, achieving multidimensionality through repeated description of the same issues from different perspectives (a technique Lawrence Durrell was to adopt in his fiction). By contrast, systematic thought achieves multidimensionality through an elaborate and more abstract architecture.

Politically, too, the Bible can be read through several prisms. In our time we have seen political scientists who have read it as a key to understanding contemporary revolutionary movements,[8] as a great game between God and humans whereby each uses His or their advantage to achieve their goals or the weakness of the other to prevent excessive departure from those goals,[9] or as a textbook for the study of leadership and the interaction between leaders and the publics or polities they lead.[10]

Even to understand the role of covenant theory, culture, ideology, institutions, and behavior, we need more than one perspective. We will look at the pervasiveness of covenant as the formative theory and practice of the Hebrew Bible, at the variety of uses of covenant in the Bible, at the uses of covenant in the designing of nations, particularly the nation of Israel, particularly the two classic regimes described in the Bible (the Mosaic polity and the Davidic monarchy). We will look at the kinds of relationships established by a covenantal system, and we will look at the biblical discussion of how God found it necessary to choose covenant form among the three fundamental models of polity available to humans.

Prismatic thought has the distinct advantage of reflecting the complexity of reality. In physics, for example, it is prismatic thinking to understand light as composed of both waves and particles simultaneously. The apparent repetition of events in the Bible (whatever the history of the original sources) is another reflection of prismatic thinking, with each account offering us a different perspective on the same incident and, hence, a different lesson to be learned from it. Given the extra complexity of human reality, there is much to be said for such an approach. The world, indeed, is far more prismatic than systematic. While this should not prevent us from seeking systematic understanding of it, such understanding can only be achieved when we begin with its prismatic character.

The political tradition that flows from all this is based upon biblical teachings: *Torah*, in Hebrew, which means teaching, especially a Divine teaching. Biblical teachings emphasize covenants, federal relationships, the frontier experience, the importance of foundings, the special character of new societies, the necessity for and problematics of civilization, the generational ordering of time, the continuous relationship of space and time, the varieties of geographic expression of human settlement, the division of humankind into nations and peoples, the necessity for and problematics of political organization of all societies and communities, constitutionalism in its republican and democratic dimensions, the importance of "way" (what moderns call culture), and the binding way of tradition. A close reading of the biblical text reveals all of these as recurrent themes.

Torah is also the term for constitution in ancient Israel. In its most immediate sense, the Torah consists of the Five Books of Moses, the first five books of the Hebrew Bible. The first four books together can be seen as a constitutional document with a long historic introduction (Genesis), a preamble, covenant, and fundamental set of laws (Exodus-Leviticus), and a historical epilogue (Numbers) that includes additional fundamental laws that grow out of the desert experience of the Bnai Israel (the children of Israel/Jacob, the ancient name of the Jewish people reflecting both the familial and federal character of the political organization). Deuteronomy is the restatement of the teachings of the other four books in more systematic and properly constitutional form, with final additions and modifications adapting the constitution to a settled life in the promised land.

Moreover, the Torah is the oldest extant political constitution in our possession. As such it is generally important for political science and is particularly important as a living example of a constitution in the covenantal tradition. Consideration of the Torah as a political constitution must begin with an understanding of ancient constitutions and how they differ from modern ones. Ancient constitutionalism is at once more comprehensive and more limited than modern constitutionalism.[11] It is more comprehensive in that it is the way of life of the polity as a whole, including matters no longer deemed to be of public concern, having to do with the behavior of individuals and families, understanding them to be of critical importance to the body politic. The Torah, for example, is concerned with the holiness of the Israelites as individuals as well as collectively as the foundation for the holy commonwealth. Because this holiness is both individual and collective, it is an important constitutional issue.

At the same time, this ancient constitution is less specific in matters of governmental institutions, allowing greater leeway for constitutional interpretation, or what Europeans and Latin Americans refer to as organic laws—less-than-full constitutional arrangements of more than normal statutory importance. These were later referred to in subsequent *halakhah*, the Jewish law derived from the Torah, as "ordinances of the time" (*takanot ha-shaah*, literally, of the hour), many of which acquired their own constitutional status as subsidiary constitutional expressions. In other words, Deuteronomy, like other ancient constitutions, has to do with the ordering of the polity, not merely of its government.

The Bible is a very rich book. Its text is relatively spare, yet every word, sentence, and paragraph is filled with nuances of meaning. The order of words, sentences, and paragraphs carries meaning. The apparent repetitions with subtle differences carry meaning. Thus, a full exploration of the text requires an intensive effort. Indeed, over the centuries hundreds of thousands of words have been written to interpret this book of constitutional statements. Our task here is only to understand the covenantal aspects of Israel's ancient constitution and to begin to expose its constitutional character, content, and ordering.

It is both easier and harder to pass over the political meaning of the biblical text than it is a piece of classic philosophy. A biblical text is not likely to proclaim itself as being political. The biblical system is one of theme and language and sound expressed through a series of stories that embody important cases and issues, bound together through sets of shared value concepts. It can be discovered only by identifying and following the threads that run through its many parts, in other words, a system best

penetrated by what in Hebrew is termed *Midrash,* the inducing of meaning from textual and other sources, rather than by syllogism. The
Midrashic method, with its emphasis on the explication and harmoniza-
tion of texts, by its very nature makes it harder for the student to uncover
that teaching but, by the same token, it requires him to delve deeper and
make a greater effort to order his thoughts. It also offers the student
greater opportunity for flashes of insight that restrain the impulse to
rush to erect comprehensive schemes that may be intellectually compelling but are far from reality.

In the effort to develop a systematic way of interpreting the biblical
text, especially the Pentateuch, for legal (including constitutional) purposes, the sages of the Talmud developed a series of rules of interpretation that reflect this attention to nuance.[12] They are:

1. Inference from minor to major, or from major to minor.
2. Inference from similarity of phrases in texts.
3. A comprehensive principle derived from one text, or from two related
    texts.
4. A general proposition followed by a specifying particular.
5. A particular term followed by a general proposition.
6. A general law limited by a specific application, and then treated again in
    general terms, must be interpreted according to the tenor of the specific
    limitation.
7. A general proposition requiring a particular or specific term to explain it,
    and conversely, a particular term requiring a general one to complement
    it.
8. When a subject included in a general proposition is afterward particularly
    excepted to give information concerning it, the exception is made not for
    that one instance alone, but to apply to the general proposition as a whole.
9. Whenever anything is first included in a general proposition and is then
    excepted to prove another similar proposition, this specifying alleviates
    and does not aggravate the law's restriction.
10. But when anything is first included in a general proposition and is
    then excepted to state a case that is not a similar proposition, such
    specifying alleviates in some respects, and in others aggravates, the
    law's restriction.
11. Anything included in a general proposition and afterward excepted to
    determine a new matter cannot be applied to the general proposition un-
    less this is expressly done in the text.
12. An interpretation deduced from the text or from subsequent terms of the
    text.
13. In like manner when two texts contradict each other, the meaning can be
    determined only when a third text is found that harmonizes them.

Appreciation of biblical prismatics as contrasted with systematic philosophy is, in the last analysis, also a matter of aesthetics. It should be no surprise that the Greeks for whom symmetry was the key of aesthetic beauty, introduced philosophy as the aesthetics of systematic inquiry (although only after laying a foundation through the Platonic Dialogues, which, while more systematic in structure than the Bible, embody a similar method, that is to say, they demand that the reader enter into the text in order to understand the argument and the principles derived therefrom). Thus, one must be prepared to recognize the different aesthetic beauty of the biblical system in order to enter into it. Biblical aesthetics is much related to process, to the necessity to read and probe, to be touched by the elegant and moving language the Bible uses to deal with prosaic matters, and the sudden insights that come with those efforts.

Well into modern times, our forefathers—Jewish and Christian alike—were able to do so because religious belief led them to a need to appreciate God's word. Most moderns are no longer able to rely on religious belief as the basis for aesthetic appreciation of the Bible. In fact, matters are often reversed. Discovery of the aesthetics of biblical thought may (indeed should) lead to an appreciation of the divinity behind them rather than vice-versa.

None of this diminishes the work of modern biblical scholarship as a means of helping to better understand the biblical text as it has come down to us. What is suggested here is that reading the Bible as a coherent whole, which speaks as if textual problems were problems of interpretation, not of composition, remains a worthwhile enterprise because it is in that way that the Bible has influenced civilization. That remains true even today when the Bible is much diminished in importance in the eyes of most of the Western world. For those who do derive ideas and inspiration from it, they do not do so because they are excited by the documentary hypothesis or because of what seem to be garbled words at certain points in the text. They are excited by the Bible's majesty, coherence, and insights, and read it through the application of their own Midrashic method, whether they understand what they are doing in those terms or not.

The Bible as Political Commentary

The Bible is an eminently political book, in the classical sense—perhaps the first comprehensive political book. By virtue of its unique concern for the establishment of the kingdom of God on earth, it could not help but be concerned with the immediate development of the holy commonwealth that was to lead to the establishment of that ultimate kingdom. Consequently, a great part of the Bible—particularly parts of the *Torah* proper, much of *Neviim* (prophets), the bulk of the so-called "historical" books, and sections of the latter Prophets—is given over to discussion of political matters, with special reference to the structure and purposes of *Adat Bnai Yisrael*—the Congregation (Assembly) of Israelites, the formal name of the Jewish people as a body politic. *Ketuvim* (writings), the third section of the Hebrew Scriptures, continues this political emphasis on a broadened basis that is, at once, deeply Jewish and broadly universal.

The discussion of politics in the Bible revolves primarily around questions of political relationships. It is (in the terminology of the Greeks) concerned with the problem of the best constitution for the establishment of a proper relationship between God and humanity, particularly the people of Israel, and the best regime for the maintenance of that relationship in the land of Israel. It deals with these problems not only in depth but with careful attention to proper and explicit terminology. This very care in terminology provides important internal evidence to the effect that the political discussion was a conscious one. And, indeed, it was a discussion, with different points of view presented, albeit within the context of a common political tradition.

Unfortunately, the passage of time and the progressive decline of overt Jewish concern with political matters after their abortive revolts against Rome in the first centuries of the common era led to some loss of this political perspective as an aid to explicating the biblical text among many of its interpreters, with certain important exceptions. For many Christians, matters of individual salvation, in a world where the second coming was expected momentarily, desacralized the prosaic details of political life and thus drastically reduced their importance. At most, political life was a transient necessary evil. Still, Christian philosophers and theologians had to harmonize their political ideas with their understanding of Scripture.

At the time of the Protestant Reformation and in the early generations of the modern epoch—in the sixteenth, seventeenth, and eighteenth centuries—the Protestant founders of modern republicanism, approaching the biblical text with fresh eyes and definite political concern, rediscovered its political implications. They made use of its great political insights in the development of their own constitutions and regimes. However, the secularization of politics that followed them, and the isolation of "theology" that accompanied this rising secularism, once again relegated the Bible to the religionists and led to its neglect as a work concerned with the political order of this world, except in the most messianic sense.

The Political Purpose of the Bible

The purpose of the Bible is to teach humans the right way to live in this world. Since its teachings require humans to live together to fulfill God's commandments, its teachings focus on living in a polity, a commonwealth designed to enable fallible humans to find and follow the right way. It does so on two levels: (1) it provides a basis for the achievement of a messianic age, and (2) it discusses the more practical problems of living in society until then.

With regard to the former, the Bible makes it clear that the messianic age will be achieved only with God's intervention, which, in turn, will come only when humans have done their full share to bring it about. On the one hand, this has led many people to read the Bible's teachings on matters of political import as applying only in the messianic age, focusing on the biblical descriptions of messianic politics, which sound better than the often harsh biblical descriptions of political realities because the former are abstracted from realities of the world as we know it. Moreover, most people know in their hearts that, as fallible human beings, they are not really expected to achieve those messianic goals, hence people often disregard these teachings that refer to the second level for which humans are held responsible.

On the second level, the Bible discusses a whole range of subjects: the organization of the Israelite polity, rules of war, ritual laws of public sacrifice, the method of providing for the poor and less fortunate—the list goes on and on. As a result, many of its most important discussions center around matters political. That is a subject in and of itself. Our concern here is to identify the ideational basis of that discussion.

We have already noted that politics has two faces, combining as it does the organization of power ("who gets what, when, and how") and the pursuit of justice (who should get what, when, and how in the good commonwealth). "Good" politics always rests on dealing properly with both elements in the combination. The Bible recognizes the interlinking of both aspects of politics and addresses itself to both. Every comprehensive society is, in fact, a polity, that is to say, it is organized politically simply by virtue of its being an organized society. That is because human relationships inevitably involve power, which must be allocated effectively and authoritatively. Politics involves the authoritative or just allocation or distribution of power. The Bible recognizes this fact in the very first chapter of Genesis where dominion over day and night is assigned by God to the sun and the moon respectively (Gen. 1:16)—introducing the first political terms in the Bible in the process—while dominion over living things is assigned to man (Gen. 1:26). Subsequently, the covenants between God and Noah, Abraham, and the Israelites at Sinai form the basis for the distribution of powers between God and human communities. By the Bible's own terms, any teaching about the good life must include teachings about the good commonwealth.

The Bible utilizes historical data to present its thesis and to demonstrate its validity, but it uses those data only insofar as they are useful to its purposes. Thus, it does not attempt to present a complete historical record of any period and says so quite openly by referring those who might be interested in the full record to other works that existed at the time and were devoted to history per se. It simply selects those incidents in the historical record that are of particular use in the development of its central idea and relates those incidents honestly and accurately as it were, but clearly from a particular point of view. Thus, the historical aspects of the Bible relate to the expression of the central idea of prophetic Judaism over time and space (i.e., in history). The historical materials are mainly illustrative in character. If one wished to "translate" the biblical approach into something roughly akin to modern academic terminology, one might call it "moral science" since it represents an effort to develop fundamental moral principles from historical examples, which, while specific in and of themselves, have an applicability in other places and other times.

An understanding of this characteristic of the Bible eliminates many difficulties. For one, it transforms the historiographic problem of apparent discrepancies, repetitions, and chronological gaps. Since the Bible attempts to be no more than roughly chronological in its sequences, it is not serious to the biblical authors if incidents are slightly out of chronological order. Since the Bible attempts to use cases to teach, it is not serious to the compiler if the same case is repeated in a slightly different version provided that each version teaches something special. Indeed, what one must look for, when one finds the same case repeated, is not the fact of the repetition per se but whether there was not some larger reason for the repetition in light of the Bible's purposes.

The argument that the Bible is a political work is not meant to suggest that it is not a religious work, a literary work, or whatever else has been claimed for it. Its prismatic character enables it to be all of these and more. Our argument is that one very important way in which it can be approached is the political.

The Bible and the Covenant Idea

The central concern that binds all the biblical books together is the prophetic concern with the maintenance of God's covenant with Israel and the working out of the relationship between the Israelites and God through that covenant and its covenant supplements. Covenant as idea and practical device is central to the whole of biblical literature. As idea, it sets forth the terms of a particularly biblical approach to the world. The entire worldview of the Bible and consequently the essential outlook of all biblically rooted traditions is built around the covenant idea. Covenant-making (and breaking) is the dominant biblical motif and descriptions of incidents of covenant-making punctuate the biblical text at decisive junctures—with Noah after the Flood, with Abraham in Canaan, with the Israelites led by Moses at Sinai and, later, on the plains of Moab, with the Israelites in Canaan led by Joshua, between the elders of Judah and Israel and David, the people of Israel with assorted Israelite kings and priests, and between Israel, led by Ezra and Nehemiah, and God. Regardless of the extent to which, as events, they are fully factual or not, members of the Jewish and Christian faith communities trace their roots back to them. Sacred history is community-defining. Through it a people acquires its form, its ethic, a system of social regulation, a lineage, and a connection to the transcendant power to which it is obligated.

A biblical covenant—the Hebrew term is *brit*—involves a pledge of loyalty beyond that demanded for mutual advantage, actually involving the development of community among the partners to it. The word *brit* appears in the Hebrew Bible 286 times.[13] The etymology of the word *brit,* while somewhat uncertain, seems to be related to or even derived from the Akkadian *biritu,* which means to bind together or fetter, an appropriate description of what covenanting is. While the word seems to be derived from this Akkadian origin, the actual Akkadian term for covenant is *riksus,* a word that also signifies binding. The ancient Mesopotamian world knew the covenant idea in some form as did the Hittites whose word *ishuiul* also signifies binding, but covenants for both represented vassal treaties between powerful monarchs and clients—usually imperial conquerers and vassal states—and nothing more. Just as the Hebrew language acquired the word indirectly and did not simply borrow the common Akkadian term, so too did the Jews shift the content of the term expanding the covenant idea to become their first principle of cosmic and human relationships.[14]

Significantly, the term used for making a covenant is *likhrot brit,* to cut a covenant. This refers in part to the original form of covenant-making, which was by sacrificing an animal, dividing it in half, having the parties to the covenant pass through the two parts, and then binding the two parts together. But it is significant that cutting (dividing) and binding, are the principal elements in the terminology and early practice of covenant-making since a covenant both divides and binds, that is to say, it clarifies and institutionalizes both the distinction between or separate identities of the partners and their linkage. This is, of course, precisely what covenants are about. In other words, the covenant relationship is to social and political life what Buber's I-Thou relationship is to personal life. Through covenants, humans and their institutions are enabled to enter into dialogue while maintaining their respective integrities within a shared framework.

The idea of God's covenant with humans is a major element in the monotheistic revolution, which raised religion from the magical to the ethical. In pagan religions, the relationship between gods and humans is natural or organic. That is to say, humans are literally procreated by the gods and owe them fealty as children do parents. Unfortunately for the children, their parents are capricious and, because they are gods, very powerful. Therefore the children must propitiate them.[15] God's relationship to Israel is deliberately portrayed in the Bible as involving creation out of earthly materials but not procreation. The bond between them is a moral one established by covenant. That is why, as Yehezkel Kaufman has put it, monotheism is not a matter of arithmetic—one god as against many—but involves a conceptual transformation of the first magnitude.[16]

Sealing a covenant involves some ritual act. In the Bible, sacrifice is the common ritual but there also were the common meal and oath. Thus, Moses, Aaron, Aaron's sons, and the seventy elders of Israel representing the entire people, shared a common meal upon completion of the Sinai covenant (cf. Exod. 24:1-12). Other forms include drinking together, gift-giving, exchange of names, sacrifices, kissing, and handshaking. The common meal is prominently featured throughout the history of covenanting. Indeed, so much so that one way to forbid establishing a covenantal relationship was to forbid eating together. The idea of the common meal becomes an important ritual in both Judaism and Christianity, with the latter emphasizing the taking of food as the means of organically linking with the Savior.

Covenanting involves the combination of pact and oath. Oaths essentially combine promises with self-cursing should the promise be violated. Since covenants rest primarily on a moral basis, the best way to secure compliance is by the invocation of curses upon oneself for violation of the terms of the agreement. Thus, God's promise of eternal faithfulness to his people in Hebrew Scriptures is often embodied in an oath (cf. Isa. 55:3). This is reflected in the New Testament as well (see cf. Luke I:72-73).

In its highest form, a covenant community is a community of souls, the highest ideal of friendship, as expressed in 1 Sam. 18:1-3: "The soul of Jonathan was bound up with the soul of David and Jonathan loved him with all his soul...and David and Jonathan made a covenant in their love for each other (which was) like the love of each for his own soul." In that sense, covenantal relationships have been compared to marriages in which the integrity of each partner continues to exist within the new community they create. On the other hand, covenants are used in far more limited but lasting relationships between former or potential enemies, as in Genesis 21:22-23, where Abraham makes a covenant with his neighbor Abimelech with regard to the sharing of water resources:

> And it came to pass at that time, that Abimelech and Phicol the captain of his host spoke unto Abraham, saying: "God is with thee in all that thou doest. Now therefore swear unto me here by God that thou wilt not deal falsely with me, nor with my son, nor with my son's son; but according to the kindness that I have done unto thee, thou shalt do unto me, and to the land wherein thou hast sojourned."

or Josh. 9:3–15, where the Israelites are tricked into a mutual security with the Gibeonites:

> But when the inhabitants of Gibeon heard what Joshua had done unto Jericho and to Ai, they also did work wilily, and went and made as if they had been ambassadors, and took old sacks upon their asses, and wineskins, worn and rent and patched up; and worn shoes and clouted upon their feet, and worn garments upon them; and all the bread of their provision was dry and was become crumbs. And they went to Joshua unto the camp at Gilgal, and said unto him, and to the men of Israel: "We are come from a far country; now therefore make ye a covenant with us." And the men of Israel said unto the Hivites: "Peradventure ye dwell among us; and how shall we make a covenant with you?" And they said unto Joshua: "We are thy servants." And Joshua said unto them: "Who are ye? and from whence come ye?" And they said unto him: "From a very far country thy servants are come because of the name of the Lord thy God; for we have heard the fame of Him, and all that He did in Egypt, and all that he did to the two kings of the Amorites, that were beyond the Jordan, to Sihon king of Heshbon, and to Og king of Bashan, who was at Ashtaroth. And our elders and all the inhabitants of our country spoke to us, saying: Take provision in your hand for the journey, and go to meet them, and say unto them: We are your servants; and now make ye a covenant with us. This our bread we took hot for our provision out of our houses on the day we came forth to go unto you; but now, behold, it is dry, and is become crumbs. And these wine-skins, which we filled were new; and, behold, they are rent. And these our garments and our shoes are worn by reason of the very long journey." And the men took of their provision and asked not counsel at the mouth of the Lord. And Joshua made peace with them, and made a covenant with them, to let them live; and the magistrates of the congregation swore unto them.

So pervasive is the covenantal system in the Bible that it is reflected in its mythic as well as historical passages. Thus, God's relationship with the natural order and lower forms of life is frequently portrayed as a covenantal one, as in Jeremiah 33:25–26:

> Thus saith the Lord: "If my covenant be not with day and night, if I have not appointed the ordinances of heaven and earth; then will I also cast away the seed of Jacob, and of David My servant so that I will not take of his seed to be rulers over the seed of Abraham, Isaac, and Jacob; for I will cause their captivity to return, and will have compassion on them."

For the Bible, nature itself is a matter of covenant. Sometimes there is a projection of the model to include the relationships between inanimate objects as being political. We already have noted the description in the first chapter of Genesis, of the sun and the moon having dominion over day and night, respectively, using the Hebrew word *mamlekhet* for rule among equals.

Whether or not such portrayals are intended to be allegorical, the Bible presents God's covenants with people as experiential events. From this perspective, *brit* is a term used to capture the Jewish myth of politics, sometimes through real covenants and sometimes symbolically. Extending the pervasive covenantal relationship between God and humans, presented as the only proper one, the Bible necessarily holds that the covenantal relationship is the only proper basis for political organization—that is, the structured allocating of authority and power among humans—as well. In a political sense, biblical covenants take the form of constituting acts that establish the parameters of authority and its division without prescribing the constitutional details of regimes. Thus, the Sinai covenant establishes once and for all God's kingship over Israel and the partnership between God and Israel in *tikkun olam* (the repair of the universe). It does not establish any particular political regime.[17] What it does do is set down the criteria that must be encompassed in a proper regime—a holy commonwealth.

Politically the covenant idea has within it the seeds of modern constitutionalism in that covenants define and limit the powers of the parties to them, a limitation not inherent in nature but involving willed concessions. This idea of limiting power is of first importance in the biblical worldview since it helps explain why an omnipotent God does not exercise His omnipotence in the affairs of men. In covenanting with humans, God in effect limits Himself and withdraws somewhat from interfering with them to give them space to be independently human. He grants humans a degree of freedom under the terms of the covenant, retaining only the authority to reward or punish the consequences of that freedom at some future date.[18]

By the same token, the humans who bind themselves through the covenant limit their powers as well. In the most immediately political sense this is particularly true of the leaders of the people whose governmental powers are limited to serving God by serving the people under the terms of the covenant without gaining anything like absolute power over the people. Thus, the idea of constitutionalism, which by definition must include the idea of limited government makes an early (if not its first) appearance in the biblical era.[19]

The Israelites may have taken the idea and techniques of covenant-making from their neighbors but they turned the idea on its head to give it an entirely different character. Mesopotamian and West Semitic covenants were designed to limit previously independent entities by making them vassals, regulating their external behavior but leaving their internal life alone. Israelite covenants, on the other hand, function as liberating devices that call into existence new entities.

The biblical covenant was not simply designed to create a dependent entity linked and owing fealty to an imperial ruler, but a partnership between the parties involved. Of course the relationship between God and the human covenanting party was not of simple equality; but it was one of equal partnership in a common task (the redemption of the world) in which both parties preserved their respective integrities even while committing themselves to a relationship of mutual responsibility. God, by entering into a covenant with humans, graciously accepts a limitation on the exercise of His omnipotence so that humans may become His free partners, thus endowing humankind with freedom. But the price of that freedom is the acceptance of an internal reform as well as external obligations. This audacious idea meant that subsidiary covenants linking human agencies or entities would, perforce, be covenants between equals in partnership. A covenantal partnership is not the kind of partnership created in private law in which the partners have very limited obligations to one another, but the most comprehensive kind of a public law partnership, which creates community and thereby involves a more extensive set of mutual obligations.

The covenant becomes the framework for mutual obligation and the basis of a new law and politics internally and externally. Consequently both the covenant itself and the ideas or principles that flow from it establish and inform a tradition. In the course of Jewish history, actual covenants and covenantal principles appear and reappear to give the Jewish political tradition both form and content.

Covenant Dynamics: Hearkening and Hesed

The radical character of the covenant idea should be apparent. Humans have gained a certain freedom. God recognizes that freedom and constitutionalizes it. He demands in return that humans accept the consequences of freedom, namely, that people organize themselves into bodies politic bound by law and pursuing justice, make themselves responsible for enforcing the law and living according to its requirements, and act accordingly. The full implications of this become apparent when it is understood that, in its capacity as a morally grounded compact, a covenant establishes a partnership linking diverse entities into a purposeful union of unlimited duration, but one in which the partners maintain their respective integrities throughout. In contemporary terms, it is a relationship that enshrines diversity within a framework of union—a federal relationship—at least for those purposes for which the covenant was instituted.

Some covenants create symmetrical partnerships in the sense that all the partners are simply equal, and some asymmetrical ones in that the quality of the partners is limited to a particular set of functions. Obviously, the covenants between God and man are asymmetrical. With all the freedom that those covenants endow man, he is still the junior partner, but a partner he is since, in matters of life on earth, he has very real power indeed.

This covenant-grounded freedom has immediate consequences. Biblical terminology expresses the true character of covenantal relationships. Thus, the Bible describes humans as hearkening (*shamoa, vayishma*) to God's commandments, hearing and choosing to respond to them—rather than simply obeying them.

Hearken is an archaism in English, featured in the King James translation of the Bible; hence, *shamoa* is sometimes translated as "obey" in more modern English versions of Scripture. But they are not the same at all, and abandonment of the older word represents the abandonment of a critical biblical concept so as to change the whole meaning of the text and the whole biblical understanding of how humans act. To hearken is very different from to obey. Hearkening is a form of consent whereby the individual receives an instruction and in the process of hearkening makes a decision to accept and follow it.

The act of hearkening is an act of hearing, considering, agreeing, and then acting. It is a sign of human freedom, of free will, whereby in order to act humans must consciously decide to do so, even in response to God. Hearkening involves the exercise of the hearkener's free will to consent rather than being forced to submit whether willing or not, or not even having the possibility to exercise free will in the first place. Indeed, there is no biblical word for "obey." The modern Hebrew word is of relatively recent coinage, for military purposes. While God can command, humans either hearken to His commandments or not.

To obey is to act on the basis of a commandment from a superior. It is essentially an involuntary response engendered by the nature of hierarchical relations between superior and subordinate, a unilateral relationship involving submission to authority. To hearken, on the other hand, involves a decision to respond. God's communications with humans involve consent.

Implicit in the Hebrew term *shamoa* is that he who hears God speak chooses whether or not to hearken to what is spoken. This is the full proof that, according to the Bible, humans are truly free. The Bible has no word for obey, humans can only hearken. God has created humankind so that they can only hearken, which means they are free to choose, indeed they must make a choice. God, as sovereign of the universe and covenant partner of humankind, reserves the right to punish them for not hearkening, but the fact that their rebelliousness is part of their very nature, limits the degree to which he can exercise that right.

If God must depend upon man's willingness to hearken to Him, man's willingness to do so is sharpened by the consequences of what befalls humanity when they do not. Man is conflicted. First, how does he know what those consequences will be; but even more important, how does he know what he must and must not do in order to preserve his federal liberty. Liberty that is not federal liberty becomes anarchy and leads to *hamas,* which can be defined as chaotic anarchy, senseless destructive anger, and social disorganization (Gen. 6:13), the kind of anarchy that brought the Flood.

The operative mechanism of *brit* is *hesed.* The biblical term *hesed* is often mistranslated as grace but is better translated as covenant love or the loving fulfillment of a covenant obligation. *Hesed* is the operative term in a covenant relationship, which translates the bare fact of the covenant into a dynamic relationship.[20] *Hesed* is a critical covenant concept. It prevents the covenant from becoming a mere contract, narrowly interpreted by each partner for his benefit alone, by adding a dynamic dimension requiring the parties to act toward each other in such a way as to demonstrate their covenant love; that is, beyond the letter of the law.

Notes

1. Cf. Karl Llewellyn and E. Hievel, *The Cheyenne Way* (Norman: University of Oklahoma Press, 1935).
2. Emil Lengyel, *One Thousand Years of Hungary* (New York: John Day, 1958); Andrew B. Urbansky, *Byzantium and the Danube Frontier* (New York: Twayne, 1968).

3. Cf., e.g., Paul Henri Mallet, *Northern Antiquities* (New York: AMS Press, 1968); Gabriel Tur Ville-Petre, *The Heroic Age of Scandinavia* (London: Hutchinson's University, 1951).
4. See Hans Kohn, *The Idea of Nationalism* (New York: Macmillan, 1961); Leo Strauss, *Philosophy and Law* (Philadelphia: Jewish Publication Society, 1987).
5. Cf. Baruch Spinoza, *Tractatus Theologico-Politicus*, trans. Samuel Shirley (Leiden: E.J. Brill, 1991) ; Leo Strauss, *Spinoza's Critique of Religion* (New York: Schocken, 1965).
6. Cf., e.g., Leo Strauss, *Persecution and the Art of Writing* (Glencoe, IL: Free Press, 1952) and *Natural Right and History* (Chicago: University of Chicago Press, 1953). For Leo Strauss on the Bible, see "Jerusalem and Athens," *Commentary* 43, no. 6 (June 1967): 45–57 and *An Interpretation of Genesis* (Philadelphia: Center for Jewish Community Studies, 1972).
7. From the perspective of the Jewish political tradition, the Bible must be read as a whole work, regardless of the correctness of the various theories of biblical criticism. What is significant about it is not the extent to which the text in our possession is an edited amalgam but that, as a whole, it presents—and represents—a comprehensive tradition. For a fuller discussion of this problem, see Leo Strauss, *What is Political Philosophy?* (Glencoe, IL: Free Press, 1959). Strauss applies his perspective in *An Interpretation of Genesis* (Jerusalem and Philadelphia: Center for Jewish Community Studies, 1975).
8. Michael Walzer, *Exodus and Revolution* (New York: Basic Books, 1985).
9. Steven J. Brams, *Biblical Games: A Strategic Analysis of Stories in the Old Testament* (Cambridge, MA: MIT Press, 1980).
10. Aaron B. Wildavsky, *The Nursing Father: Moses as a Political Leader* (Tuscaloosa: University of Alabama Press, 1984).
11. On ancient versus modern constitutionalism, see Leo Strauss, *Liberalism, Ancient and Modern* (Ithaca, NY: Cornell University Press, 1989); *Natural Rights and History* (Chicago: University of Chicago Press, 1953); Charles MacIlwaine, *Constitutionalism, Ancient and Modern* (Ithaca, NY: Cornell University Press, 1947).
12. For the rules of Talmudic interpretation, see Philip Birnbaum, *The Complete Siddur* (New York: Hebrew Publishing Co., 1950).
13. Klaus Baltzer, *The Covenant Formulary* (Philadelphia: Fortress Press, 1971), 6.
14. See George Mendenhall, "Covenant Forms in Israelite Tradition," *Biblical Archeologist* 17 (1959): 50–76. For an interesting gloss on Mendenhall, see Moshe Weinfeld, "B'rit—Covenant vs. Obligation," *Biblica* 56, fasc. 1 (1975): 120–28. For a full terminological discussion, see Moshe Weinfeld, "Covenant Terminology in the Ancient Near East and Its Influence on the West," *Journal of the American Oriental Society* 93 (1973).
15. Cf. Henri Frankfort, *Before Philosophy* (Harmondsworth, England: Penguin, 1951).
16. Cf. Yehezkel Kaufmann, *The Biblical Account of the Conquest of Canaan* (Jerusalem: Magnes Press, 1985) and *The Religion of Israel From Its Beginnings to the Babylonian Exile*, trans. Moshe Greenberg (New York: Schocken, 1972).
17. The question as to whether or not the choice of regimes is open has been much debated in Jewish tradition. That is to say, is monarchy mandated by the Torah or a matter of choice? For our purposes here we need not determine which view is correct (although this writer believes that the choice is given). The very fact that the question is a perennial one with such distinguished figures as Don Isaac

Abravanel opting for the latter view is sufficiently significant to demonstrate the point made here. For a discussion of the argument, see David Polish, *Give Us a King* (Hoboken, NJ: Ktav, 1989). For a summary of the sources, see Chaim Herschensohn, *Eleh Divrei HaBrit,* 3 vols. (Hoboken, NJ: 1918–1921) and *Malchi Bakodesh,* 6 vols. (Hoboken, NJ: 1923–1928).

18. This idea of God's self-limitation became a central idea of Kabbalah, Jewish mysticism, where it reached its apotheosis in the sixteenth-century Kabbalistic teachings of Isaac Luria, known in Jewish history as the Ari, perhaps the last great creative religious figure of premodern Judaism. Luria founded his Kabbalistic teachings on the idea of *tzimtzum* (contraction). Simply put, the theory is that in order to create the material universe, God, who encompassed all time and space, had to contract to open up time and space for the material universe that He then created. In the process of that creation, his radiance was such that the material universe could not withstand its impact and, like a clay pitcher, was shattered, thereby allowing the Divine sparks to escape and, through the breakage, releasing evil into the world. The task of humans, then, is *tikun olam,* that is to say, repairing the vessel, eliminating evil and recapturing the Divine sparks.

This theory was developed in the same century as the Puritan federal theology that saw God as self-limiting in a more political way through his covenants with humans, a very similar idea that may indeed have drawn upon Lurianic Kabbalistic influences that were widely diffused among Reformed Protestant intellectuals at the time. Lurianic Kabbalah is unquestionably an extension of biblical covenantalism and if the Puritans have not made its political implications sufficiently clear, the reader may wish to ponder them.

19. For a fuller discussion of the political institutions of ancient Israel, see Daniel J. Elazar and Stuart A. Cohen, *The Jewish Polity* (Bloomington: Indiana University Press, 1985), Epochs 1 through 6; and Daniel J. Elazar, "The Polity in Biblical Israel," in *Authority, Power and Leadership in the Jewish Polity: Cases and Issues,* ed. Daniel J. Elazar (Lanham, MD: University Press of America and Jerusalem Center for Public Affairs, 1991); Roland de Vaux, *Ancient Israel* (New York: McGraw Hill, 1965); Moshe Weinfeld, "The Transition from Tribal Republic to Monarchy in Ancient Israel and Its Impression on Jewish Political History," in *Kinship and Consent: The Jewish Political Tradition and Its Contemporary Uses,* ed. Daniel J. Elazar (Lanham, MD: Jerusalem Center for Public Affairs and University Press of America, 1983).

20. Cf. Norman Snaith, "The Covenant-Love of God," in Norman Snaith, *The Distinctive Ideas of the Old Testament,* 2d ed. (New York: Schocken Books, 1973), 94–127; Nelson Glueck, *Hesed in the Bible,* trans. Alfred Gottschalk and ed. Elias L. Epstein (New York: Ktav, 1975).

4

The Bible and Political Life in Covenant

The Federal Way of Covenant

It should be clear by now that the Bible sees it as imperative that political relationships be established by and through covenant and follow covenantal principles in order to be proper ones. The explanation of why this is so is easy enough for a believer but perhaps more difficult for agnostics or nonbelievers. All would agree that what comes through so forcefully is the strong yearning for humans to be free, yet in tune with the powers-that-be in the universe. These two aspirations, as manifestations, sometimes are quite contradictory; the tension between them is perhaps the fundamental tension of human existence, the basis for all human effort and struggle. Such is the biblical portrayal of human existence, beginning with Adam who is seemingly content to tend God's garden but cannot resist the temptation to freely eat of the fruit of the Tree of Knowledge of Good and Evil (Gen. 2-3).

There is no permanent way to resolve this tension, short of a miraculous transformation of the human race. There are only ways to control, manage, and direct it toward maximally constructive and minimally destructive ends. Those ways are federal ways. The balancing of man's desire to be free with his desire to be in harmony with the universe can only be done through covenant, through the establishment of federal liberty (the freedom to act freely but in accordance with the terms of the covenant and in covenantal ways) in place of natural liberty (the freedom to act as one pleases as long as one can survive the consequences).

God indicates the positive opportunities of federal liberty and its limits, and the consequences of violating those limits through His covenants with humankind, giving man, at the same time, a means for negotiating with God on those matters that are of mutual concern. Moreover, through covenant, God gives humans a tool that they can use to establish and regularize their relationships with each other to preserve their freedom, particularly in their political and social relations with one another.

This is the great and central teaching of the Bible. It is a teaching that must be made manifest in political life if it is to be manifested in any other phase of human existence. While, according to the Bible, God can control humans on an individual basis, if He cares to keep Himself busy doing so, humans cannot control themselves unless they live (bound by covenant) in political society, that is to say, in political relationship with one another. Here the Bible anticipates a kind of humane Hobbesianism.

According to the biblical account, political society is established by Cain, the first murderer, who founds the first city (Gen. 4:17). Cain acts on his own initiative. He does so to protect himself from those whom he fears might kill him because of the mark he bears, and also to provide a safer environment within which to raise his son. (The mark is God's punishment for killing Abel but God means it to both mark Cain's guilt and to protect him from human vengeance.) But such a political society exists without covenant and hence is not capable of remaining undegenerate. The unlimited human exercise of freedom leads to self-destruction through *hamas,* not the least of whose characteristics is unrestricted sexual intercourse between humans and other beings (6:1-5).

God is more than reconciled to human freedom; He created humans to be free, but humans, in turn, must learn to be reconciled to the need to exercise that freedom in harmony with the universal power that makes for salvation. What is God to do? He can destroy the world, and, indeed, He proceeds to do so by flood on that first occasion. But unless He wants to entirely destroy humanity, He must reconcile Himself to human reality as much as humans must reconcile themselves to God's. Humans, in order to be what they are intended to be in the universal scheme of things, must be free to choose, which means free to make the wrong choices as well as the right ones. This is true even in the case of Adam who is free to do wrong and accept the consequences of his choice.

In the antediluvian world, relationships between God and humans are portrayed in such a way that most of the time, when God speaks to man (Hebrew: *vayomer* or *vayedabber*), he does not command. Adam is commanded (*vayitzav*) only once—not to eat of the fruit of the tree of knowledge. Otherwise, when God speaks, it is up to man to respond, to hearken.

After the Flood, the Noahide covenant adds a further dimension. If humans are so free as not to be required to obey God, they certainly cannot be expected to obey each other. If their actions and relations to the Sovereign of the Universe are based upon consent, how much more so must their relations with each other be based upon consent. By agreeing together and promising, through a constitutionally binding pact supported by the highest moral authority, humans are able to define the terms of both their liberties and their polities in a spirit that, when properly applied, can bring them into harmony with the universe. From this premise flows the covenanted commonwealth based upon federal liberty.

For the Bible, this model of covenanted commonwealth is what S. D. Goitein has elsewhere termed *religious democracy,* understanding the term *religious* in the original sense of its Latin root, *religio* (binding), which has its own covenantal implications.[1] Accordingly, the heart of the classic Jewish polity is the *edah,* the congregation or organized assembly of all citizens assembled by their tribes, each of which constitutes an integral entity within the polity.

The Bible presents the *edah* as organized through a system of governing institutions, national, tribal, and local, rooted in a common constitution, the Torah, which is in itself derived from the founding covenant. These institutions are all republican in character, but republican in the special sense of a religious democracy; that is, they are established by the *edah* and God acting in tandem. God exercises His sovereignty directly within the *edah* in the classic biblical formulation, but is represented on earth by a prime minister (Hebrew: *Eved Adonai*), of which Moses and Joshua were the two greatest examples. He is supported and balanced by a court of seventy elders drawn from the tribes, a high priest with judicial and oracular functions as a counterpoise to the prime minister who was explicitly forbidden priestly functions, and the assembly of the *edah* itself with its elders and *nesiim* (literally: raised up ones or representatives).

The tribal structures are somewhat similar. The *shevet* is the tribal equivalent of the *edah,* the assembly of all citizens of the tribe. Regular business is carried out by elders and every tribe has a *nasi* as its head, as well as *nesiim* raised up for specific purposes. Locally, civic and political life is organized by township. The town government consists of the assembly of local citizens (*ha'ir*) with their elders (*sha'arei ha'ir*) who assemble at the town gates as the adjudicating body of the community.

All function within the framework of the Torah-constitution but with substantial autonomy.

This classic model is presented in full in the Pentateuch and again in the Book of Joshua. Its workings are described in the books of Judges, Samuel, and Ruth. Modified by the introduction of kingship and its bureaucratic extensions, this classic model is reiterated in Ezekiel's vision of the restoration of Israel. Over the centuries it came to serve as a model for political thinkers under various circumstances, many of whom we will meet in the course of this study.

The prophetic books of the Bible do more than portray regimes. They constitute a covenantal history of the Jewish people, a description of the fulfillment or failure of the covenantal plan informing political and military events and institutions with theological significance, the litany of covenant breaking, repentance, and deliverance as related by the prophetic historiographers. It was this history that set the stage for the deliverance of the prophetic message, which, it has been suggested, takes the form of covenantal lawsuits and, at the very least, calls Israel to account for violations of the terms of the covenant. The basis of the prophetic role is specified in the Torah itself, most specifically in Deuteronomy 18:15 ff., but see also Exodus 4:15 and 7:1 ff.

The same covenantal themes are carried over into the *Ketuvim* (Writings), the third section of the Hebrew Bible. The Psalms reflect the place of people, king, and temple within the covenantal system, poetically rehearsing the course of covenant history and reflecting on the Divine sanction through covenant of the institutions of Israel as a covenanted commonwealth. Those books of *Ketuvim* that did not explicitly utilize covenantal terminology were sooner or later interpreted as covenantal in character. The Song of Songs, for example, was included in the biblical canon by the Talmudic sages because it was understood not as an erotic love poem between a king and his beloved but as a metaphoric description of the marriage bond between God and Israel, a nonpolitical (in one sense) use of covenantal thinking but no less covenantal for that.

The Political Character of Biblical Covenants

Biblical covenants may be separable into political and nonpolitical categories, but following the biblical worldview in such matters, there is hardly a single covenant in the Bible that does not have strong political overtones or undertones. The covenant between David and Jonathan is, on its surface, a nonpolitical covenant. Yet at issue in that covenant is the right of succession to the kingship of Israel, where Jonathan is implicitly portrayed as ceding to David. While the matter is not specified in the covenant between them, the context suggests that more was involved than two friends pledging an extraordinary friendship.

Similarly, it has been argued that the covenants between God and Abraham (Gen. 15 and 17) were nonpolitical. A closer look, however, offers a strong case that they were, in the sense that they promised peoplehood and land for Abraham's descendants, thereby setting the stage for the constitutional covenants of the later period. The patriarchal covenants acquired even more direct political meaning when the Israelites settled in their land. From that point onward, there were frequent appeals to those covenants as legitimizing Israelite possession of (e.g., Neh. 9) and rule over (e.g., 1 Chron. 6) the land; defense of the polity against foreign aggressors (2 Kings 13:22-23); and the maintenance of God's law (Ps. 105). As such, they became the territorial charter of the Jewish people, affirming their right to the land of Israel.

If we look at the way subsequent generations of Jews and Christians, particularly in the sixteenth and seventeenth centuries, read those covenants, we find that they treated them as having great political significance. Their arguments rejecting the Divine right of kings, for example, stem from those covenants as well as from the covenant with Noah.

One question that arises almost immediately is the extent to which the biblical covenants between God and man are mutual or unilateral acts. The covenant with Noah has been cited both ways. Reading Genesis 9 alone, it seems that God bestowed His covenant upon Noah as an act of grace. There was nothing mutual about it. Reading the whole story (chap. 6 through 9) as a piece, however, suggests a different view. Because Noah responded to God's turning to him before the Flood, God responded in turn. So there was indeed mutuality.

The same is true with regard to Abraham, only more so. The *brit bein ha Betarim* (chap. 15) is made because Abraham demands that God make a formal commitment after his continued responses to an unseen voice. From the time he hearkens to God's voice in Haran and migrates as a result, he hears from God only once until this chapter when God reappears ready to take the next step, namely the concretization of His promise in a formal pact (covenant). Abram brings Him to that step through a negotiation, the result of which is this covenant that guarantees the land to Abram's descendants.

The evolving relationship between Abraham and God moves from one in which Abram merely hearkens to one in which he tries, successfully, to get God to formalize His commitments. Initially (Gen. 12), God tells Abram to leave his land of residence, his kith, and his father's house to go to a new land that God will show him. Abram complies and moves lock, stock, and barrel to Canaan where he wanders around unsettled and without a stake in the country. Up to this point, God has been testing Abram to see how he will respond to the challenges of building a new society by not speaking to him, leaving Abram alone to search God out. God still does not appear in person but in a vision. In fact, God appears and disappears, leaving Abram, who has staked his all on Him and who, after all, is only human, fearful of desertion. Hence the occasional—if formulary—reassurance, *al tirah,* (do not fear) here at the beginning of God's new move.

Abraham, then still Abram, responds (vv. 2-3) to God's renewed promise of great reward (v. 1) by indicating that all is meaningless if he has no natural heir who, in a patriarchal system, can succeed him as head of the enterprise. God promises Abram an heir (vv. 4-5) and reiterates His promise of a new kith to be descended from him. Abram responds (v. 6) with renewed belief that moves the dialectic further. As a consequence, God restates His promise formally and in full (v. 7). This time, however, Abram is not content with an oral commitment and (perhaps) another long silence; he wants a tangible (i.e., enforceable) one (v. 8). Here Abram clearly is the initiator. God responds with a covenant (vv. 9-10), beginning with a proper covenant ceremony involving cutting and binding. This ceremony is calculated to symbolize the reality of covenant, namely the binding of two separate entities in such a way that each maintains its own integrity even while being part of the new union. In chapter 17, it should be noted, God regains the initiative by initiating a second covenant supplementary to the first.

Subsequent to the Sinai covenant, covenants are used to link the governors and the governed under God according to the terms of the great covenant and in light of changing circumstances. The model of such covenants is found in Joshua 8:30-35 where Joshua reads the constitution to the people:

> Then Joshua built an altar unto the Lord, the God of Israel, in Mount Ebal, as Moses the servant of the Lord commanded the children of Israel, as it is written in the book of the teaching [Torah] of Moses, an altar of unhewn stones, upon which

no man had lifted up any iron; and they offered thereon burnt-offerings unto the Lord, and sacrificed peace-offerings. And he wrote there upon the stones a copy of the Torah of Moses, which he wrote before the children of Israel. And all Israel, and their elders and officers, and their judges, stood on this side of the ark and on that side before the priests the Levites, that bore the ark of the covenant of the Lord, as well the stranger as the home-born; half of them in front of Mount Gerizim, and half of them in front of Mount Ebal; as Moses the servant of the Lord had commanded at the first, that they should bless the people of Israel. And afterward he read all the words of the Torah, the blessing and the curse, according to all that is written in the book of the Torah. There was not a word of all that Moses commanded, which Joshua read not before all the assembly of Israel, and the women, and the little ones, and the strangers that walked among them.

Also, in Joshua 23 and 24, Joshua assembles the representatives of the twelve tribes of Israel and the tribal and national officers near Shechem, after the conquest and division of the land, to renew before God the covenant of Moses and reestablish the Israelite confederacy on a landed basis. As in the case of the original, those covenants also established (or reestablished) the basic distribution of authority and powers but did not include a frame of government per se, simply accepting the frame of government established earlier.

With the introduction of the monarchy, which represented a major shift in the structure of authority within the nation, a new covenant was made (2 Sam. 5:1-3; see below). Similar covenants were initiated or renewed after every major political change or reform in the biblical period, such as when the High Priest Jehoiada restored the legitimate monarchy after Athaliah's usurpation (2 Kings 11:17-20) and Josiah promulgated his constitutional reform (2 Kings 23:1-3).[2]

Covenant as the Foundation of Justice, Obligations, and Rights

Fundamental to any Jewish conception here is the principle that God is the creator and sovereign of the universe, all of which ultimately belongs to Him— "*Ki li kol ha-aretz*" (because the whole earth is mine)— including all life within it. Humans have what we call rights and liberties by *reshut;* that is to say, by the authority of God.

The special significance of this is that, while humans have nothing other than what God grants or covenants with them, as God's possessions no human instrumentality, certainly no state, can legitimately interfere with their God-given rights, liberties, protections, or obligations. Once God has commanded or covenanted—and His commandments are based upon His covenants—no human authority or agency has the right to interpose itself without the consent of those commanded or those who are partners to the covenant. As we all know, this, indeed, is the foundation of the modern development of rights, growing out of sixteenth- and seventeenth-century Reformed Protestantism, which took these matters very seriously indeed.

The Bible projects an omnipotent, omniscient, and eternal God while all humans are mortal and limited, even after eating from the tree of knowledge. The partnership between them, although based on a measure of equality between them, is essentially a functional one, confined to certain tasks of *yishuv ha-aretz* (the settlement of the earth) and *tikkun olam* (the repair of the world); in other words, the earthly tasks of this world where humans increasingly have played a major role in God's scheme of things. It is by virtue of that partnership and the obligations which flow from it that humans have rights that are real rights, not at all diminished by being derived from obligations. Nevertheless, because they are rights that flow from God's covenant with humans, they are to some extent conditional on humans' maintaining their part of the covenantal bargain. In the language of the Puritans, they have a federal obligation, fulfillment of which guarantees their federal liberty.

One critical question that must be asked is whether covenant is also the foundation of justice, with its concomitant obligations and rights, according to the biblical worldview, or whether justice is built into the world from its beginning or creation; that is, natural. Is there a natural law of justice in the biblical worldview?

One may find in the Bible references to three possible positions. In Genesis 4, the story of Cain and Abel suggests that there is such a thing as natural justice built into the world. Verse 10 is the proof text. After Cain asks God whether he is his brother's keeper, God turns to him and says: "What has thou done? The voice of thy brother's blood cries to me from the ground" (*Kol damai akhikhah tzoakim alai min ha-adamah*). This is by far the most significant biblical passage speaking to the existence of natural justice and has been quoted to that end by generations of commentators.[3]

Far more ambiguous are passages such as that beginning in Job 38:4, when God, speaking out of the whirlwind, asks Job the famous question: "Where were you when I founded the world," and then proceeds to set forth a description of God's creation and systematization of the natural order. However, the upshot of God's answer is to suggest that while there is a natural order, there is no natural justice; that God behaves according to His own will in ways that may seem to humans capricious in meting out justice. The closing verses of Ecclesiastes 12 (Kohelet) suggests the same but in a more positive tone, that God has ordered the world and therefore has redeemed humanity from the desperately cynical conclusion that all is vanity, presented throughout the rest of the book.

Apparently refuting the claim that the Bible rests on natural law is Genesis 9, which describes God's first explicit covenant, with Noah and his descendants after the Flood.[4] That covenant sets down the basic rules that God expects humans to live by and provides for the establishment of means of enforcement of those rules.[5] It binds all humans forevermore.

One can conclude from the foregoing that while there may be natural justice built into the universe, law is entirely a product of God's commandments, which, except for a few basic commandments that God gave Adam, such as to be fruitful and multiply, to be His steward in the Garden of Eden, and not to eat of the fruit of the forbidden trees, are all mediated through God's covenants, first with all humanity through Noah and then through segments of humanity beginning with Abraham. Thus, *brit* is required for the ordering of the world (for humans) in matters of *tzedakah u'mishpat*. This, indeed, is the conclusion in Kohelet referred to above.

From reading the first chapters of Genesis one can theorize that it is possible that God tried natural justice before the Flood and found that it did not work, that human nature itself included too much egoism, appetite, and self-interest for humans to act justly without the necessity to do so, and that, prior to His covenant with Noah, God had to intervene personally in every instance to assure just behavior or to punish injustice. In order to eliminate the necessity for such massive personal Divine intervention, God acted, through His covenant with Noah, to establish an order that included the requirement for human enforcement of *tzedakah u'mishpat*. This would make God's initiation of His covenant the first major step in the transfer of his active authority in this world to humans, essentially providing that in matters of ordinary law humans would be responsible, with His involvement confined to extraordinary situations or where human institutions failed to perform according to the terms of the covenant and God's justice.

Covenanting is a most appropriate instrument for this transition. The putative covenant with Adam refers to him as God's *shomer* (steward) in the world (Gen. 2:16) and in the covenant with Noah (Gen. 9), where the specific terms are not used, examples of the retribution necessary to maintain justice are given. In the first covenant with Abraham (Gen. 15) the term *tzedakah* is used. The second covenant (which uses the word *shamor*) is followed immediately by the story of Sodom (Gen. 18), in which one of the most famous justice-related verses in the Bible is presented. *Hashofet kol ha-aretz lo ya'aseh mishpat* (Will the judge of the whole world not do justice?) The culmination is in the Sinai Covenant, which provides the details of what constitutes *tzedakah, hok u'mishpat.* This pattern continues in Joshua's covenant (Josh. 24), which refers to *hok u'mishpat* and David's (1 Chron. 16:7-43), in which David refers to *mishpatay piv,* the justice or just judgements from God's mouth. Every *brit* is an agreement that requires from both parties *shmiya* (hearkening) and *shmirah* (observing). The combination of *shmiyah* and *shmirah,* hearkening and observing, is the way that humans are expected to respond to God's *mitzvot* (commandments). Since the Bible holds that human beings are free to hearken to God or not, and to observe or not, covenant is needed to bind them by sworn promise to do so. Since every *brit* includes the obligation to justice through law (or just judgment), in Hebrew *tzedakah u'mishpat,* whether there is natural justice or not becomes a moot question after God's covenant with Noah.

Three Forms of Justice, Obligation, and Rights

Turn, now, to the three archetypes of political organization in the world—hierarchical, organic, or covenantal. Each can be said to establish a different basis for justice and obligation and source of rights. In hierarchies, one is obligated to those senior to oneself in the hierarchy and ultimately to the person or institution at its top. Under such circumstances one's rights are derived from one's place in the hierarchy. Feudalism is an excellent example of constitutionalized hierarchy where both obligations and rights are clearly demarcated.

In organic polities, one is obligated first to one's primordial group, which has developed organically out of kinship over time, and one's rights are based on one's standing in that primordial group. Tribal societies are excellent examples of the organic model, with tribal custom fixing one's obligations and rights. In covenantal polities, justice is determined by the moral principle upon which the covenant is based. One's obligations are to one's covenant partners and one's rights are derived from and defined by the covenant itself.

While each of these models can be seen as an ideal type, in the real world models are often, perhaps usually, mixed. Thus, the Bible presents Israel as a combination of kinship and consent, beginning, if you will, with God's covenant with Abraham, to produce a family of nations that would be blessed through him. Abraham's immediate descendants form such a family, with Israel emerging out of the line of his grandson Jacob and his twelve offspring who are reunited around a common commitment to God's justice and moral law through the Sinai Covenant, which provides the specifics missing from the Noahide Covenant. In keeping with the organic character of the twelve-tribe kinship group, before Sinai the tribes were governed by customary law. Through the Sinai Covenant God changes the moral basis of the Israelites' obligations and rights as much as He changes their content.[6]

The biblical history of the covenants between God and humans suggests a movement from hierarchical to fully covenantal relations between God and man. At first, God takes the lead in initiating His covenants, establishing His covenant with the patriarchs, perhaps Adam, certainly Noah and Abraham. It is clear from the biblical account that Abraham's role as father of multitudes includes Israelites and others, for example, the Ishmaelites, descended from his son by Hagar. But the Bible carefully distinguishes between the *brit* that Isaac is to reaffirm and continue, and the *brakhah* (blessing) that Abraham confers on Ishmael and the other peoples (or religious communities) descended from him.

In the second stage God seeks to gain popular consent to covenants that He initiates through His designated servant (*Eved Adonai*) who is the principal leader of the people. God's first attempt to do this can be found in Exodus 6, where He has Moses approach the governing elders of the Israelites enslaved in Egypt to renew the covenant of their forefathers, a step that they reject.[7] This technique is successful at Sinai where God initiates the covenant but through Moses requires the popular consent of the Israelites expressed three separate times before the pact is made (Exod. 19:1-9, 24:3-8).

In the third stage, the principal leader turns to God and to the people to covenant or recovenant. Moses is presented as initiating this process in the Plains of Moab at the end of his tenure (Deut. 28:69–33:47). Joshua's initiative is of this type in Joshua 24. Indeed, it may be an older account of that type of initiative than the one we have in Deuteronomy. David does the same after he brings the Ark of the Covenant to Jerusalem (1 Chron. 16), as did Hezekiah after the destruction of the northern kingdom (2 Chron. 29–31), and Josiah in the seventh century (2 Kings 23).

In the fourth stage the people themselves initiate a covenant renewal. This occurred in the days of Ezra and Nehemiah, as described in Nehemiah 8. They turn to their leaders who simply serve as organizers of the act. While God is the object, the description of the event does not involve His direct intervention as it does not in any of the covenants after Sinai. Applying the themes of our initial model, we see that the Bible portrays God's initial covenants with humans in a hierarchical mode. God initiates and acts through patriarchs. Covenanting then enters an organic mode; God covenants with a kith, presented as descending from common ancestors, that becomes a people through the combination of kinship and consent. Only in the final stages does covenanting itself become fully covenantal, that is to say, initiated by all of the partners. Thus, even within the covenantal model there are echoes of the other models.

Covenantal Justice Based on Obligation

Biblical covenants have three dimensions. They contain a theological dimension, either a direct connection with God or with God as a witness; a national-political dimension relating to Israel as a people (*am*) or an organized body politic (*edah*); and a normative dimension dealing with foundation or maintenance of justice, either *tzedakah u'mishpat* or *hok u'mishpat* (law and justice), which includes within it a framework of obligations and rights. This is particularly true of those covenants that establish new frameworks, in Hebrew the covenants of *bnai brit*. It is somewhat less true but still frequently true of those covenants that regulate international relations, where the covenant remains subordinate to its partners, covenants of *ba'alei brit*.

Sinai, the culminating covenant, makes clear what has been the critical primal element of covenantal partnerships from the first, namely, that covenants establish justice through mutual obligations, indeed, systems of mutual obligations, whence are derived (in modern terms) the partners' rights. Under the covenantal system there are no rights that are not derived from obligations. Covenantal obligations are twofold: to be holy and to be just.[8] Hence, they are excellent sources of what moderns define as rights, but covenant also keeps rights conditional on one's maintaining one's covenant with God, which establishes basic morality, justice, and law, at the very least, transforming natural justice into law.

Just as covenants establish different levels of obligation, so, too, they make possible differentiation in rights among those who are covenant partners or those who are partners to different covenants or covenants of different scope. As in the case of the biblical view of covenant obligation, this is not designed to invidiously discriminate among humans but to allow humans to decide for themselves by which covenants they are bound, which obligations they take upon themselves, and, hence, what rights are available to them. In the biblical worldview, all humans are expected to be bound by the Noahide covenant, which obligates them to recognize God's sovereignty, protect human life, and pursue justice on earth, and also endows them with all the basic human rights.

Those who refuse to be bound by accepting the obligations of the Noahide covenant are thereby not entitled to those basic human rights because they have proclaimed themselves outlaws. But it is their choice. Although they can be punished for violating the terms of the covenant, as humans, they cannot be outlawed by others except perhaps for the most blatant causes (what contemporaries would describe as "inhuman").

All human beings can also accept the covenant of Abraham, that is to say, join one of the monotheistic faiths and accept its obligations and gain certain rights thereby. They may also accept the Sinai Covenant and become Jews, thereby taking on even greater obligations and winning the right to be numbered among God's singular people (*am segula*), that is to say, to have the full *brit* and not merely benefit from Abraham's *brit* and *brakhah*. These are all matters of individual human choice.

For Jews, who are further bound by the covenant of Sinai, there is a further obligation of holiness (Deut. 19–21) as the highest form of imitation of God. Whether or not the Jewish people in this respect were to be the pioneers for the rest of humanity is a question that has been the subject of some discussion. (Many Christians see themselves equally bound but with a twist.) While it does have a bearing on rights of citizenship, what bearing it has on human rights is an open question. On basic matters of human right to life, sustenance, property (within limits), and justice, the Bible explicitly provides that "the stranger within thy gates" has the same rights as Israelites, even in the land of Israel. What the outer limits of those basic rights are has been a matter of some discussion over the years.

What is critical about the relationship between rights and obligations in the biblical tradition and in subsequent Jewish tradition is that those covenanted with God are obligated to their fellows under the terms of the covenant to do them justice, from which derives their right to justice. The covenant partners are obligated because they are covenant partners. For Jews the obligation is that they must do justice to the widow and the orphan and the stranger in order to be holy. So it is not that the widows, orphans, and strangers have rights per se, but that they can call upon the Israelites to live up to their obligations. Is this merely a semantic point? I think not, because Israelites are equally obligated to do justice in the form of punishing those who are violators of God's covenant, who cannot claim some a priori natural or human right to be protected against such punishments. What they can claim on constitutional grounds is that the Israelites must live up to their obligations. In some respects that is an even stronger claim than a rights claim. But, however it is perceived, it is a different one.

Even more than that, rights themselves are expressed as obligations. Thus, humans have an obligation to remain alive and to preserve the lives of others. From this can be inferred what moderns would refer to as the right to life, but in classical Jewish sources it is expressed as the duty to maintain life, one's own and that of others, a covenantal obligation, as it were. Thus, the duty to preserve life is derived from the belief that it is God who bestows human life and therefore only He can prescribe the ways in which it can be taken away. Every human has a duty to preserve his or her life as part of his or her duties to God.

The issue is even more clearly joined in the case of property. The right of humans to own and use property can be derived from many scriptural statements of obligations, not the least of which is the commandment, "Thou shalt not steal." Scripture also clearly states that all land and other property ultimately belongs to God who prescribes the parameters of its use by humans. Thus, for example, people can own land. If that land is another Jew's *nakhalah* (biblical inheritance), it must be returned to the family at the appropriate jubilee year. While in a person's possession, agricultural land must be governed by rules providing for the poor to glean and the worker to eat of its produce.

Over the years these restrictions on property rights were interpreted broadly rather than narrowly to create a set of environmental rights that recognized the special needs of individual humans. These included protections of the right to sunlight that existed when a property was acquired, even at the expense of preventing another from building on his adjacent property in such a way that would interfere with that sunlight, or a right to ventilation protected in the same way. Whether formally defined that way or not, these were essentially duties/rights of *re'ut,* that is to say, neighborly comity of the kind described in Deut. (e.g., 22:1-26) as constitutionally required of Israelites in the Torah. *Re'ut* is an extension of *hesed* and as such is an obligation of holiness on the part of covenant partners.

The Torah tends to be uncompromising in its expression of the obligations of humans in general and Jews in particular. The other books of the Bible introduce loopholes, the most important of which are associated with the *mishpat hamelekh* or *hamelukhah* (the law of the king or of the kingdom), derived particularly from 1 Samuel 8 where the prophet Samuel warns Israelites against seeking a king because of the powers a king inevitably has. It seems that even in biblical times kings exercised power over and above Torah constraints. Subsequently, the idea of the *mishpat hamelekh* as a loophole developed, especially against stringent aspects of the criminal law.

What emerges out of the biblical approach are a series of protections and limitations that can roughly be translated into rights and obligations as when the poor are given rights to glean the fields during the harvest. Thus, many of these protections and limitations become what we would call rights, as protected through the Torah as any constitutional right is today. The result, as already noted, are rights and obligations stemming from the federal relationship between humans and God, what John Winthrop, the great Puritan governor of Massachusetts, was later to define as "federal liberty."

In the last analysis, while there may not be natural rights in the Bible, there are fundamental rights in the sense that all humans are bound by covenant with God, at least through the Noahide covenant (some Christians would claim an earlier covenant with Adam as well). These fundamental rights are in that sense constitutional or federal rather than inherent. They certainly are not like the vulgar modern conception of rights as the individual's right to do whatever he or she pleases, perhaps limited only by how an individual's actions affect others, but maybe not even by that.

This leads to another question, namely, who can be obligated and how? We have already touched upon this question to some extent in the preceding paragraphs, but it deserves to be sharpened because it has to do with rights that are other than fundamental. With regard to those obligations associated with what we understand to be rights, the Talmudic sages raise the question as to whether those obligations extend only to fellow Jews or to all humans. This led to the famous discussion between Rabbi Akiva and Ben Azzai, in which Rabbi Akiva states that the most important verse in Torah is *veahavta l're'akha kamokha* (love thy neighbor as thyself), while Ben Azzai claims that even more important is the verse *elle toledot ha-adam* (these are the generations of Adam) because *rea* (neighbor) has been interpreted by some to apply only to fellow Jews while the second verse clearly refers to the common descent of all humans and hence their common equality before God.

Re'ut (neighborliness) is a good example of a biblical concept related to what we could call rights. It is a very important covenant concept, dealing with those to whom we are obligated beyond the letter of the law, what in Anglo-American jurisprudence is referred to as comity and in German as *treu*. In that way it also reflects a certain right that *re'im* possess toward one another. Thus, it is important to establish who is a *re'a* to determine the scope of our obligations toward him.

What is clear is that biblical terminology dealing with these concepts is not our terminology. The biblical term expressing obligation is *hesed,* which is appropriately translated "loving covenant obligation." *La'asot hesed* (to act out of loving covenant obligation) reflects the way the burden is on him who is obligated to do what he does because of his covenant obligations and is connected with holiness. No other biblical word relates to what we call obligation. The contemporary word for obligation, *hovah,* comes into use only in the Middle Ages.

Hesed is a very powerful word and a very covenantal one. It cannot be understood apart from its covenantal dimension and the moral authority embodied within it is a very heavy one. There are three related biblical terms that relate to the concept of rights: *yosher, tzedek,* and *mishpat. Yosher*, from *yashar*, has to do with being honest—with somebody or in one's own behavior. *Tzedek* is concerned with doing justice and *mishpat* with fulfilling the law. All three clearly refer more to the obligated party than to the possessor of the right. *Yosher* may possibly have some relationship to the latter as in Judges when Israelites are described as *kol ish asa et ha-yashar b'einav* (every man did what was right in his eyes), but that has to do more with what is defined as the straight path than with the possession of a right.

In sum, the Bible sets forth a comprehensive covenantal system, establishing a framework for both justice and rights in this world, one that offers the civil and social protections of contemporary rights theory without succumbing to the excesses of that theory. It does so by providing constitutional means for guaranteeing rights and controlling the demand for rights by deriving them from obligations.

God's Federal Universe

While the foregoing examples represent the most important uses of covenantal arrangements in the Bible, the term *brit* and the practice of covenanting involved a wide variety of situations, ranging from what were designed to be lasting or perpetual international treaties to secondary contractual obligations between rulers and ruled. This flexibility of usage is consistent with the biblical worldview, which sees the universe as built upon an interlocking and overlapping system of covenantal relationships, each with its own measure of demands and equivalent measure of responses; in sum, a kind of federal system of the highest order.[9]

The biblical grand design for humankind is federal in three ways: 1. It is based upon a network of covenants beginning with those between God and man, which weave the web of human, especially political, relationships in a federal way; that is, through pact, association, and consent.

2. The classic biblical commonwealth was a fully articulated federation of tribes instituted and reaffirmed by covenant to function under a common constitution and common laws. Any and all constitutional changes in the Israelite polity were introduced through covenanting and even after the introduction of the monarchy, the federal element was maintained until most of the tribal structures were destroyed by external forces. The biblical vision of the restored commonwealth in the Messianic era envisages the reconstitution of the tribal federation (Ezek. 47:13-48:35).

3. The biblical vision for the "end of days," the messianic era, sees not only a restoration of Israel's tribal system but what is, for all intents and purposes, a world confederation or league of nations, each preserving its own integrity while accepting a common Divine covenant and constitutional order. This order will establish appropriate covenantal relationships for the entire world. Each of these elements has had a direct impact on subsequent political thought and, in a number of significant cases, action.

It is no exaggeration to say that the contrast between the statist and the federalist approaches to political life reflects the difference between the systematic and prismatic approaches to understanding civil society. The systematic approach seeks to define everything precisely, to set boundaries that cannot be crossed; hence, the statist approach emphasizes questions of sovereignty as a means of defining ultimate boundaries. The federalist approach, recognizing how all of God's universe is interconnected, seeks, rather, to establish separate cores and to understand how each core has to be perceived and responded to differently from different perspectives. Boundaries need not be so clear. Interaction is more important than definition, which explains the federalist emphasis on multiple polities related to one another, united yet separate, a logical contradiction from the perspective of systematic philosophy, but a clear reality from the perspective of prismatic thought.

Notes

1. S. D. Goitein, "Political Conflict and the Use of Power in the World of the Geniza," in *Kinship and Consent: The Jewish Political Tradition and its Contemporary Uses,* ed. Daniel J. Elazar (Ramat Gan: Turtledove, 1981).
2. All biblical usages of the term *brit* have been assembled and classified in *HaMunach "Brit" BaTanach* (The Term "Covenant" in the Bible), a guide published by the Workshop for the Study of the Covenant Idea and the Jewish Political Tradition co-sponsored by the Center for Jewish Community Studies and the Department of Political Studies of Bar-Ilan University.
3. Gen. 4:10.
4. There are those, especially Christians, who argue that God established an implicit covenant with Adam, which is only reaffirmed by the covenant with Noah. They base their argument on Gen. 2:16, but that conclusion must be derived by heavy interpretation of the verse in question. It would, of course, moot the question of natural justice since all other references come after Adam.
5. This contains the requirement that thereby human mechanisms for the punishment of murderers is embodied in the plain text (Gen. 9:5–6). The sages of the Talmud concluded from these verses that God required institutional mechanisms,

such as the establishment of courts of justice. They derived from this chapter the seven Noahide commandments, holding that God's covenant with Noah bound all humanity to a set of basic Divine commandments, ranging from the practice of monotheism to the prohibition of theft and the establishment of a just polity. See Maimonides, Mishnah Torah (Melakhim 8:10-11, 9:1-14, 10:11-12). A good discussion of the Noahide commandments can be found under the entry of that name in the *Encyclopedia Judaica*.

6. The Bible indicates that the beginnings of the process of the transformation from customary to covenantal law are to be found at Marah (Exod. 16:23-26). See verse 25: *sham sam lo hok u'mishpat* (there He made for them a statute and an ordinance). Cf. Nachmanides, commentary on Exod. 16:25.

7. Here God also introduces a dimension of popular involvement in the initiative by indicating that He is responding to the people's groaning (*Shamati et naakat bnai yisrael...v'ezkor et briti*—I will remember My covenant, Exod. 6:5). In other places in the Bible, God's response is triggered by the people's *zaakah* or crying out, whereupon God remembers His covenant and comes to their aid.

8. Daniel J. Elazar, "Deuteronomy as Israel's Ancient Constitution: Some Preliminary Reflections," *Jewish Political Studies Review* 4, no. 1 (Spring 1992).

9. Daniel J. Elazar, ed., *Federalism as Grand Design* (Lanham, MD: University Press of America and Center for the Study of Federalism, 1987), Introduction.

Part II

Torah: Covenantal Teaching

5

Bereshith: The Covenants of Creation

Bereshith, or Genesis, the first book of the Torah, establishes the conceptual setting for the world of covenant. Not only does it introduce the idea and concept of covenant but it provides the linguistic and conceptual basis within which to understand covenant and covenantal systems. Constitutionally, it is like a long definitional preamble to a basic law, only rather than being presented as a dry list of definitions it consists of a series of very human tales with strong moral messages set in a historical framework that, after the creation itself, locates the unfolding history in a particular spatial-temporal-cultural location. It is this concreteness of biblical thought that is so striking. We are not dealing with abstract definitions but with meanings that arise out of particular contexts and that can be understood and developed only by understanding the context in which they are set. Thus, Bereshith is an introduction to the covenantal perspective of ancient Israel that was to be so influential in the Western world and its constitutional extension.

Textually and historically, the text before us is not without its share of problems. For our purposes, however, we may read it as a single whole for what it is designed to teach us, regardless of how and when it was written, compiled, and edited into its final form. While explicitly advocating covenantal ties as the basis for a good life, Bereshith presents those ties in the context of requisite organic connections among families and peoples needed for human society to work properly. The text expresses the interplay of organic and covenantal ties, showing where covenants rest on organic connections and where they are designed to cut or replace such connections. It presents the descent of the family of man from a single common ancestor to demonstrate the unity and basic equality of all humanity, the binding of all humans through God's covenant with Noah, the subsequent separation of humanity first into different

97

groupings and then into nations, the further separation of those nations by the development of separate languages, culminating in the separation of one man, Abraham, from his family to establish a new nation by covenant.

Creation as Making Distinctions

The first chapter of Bereshith presents the biblical message of creation, designed to undermine and replace the pagan creation myth. It emphasizes God's role as Creator in relation to all the various parts of the visible universe. It is devoted to making distinctions and separations, to teach that God is the sole Creator and that distinctions and separations are the basis of all creation.

The chapter begins with the distinction and separation between God the Creator and His creation (v. 1). There follow the distinctions within the creation itself, such as the separation of heaven and earth (v. 1), light and darkness (v. 3), day and night (v. 4), firmament and seas (v. 6), the dry land and waters (vv. 9–10). Third, there is the distinction between the immobile elements of creation and those possessing local motion (v. 10ff.). Fourth, there is the distinction between those elements that can only move in fixed courses (the heavenly bodies) and those that can move as they please (living creatures) (v. 14ff.). Finally, there is the distinction between man, who may turn from the right course, and other living creatures (vv. 26–28).

We are told, in effect, that the universe rests upon making and maintaining proper distinctions whose roots go back to creation. The existence of those distinctions recognizes the multifaceted character of the universe and the need to choose the right path or way. Thus, the stage is set for the subsequent discussion of the first concern of ethics and politics, namely, what is the right way and how humans must organize themselves to follow it.[1]

God creates by speaking. The Bible begins (v. 3) by indicating the creative power of words, an idea repeated in various contexts throughout subsequent chapters. God does not command, he speaks, calls things into being, or blesses. Nor does He command His human creations but speaks to them as well (v. 28). God blesses and instructs them to be fruitful and multiply but they must respond. At first, then, they are spoken to, not commanded. At any place where the term commandment could have been used, the word used is *vayomer* (said or spoke), suggesting God's use of His word is sufficient. Later interpreters of the Bible, Jewish and Christian, saw this as evidence that God had already covenanted with Adam even though the first actual use of the term is in connection with Noah (6:18). Since speaking demands a response freely given, it already suggests the mutuality of covenant. Humans, separated so thoroughly from God by the separations of creation, are to be reunited with Him through covenant.

This first chapter of Bereshith introduces two important political terms. The first is *memshelet,* the construct of *memshala,* which in turn comes from the root *mashol,* meaning governance (v. 16). It is used in reference to the assigned tasks of the sun and the moon, the first governing the day and the second governing the night and the stars. The second political term used is *redu,* from *rado,* dominion (v. 28), used when God grants man dominion over all other creatures.

Memshala, the generic term for governance in biblical and post-biblical Hebrew, implies the rule of like by like, if not equals then at least potential equals in some important and relevant way. From the context we immediately learn that such rule can be shared, such as the fact that the sun rules by day and the moon by night; and such rule can also be limited, as the sun, moon, and stars are limited in their courses. *Redo,* on the other hand, deals with the dominion of unequals over unequals, in this case of humans over nonhumans (indeed subhumans). Out of it grows the later term *rodan* (dictator), a ruler who exercises human dominion based on the principle of inequality. From the context here, however, we learn that such rule is not a fitting relationship between humans, who are, above all, equals or potential equals, all having the same common parentage. It is therefore a usurpation when applied within the human community. Even God does not rule humans as a *rodan* according to Scripture. Thus, the introduction here of the two terms is accompanied by the implicit distinction between the two principal forms of rule.

Humans are not only given dominion over other living creatures but are blessed and instructed (not commanded) to populate and subdue the earth. This puts the Bible squarely on the side of what is today called development, but within clear limits. Not only are the distinctions of creation to be maintained but humans and other creatures are to be vegetarians. Thus, while the terminology used is very strong, it is not, as some have suggested, a command for man to be rapacious. Quite to the contrary, it commits (or at least strongly urges) man to the enterprise of pushing back frontiers but within the Divine framework. The opportunity itself is considered a blessing, the very first blessing of mankind. In subsequent chapters and books, the Bible is to chronicle and evaluate the frontiersmanship of humans, giving us a full teaching about our roles and responsibilities in pursuing this task and thereby fulfilling our blessing.

Crucial to this chapter is the interweaving of the relationship between time and space and what is effectively a subordination of space to time. It is the progression of days that brings changes that are played out in the arena of space. This is made even more clear at the beginning of chapter 2, where the Bible simply acknowledges the completion of the structuring of space (never separate from its inhabitants, it should be noted) and then proceeds to describe how God blesses or sanctifies time by setting aside the seventh day as Sabbath.

Principles of Organization and Relationship

The second chapter teaches about four elements presented by the Torah as basic to human existence: the Sabbath, the generational rhythm of time, the importance of language, and the essence of the family relationship. The first two organize human time, the third and fourth organize the context of human relationships.

The chapter begins with the sanctification of time through the Sabbath. God has worked six days and now He rests. That is followed by a recounting of the story of creation from a second perspective to emphasize the emergence of human beings and their relationship to God. Verse 4 introduces the term *toledot* (generations, also history). The biblical concept encapsulated in the term is the sense of the movement of time from generation to generation, its organization in a generational progression with each generation distinct in the sense that it confronts its own set of challenges within its own particular context (e.g., the generation of creation, the generation of the Flood, the generation of the wilderness), yet biologically not fully separable and thus linked to all others before and after it.

The biblical organization of time is consistently generational and its conception of history is a record of the activities of successive generations. As an organizing element or building block, the generation, which links the biological, cultural, and historical dimensions of humankind, is indeed the most satisfactory. All of human history can be mapped according to the rhythm and progression of generations. Thus, according to the Bible, every tenth generation begins a new epoch: from Adam to Noah, from Noah to Abraham, from Abraham to Moses, from Moses to David.

The subtle interplay of linkage and separation continues. Humans are intimately linked with the natural processes at the very outset, but are simultaneously separate and distinct. This process of distinction with linkage is emphasized in the relationship between man and the soil, both in his role as a product of the earth and as steward of the Garden of Eden. Finally, it emphasizes both the distinction and linkage of man and woman. Woman is described as *ezer k'negdo*—man's helper and opposite number—a helper who stands with man but apart from him.

In keeping with this view of distinction and linkage, chapter 2 also indicates the beginning of man's active partnership with God (v. 15ff.). The first chapter has set the basis for their partnership at least prior to Adam's disobedience, namely, God's instruction to man to dominate all other creatures. In the second chapter, man is made God's steward in the Garden of Eden, a role that allows him some free choice and then gives him a more important task, that of naming all living creatures (vv. 19-20). Parallel to the biblical emphasis in chapter 1 on the creative power of speaking, here the Bible indicates the power of language as the foundation of reality because it is the foundation of the cognition of reality. Adam's power to name, to organize his reality, is the worldly basis for his power to rule.

Jewish tradition emphasizes this role of language, including it as a fundamental science and, indeed, viewing the universe as constructed out of the combination of letters into words. Students of culture have come to understand the importance of language as the foundation of all culture, as a means of linkage and distinction. In effect, they are merely elaborating on the biblical teaching.

The one potentially political term introduced in this chapter is *vayitzav* (from *tzavo*, to command) (v. 16). God commands man, for the first time, regarding the use of the fruits of the Garden of Eden. Up until now, God has "spoken" to or instructed man. Here, however, God commands man not to do something, namely, not to eat of the fruit of the tree of the knowledge of good and evil (which from the context may refer primarily to sexual knowledge). This is the first negative commandment in the Bible and involves the first prohibition on man's activities. Subsequent human disobedience to this commandment may be the Bible's way of indicating the problematics of commanding rather than securing consent. No command can be more powerful than God's but humans are willful and can disobey. Thus, commanding is no better than speaking.

The Bible, like the Greek philosophers, takes the family as the starting point for political organization. Its conception of the family is the basis of its theory of the polity. The essence of the family relationship in the biblical view is the conjugal link between husband and wife (v. 24). The conjugal tie, based on a pact — later to be called the covenant of marriage — precedes the tie of kinship. The natural history of the family is for husband and wife to raise children until they reach maturity and then help them establish their own families (through covenant) so that the process may be repeated. Such a family is referred to as a *bayit* (household, cf. 7:1). The *bayit,* based on both consent and kinship, is the basis for all political and social organization. It includes the natural family and those adopted or otherwise absorbed into it because of their positions in the household economy.

Proper political associations are essentially unions or federations of households in which the latter retain their respective integrities. There is an implicitly federal relationship here throughout, not only between man and woman who are united in a union that establishes a new entity while allowing each partner to maintain a separate integrity, but between generations within a family whereby after children pass through a period of colonial dependency, they become autonomous units through union with a member of the opposite sex from another conjugal union, yet remain linked to the extended family. The federal process here is not simply one of children growing up and becoming independent of parents, but that children can become independent of parents only when they form unions with members of the opposite sex and thereby establish new family units. Throughout the Bible, we see a pattern of nucleated units formed by conjugal union and linked with one another through kinship in permanent relationship in such a way that all maintain their respective integrities and even are able to perpetuate themselves by generating new units.

Human Choice Determines Human Destiny

The next step in human development is the acquisition of a sense of moral distinction. Chapter 3 recounts how God's prohibition came to be violated when the serpent tempts Eve to eat of the forbidden fruit and then Eve convinces Adam to do likewise, and its consequences for the principals involved and for humanity as a whole. In this chapter we not only see the limits imposed by God on humans but those imposed upon God by His entering into a relationship with man and how He copes with those limitations.[2]

The account of Adam's acknowledgement of his violation of God's prohibition (vv. 9-12) does not place man in a heroic light. Adam states the factual truth but in a manner that is designed to place the moral responsibility on his partner. God will have none of that. When Eve tries the same tactic (v. 13), God's reaction is similar. Here, the Bible emphasizes that every individual carries his or her own moral responsibility no matter what the sources of the temptation to violate commandments.

At the beginning the Bible portrays men and women as essentially equal, not only because woman is created from man (2:22), but because both can be held morally accountable in equal measure. The Bible certainly emphasizes the distinctions between men and women, but these distinctions operate within a framework of fundamental equality. This is all the more striking when we look at the punishment God metes out to the three principals in this event (vv. 14-19). The punishment for men and women are punishments befitting men and women and are essentially equal, differing only in that women's punishment seems to be harsher because woman played a more important role in violating the precept, by responding to the snake's temptation and then by tempting another, her husband. The punishment meted out to the snake, on the other hand, reduces him to the level of all other nonhuman creatures, even though he occupied something of an intermediate position between ordinary beasts and men at the outset of the chapter. In fact, his punishment is to be reduced to the lowest rung in the order of beastly prominence.

The woman's punishment is to be made subordinate to her husband within their union (v. 16). The Bible uses the term *yimshal* to describe man's rule over woman. In other words, it is a rule of equals over equals and is based at least in part on a change in woman's appetite, namely that women will have sexual desire, something that flows directly from the sexual connotations of the fruit of the tree. That desire will be directed toward her husband and will enable him to rule over her. The Bible seems to be saying here that sexual desire is a source of interper-

sonal power relationships between the sexes, an observation that has
since been made with some considerable force and given some reasonable documentation by twentieth-century dynamic psychology.

Man's punishment is predicated on the fact that he hearkened to his
wife's voice (vv. 17-19). The Hebrew word is *shamata* from *shamoa*—to
hearken. This term is used in response to the term *vayitzav* or *tzavo* in
the previous chapter. The linkage between the two terms is made more
immediately specific later in the Bible, but it is important to note it here
because of what it tells us about man's primordial independence in the
Divine scheme of things even before the acquisition of the knowledge
of good and evil. While this chapter recounts the ending of man's innocence by the acquisition of sexual knowledge and passion as the basis
for making certain kinds of moral distinctions, man's ability and freedom to choose antedate the encounter with the tree; they seem to be
built in with his creation.

This concept of hearkening is linked to the fundamental premise of
biblical thought, that relationships are covenantal. Here Adam hearkened
to his wife, his partner in the union of man and woman. By doing so he
consented freely to participate in her act and is punished accordingly.
Man's punishment is in line with his role as steward of the earth. He
remains God's steward, indeed that is the reason for his creation, but his
stewardship is rendered more difficult. Rather than being the custodian
of a well-watered fertile garden, he must now exercise his stewardship
with difficulty over a recalcitrant earth reluctant to respond to his most
intense efforts. Moreover, the culmination of his stewardship will be
death, the punishment that God initially promised for violation of his
single prohibition, postponed but not eliminated. God makes certain, by
driving him out of the Garden (vv. 22-24), that man will not through his
own efforts attain immortality by eating from the tree of eternal life.

The whole question of the human role in the universe is elucidated in
chapters 2 and 3, particularly chapter 3. God creates man to be His steward on earth. In doing so, He creates him from the earth itself but breathes
into him from His own spirit, a godly soul. Thus, man is suspended
between the two poles. As a consequence, man has a certain independence of mind and freedom of choice from the beginning. God takes
care to limit this freedom of choice by denying man and his helpmate,
woman, sexual passion and cognition, and the knowledge of good and
evil that flows from sexual drives. Man's very independence of action,

however, leads him to violate God's single commandment by choice and thus launches him on a course that is to lead him from rebellion against God to challenging God's very omnipotence and then authority. In effect, God recognizes that man has embarked upon this path as a result of the acquisition of sexual drives and the knowledge that can come from sublimating them and takes steps to prevent the likely ultimate consequence of man's newfound drive, namely, man's acquisition of immortality. Thus, by the end of chapter 3, the stage is set. Man's tasks are delineated and the lines of his rebellion are clearly suggested. Perhaps it is significant that when they first discover that they are naked, man and woman clothe themselves in fig leaves. But after God punishes them, God himself clothes them with skins, killing for the use of the two humans as they enter their new world.

The Biblical Organization of Time

Expelled from Eden, the human race begins a series of "firsts" or foundings that give form to human civilization (chap. 4). The Bible portrays civilization emerging as a result of discontent. First is the introduction of sacrifice, murder, and urbanization into the world, which led to the beginning of human invention in the arts and sciences. The Bible clearly links all four. Adam's sons, Cain and Abel, compete over the offerings they bring to God and, in his jealousy, Cain kills Abel. God's punishment leads Cain to found the first city, to protect his son, and to establish his line there, which becomes the source of all invention.

The Bible places these events in the generational context. Biological and social time are linked through foundings, which by their nature establish common beginnings.[3] The Bible is very much concerned with foundings. Foundings establish lines of development, which persist as shaping forces until a refounding, if not beyond. They also serve as temporal benchmarks and points of generational unification, which help give meaning to each historical generation. Foundings also serve to establish the basis for the regularized progression of generations by setting an order to the course of events. Founding acts establish the framework and direction of the generation and those involved in them tend to remain the generation's central figures. Thus, their active life spans give shape to the whole. The founding events of each generation set in motion a train, which leads to a series of climactic events in mid-generation and culminating events to mark its end. The oft-used biblical phrase "forty years" is the idiom for a generation, representing the outer limits of a generation's time span. Empirical studies subsequently have shown that the time span involved in a historical generation is between 25 and 40 years, as the Bible itself frequently suggests.[4]

The Bible suggests that every person not only fits into the overall generational rhythm and progression of history but personally is part of the generational cohort into which he is born. Noah, for example, is described as "righteous and whole-hearted in his generations" (6:9). This phrasing has provoked endless discussion among subsequent generations of commentators as to whether Noah was to be counted among the truly righteous or whether he was simply relatively righteous, head and shoulders above his peers.

A person's "generation" refers to the generation of his maturity. A normal lifetime, according to the Bible, is essentially two generations in length and a full three generations (120 years) is the Bible's upper limit (6:3). In a 70- or 80-year life span, the first 20 to 25 years are essentially years of development into adulthood and the last 10 to 20, years of retirement. The 40 years in between, the years of adulthood when the person is a productive member of society, represent the years of his generation. (Thus, Noah, the last of the fabulously long-lived antediluvians, is described as living over "generations.")

The generations seem to follow a pattern of triads. There is a founding generation that sets out the beginning steps for a particular century or epoch, a second generation that either advances or perverts those beginning steps, and a third generation that rounds out the events. Here, for example, Adam represents the founding generation, and Cain, Abel, and Seth the second generation, when man's initial attempts at agriculture and the domestication of animals is brought to naught by man's own folly. Cain is the focus of the action, compounding Adam's sin and bringing the concrete results of founding a city. Enoch and Enosh represent the concluding generation of this triad during whose time organized religion emerged (4:25-26).

The next generational triad—Erad, Mechuyael, u'Metushael—are mentioned without comment. Lamech, the founder of the third triad, is presented as a founder. The second generation in that triad is the one that, like Cain's, is inventive, being responsible for the domestication of cattle and the establishment of a cattle-based nomadic line, the introduction of the arts via music, and the introduction of metalwork, particularly weaponry (invented by Lamech's son and Cain's namesake, Tubal-Cain). With the introduction of the latter, we have the recrudescence of violence on a new scale as verses 23 and 24 deal with Lamech's lament to his wives. Noah is the first person born after the death of Adam, thus reinforcing the biblical intent to show that he begins a new epoch.

The organization and proper use of time is, for the Bible, one of the great human enterprises, a basic frontier experience for humans no less than the taming and organization of space. Indeed the two are inevitably linked. Thus, by the end of chapter 5 we have all the elements for organizing time: the generation, the generational triad (which is to become the equivalent of a century when ordinary time is introduced), the triad of triads (which, in normal time, will cover approximately 300 years and be an epoch), and the millennium (which, in normal time, will be a triad of epochs). All that remains is to have the proportions reduced to human scale, which is done in the next chapter. True, the antediluvian period is one of fabulous life spans according to Scripture but the unnaturalness of that situation is reflected in the discussion of the 120-year (three 40-year generations) life span imposed in 6:3.

Cain and Abel are presented as being involved in civilized pursuits (v. 2), Cain as a farmer and Abel as a sheepherder. The Bible is suggesting that both of these activities appeared at the same time. Is it suggesting that agriculture preceded sheepherding? It is hard to say since, although Cain was the older brother, the Bible presents the issue by mentioning Abel's sheepherding first.

In any case, Cain's punishment includes his forced withdrawal from agricultural pursuits (vv. 11–12). Since Abel's murder ended sheepherding, what the Bible seems to be describing is an abortive start toward sophisticated agricultural civilization that is only renewed by Cain's descendants considerably after the founding of the first city. This seems to reverse the accepted notion of a linear evolution from agriculture to urbanization. However, research and more sophisticated analysis have led to a better understanding of how cities as centers of commerce have been crucial in promoting agriculture. In opposition to simpleminded agrarianism, we have come to learn that commercial interests are not parasitical middlemen but the developers of markets that have encouraged the expansion of agriculture. Thus, the order here makes eminent sense.

The biblical chronology is given in verses 17 through 21. It is not until the sixth generation after Cain (or the eighth generation of mankind, which in biblical chronology means toward the end of the first human epoch) that we find reference to an advance in agricultural pursuits, in this case the domestication of cattle, which came in the same generation as the development of music and the introduction of metalwork.

It cannot be accidental that Cain, the first murderer, also founds the first city. In some respects, this can be seen simply as the linkage between urbanization and violence upon which many have commented.[5] But the biblical story is more subtle than that. Cain murders out of passion. He is not a premeditated killer. Men who commit violence need to protect themselves and their families against retribution. Cities in the Bible are primarily places of protection.[6] *Ir*, the Hebrew word for city, is derived from the Akkadian *uru*, which means tower, and historians of the ancient Near East generally agree that cities originally came into existence for defensive purposes, as places where the inhabitants of a region could come together to collectively defend themselves.

The Basic Flaw in Human Impulses

The description of the second epoch of human history, that of Noah and his heirs, begins by recounting the spread of wickedness on the earth, the Lord's disgust with that wickedness, and his plans to deal with it by destroying all living creatures except for Noah and his immediate family and an equivalent representation of each species (chapter 6). Up to now, political authority exists only as patriarchal rule within extended families. Beyond the extended family, anarchy has degenerated into random senseless violence (*hamas*).

Before introducing the idea of covenant, the Bible introduces the concept of *hamas,* chaos-producing violence. In the Bible, comprehensive destruction is always a response to *hamas.* The one thing that can provoke God's virtually unlimited wrath is the sense of chaos implied in the term; the kind that utterly destroys all covenantal relationships and the rule of law.

Derekh (way) is another basic biblical concept introduced in chapter 6. *Derekh* precedes *brit* (see v. 18), which complements it. Every creature has his own *derech* that either represents his biological heritage or, in the case of humans, the synthesis between their biological and cultural heritage. It is the biblical parallel to the Greek concept of nature, but, unlike the latter, recognizes how impossible it is to separate nature and culture and is dynamic rather than static. Way or path denotes movement that, although to some extent fixed, also provides for change or development, not simply the filling out of a prefixed form. The reference here is to the fact that all flesh had corrupted their way, that is to say, the path common to all humans. This leads God to decide on the drastic step of destruction and refounding.

God sees that the problem with man is his *yetzer* (impulse), as stated in 6:5, *yetzer mahshevet libo* (literally, the impulse of his heart's thinking).[7] Here the Bible addresses itself to the psychological basis of the human condition, restating the classic philosophic problem; how could a good God create evil. The Bible only hints at the problem, namely, that the qualities with which it was necessary to endow humans to fulfill their role in creation included impulses that humans could not control. The political implications of this are extraordinarily important. Man is not naturally good but, as Freud put it, is a bundle of impulses in desperate need of expert management. If God cannot control man's prior actions through what He has implanted within human beings, then any effort to establish a political framework for humanity must be based on this reality. Evil as well as good impulses must be recognized as inevitable and arrangements must be instituted for their management.

The problem is reflected in Noah's first action after leaving the ark and God's response. Noah takes one of the surviving creatures and sacrifices it to the Lord, whose response is extremely cryptic. He is portrayed as smelling the sweet savor of the sacrifice and, as a result, promising not to curse the ground anymore because of human actions (Adam's punishment) nor again destroy the entire living world (the punishment of the generation of the Flood). He explicitly reaffirms that the natural order will continue uninterrupted, both the seasons and the cycle of days. But He does so on the grounds that man's *yetzer* is irreparably flawed from his youth. In other words, He seems to be rendering a judgment on some aspect of Noah's behavior. The reference to evil inclination from one's youth implies that sexual maturity has some role to play in the matter, but the issue is not developed.

God must now revise His basic plan. He began with Adam as an innocent, placing man and woman in a near-perfect environment that would allow them scope for their faculties without requiring that they lose their innocence. Those same faculties bring them to the loss of that innocence so God tries hard work and pain as devices to control the newly knowledgeable race. But human ingenuity and inventiveness reduce the burdens of labor (through technology) and pain (through music) to tolerable levels so that people once again can turn to their evil ways. In both cases, those evil ways are somehow connected with vaguely illicit sexual activity. God then decides to destroy life and start again with the best available candidate for the renewal of the human race only to find that the hereditary flaw built into the race persists. What follows (chapter 9) is a discussion of God's third plan, His general covenant with mankind.

From the beginning, God does not command Noah; He speaks to him to give him an instruction. Noah is free to respond or not. This emphasis on freedom is to reach its full expression in the idea of the covenant between God and man, which can only be entered into freely by the partners. Noah's response is to act on God's word, to respond to it, which opens the way to God's promise to covenant with him (v. 18). Speaking, using words, is a power but, when used in connection with humans, still is a limited one. When God speaks, He evokes a commanding presence but He does not command. God's promise is not unilateral; it comes after Noah has responded affirmatively to His instructions regarding the ark. Covenanting demands mutuality.

God promises to establish his covenant with Noah and his descendants. The term *brit* is introduced in this chapter where it complements *derech*. If the latter is built into humans, the former represents man's ability to freely make choices and commitments, and to build human civilization on the framework of choice as much as necessity. Humans are engaged in a constant effort to relate *brit* and *derech* in the building of civilization, its peoples and polities. Covenanting is not simply a matter of swearing an oath or signing a document. Rather, it is a dynamic process designed to produce an ideal result as best as humans can. The concepts introduced in connection with God's covenant with Noah express both.

The Noahide Covenant:
The Biblical Basis for Human Political Order

In biblical terms, God relates to his universe and the creatures within it, including man, through a system of covenants. We are all familiar with God's covenants with the patriarchs and Israel. Yet the Bible teaches us that God's covenant with Israel must be viewed in the larger context of God's covenant with all humans. The sages of the Talmud and the Church fathers taught that the beginning of this covenant relationship is implicit in God's relationship to Adam, particularly after man acquired knowledge of good and evil, a position shared by most medieval and early modern theologians. But the first formal covenant was made with Noah after the Flood (Gen. 9:8–16):

> And God spoke unto Noah, and to his sons with him, saying: "As for Me, behold, I establish My covenant with you, and with your seed after you; and with every living creature that is with you, the fowl, the cattle, and every beast of the earth. And I will establish My covenant with you; neither shall all flesh be cut off any more by the waters of the flood; neither shall there any more be a flood to destroy the earth." And God said: "This is the token of the covenant which I make between Me and you and every living creature that is with you, for perpetual generations: I have set My bow in the cloud, and it shall be for a token of a covenant between Me and the earth. And it shall come to pass, when I bring clouds over the earth, and the bow is seen in the cloud, that I will remember My covenant, which is between Me and you and every living creature of all flesh; and the waters shall no more become a flood to destroy all flesh. And the bow shall be in the cloud; and I will look upon it, that I may remember the everlasting covenant between God and every living creature of all flesh that is upon the earth."

Through Noah, the sages teach that covenant is binding on all people as the basis for universal law.

Genesis 9 is one of the key chapters of the whole Bible, describing as it does the first covenant between God and man and the foundation for the moral obligations of all humans. It is also the chapter in which, according to the Talmud, the principle of formal government was introduced as one of God's seven commandments and part of His covenant with Noah. In essence, it is the chapter that describes the new foundation of the postdiluvian earth on a more formal and structured basis.

The seven commandments of the sons of Noah are binding upon all men. Their observance entitles non-Jews to recognition as *hasidei umot ha'olam,* usually translated as the righteous among the gentiles, but better understood as those among the gentiles who accept the obligations of the covenant bond, which is what *hasidim* are. To the sages, the term *bnei Noah,* the sons of Noah, is the generic term for mankind (more so than *bnei Adam,* the sons of Adam, which has become the colloquial term in modern Hebrew). This should be understood as a reflection of the importance of the covenant idea to them.

All humans qua humans are sons of Adam, but humans as people standing in serious relationship to God are sons of Noah because Noah is the first to be explicitly bound by covenant and to have the opportunity to consent to God's commandments.

The two principal sources for the rabbinic discussion of the Noahide covenant are Tractate *Sanhedrin* 56 through 60, in the Babylonian Talmud, and Maimonides's *Mishneh Torah,* Book of Kings, chapters 8 through 10. Maimonides introduces the term *ben brit Noah,* the son of the Noahide covenant, as the equivalent of a *ger toshav,* that is to say, a resident alien within the framework of Jewish society. Both sources emphasize that these seven commandments are the minimal moral duties enjoined upon all men. While there is some disagreement as to precisely which commandments are included, it is generally agreed that idolatry, blasphemy, shedding human blood, sexual sins, theft, and eating parts from a living animal are the six prohibitions, while establishing a legal order is the one positive injunction. Of course, each of these seven is interpreted to cover an extensive range of commandments. Theft, for example, is interpreted in *Sanhedrin* to include military conquest and dishonesty in economic life. The rabbinic discussion makes it clear that the establishment of a legal order and a system of governance is crucial to the maintenance of human society along the lines required by the other six commandments.

While the phrase *hasidei umot ha'olam* is translated and understood to mean the righteous among the gentiles, a more literal translation would be the keepers of the covenant among the nations of the world. *Hasid* is derived from *hesed.* Thus, a *hasid* is one who takes it upon himself to unstintingly fulfill his covenant obligations. The term is a standard one in the Jewish lexicon in all epochs.

God's covenant with Noah follows on His promise before the Flood in chapter 6. It is at this point that relationships between God and man become constitutionally ordered, based upon a formal partnership between them. A covenant is a constitutional ordering of relationships (although it is not necessarily a constitution). From the biblical perspective, all human covenants must flow from the covenant in which God established His relationship with humankind. It is on the basis of God's pact with Noah that people in turn establish relationships with each other. In one sense, this is a step forward in man's relationships with God. In another, it reflects a stepping backward on the part of God in His hopes for man.

God's relationship with Adam is essentially one-sided. God creates Adam, appoints him His steward in the work of maintaining the earth, and punishes him when he violates the prohibition against eating the fruit of the tree of knowledge of good and evil. Subsequently, God establishes brief "personal" relationships with selected descendants of Adam. The action on either side is unilateral, that is to say, God chooses to act or man chooses to act, each separately and discretely. Generally, God chooses to instruct, command, or set things in order, and man is willful and chooses to act in violation of God's commandment or some principle of natural justice. The relationship is not only asymmetrical, but segmented. In the end, this leads to the spread of aimless violence (*hamas*) and God's decision to destroy all life on earth with the exception of Noah and the inhabitants of the ark.

The destruction completed, God looks to Noah to make a new beginning, only to find that Noah, in part out of the goodness of his heart, shows the same human qualities and weaknesses that had existed before the Flood. God then determines, if we read the story carefully, that unless He wants to blot out man altogether, he must accommodate himself to man's weaknesses. He decides to do so in two ways: (1) by establishing a partnership between Himself and mankind (the sons of Noah) that will recognize man's ability to choose and grant him a formal role in the choosing, that is to say, freedom and status as a partner, albeit a junior partner, with God; and (2) by binding men through law in an effort to curb their inclinations or passions and to enable them to organize themselves into civil society in order to do so. These are the two sides of God's covenant with Noah presented in chapter 9.

A detailed analysis of Genesis 9, in which God covenants with Noah, is in order. The chapter begins with the third restatement of the first of God's blessings to mankind: to be fruitful, multiply, and fill the earth. These repetitions reflect the intensity of the biblical commitment to man's task as settler of the planet. Moreover, the blessing is directed to Noah and his sons, that is, to all of humankind as his descendants so that there will be no ambiguity as to its application.

But there is a change from the first time this instruction is given to Adam (Gen. 1:28–31). Before the Flood, humans and other living creatures were to live in harmony, in a peaceful hierarchy based on a common vegetarianism. After the Flood humans are allowed to be carnivorous as well as herbivorous, hence the fear and dread of man shall be upon all other creatures, land, sea, and air (vv. 2–3). The original authority relationship between man and other living creatures remains but with a new and dreadful power attached to it.

There is another side to this equation (vv. 5-6). If man can kill beasts, beasts can kill man. But murder is prohibited; men and beasts can kill for food or in self-defense but not wantonly. Murder is to be punished by death, for which reason the sages hold that courts of justice must be established to determine the crime and the punishment, and government instituted to control and direct society.

On another level, in the comparison of 1:28-31 and these verses, we are given a first look at the biblical understanding of the relationship between authority and power. The initial blessing and its repetitions are grants or reaffirmations of a grant of authority whose powers are also defined at the time of the grant. Here God reaffirms the grant of authority but changes (and expands) the powers attached to it. The difference between the two is that the authority flows from God's will and determines what is legitimate while the powers are recognitions of man's capabilities and his intention to exercise them. Since, in the biblical view, all flows from God, the latter must be accounted for as well as the former.

God then establishes His covenant with Noah, Noah's sons, their descendants (*zar'echem,* your seed), and with every living creature that came out of the ark (vv. 8-11). He does so by speaking (*vayomer*) with Noah and his sons (v. 8), who, by the context, are agents for their descendants and for the other living creatures. God indicates that this is His undertaking in return for His new instructions to mankind. *Hineni mekim et briti* (Behold, I establish my covenant—the covenant-making expression is *mekim brit* [establish a covenant]) indicating that, while it is God's reaction to Noah's response, the covenanting itself is done by God unilaterally.

The first clause of the covenant is that never again shall God destroy all life on earth through a comprehensive Flood (v. 11). God makes the rainbow the sign of this covenant (vv. 12-17). Man needs symbols for reassurance and God recognizes this need by choosing the symbol that the rain has ended for this purpose. The rainbow will trigger God's remembrance, which is, in turn, a triggering mechanism for action under the terms of a covenant (v. 15).

The matter is strongly reinforced in verse 16 with the phrase *U'reitiha lizkor brit olam* (I will see it and remember the everlasting covenant).

Olam, used here to signify everlasting or eternal and used in other contexts as universe, is another key word in the constellation of biblical conceptualizations. It combines within it the concepts of space and time as two dimensions of the same unity, hence it truly expresses the concept of universe. Here, for example, the covenant is explicitly applied to all the earth forever.

Note that humans can eat everything (v. 4), unlike the Jews who are yet to emerge as a separate group, who are to be restricted to specifically permitted foods after their special covenant with God in Shemoth (Exodus). The one restriction in matters of food is that humans may not eat flesh with the blood still in it, which is interpreted by the sages to mean from a living creature. Blood is here described as the bearer of the soul.

Remembering is the triggering mechanism for the fulfillment of the terms of a covenant. *Vayizkor Elohim et habrit* (God remembered the covenant) is the usual biblical phrase. The concept of God remembering those with whom He has covenanted is a basic one in the language of covenant.

The Emergence of Peoples, Polities, and Empires

The story of the Flood concludes with Noah's curse and blessing to his sons. The first of a series of biblical fathers guiding the future through such blessings, Noah spells out the biblical order of precedence of humanity in its three basic divisions. Canaan, the son of Ham (who is not mentioned), is to serve Shem and Japheth; Japheth is to be the largest grouping but is to "dwell in the tents of Shem." The three divisions cannot be racial since all are descended from the same father. Rather, they are kinship-cum-cultural divisions.

Japheth, as will be seen below, represents the Indo-European peoples and Shem the Semitic ones. Japheth dwelling in the tents of Shem has been interpreted by later Jewish sages as reflecting the Semitic source of the great monotheistic religions and the harnessing of philosophy and science (developed by the Ionian Greeks—Yavan, the descendant of Japheth) to faith, not unreasonable given the overall thrust of the Bible regarding what is of central importance.[8] Canaan's servile role was used in the past to justify Negro slavery, a clear distortion of the political implications of the passage for the Israelites where it laid the groundwork for Israel's claim to the land of Canaan.

Chapter 10 serves as an introduction to the discussion of the spread of mankind throughout the world in the postdiluvian generations by tracing out the families of Noah's sons and their various branches.[9] The lists of eponymous names have the familiar ring of peoples and countries of central and western Asia, Mediterranean Europe, and north and east central Africa—the world of the Bible. Tracing the identities of the people and places mentioned is a fascinating exercise in ancient geography and in the biblical understanding of how the world was divided into nations on the basis of separation of families into branches as population increased and people migrated to find suitable homes. The reader is left with the sense that this discussion is by reference only, that is to say, it is addressed to an audience that knows this history and is designed to place it within the proper context.

The Japhethites, the Hellenic and Ionian peoples, are listed first since they nearly disappear from the biblical scenes that follow; hence, it is simply necessary to account for them. The Hamites are treated in slightly greater depth because of their role in establishing the setting in which the subsequent narratives take place, both on the east where Abraham is to come from and on the west in the land of Canaan. The Semites are listed in such a way as to point us toward Abraham.

In the biblical way, the emphasis here is more on relationships than on mere classification. The nations are presented in family groups with the primordial relationships between them clearly indicated. Beyond that, the relationships between the three principal human families are indicated, as well as the relationships between peoples, their languages, and their lands.

The chapter introduces several important terms and concepts: *goim* (nations)—the first use of the standard term is given with a definition (*b'artzotam ish lil'shono l'mishpahotam*—in their lands each one in his own language, according to their families). Thus, the Bible defines a nation as consisting of a kinship group with its own land and language. This definition remains standard throughout the Bible and reflects the biblical emphasis on the primordial yet cultural character of nations.

Goy is one of the generic terms in the Bible and a very important one.[10] Its definition does not explicitly include a political component but, rather, describes the ethnic basis to which political organization can be added. While the Bible requires humans to establish political institutions for the sake of an orderly and just life and assumes that nations are either organized politically or fall within some larger political organization, polity itself is not primordial but civil in origin—it must be established and does not just happen.

The Bible suggests that all polities are established through the exercise of human will, although, as befits its covenantal grounding, it emphasizes that *good* polities are established by (and governed through) consent. The very basis for political institutions is established in God's covenant with Noah, suggesting that pact is the preferred way. The theory of the origins of the peoples named here emphasizes organic development, which is consistent with this account.

The sons of Ham (v. 6) include the peoples of northeast Africa with their two Asian branches, the Canaanites and the peoples of the Yemen and the Persian Gulf (apparently the Sumerians). The Canaanites are related to the Egyptians (*Mizraim*) but are not descended from them. Here the Bible mentions the origins of the first polity established by conquest and force. Cush, the son of Ham, produces Nimrod (whose name suggests *rado*, dictatorial rule), the first imperialist. Nimrod is described as the ruler of cities, not a founder, suggesting that he conquered them to build his empire. The cities mentioned as the cornerstones of that empire include the three great capitals of ancient Mesopotamia, an indication of Nimrod's power and greatness. The location and development of an early empire, beginning with the area of the Sumerian settlement in southern Mesopotamia and spreading northward, are confirmed by independent archeological and historical research.

Both major sources of ancient Near Eastern civilization are Hamitic according to the Bible, through Ham's two sons Cush (Ethiopia) and Mizraim (Egypt). It is the Cushite or Ethiopian branch of the Hamites who are presented as the founders of Mesopotamian civilization and with it empires and great cities. This is presented as a matter of fact, neither praised nor condemned.

Nimrod, the son of Cush, is presented as a *gibbor* (v. 9). The term is related to *gevurah* (power) and suggests powerful political or military leadership.[11] Implicit in this and the following two verses is a delineation of the character of conquerors and empire builders. Included in it is the sense that their power is multifaceted, including personal power (magnetism), ruthlessness (as a hunter), and ability to impose their will on others (v. 10). This is elaborately reflected in later Jewish legends about Nimrod, who emerges as a fascinating character in Jewish *Midrash* and folklore both. From the context, it seems that Nimrod was a known figure in the ancient world since the verse quotes what is apparently a folk saying about him.

The *Midrash* builds upon these verses to portray Nimrod as the one who initiated the human rebellion against God (his name also suggests *mered,* rebellion), a result of his success at empire building. This led him to challenge Heaven as manifested through construction of the Tower of Babel, which he is reputed to have initiated. He is counterposed to Abraham whom he tried to have killed as a threat to his rule. The *Midrash* links killing men and empire building in the case of Nimrod just as the Bible does with killing men and city building in the case of Cain.[12]

The relationship of Nimrod to both *mered* and *rado* may be a double play on words to suggest that one who rules dictatorially rebels against God. Whatever the meaning of Nimrod's name, the Bible describes his regime as a *mamlakha,* using the term for a polity of equals since humans obviously are fundamentally equal no matter what.

Asshur, the eponymous ancestor of Assyria, is identified as the builder of the great cities of Assyria (vv. 11-12). Building cities implies not only founding but recruiting settlers, which, in turn, hints at founding by some form of pact. External evidence suggests that pacts between various parties were features of early Assyrian life. Asshur came out of Nimrod's empire but, as indicated in verse 22, he was not a Hamite but a Semite. The verse suggests what external evidence seems to confirm, that the Semitic cities and empires of northern Mesopotamia learned their civilization from the non-Semitic Sumerians of the south.

Challenging God: A Breach of the Covenant

The Bible not only starts with mankind's common ancestry but emphasizes subsequent intermixtures of nations and civilizations as a normal part of human history. In the last analysis, however, while all humans are descended from Noah and human history continues to flow in a generational rhythm, after the Flood that history will be one of separate nations on a divided earth. This is made clear in the moral case study of the Tower of Babel (chapter 11) explaining the dispersion of mankind and suggesting that human efforts to be like God, to exceed their position as covenant partners, constitute an improper relationship between the two.[13]

God's response to the Tower of Babel suggests the decisive biblical rejection of the world-state as a single entity. At no point does the Bible diverge from this position. Later prophecies regarding the messianic era call for or forecast what properly may be termed a world confederation of God-fearing nations federated through their common acknowledgment of God's sovereignty and dominion, with Jerusalem, where all go up to worship God, as its seat. Such a confederation is like the original confederation of Israelite tribes writ large; it is the antithesis of the world-state attempted through Babel or projected for the future as the Roman or Christian ecumene that will unite all nations into one people. The biblical position has remained that of the Jewish political tradition ever since, in opposition to the ecumenical stance of much of Christianity. The reasons for the biblical view are made explicit; such a world-state would be, by its very nature, an impious act since it would lead humans to overestimate their power, especially vis-à-vis God, and, by implication, misuse it vis-à-vis each other (this last point is a favorite theme of the *Midrash*).[14]

The tower is not presented as the expression of the human effort to come closer to God for purposes of worship, but to challenge Him. It is presented as *migdal* (tower, from *gadol*, big or great), not as a watch-tower (11:4). Humans here clearly overstep the bounds of the permissible in their relationship with Heaven and are swiftly punished for it. This is not only a classic tale of Divine response to what the Greeks termed *hubris* but a message about the inability of humans to limit themselves once they break out of external limitations.

The issue is presented straightforwardly as one of power; humans challenge God to enhance their power but God is the ultimate power holder and responds accordingly in what can only be called a naked power play. Contrast this with God's relationship with Noah. Noah does things of which God does not approve but does not directly challenge Him. In essence, God offers mankind a partnership in the polity and economy of the world, and is even willing to covenant to that effect. It is a partnership in which human power is great but not great enough to challenge Heaven. Nor should it be; God will view such a challenge as a breach of the partnership and its covenant and will react accordingly. The people at Babel in effect reject partnership for pursuit of their own visions of power and are punished in such a way that the original covenant remains but humanity is no longer able to form a single bloc against

Heaven. Thus, the incident brings a rupture between God and man, after the new arrangement following the Flood. Each nation must now find its own way back to a proper relationship with God.

Once again the Bible does not deal kindly with cities. Here they are seen as expressions of overweening human ambition and impiety as well as concentrations of power, even worse than (albeit closely related to) earlier views of cities as the artifacts and refuges of murderers (4:17) and fonts of empires (10:10). The city is clearly an artifact in the biblical understanding of things; it responds to elements in man's *derekh*/way but is not a product of nature. Like so many human artifacts (and, for that matter, natural phenomena) it has a strong potential for evil or at least misuse. This is one such example. Yet at the same time it is needed precisely because of the way it develops and concentrates human skills and power. The connection between 10:10 and this case study becomes clear in verse 9 where it turns out that the city of this account is the first city in Nimrod's empire. Putting the two accounts together, we see that God reconciles Himself to cities as long as there are many of them so that no one can become so dominant as to challenge Heaven.

Language is also an artifact according to the Bible (2:19-20) but, unlike cities, one that God Himself induced man to invent (11:7). God Himself intervenes here to limit the power humans derive from language. By confounding their language and scattering them, He succeeds in stopping their city-building efforts (v. 8). Still, God Himself must scatter them; they do not move away by themselves. Apparently the "herd instinct," which, at the lowest level, leads people to crowd together on a beach, could only be overcome through Divine intervention, even after they ceased to understand each other.

Beginnings of the Westward Movement

This God-induced dispersion is related to the beginning of the westward movement that produced Western civilization. In the biblical account, it begins at the end of chapter 11 with the migration of the sons of Eber (the Hebrews?), great-grandson of Shem, beginning with Terah who starts out from Mesopotamia for Canaan and gets as far as Haran in what is today north central Syria, at the beginning of what were then known as "the lands of the West."

Terah's migration, which many scholars believe took place in the nineteenth century before the common era, marks a turning point in more ways than one. Until this point, all the migrations mentioned in the Bible have been eastward (3:24, 4:16, 11:2), or, in one case, northward (10:11). Terah is portrayed as initiating the westward migration or movement of what has become Western civilization, which is to continue for some 3800 years and is to become one of the major factors in shaping the West as well as one of its most common themes.

That migration is to take Western man to and across the Mediterranean Sea, Europe, the Atlantic Ocean, and the American continents to the Pacific, while an offshoot is to turn northward across the Black Sea, the European steppes, and then eastward across Siberia and Alaska as far as northern California. There at the very beginning of the nineteenth century of the common era, after circling the globe, the two strands are to reunite at Ft. Ross, a Russian outpost in northern California, at the edge of Spanish territory then about to be penetrated by Americans. The linkage there was made by representatives of the three great branches of Christianity: Orthodox, Catholic, and Protestant, a daughter religion of that founded by Abraham, the son of Terah, who participated in that first migration and who is seen by Christians as their spiritual father. It reflected the conquest of the world by the West, a conquest that was to become very apparent in the course of the nineteenth century, during which the Jewish people, the children of Abraham, were to reach the uttermost limits of the West and begin their return to the land promised to him by God.

Notes

1. We are indebted to Leo Strauss for this insight. See his "An Interpretation of Genesis," *Jewish Political Studies Review* 1, nos. 1-2 (Spring 1989): 77-92.
2. Despite His earlier threat, God is unable to carry out His threatened punishment of instant death without frustrating His intentions for creation. The snake made his case to Eve by pointing that out (vv. 1-5). But God can find other means of punishment, which over the long run are perhaps worse than death since they involve recurring pain and suffering. Even then, death is only postponed to the end of each individual's road rather than instantaneous obliteration. Thus, God does execute His sentence, but not immediately.
3. On the scientific and philosophic study of the question as the basic unit of biosocial time, see Daniel J. Elazar, *American Mosaic* (Boulder, CO: Westview Press, 1993); "Generational Breaks," in *When Patterns Change: Turning Points in International Politics,* ed. Nissan Oren (Jerusalem: Magnes and St. Martin's Press, 1983); *American Federalism: A View from the States,* 3d ed. (New York: Harper & Row, 1986); "The American Cultural Matrix," in *The Ecology of American Political Culture: Readings,* ed. Daniel J. Elazar and Joseph Zikmund II (New York: Thomas Y. Crowell, 1975), 13-42.

Cf., e.g., Leo Strauss, *Persecution and the Art of Writing* (Glencoe, IL: Free Press, 1952), and *Natural Right and History* (Chicago: University of Chicago Press, 1953). For Leo Strauss on the Bible, see "Jerusalem and Athens," *Commentary* 43, no. 6 (June 1967): 45–57 and *An Interpretation of Genesis* (Philadelphia: Center for Jewish Community Studies, 1972).

4. For studies of the generational rhythm of human affairs, see Julian Marias, *Generations: A Historical Method,* trans. Harold C. Raley (Tuscaloosa: University of Alabama Press, 1970); Marvin Rintala, *The Constitution of Silence: Essays on Generational Themes* (Westport, CT: Greenwood Press, 1979).

5. Cf., e.g., Louis Mumford, *The City in History* (Harmondsworth: Penguin, 1966).

6. *Ir,* the Hebrew word for city, is derived from the Akkadian *uru,* which means tower. Historians of the ancient Near East generally agree that cities originally came into existence for defensive purposes, as places where the inhabitants of a region could come together to collectively defend themselves (Frankfort, Childe). The Bible itself gives a clear picture of the process of urbanization in the story of the Tower of Babel (chap. 11). There the meaning of *ir* as a focal point is clear. The word itself is parallel to *migdal* (tower, as in v. 4). As the account indicates, a city is not so much an enclosed space set apart from the surrounding countryside but a center that draws the surrounding area toward it. In an arid or semi-arid environment, it is an oasis, perhaps an artificial one, made by man to serve the people of a particular area; hence, the tower is its focal point.

7. On the use of "heart" in the Bible, see Moshe Weinfeld, *Deuteronomy and the Deuteronomic School* (Oxford: Clarendon Press, 1972), esp. p. 304. Cf. also Charles Webb Carter, *The Biblical Ethic of Love* (New York: P. Lang, 1990).

8. See Midrash Tannaim 73.

9. Cf. Gen. 10: 1–32. See also A. Heidel, *The Gilgamesh Epic and the Old Testament Parallels,* 2d ed. (Chicago: University of Chicago Press, 1949); S. N. Kramer and E. A. Speiser in *Ancient Near Eastern Texts Relating to the Old Testament,* ed. James B. Pritchard, trans. W. F. Albright (Princeton: Princeton University Press, 1969); Nahum M. Sarna, *Understanding Genesis* (New York: Schocken, 1966).

10. See E. A. Speiser on "'Goy' and 'Am'" in *Oriental and Biblical Studies: Collected Writings of E. A. Speiser,* ed. J. J. Finkelstein and Moshe Greenberg (Philadelphia: University of Pennsylvania Press, 1967), 160–70.

11. For an article on Nimrod, see Heinrich Schuetzinger, *Ursprung und Entwicklung der arabischen Abram-Nimrod-Legende* (Bonn: Universität Bonn, 1961).

12. See Midrash Aseret Melakhim, 38-39; Midrash Rabbah Gen. 10:8.

13. On the Babel story, Hugo Grossman, *The Tower of Babel* (New York: Jewish Institute of Religion Press, 1928); Andre Parrot, *The Tower of Babel* (London: SCM Press, 1955); Hubert Bost, *Babel: Du Texte au Symbole* (Geneve: Labor et Fides, 1985).

14. See Midrash Rabbah Gen. 11:8; Midrash Abraham 46.

6

Abraham and His Children: Migration and Covenant

Migration and the Founding of a New Nation

The beginning of the westward movement is also the beginning of God's effort to control human weakness without destroying humanity, through the singling out of a single person and his descendants who will come under His special providence. It is the first step toward what will be the focal point of the Bible, namely, the founding and development of a new society, Israel, living under a Divine constitution in a land chosen for them by God, and in covenant with him. With Abraham, God tries a fourth plan after His earlier failures.

God's first effort, with Adam, was to create a creature with sufficient intelligence to manage His garden but naturally innocent and thus uninterested in challenging Heaven. The combination of man and woman, however, undid God's plan. Humans lose their innocence by gaining knowledge of good and evil, thereby arousing God's fear that they will indeed challenge Him.

God tries to remedy this by requiring humans to work hard and make their way in the world only with pain; this is His second effort. But humans show their mettle, are inventive, and soon are in liaison with beings from heaven, gaining in power without any moral restraint. So God wipes them out by flood, saving only one family for a new beginning.

God makes a third try with Noah and his sons. This time He decides to harness man through a pact that firmly establishes the partnership and its moral basis. Not only does Noah disappoint Him but, worse, humanity as a whole challenges Heaven at Babel. As we have seen, God strikes back forcefully.

The story emphasizes two decisive themes: (a) the relationship between migration and new starts and (b) the relationship between the Israelites as a people and Canaan as a land to the two great pillars of the ancient world, Mesopotamia and Egypt. In dealing with them, it also spells out the elements of primordial human linkage while presenting the first step toward repairing the breach between God and humanity brought about by man's attempt to challenge Heaven at Babel.

The story begins by emphasizing relationships: (1) God's relationship with Abraham, which is presented as one in which Abraham shows unquestioning responsiveness or hearkening to God's statements; (2) Abraham's first relationship with the land promised to him; (3) his relationship with Sarah his wife; and (4) his relationship with the Pharaoh. Sarah apparently hearkens to Abraham as Abraham hearkens to God although this is not always to be the case. Indeed, Abraham is later to hearken to her (Gen. 16) at God's behest. Abraham's relationship to the Pharaoh is strictly human in which Abraham dissimulates unsuccessfully, apparently offending God in the process.

God tells (*vayomer*) Abraham to go forth from his land, his kith and kinship network, and his father's household (Gen. 12:1), that is to say, the environment of his extended family, to a new Divinely indicated land. As in previous accounts concerning Adam and Noah, God speaks and Abraham the addressee chooses to respond—there is no commanding and no obeying but speaking and hearkening.

Note the elements of primordial human attachment specified here: (*eretz*—land, *moledet*—kith or kinship network, and *bet av*—father's household). Founding a new society requires detachment from all of these factors, which are the principal sources of cultural ties and transmission. At the same time, humans cannot live without these primordial attachments; hence, they must be replaced in the new society by new attachments of equal weight (Gen. 12:2-3). God will do this by covenanting with Abraham (chap. 15) to give him and his descendants a new land, make those descendants numerous enough to constitute a great kith, and prosper Abraham sufficiently in his own household, all within the context of a culture-transforming Providence.

Moreover, "through you all the families of the earth shall be blessed"— the ultimate in family replacement. Here is expression of the purpose of Abraham's migration and the new nation it is to bring about. Every new society or nation must have a purpose that motivates its founding and informs its existence. That purpose then becomes rooted within it and remains part of its fundamental constitution.

The transformation of culture is possible only through new frameworks established by the combination of a great faith and great founders who are themselves transformed by the faith and who can lead in the establishment of a new society informed by it. The story of Abraham is illustrative of this and should be understood as a paradigm of both the phenomenon and the process. The founder or founders must be exemplary expressions of the new faith and the behavior it demands, human but with an unusual nobility or virtue.

Such transformations only come when migration is part of the process. Despite all the grand revolutionary slogans, people do not build new societies on the ashes of the old because as long as the people who grew up within the context of the old ways still live in the same environment, too much is carried over. That is why revolutionaries seeking to radically transform their societies usually end up resorting to great cruelty. Burning with idealism, they seek to transform their peoples "in place" as it were, and must resort to the most drastic measures of upheaval and destruction to do so. Even then they do not succeed.

Even migration cannot eliminate all the old cultural baggage but, if combined with the right circumstances in the new land, it makes possible the reintegration of those elements around a new set of beliefs and principles and a new way of life. Thus, all successful truly new societies or nations began with a great migration (to use the word used by the Puritans, another covenanted people, who emigrated to Massachusetts Bay in the seventeenth century). More than that, migration requires the establishment of new frameworks in new territories where those who settle and survive have a strong claim to equality. Thus, they demand an equal share in those new frameworks, which they gain through the pacts—covenants—that establish political order. Hence, there is an existential connection between migration and the founding of new societies by covenant.

The need for a great faith to be willing to take the risks of migration and founding explains why religion is more often the cause of cultural transformation than such well-hawked modern explanations as the class struggle. It was only when the idea of the latter was made the cornerstone of a secular faith, communism, that it acquired revolutionary force, and even then for no more than three generations. On the other hand, socialists who believed in the existence of the class struggle but not as an article of faith, were never able to use it to motivate fundamental changes in society; it helped in the struggle for social reform but no more. Even the once-powerful Marxist-Leninist faith, when it went bankrupt, could not hold the dikes against normal human desires for life, liberty, and the pursuit of happiness.

The idea of the special worth of founders is common in the ancient world. It is replaced in the modern world by the idea of progress, which diminishes the worth of previous generations, and in the contemporary world by the notion of development, which essentially eliminates the nature of a polity's or people's founding as an important factor in shaping its character.

The Bible is not slavishly faithful to the ancient emphasis on founding as an exclusively important act and it hardly rejects the idea of progress, given its linear view of history. It holds founding and founders to be of central importance in human development but includes the possibility, even likelihood, of refoundings. Founding, for the Bible, is not a one-time act, a matter of a lawgiver bestowing a constitution as in ancient Hellas, but a set of decisive acts by founders, followed by not simply direct linear development, that is, by "ups and downs," and then by another set of decisive acts by founders, more ups and downs. Each refounding comes by virtue of the previous founders' merit and builds upon it. Later the Bible is to state that such merit persists for a thousand generations, nearly forever.

The Bible distinguishes founders by the title *eved adonai* (servant or minister of God). This term (or a variant of it) is used in connection with Abraham, Moses, Joshua, and David, all founders. It reflects the authority granted them by God to cross normal boundaries: (1) in their relationships with Him; (2) in their relationship with the *am*; and (3) in their relationship with the other elements of the *edah* (the *am* constituted as a polity), particularly in crossing the traditional division of powers between the three Divinely segmented domains of authority: *Torah* (interpreting God's teachings and their interpretation), *malkhut* (leading the civil government), and *kehunah* (performing acts of priesthood). Abraham combines those functions in his person as the first of God's people. So will Isaac and Jacob as his successors. After the patriarchs no other founder will do so, but Moses will exercise the powers of the first two and organize the last, and Joshua will also exercise the powers of the first two. David's is more a claim that is partially fulfilled; hence, he does not actually exercise authority other than the *malkhut* but he reorganizes or causes the reorganization of the other two domains around his new court in Jerusalem.

Abraham (then still Abram) responds and begins his new life. The first stage of Abraham's migration involves his getting to know the land of Canaan without settling down. He builds his household while wandering through the central hill country and toward the Negev. Wherever he stops, he builds an alter and prays to God as a means of establishing his legitimacy in the land. God appears to Abram at Elon Moreh, one of the altar sites, and, without covenanting, reiterates his promises to Abram.

There follows the first contact between Israel and Egypt, a brief (and problematic) sojourn. The text reveals an Egypt and its Pharaoh innocently involved in violating the norms against adultery because of the dissimulation of a leader of a band of nomads seeking relief from famine in the breadbasket of the ancient world. If anything, it is the Israelite who is less than honest with his hosts, albeit for understandable reasons—to protect his woman (alternatively, there is Speiser's theory about the Hurrian custom of adopting one's wife as a sister). The Pharaoh acts honestly and, as the wronged party, expels Abram and his household from Egypt. How does Abram come into the Pharaoh's presence? We are not told, although we are told that the Pharaoh seeks him out after falling sick inexplicably. Sarah is originally discovered by the Pharaoh's officers (v. 15). Of course from the Bible's perspective, Abraham is not simply another minor nomad leader from the lands to the northeast as an objective observer might view him or a barbarian chieftain as he might have been viewed by the Egyptians, but God's chosen and hence at least on a par with any Pharaoh.

On first reading, this is a curious account that seems to be the remnant of an ancient tradition whose meaning had been lost but which was sacred because of its antiquity, hence its inclusion. That is too simple by far. The story tells us how Abram had to learn how to be a new man. Abram behaves here in a normal way for a person of his cultural background. God does not back him up but neither does He punish him. There is no miraculous intervention to prevent Pharaoh from discovering the deception; quite to the contrary, God visits the Pharaoh with sickness, causing him to inquire as to what has happened and to force the truth out of Abram. It seems as if Abram has not yet learned how to be a new man, the archetype of a new nation. God forces him to confront his weakness so as to teach him but does no more to punish him than allow the Pharaoh to expel him from Egypt. As we see in his subsequent behavior, Abram learns from the experience, but not easily.

There is an added meaning to this episode that is to be found when it is compared with Abraham's second contact with kings in chapter 14 where he meets them in a public capacity, whether in his relations with the king of Sodom or in his war with the four invading kings, reflecting how he has learned to become more than a private householder, to be the head of a public on its way to becoming a nation. The sharp contrast between the strictly private relationship here and the public leader in chapter 14 helps throw this incident into proper perspective in this series of case studies of nation building.

Exercising Power in the International Arena

Abraham's first covenant is conventional, an alliance with two local Amorite clans near Hebron who became his *ba'alei brit*. With them, he is ready for his first venture into the international arena as an independent force (chap. 14). A nation is politically complete only when it can conduct its own foreign policy and take military action on its own initiative; that is to say, when it has a sufficiently developed political organization and can mobilize sufficient power to do so. While this account still portrays Abraham as Abram leading the men of his (now grown) household in a war against the expeditionary force of four invading kings, it marks the first step in that direction.

After the five cities of the valley of the Salt Sea (today, the Dead Sea) joined to throw off their common overlord (vv. 2-4), a punitive expeditionary force from Elam and its allies (v. 5) successfully intervened to restore the status quo ante. The five rebel kings were defeated and their cities pillaged (vv. 8-11). The whole account is very matter of fact. No issues of morality are raised. Empires or powerful states subdue weaker ones and force them into vassalage, which means essentially keeping the peace and paying tribute, not interfering in their internal affairs. Sometimes the latter revolt and the former try to repress such revolts. The issue is treated as international politics in its most amoral sense because none of the parties here has any special virtue.

Until now, Abraham has dealt with a king (the Pharaoh) only on a strictly private basis (chap. 12) and his public activities have been limited to building altars to establish claims to various parts of the land. Now there is a quantum leap forward. Abraham is not yet the leader of a nation; it is not even clear that he is the leader of a public; that is to say, a community sharing multigenerational externalities characterized by its civic character and political expression. His is, by now, a large household with hundreds of people linked to and dependent upon it, but it remains a household, not a polity. However, he can mobilize a fighting force capable of taking to the field and saving the cities of the plain, which makes him a factor in Canaanite politics. Abraham's nephew, Lot, who in the interim had moved to Sodom, is taken captive in the struggle (vv. 12–14), bringing about Abraham's intervention. The military campaign is simple and swift (v. 15), resulting in a decisive victory by Abraham's force.

The case study is important for what it teaches about international relations from a covenantal perspective. First of all, entering the international arena is also a matter of relationships, several kinds of which and the distinctions among them are referred to, including:

1. The league of imperial states (v. 1), a standard military alliance;
2. The vassal relationship between Elam and the cities of the valley of the Salt Sea (v. 2);
3. The alliance of the five cities of the plain, denominated in covenantal terms;
4. Abraham and his Amorite confederates (vv. 13, 24) as *ba'alei brit*;
5. Abraham and his household (v. 14);
6. *Am* as a *goi* bound by a special relationship to a specific higher authority (v. 16);
7. Abraham and Melchizedek (vv. 18–20), an ideological ally from a different polity and people;
8. Abraham and El Elyon (v. 22);
9. Abraham and the king of Sodom (vv. 22–24), how to handle sometimes necessary relationships with morally repugnant entities.

Abraham refuses to profit from the campaign because of the morally repugnant character of Sodom, the regime his efforts have restored (vv. 22–24). Given the ways of the world and international relations, good peoples sometimes must intervene on behalf of those who are morally repugnant to them in order to secure some proper interest or end. It is reasonable and acceptable to God that they do so, but they must do so in such a way as to minimize the moral taint and make clear their moral position vis-à-vis their associates. Two ways to do so are presented here:

(1) devotion of a share of any gains to Divine purposes and (2) refusal to profit from any of the rest. This demonstration involves more than words. At the same time, reimbursement for expenses incurred is quite legitimate. The foregoing applies only to morally obligated peoples; their morally neutral allies such as the Amorite chieftains can expect to receive their share (v. 24).

Implicit in this account is the division of polities into three kinds: those that are morally good (or at least are obligated to be), covenanted; those that are morally neutral, guided by appropriate codes; and those that are morally wicked, socially and politically corrupt. Abraham and his household and probably Melchizedek's Salem are presented as morally good; the Amorite tribes and, perhaps, even the four invading polities are presented as neutral; and Sodom and, probably, the other cities of the plain are presented as wicked.[1]

Sodom is presented here as a city of the wicked (13:14), the paradigm of the city that has adopted immorality as the foundation of its regime, placing itself beyond redemption. It is the second of the four archetypical cities presented in the Bible: Babylon, Sodom, Jerusalem, and Nineveh. Babylon is presented as the paradigm of the cosmopolitan city, united by the ambitions, enterprise, and great expectations of its residents. It is morally neutral and this is its fatal flaw. Jerusalem is presented as the city founded on piety, justice, and morality and that consequently has an extra measure of obligation. Nineveh will be presented in Jonah as the paradigm of the cosmopolitan imperial city capable of repentance and, hence, redemption.

Brit Ben Habetarim: The Covenant of Land and People

The use of ordinary covenants leads to the transformational covenant between God and Abraham. In chapters 12, 13, and 14, Abram (Abraham's original name) hearkens to God's word, undergoing certain vicissitudes in the process and at the same time prospering and developing. In chapters 15, 16, and 17, God responds with two covenanting acts.

While the *brit ben habetarim* is specific to a particular person and kith, God's universality is expressed in His statement that He judges other nations (v. 14). This element of being under judgment is basic to biblical morality and is a reflection of God's role as judge. What is implicit here is made explicit elsewhere in the Bible, namely, that the universe is *malkhut shamayim* (the kingdom of heaven). God is the only holder of sovereignty in His kingdom and is its king, legislator, and judge (Isa. 33:23). The political imagery is essential to the definition of God's role; He is not so much a savior of individuals but a governor of nations, peoples, and polities.

The covenant of circumcision, God's second and final covenant with Abraham, is described in chapter 17. It is essentially a repetition of the triad of promises enunciated by God regarding the relationships between God and Abraham, Abraham and his descendants, and Abraham and the land, all growing more intimate. It includes the fullest promise of descendants, dealing with both quantity (*hamon goyim*: a multitude of nations, v. 5) and quality (nations and kings, v. 6) and sealed by God's changing Abram's name to Abraham (father of a multitude), a classic act in the ancient world where name changes are devices to mark and seal great personal changes. This is coupled with a transference of the covenant ceremony from a cutting of animals to a cutting of men. Thus, it is a counterpoint to chapter 15, a completion of the covenant process begun in that chapter. There Abraham secures a covenant from God; here God comes back to Abraham and offers him the same covenant with terms, thereby regaining the upper hand. To do so, He even goes so far as to reveal Himself to Abraham for the first time.

Here Abraham is necessarily more submissive, no doubt overawed by God's visible presence, but not entirely subdued since he laughs to himself when God promises him a son by Sarah (v. 17). Throughout his relationship with God, Abraham retains his integrity, freedom of thought, and freedom to speak and respond. This, too, is part of the biblical model of the relationship between humans and God, respectful but not servile. This model is to acquire even sharper expression in Abraham's effort to save Sodom from destruction by negotiating with God (chap. 18).

All this time Abram has responded to a truly unknown God, unseen and unnamed. Earlier Abram has tried to identify the God who spoke to him and whom he has followed with Melchizedek's *El-Elyon* (chap. 14); we could even feel the hope and anxiety combined in his doing so. Even in chapter 15, where Abram succeeds in pinning God down to a firm pact, he has continued to deal with God the unknown. Now God chooses to reveal Himself.

The covenant is with Abraham and his descendants, generation by generation (v. 7); hence, it is a *brit olam* (eternal covenant, in time and space). The phraseology here not only reflects the generational structure of history but suggests that each generation is bound collectively by the covenant. This acquires concrete expression in the recovenanting ceremonies required and described in the later books of the Bible. The essence of the covenant is that God will be the God of Abraham and his descendants. That is the condition attached to the promise.

This is made even more explicit in connection with the renewed promise of the land (v. 8). Canaan, too, is given to Abraham and his descendants as *ahuzat olam* (an eternal landhold) on condition *v'hayiti lahem laelohim* (I will be your God). The terminology is still one of consent and not of command. The idea of keeping (*shamor,* v. 9) the covenant is part of this consensual structure. The explicit sign of the covenant to be kept (*tishm'ru*) by Abraham and his descendants is the circumcision of every male (v. 10). Circumcision is to be the *ot brit* (sign of the covenant), a necessary element in the covenanting. Circumcision applies to natural born and adopted males alike (vv. 12–13), indicating that the patriarchal household in both its elements is now united by the covenant with God. Kinship remains important but not decisive. It is remaining uncircumcised that is an explicit violation of God's covenant (v. 14). Abraham follows God's instruction precisely and circumcises all the males of his household. He, too, is circumcised, only after which he is able to bring Sarah to conceive.

Abraham as Partner, God as Judge

The new partnership between God and Abraham is given bone and sinew in chapter 18. Before the two covenants, both God and Abram were presented as acting alone with the other simply responding. God is a vision or a voice, no more. Now God appears to Abraham twice, the second time to consult with him about a third-party action, namely, the fate of Sodom and the cities of the plain, indicating that He does so because of the special relationship between Him and the nation that is to develop from Abraham. The character of the partnership is delineated in this case: God consults with Abraham, who can freely, if respectfully, argue or negotiate with Him, but God reserves the final right of decision. It is a partnership but not of full equals.

What follows is in the nature of a trial whose procedures are carefully set out, as a case study in applying the principles of God's justice to concrete situations. The matter is presented as one of *tzedakah u 'mishpat* (justice and righteousness), the biblical phrase for the complex of obligations and rights that are the essence of the just society. God's intervention comes when the earth (or some part of it) cries out (*za 'akat*) against injustice (v. 20). This is parallel to the situation with regard to Cain's murder of Abel whose blood cries out from the earth (4:10). God does not simply intervene; He must be summoned. Before taking punitive action, God investigates the charges (18:21–22 and chap. 19). God's three messengers proceed to Sodom to conduct the investigation.

Abraham approaches God (*vayigash*—he drew near) for purposes of discussion, a daring concept reflecting his new position under the covenant. He seeks to defend Sodom from destruction, not by denying its general sinfulness but by trying to find reasons for God to be merciful despite it. What follows through to the end of the chapter is a negotiation between Abraham and God regarding the basis for acting mercifully with Sodom, one in which God concedes a great deal to Abraham who, in the end (after God's messengers inspect the city), must concede that Sodom is beyond redemption. The course of the negotiation tells us a number of things about the low level of biblical expectations of humanity by this time. Fifty righteous men in a city of probably several thousand is reasonable to offset grievous sin; even ten is an acceptable number.

With the story of Abraham the full interplay between kinship and consent acquires expression in several ways. Abraham builds a household, most of whose members are clearly not organically connected to Abraham's family since Abraham was childless and his nephew Lot, the one relative mentioned as having accompanied him out of Haran, separates from him because of competition among lesser members of their two households for scarce resources. Lot settles in Sodom and, while he more or less retains his honorable code of life, sees his family corrupted, losing his locally intermarried daughters and his overcurious wife when the city is destroyed and ending up as the father of two of the nations neighboring Israel, Moab and Ammon, through an incestuous relationship with his surviving daughters.

This is the first of several discussions of the origins and character of Israel's neighbors. All are presented as related to Israel, reflecting the sense of common origins that pervaded the peoples of the West and also giving more detail of how new kiths and nations emerge from families of common descent. None of the discussions is flattering.

The discussions of covenants of alliance and covenants of founding and their implications, are interrupted by yet a third, God's promise to Hagar and Ishmael. Ishmael, the first product of Abraham's loins through Sarah's handmaiden Hagar, ultimately is denied his birthright by the birth of Isaac, who is designated by God as Abraham's proper heir. Ishmael receives his own promise from God (via his mother) for nation-hood, not fully covenantal, whose quasi-covenantal character prefigures the quasi-covenantal relationships in the Arab world.[2]

Ishmael is the father of the Arabs. As the Bible indicates in 16:10, he fathers a kith, not a single nation. He is inappropriate as Abraham's heir to continue the Abrahamic chain because he is wild and feuds with all, a character trait the Bible carefully weeds out. In a sense, one of the possibilities opened by covenant is to minimize the negative impacts of a strict kinship system by eliminating those inappropriate to the task at hand and provide a means for those who are appropriate to be authorized and empowered as they should be.

But the matter is more problematic than that. When the patriarchs seek wives for the sons who are to be their heirs, they go back to their family outside of Canaan. Their sons need mates. Should they take local mates they would introduce all the Canaanite influences into the family, thereby violating the entire intention of the migration, which was to detach Abraham and his heirs from a polytheism that was so much rooted in the worship of the gods of particular places. By going back to the original family at least that is avoided and no doubt it is hoped that by detaching the prospective wives from their original places they, too, will be more or less detached from the religions of those places.

Even a tribal household is constituted through the combination of kinship and contract. A wife is acquired by contract, her children belong by virtue of their kinship. If she is childless, she can seek to maintain her status by offering her husband her handmaiden, acquired by purchase, as a surrogate to provide him with her share of his heirs. The handmaiden is not simply a surrogate since her status must be formally changed as well (v. 3). The resultant issue is kin but not fully; his status must also be affirmed by some act at some point.

Abraham is presented in Bereshith as father of a number of separate peoples. Even the greatest Jew will transmit his Jewishness only to part of his line. The Jews make a double contribution—a continuing collective one through the Jewish people and a periodic fertilizing one through individual founders who are hied off into the larger world—Lot in a very small way, Ishmael in a larger one, on to Jesus and to Marx, and indirectly to Mohammed.

At the same time, it is another expression of the biblical teaching that neither kinship nor covenant are sufficient unto themselves. Only those of Abraham's descendants who are heirs to his covenant with God (usually directly reaffirmed in some way) carry on the line. The others are spun off; some become separate peoples who partake of "Jewish energy" (the influence of heredity) but not necessarily for the highest, or even respectable, purposes. Still others—Christians, in particular—later claim a covenantal connection with Abraham but, without adopting kinship, they are not Jews.

Territory Gained Through Covenant

Abimelech, seeing that Abraham plans to remain in his vicinity and in view of his earlier experience with the Hebrew, decides that he had best protect himself by regularizing their relationship through a treaty (covenant) of alliance. The way Abimelech approaches the issue is instructive with regard to covenant negotiations. Abimelech's decision seems to be based, at least in part, on military considerations (and perhaps reflects his effort to threaten Abraham militarily to encourage him to agree).

Most of all, it is based on strategic planning. Since God prospers Abraham in all he does, Abimelech sees the need to protect his rule, his dynasty, and his land. He claims a response from Abraham equivalent to his in their first encounter. The terms used are covenantal. Abraham is asked to take an oath before God, to make a covenant promise to return an equivalent *hesed*. *Shevuah* or oath is a covenant term throughout the Bible.

Abraham agrees to the oath, the covenant, but uses the opportunity to negotiate water rights. He opens the negotiations by putting Abimelech on the defensive in a careful way by reproving him for the acts of his subordinates (as if Abimelech himself bore responsibility for the problem). Abimelech responds in kind. He claims not to have known of the situation principally because Abraham never brought it up to him.

Abraham then gives Abimelech livestock and the two of them cut a covenant. Abraham establishes his claim to the disputed well through a symbolic gift through which he indicates that he dug the well. The gift is a form of payment for the rights, perhaps symbolic (i.e., the proverbial dollar to bind a conveyance), and also an inspired pun that reminds both of the covenant, namely, seven (in Hebrew, *sheva*) ewes. *Sheva* sounds like and is spelled in the same way as the word for oath taking. By taking it, Abimelech acknowledges Abraham's claim. He can afford to do so since the area in dispute is toward the interior of Canaan, in the borderlands of his domain, and he no doubt feels that getting Abraham to settle there under a binding treaty will protect his principal holdings close to the coast. The symbolic pun is continued in the naming of the site *Beer-sheva*, Beersheba, which is presented as meaning the well of the oath.

The covenant is made and Abimelech and Phicol return to the heartland of their territory. Abraham marks his permanent settlement in Beersheba with the planting of a tree. That act reflects the successful outcome of the negotiation from his point of view; namely, confirmation of his rights in Beersheba by Abimelech, the local suzerain. Thus, Abraham acquires a legal territorial right in Canaan for the first time and he does so through political means.

The Akedah

Isaac is the second of the patriarchs. He is a shadowy figure, and is generally presented in the Bible as a passive one. Things happen to him and he accepts them or responds minimally, so much so that biblical critics have called into question his very existence as a separate person, more so than in the case of Abraham and Jacob. In essence, the climax of Isaac's life comes in his youth with his near sacrifice to God by his father.

The story of Abraham's near sacrifice of Isaac is known in Hebrew as *akedat Yitzhak*, the binding of Isaac. The key term, *akedah*, appears in v. 9. Binding is, of course, an element of covenanting and the choice of that term to describe this critical, poignant, and moving event is another reflection of the pervasiveness of covenantal thinking in the Bible and Israel in all its generations. Isaac is the first full *ben brit*, son of the covenant; he is circumcised—cut—according to God's command and then he is bound over to God. Later generations of Jews were to add symbols of binding (e.g., the wimpel in the Germanic world) to the circumcision ceremony to reflect the combination of cutting and binding.

This climactic chapter focuses on several crucial relationships. It emphasizes the willingness of all parties to fulfill their covenant obligations and the restraint that willingness must impose on each other's demands. The story in its spare, stark, poignant telling expresses the problem of all fathers who must send their sons out on potentially fatal missions, such as to do battle, whereby the sons not only go to what may be death but must carry with them the tools of their possible destruction. God speaks to Abraham who responds with one word, *hinneni* (here I am), and moves rapidly and decisively to fulfill God's will. He leaves early and fully equipped. He is with Isaac and his thoughts for three days of travel.

Isaac speaks for the first time (indeed for the first time in the Bible) as he and his father walk the last steps to the place of sacrifice. He calls out to his father who answers him with the same *hinneni* with which he had previously responded to God, adding *b'ni* (my son). Both the symmetry and the difference in the relationships is clear. Both kinship and covenant demand a *hinneni* response but a covenant with God takes precedence. Isaac's question as to where is the being to be sacrificed is a natural one that sharpens the poignance of the telling.

The story describes Abraham's final preparations step by step: reaching the place, building the altar, arranging the wood, binding his son, and, finally, placing him on the altar. At the final moment, the messenger of the Lord calls out to Abraham by name, twice as if in an urgent, agonized way, and Abraham, as always, responds with a *hinneni* (here I am), thus halting the act. There is a Midrash that Abraham demanded of God that He, Himself, revoke the decree and reiterate his covenant promises. Indeed, in 2:12 it seems to be God speaking rather than His messenger. (As in the Sodom story, God and his messengers, angels, merge into a single multifaceted personality, emanations from the Godhead who emerge and resubmerge as needed.)

At the end of the story, God's blessing is further extended beyond the new nation to include the nations of the world that are to be blessed through Abraham's seed. This adds another whole dimension to God's design, albeit a logical one given God's desire to give humanity as a whole the tools by which to redeem itself. Israel is to be a principal tool. This verse has, needless to say, attracted the attention of Christians over the centuries, who see in it a prefiguration of Jesus in the same way that Muslims transform the story by giving Ishmael Isaac's role. Abraham's role as the common father of the monotheistic religions is hereby delineated. The blessing itself is a response to Abraham's hearkening to God's voice. The importance of hearkening—consenting and doing—is made explicit.

Isaac's subsequent career remains within the shadow of the Akeda. Not surprisingly, the boy seems to have been traumatized by his near-sacrifice and grows up to be a man who is manipulated by his wife as he was by his father. Nevertheless, he is Abraham's heir and the second patriarch, inheriting the covenant and its promises.

Just as Isaac is a passive adjunct to the Abraham story, so he becomes a weak adjunct to the story of Jacob and Esau. The only story in which we see Isaac taking a leading role, it is a near duplicate account of the encounter between Abraham and Abimelech (Gen. 26), this time with Isaac as one of the two principals. It is one of the reasons advanced by some biblical critics to support their theory that Isaac is entirely legendary, a composite of other characters. Following our principle of taking the text as a coherent whole, we are left puzzled by this chapter except as a reflection of the ancients' respect for received texts and traditions. The text even shows awareness of the problem in v. 1 where it refers to Isaac's famine as distinct from that of Abraham. In general, this seems to be a later account on the basis of the terminology used. God appears to Isaac as a patriarch for the first time to tell him not to go down to Egypt. Isaac is the only one of the patriarchs who spend his whole life in Eretz Israel, not even leaving briefly.

God is presented as renewing His covenant with Isaac in chapter 26 where Isaac hearkens and promises to observe the forms of the covenant. *Shama* and *vayishmor* (hearken and observe) are the key words indicating covenantal response. Here we have the first appearance in the bible of the phrase *mitzvotai, hukotai, v'torotai* (my commandments, my constitutional laws, and my teachings), the three elements of the Torah as constitution.

Isaac also enters into a treaty-covenant with Gerar. Here another term for covenant, *ala*, is introduced (26:28), a synonym for *brit* that appears from time to time in the Bible, especially in connection with the secular pacts. The importance of the covenant idea is reflected in the number of synonyms for *brit* that can be found in the text, such as *ala, amanah, edut,* and *shevu'a.*

Isaac benefits both from God and from his neighbors because of his father, the founder. Here the Bible strikes the theme of heirs enjoying God's favor by virtue of their founding ancestor, a theme that is to be continued and expanded. The one thing that stands out is that Isaac is more active in naming places in Canaan than is Abraham. Abraham, an immigrant, readily accepted the names given to places by others until near the end of his career when he and Abimelech together named Beersheva. Isaac, a native, is portrayed as namer of places as well.

Isaac's final appearance in the Bible is when he is deceived by his wife, Rebecca, and his son, Jacob, with regard to his patriarchal blessing. In his childhood and innocence, he was deceived by his father for reasons of faith. Now in his old age and blindness, he is deceived by one of his sons for personal gain.

Notes

1. This division corresponds quite closely to the Aristotelian idea of three kinds of constitutions (in the sense of polities): the one that leads to the good life in absolute terms, those that are not absolutely good but are good for the peoples they serve, and those that are deficient by every ethical standard even if they fit the people they serve.
2. The story of the relationship between Abraham, Sarah, Hagar, Ishmael, and Isaac is presented in the Bible with keen psychological insight. Sarah, who initiates the relationship out of sympathy for her husband's desperate desire for an heir of his own flesh and blood, almost immediately regrets her sympathetic act as she sees her husband sleeping with and impregnating Hagar. Her anger is described as senseless (*hamas*) but is nonetheless real. God, committed as He now is to Abraham and Sarah, takes Sarah's side but provides a compensatory promise for Hagar and Ishmael.

7

Federal versus Natural Man

Jacob and Esau: The Struggle Continues

The Bible, as is its wont, is not simply concerned with the technicalities of covenanting and covenantal obligations but with the larger implications and purposes of the covenantal way. Chief among them is the harnessing of the natural wildness of humans through covenants to deal with the problem of how to preserve human liberty without encouraging license. It is this double task that makes the covenantal way unique.

Most, if not all, theories of civilization begin with an understanding that humans are born natural, free, and wild. To remain free, indeed to even survive, they must somehow harness that natural wildness. They must replace the external restraints of an often cruel nature with internal ones.

This problem is additionally complicated by the fact that the wildness is often attractive, at one level of understanding, to all of us, and at another level, to many. Moreover, the bonds of civilization are frequently unattractive and those who take the lead in maintaining them may do so to gain power for their own ends. When the Bible deals with this issue as it does over and over again (we have already seen the cases of Cain and Abel and Ishmael and Isaac), it does so with honesty, sensitivity, and sympathy to both expressions of humanity although it leaves no doubt as to where it comes out. Indeed nowhere in the Bible is the tragic reality of life better expressed than in the scriptural rejection of these bluff, hearty, natural men in favor of federal men with their own weaknesses and problems.

Jacob and Esau are perhaps the most important paradigms of federal and natural men in the Bible. They are introduced as struggling (*vayitrotzetzu*) with each other from the womb (Gen. 25:22). The homiletic treatment of this has been extensive, considering the way each has come to symbolize conflicting dimensions of power and authority. The common element uniting both is their tremendous energy, which must be directed and harnessed. Jacob is to become Israel (literally: one who struggles with God), whose energy is directed by the covenant, while Esau will struggle with men and animals (nature) to become, in the eyes of the Midrash, the exemplar of a non-Jewish imperial ruler.

The future of the two struggling fetuses is foretold by God and is stated in ethno-political terms. The fathers of the two nations—*goiim* and *leumim* are the terms used—are struggling. Jacob emerges as he is to live, as Yaakov, one who grasps at the heel of his brother, trying to get out first and, as he is to live the first half of his life, struggling for personal advantage.

The description of Esau as a hunter and man of the field fits with the description of his appearance at birth, but that of Jacob as a quiet man, dwelling in tents, contradicts the first description of him. Given what follows immediately, one senses an irony in this description, although it may indicate the other dimension of Jacob's personality, which also stays with him, namely, the desire for a calm existence that remains his strong arm through all his struggles.

Jacob takes advantage of Esau's weakness, an unthinking impulsiveness, to press his advantage in a most unbrotherly way, first acquiring Esau's *b'khora* (birthright) for a bowl of lentils and then his father's blessing through a trick. The birthright has to do with inheritance of goods and position both. The tale is typically biblical. The "bottom line" is that by his actions Esau demonstrates that he does not deserve to be the one who continues Abraham's responsibilities and rewards under God's covenant since he does not have the steady, thoughtful qualities that are required. Rather than getting his own food—after all, he was not really starving to death and Jacob's was not the only kitchen in the encampment—he responds impulsively to a good smell and, in the words of 25:34, "despises his birthright."

Jacob shows his wiliness as well as his greater intelligence and forethought. Jacob's eye is always on the main chance; he sees his advantage and takes it, perhaps not believing the foolishness of his despised—and despising—rival. What he does is not quite honorable, though not illegal. The title he gains is at least partially valid, although he is insecure enough about it to conspire later with his mother to deceive his father so as to gain the blessing for the first-born as well (chap. 27). In short, he is what nineteenth-century Americans would call "sharp," a characteristic associated with the products of covenantal cultures ever since.

Much later, Esau marries two wives, both Hittite women, locals, in violation of Abraham's (and God's) injunction. Again, one gets the sense of a headstrong person who acts impulsively, without sufficient forethought (26:34–35). His marriage is described as a vexation to both Rebecca and Isaac. Even his father, who has strong affection for him (opposites attract), is hurt by his act. This action forever rules out Esau as the bearer of patriarchal continuity. Esau could have overcome the sale of his birthright; as we see in the next chapter, Isaac was still prepared to give him the blessing due the firstborn. But acquiring foreign wives meant the detachment of his children from the Abrahamic line.

Both the personal and psychological and the public and national dimensions of the rivalry between the two brothers are noteworthy. Despite the dreadful deception on the part of Jacob and his mother to gain Isaac's patriarchal blessing, Jacob's vocation as Isaac's legitimate heir in the continued founding of the Jewish people is reaffirmed. In essence, the Bible tells us that a bright, calculating person who, at times, is less than honest, is preferable as a founder over a bluff, impulsive one. Jacob continues to display characteristics of "sharpness" that are later to become part of the non-Jewish stereotype of Jews (although they are only prominent, not typical—witness the very different characters of Abraham and Isaac), while Esau continues to display characteristics of involvement in violent behavior that are later to become part of the Jewish stereotype of non-Jews (*goyim*).

The public and national purposes of this story are, by now, self-evident. That the Esaus of the world cannot assume the mantle of Abraham because of their personal deficiencies is already brought to our attention. At the very least, the Jacobs are the lesser evil because they can be chastened, educated, and redirected. In subsequent chapters God is to test and temper Jacob to turn his intelligence and cunning to moral ends.

In essence, what we have here is a struggle between natural man (Esau) and covenantal (or, in sixteenth- and-seventeenth century terminology, federal) man (Jacob). Both are presented realistically, "warts and all," in the Bible's way. Thus, it is not a confrontation between good and evil but a choice between two limited and flawed human beings. Esau has the good and bad qualities of natural man—principal among them, generosity and impulsiveness, the characteristics of natural liberty. Jacob's character is at least equally mixed, joining intelligence with guile.

Isaac, passive and insecure—he seems traumatized since the *akedah*—is drawn to Esau who as an active person seems so different but who also shares his father's insecurities. God, however, chooses Jacob since He can bind him by covenant and hopes to restrain his sharpness through the constraints of federal liberty—liberty in accordance with the terms of the covenant—while natural man simply cannot be restrained except by force. Once again, God's choices are limited by the realities of human frailty. He makes the best choice that He can but we need not exaggerate the goodness of one or the badness of the other.[1]

Covenant or Contract?

Jacob begins his spiritual journey after having been presented to us in the worst possible manner as a liar and a thief who lies outright to steal Isaac's blessing. After Jacob steals his father's blessing, arousing Esau's murderous wrath, Isaac responds to Rebecca's request by sending him off with his blessing and actually commanding him not to take a Canaanite wife and to go to the family hearth for one instead. The Bible conveys the sense of a not very strong person, much influenced by his wife, attempting to play a role of strength by issuing commands (v. 1, *vayetzavehu*), something that even God does not ordinarily do. The reader knows how absurd it is for him to be commanding Jacob to do what Rebecca set him up to do in the first place to save Jacob's life. Isaac transmits Abraham's promise to Jacob for the first time. His blessing includes both personal fertility and national promise.

Up to this point, whatever legitimation Jacob has obtained has been obtained by deceit. Here, for the first time, he obtains a blessing more or less on his own. Whatever the source of the suggestion and the reasons behind it, Isaac knows it is a valid one. Perhaps it also brings with it recognition that, with Esau's marriage to a Hittite woman, only Jacob can be the bearer of the *brakhah*. Isaac gives it fully.

Shocked by his father's blessing Jacob, Esau suddenly realizes what his Canaanite wife has meant to Isaac. He makes one last attempt to remedy the situation by also marrying a first cousin, the daughter of Ishmael. The effort to parallel Jacob is both clear and insufficient. Ishmael's is not the favored side of the family.

Jacob leaves home to avoid Esau's wrath and his transformation into a man suitable to carry on God's enterprise begins (chap. 28). While Esau is left trying desperately to please his father, Jacob confronts God for the first time. God profers His covenant to Jacob, who, lacking understanding, immediately turns it into a contractual arrangement. The careful reader of the biblical text cannot fail to perceive that the clever, often devious younger brother needs to develop a new higher dimension of the spirit. He has begun his testing.

Jacob's first encounter with God (28:10-22) in a Divinely inspired vision is perfectly appropriate: a ladder set up on the earth and reaching to heaven. No one is more of this world than devious, scheming, jealous, ambitious Jacob who is here called to raise himself heavenward. God could hardly appear to him directly; first He had to get his attention, hence the device of the ladder and the heavenly beings going up and down, bringing Jacob's gaze and thoughts toward heaven.

God then becomes very personal in His guarantees and promises to Jacob; again, knowing his customer, as it were. God's revelation to Jacob is a reaffirmation of the promise to Abraham, in even more practical and earthy terms suitably attractive to Jacob, given his character. The promises of territory and kith are repeated, along with the statement that all the people of the earth will be blessed, legitimized through Jacob's descendants.

Jacob's response is equally in character. He is awed by God's presence but still tries to make a deal with Him by vowing that if God keeps His promise in four specifically personal ways (protection on his way, food, clothing, and a safe return home), he will acknowledge Him and even reward Him by tithing—to "sweeten the pot" for God, as it were, a sure sign of Jacob's contractual approach to the matter. Jacob understands that God is not Esau, to be taken advantage of in a bargain. Nor is he Isaac, to be deceived. God is a real power; hence, the deal should be a good one for him. God does not respond to all of this. What is most notable at the end of the chapter is God's silence.

The foregoing chain of events is not a covenant and is not described as such but is clearly presented as having all the elements of a pact. It is, indeed, a reaffirmation of the covenant with Abraham on God's part, which is turned into a kind of contractual arrangement by Jacob. Jacob is not morally ready for a covenantal relationship. His transformation may have begun but it has just begun. God offers him a great promise for the future and Jacob concentrates on the details of his present well-being. (Notice that he makes no reference whatsoever to the covenantal future in his vow.) Significantly, God, understanding Jacob, offers both possibilities. He needs Jacob to continue the unfolding of His plan; hence, He must educate him and bring him along.

The whole incident teaches us about the similarities and differences between covenant and contract, how they can be confused with one another because of their common emphasis on the freedom and integrity of the partners, their roots in negotiation, and the resultant mutual obligation, yet how they differ in their scope, in the basis of the obligation incurred, and, perhaps most important, in the spirit that surrounds and informs them. This relationship between the two species of pact is an enduring one, encountered in every situation where one or the other is used. There is place for both in our imperfect world, not only by using a contractual relationship as a way station toward a covenantal one but also for each in its own place and situation. However, as much as their relationship to one another should be understood, they should not be confused.

Jacob goes on to meet a greater artist at deception than he, his uncle Laban (chap. 29). First, he is deceived in his marriages, thereby acquiring two wives, Leah and Rachel, and their handmaidens—who are to mother the tribes of Israel—and then in his work relationships. Jacob's hatred for Leah is not explained. One is led to deduce that her very presence is a constant reminder to Jacob of how he, the deceiver, was deceived in turn, forced into an unwanted marriage and seven years' additional free service to his uncle, in order to claim his beloved Rachel. Given what we know about Jacob's concern for his personal well-being, this was a deception that hurt greatly. Hence, there is nothing that Leah can do to win her husband's love.

Here we have another example of Jacob's callousness toward other human beings. Leah is caught in a tragic web no less than Esau, and Jacob, while not the weaver of either, is very much involved in heightening the pain of their respective tragedies. In the end, each is somewhat compensated by God; Esau becomes wealthy and powerful in his own right (chap. 36), Leah (and her handmaiden) provide most of Jacob's sons. Jacob, while winning, suffers greatly. He loses Rachel (chap. 35), lives for years in the belief that Joseph, his favorite son, is dead (chap. 37), and finally is forced to end his days in Egypt (chap. 46). It is through Jacob's tempering by life that he is transformed to become Israel, literally, someone who wrestles with God (Yisrael).

After twenty years, Jacob and Laban reach the parting of ways, not without bitterness, fear, and further deception, causing God to intervene to protect Jacob and his household. The end result is a covenant between the two men, defining their future relationship by separating them one from the other. Up to this point, covenants have only been used to bind; here we learn that they can be used to separate as well. There are certain relationships that are best preserved from a distance and this is certainly one of them. In a sense, the covenant is a sign of the good sense of the two principals, who are both crafty and prudent.

The covenant is made in the traditional manner. Laban suggests making a covenant that will end their confrontation and will also be a mutual promise to stay apart (31:44–52). Jacob responds positively to the overture. First, God is evoked as a witness, then the gods of the principals' respective forefathers. The two men agree on the terms of the covenant that they shall end their confrontation and stay apart in the future. Laban also requires Jacob to promise that there will be no new wives, that is to say, that Laban's property will not go to heirs other than his own descendants. A pile of stones is erected to mark the covenant, referred to in verses 47 and 48 by both its Hebrew name *gal-e.* literally, a heap of witness, and by the equivalent Aramean term. The covenant ceremony is concluded with a sacrifice and ceremonial meal eaten by the parties involved.

Jacob Becomes Israel

Jacob moves out of one dangerous situation toward another, both with members of his family—Laban and Esau—and, on the way, decisively confronts God (chap. 32). Through that very mysterious confrontation, crafty, self-centered Jacob becomes one who strives or wrestles with God (*yisrael*), thereby establishing the destiny of his heirs forever. This destiny is to be embodied in the name of the people who inherit him. A new higher relationship is thereby established, one of striving with God.

There are those who, like Abraham, hearken to God and those, like Isaac, who passively accept God's dictates. Jacob has none of the characteristics appropriate for either role; witness how he has tried to contract with God for protection. But he can be brought to at least strive with God, wrestle with Him in the spirit of his heritage. Thus, Jacob's wrestling with God completes the patriarchal cycle of relationships with the Almighty, from Abraham's powerful and dignified service to Isaac's submissiveness to Jacob's ambivalence. Earlier covenant negotiations give way to wrestling and bargaining for a blessing.

Jacob completes his arrangement with Laban only to learn of Esau's approach with a large body of men at his side, frightening Jacob, who takes steps to save as much of his people and property as he can in case there is trouble, without resorting to force of arms. Jacob has no military resources at his disposal so he can only maneuver, another paradigm of the Jewish condition throughout much of Jewish history.

He then turns to God in a very carefully phrased prayer (as we would expect, since his every move and word reflects forethought), which: (1) invokes his fathers (v. 10); (2) reminds God that he is returning to his land and kith at God's request (v. 10); (3) emphasizes his unworthiness (certainly true in this case) to be one of God's *hasidim* (v. 11); (4) indicates that he had taken what steps he could to protect his camp (v. 11); and (5) asks God to save him, and especially his sons (v. 12), from Esau because of his promise to multiply Jacob's descendants (v. 13).

Every element is appropriate in a petition, which is, at the same time, the opening of a negotiation. Jacob terms God's response to his servants the patriarchs, *hasidim* or loving expressions of covenant obligation and *emet* or true manifestations of covenant loyalty.

The third element in Jacob's preparations is the assembly of gifts for Esau on a grand scale and the arrangement for their presentation in the most effective way, prior to their meeting and in waves, to soften him up for the actual encounter. What we have before us is vintage Jacob in a defensive posture—prudent, crafty, careful, covering all his bets. He divides his camp so that at least half of his wealth is likely to be preserved, he asks God's help in a carefully constructed prayer, he not only arranges to present Esau with abundant gifts but takes care to arrange the manner of their delivery, and then he secretly transfers his immediate family to safety, just in case.

Finally, alone by his own doing, Jacob is now open to the climax of his life, the encounter with the mysterious stranger who speaks in the name of God. In the wrestling that follows, Jacob displays two of his strongest characteristics—tenacity and the ability to make it pay. Jacob wrestles the stranger to the point where he can ask for a blessing.

As his blessing, Jacob's name is changed to Yisrael. Unlike the firm faith of Abraham and the accepting faith of Isaac, Jacob wrestles with God all his life, doing his will only after that wrestling. This becomes his people's destiny until the end of time. Thus, it is the unique destiny of the Jews, Israel, to wrestle with God as well as be partner to his covenant. Israel's future is not one of blind faith and obedience to God's will but one of difficult covenant partnership, of wrestling with their own inclinations and doubts in the face of a mystery that will not fully reveal itself. Covenants do not necessarily end strife; they contain it within a framework or, better, within certain bonds. In that sense, the imagery of the conflict between Jacob and the stranger is paradigmatic. The Jews are still holding the mystery in their arms while it grasps the hollow of their thighs and will not let it go without a blessing.

Jacob perceives what has happened to him—that he has seen the face of God and that his destiny is now changed. At the same time, he is left with a limp; his thigh has been permanently damaged. One does not emerge from such a conflict without some scar.

Jacob, now Yisrael, is ready for his confrontation with Esau—prudently prepared by his own agency and properly chastised yet blessed by Divine agency. The confrontation continues the saga of the complex relationship between the two brothers and sharpens the biblical description of natural versus federal man. Esau remains as open and impulsive as Jacob is prudent and crafty. Jacob determines to make peace between them but to keep their relationship at arm's length. Esau, forgiving, seems happy to do the same. And so it is. The text, however, is ambiguous in its tone. Is Esau simply trying once again to restore brotherly harmony in light of his generous nature or does he have ulterior, and less generous, motives? Is Jacob's response based on an assessment of Esau's motives or a reflection of his own feelings of guilt? If the former, is it a correct assessment? In terms of a political teaching, what is important is the example of how ambiguous such situations appear when one is within them and how decision making must take place under such conditions, with all the uncertainty embodied within them. Intentions are difficult to divine, mixed motives abound, consequences are unclear, but decisions must be made and actions taken. Part of the truth of the Bible lies in its faithful portrayal of the human conditions in such matters.

After his three confrontations—with Laban, with God, and with Esau—Jacob reaches Canaan and begins to settle in. The Bible states *vayavo Ya'akov shalem* (Jacob came in peace). *Shalem* (wholeness, intact) and *shalom* (peace) are relative terms, both part of the Bible's covenantal vocabulary with its emphasis on the relationship between wholeness and peace as a coming together. He camps near Shechem, a trading center where he can do business, far enough from both Isaac and Esau.

Jacob immediately buys a piece of ground to live on. Here we have another parallel to Abraham's experience, the link between acquisition of land by purchase and the further legitimation of the Israelite claim to the land. But here, too, the parallel is based on a reversal. Abraham purchases a burial site while Jacob purchases a campsite, a place upon which he intends to live. Parallel to acquiring a homesite, Jacob establishes a place of regular worship as part of settling in (33:18-20).

Hierarchy: The Contrast with Covenant

One consequence of Jacob's character is that life never goes smoothly for him. Chapters 34 and 35 chronicle the trials and tribulations he encounters on his return to Canaan, the most prominent among them being the sack of Shechem by his sons, forcing him to flee once again, and the death of his beloved Rachel in childbirth while underway. Jacob renews his ties with God, who renews his new name. At the end of chapter 35, Jacob and Esau come together one last time to bury their father. Jacob's son by Rachel, Joseph, then becomes the principal point of focus of the book.

Joseph, the first Israelite to make his career in government, is born with a hierarchy-oriented personality, and his career is in Pharaonic Egypt at the top of its governing hierarchy. His story can be read as an example of how a successful courtier climbs to almost the very top of a governmental hierarchy and then uses his position to simultaneously bring advantage to the ruler at the top of the pyramid, whom he serves, and his people whom he wishes to save. On the surface it seems to be a remarkable "rags-to-riches" tale of a young man's success. Read more deeply, it raises some moral questions as to what is permissable in government and politics.[2]

Joseph's ambitions are there from the beginning; as a youth he is tactless in revealing them through his dreams, made public within the family circle (chap. 37). By being tempered through suffering, he learns to acquire the tact necessary to move his ambitions forward. Despised by his brothers and so boastful as to anger even his doting father, his brothers actually contemplate killing him and compromise by agreeing to sell him into slavery. He finds himself a household slave in Egypt where he is favored with good connections and tested by a woman bent on adultery, a classic weakness of political leaders (chap. 39).

Imprisoned on a false charge, Joseph's Divine favor does not desert him in prison. Quite to the contrary, it is manifested by both God's covenant love toward him (*hesed*) and God's grace toward him (*hen*). In other words, God goes beyond his covenant obligation to Joseph's family to grant Joseph special grace.

Once again Joseph rises quickly to be the overseer of the other prisoners under the prison warden, and once again all prosper. Joseph moves from amateur dream interpretation to interpreting two dreams of fellow prisoners in such a way that he is able to escape his confinement and to bring his third and decisive rise to power (chap. 40).

Joseph's contacts pay off (chap. 41). His previous experience in dream interpretation brings him into the royal court and his previous experience in management enables him to succeed in the tasks assigned him. He becomes the quintessential senior official operating in a hierarchical system, combining good management and faithful service to his sovereign to achieve the security of the kingdom in a time of crisis. He uses the opportunity present to centralize power in the hands of his ruler and to strengthen his own position by doing those two things.

Not only does Joseph successfully interpret the Pharaoh's dream (41:15-16), but at the conclusion of his interpretation, Joseph goes beyond what he is asked, capitalizing on the opportunity to suggest a plan of action, relying upon his having convinced the Pharaoh of the accuracy of the interpretation to establish himself at least as a valued consultant. He recommends that the Pharaoh appoint "a man of discernment and wisdom" (v. 33) and give him responsibility for preparing for the famine. This overseer should be supported by regional overseers subordinate to him who will be responsible for collecting a fifth of the crop for each of the seven years of plenty to be stored away under the Pharaoh's control for the years of famine.

Joseph's plan is utterly in keeping with the character of the Egyptian polity. The Pharaoh is to establish a new bureaucratic hierarchy under Joseph's control whose task it will be to store up the food supply. In other words, it offers a further centralizing potentiality. The Pharaoh likes the plan, consults with his advisers, and they like it also. He chooses Joseph to be his chief overseer, delegating to Joseph complete power over his household and his people, retaining only the superiority of the throne. Joseph goes from being an ad hoc consultant to achieving the highest possible appointment in the land in one quick jump.

The Pharaoh's act is not as capricious as it might seem at first. Having been persuaded that Joseph is correct in the necessity for a strong hand at the helm to carry out such a difficult project as taking one-fifth of each harvest by eminent domain from a people not as fully under Pharaonic control as he would like, he needs someone to undertake that task who will have no local ties that might prevent him from being as ruthless as necessary, yet also totally dependent on him and unable to threaten his rule. Joseph, who has conducted himself well, is a young Hebrew; hence, any position he will have in the court will be utterly dependent on the Pharaoh's support. In other words, he is the safest possible candidate from the Pharaoh's point of view. The Pharaoh drives the point home to Joseph, saying to him, "See, I have put you in charge of all of Egypt" (v. 41). The "I" is as important as every other part of the sentence here and Joseph no doubt understood full well that it was the Pharaoh to whom he was obligated and upon whom he was utterly dependent for this great power and new status.

By the time the famine comes as predicted, Joseph has done his job. He then proceeds to deprive the Egyptians of their liberty and independence step by step. Rather than use the food he has had stored to enable them to survive on their own lands, he deliberately bankrupts them, takes their land in the name of the Pharaoh, his master, and even relocates them so that their local ties will be severed (chap. 47). Only the powerful priests are left untouched. This is hierarchy with a vengeance, the absolute contrast to *brit* and *hesed*.

Joseph proceeds step by step, taking advantage of the Egyptians' need for food to lead them to the point where they must sell their liberties at their own initiative. First, he acquires all their money for the Pharaoh in payment for food supplies. The Hebrew term *vayehket* (he gathered up) denotes comprehensiveness, or to the last bit.

Once there is no more money available, Joseph trades food for livestock and thereby acquires the "horses, flocks...herds...and asses" of Egypt by the end of the first year. All the hungry Egyptians have left to trade for food are their bodies and their lands and they are prepared to sell both rather than die of starvation. Thus, the Pharaoh acquires the land and the people, through Joseph.

Joseph then asserts the Pharaoh's new prerogatives over his newly acquired serfs, moving them off their land across the face of Egypt, to detach them from their old roots and increase their dependence on their rulers. He gives the serfs seed and commands them to sow the land, instituting a sharecropping arrangement whereby the Pharaoh is permanently guaranteed 20 percent of their produce. The people agree to this arrangement. The entire matter is presented in contractual terms from the exchange of property to the agreement on the terms of serfdom, slavery by contract, as it were. Then the new arrangement is embodied in legislation of constitutional status.

What we have before us is a paradigmatic description of the centralization of power without violence through control of critical resources. It is presented as the transformation of Egypt from a hierarchical state of freeholders to an even more hierarchical state of royal serfs. Our knowledge of Egyptian history suggests that this was a recentralization, after the fragmentation caused by the invasions of Asian peoples at that time.[3] But the accuracy of the story is far less important than the paradigm it presents and the political lessons to be learned from it. Hierarchy leads to serfdom, one way or another.

The story shifts back to the Israelites, who, protected and aided by Joseph, are brought down from Canaan to settle into the land of Goshen and take possession of it (*vayaahazu*) just as the Egyptians are losing possession of their lands. There they prosper mightily and multiply. If there is any better opening for later Egyptian anti-Semitism, it would be hard to find. Even if all this happens innocently, the taste remains. The realities of power are what they are but that does not make the results more palatable to the losers.

The question should be asked as to why the Pharaoh and Joseph wanted to do what they did. It was not inevitable; the government could have acted to support the people in their hour of need without exacting such a price. What we have witnessed is the way in which hierarchical systems work to reinforce hierarchy. Their leaders can think of no other way.

Joseph should have known better, given the political culture in which he grew up, but his personality had clear hierarchical inclinations as reflected in his childhood dreams. One way in which the Joseph story can be real is as a clash between culture and personality. Every culture has its deviants. Joseph, a clever deviant, managed to use his deviance to gain control. By bringing his family down to Egypt where he could feed and dominate them, he was able to change the environment in which his family lived rather than leaving them.

Two Excurses: Esau Becomes Edom; Judah and Tamar

Interspersed between these stories are two important excurses seemingly out of place but actually foreshadowing later events. In chapter 6 Esau becomes Edom. The natural man tames his wildness sufficiently to become a founder in his own right, independent of the patriarchs, in his case through organic descent rather than by covenant. Esau's new nation also stands in contrast to the hierarchical organization of Egypt that we find in connection with the immediately subsequent Joseph story. Edom is the organic creation of the scion of the patriarchs who married two Canaanite women and an Ishmaelite woman. Through Esau, the patriarchs are organically connected to the peoples of greater Canaan. For this, Esau has paid a price since he has lost Jacob's inheritance and must leave the land to settle in Seir to its southeast where he fathers twelve families parallel to Jacob's including a semi-legitimate descendant, Amalek, who is to become Israel's legendary worst enemy.

For the Bible, the Edomites remain the embodiment of natural men, warriors and hunters, in the very unpredictable branch of the family. But the story does not end there. Some 1,700 years later in the days of the Hasmoneans, Israel was to conquer Edom and forcibly convert the Edomites to Judaism, thereby introducing the Herodians into the Jewish people with fateful consequences.

With regard to Judah and Tamar, we see Judah, whose descendants in the biblical story are ultimately to supersede those of the Joseph tribes and to inherit the mantle of God's kingdom, also involved in responsibilities derived from familial and kinship relationships. He, however, perhaps because he lives in Eretz Israel, does not succumb to outside blandishments. As leader of his family he plays according to the rules even when he is embarrassed by the results, thereby proving his worthiness to provide the family that will be the ultimate heirs of the patriarchs.

All three of the stories relate to kinship. In the Joseph story, Joseph himself climbs the hierarchy so as to be able to save his kin by asserting his superiority over them. The emergence of Edom suggests that in the end nobody can be responsible for all of his relatives. The story of Judah and Tamar suggests how even a leader who errs can act responsibly within a kinship system. Here we have the two alternatives to covenant, both of which have their advantages but are ultimately found wanting.

The Tribes Are Founded

A principal purpose of the Jacob and Joseph stories is to explain the foundation of the twelve tribes of Israel. Bereshith gives an account of the birth of Jacob's twelve sons; eight from Leah and her concubine Zilpha and four from Rachel and her concubine Bilhah. While those twelve sons of Jacob may have been the ancestors (real or eponymous) of the original twelve tribes of Israel, in fact history indicates that while the number remained the same, the identities of the twelve tribes shifted. The beginnings of the shift are described in Bereshith. In the process we have the final dimension of covenant developed in Bereshith, namely the establishment of the basis for a covenantal polity, a tribal federation.

The story in Bereshith elevates Joseph and Judah over their older brothers to center stage, reflecting the subsequent division of the Bnei Israel into two groupings, one based on the tribes of Ephraim and Manasseh, the sons of Joseph, and the other on the tribe of Judah. This is one of the ways in which Bereshith is a preamble to the other four books of the Humash, which constitute the Torah. The task of Bereshith is to explain the coming into being of the universe, the world, humanity, the peoples into which humanity is divided, and finally the Jewish people, and to designate the order of power relationships within each.

In the case of *Adat Bnei Israel,* Bereshith portrays the power relationships in such a way that Joseph is most visible, with Judah playing a continuing, if secondary, role. This inheritance is bestowed by Jacob himself who adopts Joseph's two sons as his own, thereby making them eligible to be *Bnei Israel* in the most direct sense. He explicitly emphasizes that Ephraim and Manasseh will be to him as Reuven and Shimon. In a sense the verse reflects not only an adoption but a displacement since Reuven and Shimon disappear as other than residual tribes early in Israelite history.

The fact of the displacement suggests the importance of maintaining the twelve-tribe arrangement rather than simply adding new tribes. A covenanted people should have a proper federal structure. The story once again suggests the somewhat polyglot origins of the Jewish people, which required the combination of kinship and consent even prior to Sinai.

In his last days, a transformed Jacob recapitulates his original confrontation with God at Beit El in chapter 48 (vv. 3–4), and God's promise to him, which has two components: his descendants becoming a *kehal amim* (a community of peoples) and his seed acquiring permanent possession (*ahuzat olam*) of Canaan. The phrase *ahuzat olam* stands in contrast to the last verse in chapter 47 (v. 27), which describes how Israel possessed (*v'yahazu ba*) Goshen. From one perspective the phrase *kehal amim* can be interpreted in reverse—not that Jacob becomes the father of a community of peoples but that he is given to them in some way, that is to say, his promise is given to them, with the reference being understood as including not just *Am Yisrael*, but the monotheistic peoples of the world. In that interpretation *kehal amim* would be another term for the league or confederacy of nations that will come about in the messianic era. If understood in this way, then there is a contrapuntal relationship between that promise and the promise of Canaan to Jacob's specific descendants, that is to say, *Am Yisrael*.

On the other hand, the text can be interpreted more narrowly as referring only to *Adat Bnai Yisrael* with each to be considered an *am* and *kahal amim* referring to the *Edah* as a whole, a generic term for federation. The reference in v. 19 to Manasseh's descendants becoming an *am* suggests this alternative reading for *kahal amim*, to describe the forthcoming federation of the tribes descended from Jacob's sons. Either way, *kahal amim* may be one of the few generic political terms in the Bible.

In the book's finale (chap. 49), Jacob gathers his sons and envisions their long-term future. This is presented as the first of those federal messages that recur in the Bible, which reaffirm the unity of *Adat Bnei Yisrael* and, simultaneously, the separate character of each of the tribes. In it, Jacob sums up the history of his offspring to that time and projects forward from that history. The end result is a vision of reordered power relationships, not all of which are entirely clear to us even now. The animal and other symbols brought in the passages become the basis for the tribal standards and banners and remain so to this day.

While Bereshith emphasizes the limitations even of God in changing the ways of the world including the human way, it also demonstrates that covenant comes to harness what we would call nature and to help God in His effort to work against custom or social necessity. Since *derekh* includes both, it is not surprising that *brit* is a way to modify or even change both. If necessity or custom reign, then God is not needed. If they are changed, then it can be done successfully only through greater free choice, more room for voluntary decision and action, which is the essence of covenant.

Bereshith teaches about the interrelationship between covenant, kinship, and hierarchy, the three sources of political organization. It makes it clear that covenant is necessary for proper human organization and that covenants are made first with the family of man and then with families of men. While kinship is not enough, humanity cannot live without it. Covenant comes to direct families in the right path. Alone, it, too, is insufficient. At least some humans have a propensity for hierarchy, but hierarchy contradicts covenant and may even pervert covenanting. Covenant, on the other hand, properly used, can restrain hierarchy or at least its impact. The message of Bereshith is that humans must grapple with all three and must not only choose between them but learn how to combine them as well.

What, then, is one of the principal overall messages of Genesis? God establishes His initial relationship with human beings on the basis of hierarchy. Adam is His creation and His steward on earth. He is intelligent enough to name all the animals, to have authoritative control (*radah*, in Hebrew) over them, but is prohibited from eating of the tree of knowledge, which is often interpreted as sexual knowledge, or the tree of life.

Adam stands in relationship to his helpmate Eve as God stands in relationship with him, essentially hierarchical but with the subject too intelligent for the relationship to be simply hierarchical. Indeed, in both cases that intelligence leads to the failure of simple hierarchy and its abandonment, both by God and by Adam. Eve is convinced by the serpent to eat of the tree of knowledge and she, in turn, convinces Adam. God intervenes only after the fact, not only to punish them but to reorganize His system in light of the new reality.

At first God assumes that He can maintain hierarchy by decreeing hard work and childbirth on His human subjects, but again, humans are too clever. In the course of eight generations they manage to use their inventive skills to invent technologies that make life easier and more pleasant. Moreover, the Bible tells us that it is precisely the Cain family, founded by the first murderer, that has the requisite inventive ability.

Both technological and aesthetic inventiveness, then, are tied to murder and urbanization by the Bible. Both have their glories but also their shame in the sense that humanity becomes corrupted and God must again step in. He tries a drastic measure, the Flood, to wipe out all of humanity but one family whom He deems appropriate to save. Subsequently, he unilaterally establishes a covenant with Noah, the head of that family, and his descendants, but only after Noah has indicated that he consents to God's leadership by following God's commands in preparation for the Flood. But, just as God admitted defeat with Adam by accepting the changed circumstances after Adam's disobedience and making allowance for them in His plans, so, too, does God recognize His defeat with Noah and He concludes by the behavior of Noah and his sons after leaving the ark (Noah's sacrifice and drunkenness and his son Ham's response to that drunkenness) because "the inclination of man's heart is evil from his youth" (Gen. 8:23) and determines to reconcile Himself to that reality, using covenant as a means to shape humans not only in His image but to His liking.

God subsequently refines this hierarchical approach by forming a special nation to be His people, to pursue His purposes. To do so He chooses Abraham as patriarch to establish that people out of his own family by migrating from his native land, his kith, and his father's house to a new land. Here Abraham serves as the civil head of his people (keter malkhut), their channel of communication to God (keter kehunah), and as God's channel of command to them (keter torah). Examples of all three forms of behavior are found in Genesis 12, verses 4-9.

But humans are still mortal and Abraham the patriarch, who, though flawed, still is exemplary, has to pass on his mantle to a son. The choice between Isaac and Ishmael, painful as it may be to Abraham, is relatively easy because Issac is born from a legitimate wife while Ishmael is not; and Isaac, perhaps because he is traumatized by Abraham's offering him to God as a sacrifice, turns out to be a very quiet and faithful successor to Abraham. He essentially repeats his father's life pattern with somewhat less excitement and verve.

When the time comes for Isaac to pass on the succession, he has a more difficult problem, for God has to choose between Esau, a bluff, hearty, yet irresponsible man, and Jacob, an intelligent, clever, yet devious one. God makes His painful choice and creates situations through which it is ratified by Isaac with the help of Rebecca, who is the more important center of action in all of this. But once God has chosen Jacob, He must temper him through experience to bring out his better qualities and help him suppress his less favorable ones.

Abraham's choosing of Isaac and Isaac's choosing of Jacob have already added another dimension to the original hierarchical system, for patriarchy is now embedded in an organic community of fathers and mothers and sons and wives. (One of the reasons for God's choice of Jacob over Esau is that Esau has married Canaanite women while Rebecca is about to send Jacob to her brother Laban to find a wife.) But just as hierarchy alone cannot provide a mode of government because it is deficient in its ability to reckon with the God-given independence of all human beings, even when modified by covenant (cf. Gen. 15, 17), an organic dimension is added. While it is possible to pass the authority and powers of hierarchy through an organic chain, choice is still required to choose among the potential successors to the patriarch in each generation. Yet such choices require either direct Divine intervention or human reflection.

This becomes even more necessary with Jacob and his sons, where there are twelve and not just two among whom Jacob has to choose. Once again, one son comes to the fore, this time not the son of the one official wife, as in the case of Isaac and Ishmael, but the oldest son of Jacob's beloved Rachel, acquiring the position not only as a result of Jacob's choice but through his own ambition and ability to pursue that ambition despite adversity.

Joseph marks the end of God's experiment with hierarchy as a system of governance by demonstrating that he, while sufficiently talented to be a ruler, is not morally fit. Joseph's rise to high places is accompanied by private moral correctness (as in the case of his refusal to sleep with Potifar's wife) but serious public moral compromise as when, following Pharaoh's instructions, he marries the daughter of a priest and on his own initiative uses the region's seven lean years to consolidate Pharaoh's power as the totalitarian ruler of Egypt, impoverishing, displacing, and humiliating the Egyptians in the process. God apparently decides on a new course.

After Joseph's death the Jews are reduced to slavery (could this be a punishment for Joseph's enslavement of the Egyptians?), only to be later redeemed after ten more generations on a new covenantal basis, one that promises no more hierarchy and even a diminution of reliance on organic ties, which continue to exist but are subordinated to a new covenant at Sinai that sets the national path for the Jewish people. Under that covenant and, indeed, even prior to it in part, the three *ketarim* are separated, with the *keter malkhut* becoming the province of tribally based elders and magistrates and nationally based judges and officers, the *keter kehunah* is given by covenant to Aaron and his sons assisted by the

Levites who are other members of Aaron's family, and the *keter torah* is not only given a slightly prior position by the fact that Moses is its principal occupant (he is given the singular designation *eved adonai* or God's minister or servant), but the position is made a matter of God's choice solely through the granting of His charisma, thereby eliminating every hereditary dimension.

Thus, the Book of Genesis gives us the movement from hierarchy to covenant as the best means of governing humans. Later on, the Bible recognizes that covenant alone is also not sufficient and reintroduces a measure of hierarchy through kinship, only man is subordinate to covenant, even to several covenants, Divine and human, and must share his authority and powers with the other *ketarim*. At the very end of scriptural history, even that modification is modified as the hierarchical dimensions of the Jewish polity are removed from the monarchic principle and made a matter of human and Divine decision on a recurring basis.

Notes

1. The Talmudic sages do just that, probably because they were in a life-and-death struggle for the souls of Jews in confrontation with the later Roman Empire, a society that glorified "natural" behavior, meaning that everyone should do what gave him or her pleasure. The hedonism of Rome no doubt was attractive to many Jews who abandoned their covenant in pursuit of pleasures. The sages fought back by glorifying Jacob and identifying a blackened Esau with Rome.
2. See Aaron Wildavsky, "What is Permissible so that this People May Survive? Joseph the Administrator," *PS: Political Science and Politics* 22, no.4 (December 1989): 779–88. See also Aaron Wildavsky, *Assimilation versus Separation* (New Brunswick, NJ: Transaction Publishers, 1992).
3. On Joseph's Egypt, see Henry George Tomkins, *The Life and Times of Joseph in the Light of Egyptian Lore* (London: The Religious Tract Society, 1891).

8

Freedom and Covenant:
Exodus, Sinai, and Sefer Habrit

The Bible offers a series of paradigmatic political covenants that have animated the covenantal perspective in politics since biblical times. We have already examined the first of those, the covenant with Noah, which defines the basic relationship between God and humankind, the charter of federal liberty for all humanity. We also reviewed the covenants with Abraham establishing God's intention to found a specially covenanted people who will build a new society to set the pace for humanity as a whole. This new nation will ultimately be given a constitution in the form of the Torah, which combines God-given *hukkot*, constitutionally binding but not explained, often ritual commandments, and *mishpatim*, civil and social laws, in part based on prior custom, and is anchored in a series of covenants of which these two are the first. The third paradigmatic covenant of the Bible is at Sinai. It establishes an *edah* prepared to receive a constitution. The fourth is on the plains of Moab, a covenant set within the constitution itself, adapting it to settled life in the land of Israel.

Part of the evidence for the emphasis on covenant and its connection with constitutionalism in Scripture lies in the extensive and precise terminology used in the Bible to deal with constitutionalism and constitutional matters. Following the biblical terminology and references, the following emerge as key constitutional terms, some of which we have already encountered:

* *brit*: covenant;
* *bnai brit* (sons of the covenant): partners in a new common entity established by covenant;
* *baalei brit* (masters of the covenant): allies in an alliance established by covenant;

- *goy*: any nation;
- *hesed*: loving covenant obligation;
- *am*: a people, in other words, a nation with a vocation;
- *shamoa*: to hearken.

In this chapter we will move from covenantal terminology to the constitutional terminology derived from the covenantal world view, such as:

- *Torah*: the comprehensive term for constitution, emphasizes constitution as teaching;
- *mitzvah*: Divine commandment;
- *hukkot*: constitutional laws commanded by God for which no explanation is given, often ritual commandments;
- *mishpatim*: civil and social laws including corpuses of law, as well as *mishpat hakohanim* and *mishpat ha-melekh/melukhah*, corpuses for priests and kings or civil rules, respectively;
- *hok u'mishpat*: a constitutional jurisprudence, consisting of *hukkot* on matters between man and God and *mishpatim* on matters between man and man, the latter of which include special legal codes or corpuses for at least two of the three authoritative domains provided for in the Torah (which will be discussed later), all obligating humans to hearken to and observe *mitzvot* (God's commandments).

This chapter also addresses human collectivities other than the human race as a whole, and individuals within it, utilizing the following terminology:

- *Am Yisrael*: the people of Israel, described as a nation whose vocation is to hearken to God (Moab, on the other hand, is described as the *am* of Chemosh, the chief god of the Moabites);
- *kahal*: assembled congregation (in the original sense of an assembled people), the closest generic term for polity in biblical Hebrew;
- *edah*: congregational assembly, in the republican sense of a governing body that meets at regular intervals (*moadim*);
- *Adat Bnai Yisrael* (the assembly of the sons of Israel): *Am Yisrael* in its organized political capacity;
- *eved adonai*: God's servant or prime minister;
- *nesiim*: those elevated or selected from among the people;
- *zekenim*: elders;
- *shofetim*: judges in the sense of those who administer justice;
- *shoterim*: officers—the civil service;
- *kohen gadol*: high priest;
- *kohanim*: priests;
- *leviim*: Levites, the officers of the *kohanim*;
- *ezrach*: citizen.

Sinai: The Paradigmatic Constituting Covenant

The paradigmatic constitutional covenant is that between God and Israel at Sinai, whose centerpiece is the Decalogue, known in Hebrew as *aseret hadibrot* (the ten statements) engraved on the *lukhot habrit* (tablets of the covenant). It is the great covenant of the Jewish people (Exod. 19:1-20:23, 24:1-38). It is the classic example of covenanting as a theo-political act, which establishes the basis for subsequent constitution making. Although there is some argument among biblical scholars, it seems safe to say, following Mendenhall, Hillers, Weinfeld, and others, that it is a classic covenant following the style that evolved from the vassal treaty.[1] It is not, in itself, a constitution, but a pact that establishes an organized people—by establishing a relationship between God and a particular nation—thereby establishing the basis for the constitution, which is presented as the Book of the Covenant immediately following the Theophany (Exod. 21:1-23:33).

The covenant at Sinai is the climax of the Exodus story—one of the world's great stories of national liberation. Told in the Book of Exodus, it has served as a stirring paradigm and inspiration in the popular struggle for freedom, not only for Jews throughout all of Jewish history, but for the entire Bible-reading world—whether the Protestants of the Reformation, the secular makers of the French Revolution who came out of the Catholic tradition, black slaves in America who sang "Let my people go," twentieth-century, left wing, socialist radicals like Lincoln Steffens, and on and on.[2]

The story, as told in the Book of Exodus, tells of the Israelites enslaved after the death of Joseph, treated as potential fifth columnists, and subjected to genocide through the Pharaonic decree to destroy all male babies born to them, who are liberated by a leader who was saved from death as a result of God's concern but not miraculously, raised in the Pharaoh's household, and who later rediscovers his roots. The paradigm presented in the Bible has since been elaborated on through historical and social scientific research into the liberation of oppressed peoples. The need for a leader who is of his people yet familiar with the world of the oppressors, whose strong sense of the justice of his people's cause makes him willing to take the risks needed in pursuit of his goal. Also paradigmatic are: the difficulties of mobilizing an enslaved population who, while very discomfited by slavery, are even more afraid of changing their status quo; the way the leader must pass through a period of toughening before he is strong enough to confront the ruling oppressors; the struggle with the oppressors whose hearts are hardened; and the final dramatic steps of the liberation.

Moses demonstrates his sense of justice when as a young adult he kills an Egyptian overseer who is beating one of the Hebrew slaves. His people show their capabilities for dissension in the way they respond to him—showing no national solidarity, only individual self-interest. He flees to Midian where he marries into one of the leading families and settles down to a life as a shepherd and an exile. God appears to him through the burning bush and instructs him to return to Egypt to liberate his people. Moses is very reluctant, but through a combination of cajoling, threats, and promises God prevails. Upon his return to Egypt, Moses seeks the elders governing the Hebrew people by invoking the traditional covenants with the patriarchs. The elders will have none of it in an important step that paves the way for the new covenant at Sinai.

To establish or conclude such a new covenant, God understood that it would be necessary to: (1) demonstrate His saving power, thereby filling the people that He has chosen with awe and gratitude toward Him, and (2) to bring them out of slavery so that they will become a free people, freely able to consent to a covenant.

Covenants cannot be made by slaves because they require free consent and a free people will only enter into a covenant if they see a reason to do so.

After noting the skepticism, even fear, of the Israelite elders, Moses, with his brother Aaron, his designated (by God) spokesman, takes the initiative to mount the campaign against the Pharaoh as God's representative. Following a series of escalations of the conflict marked by various plagues, the Pharaoh is finally broken by the demands of his people that the Israelites be expelled before all Egypt is destroyed (even in hierarchy sometimes things go so far that the people will cry out). He consents to let the Israelites go, but when they actually try to leave, he changes his mind and pursues them with his army. According to the Bible, the Israelites are miraculously delivered by God, enabling them to cross the Sea of Reeds (mistakenly referred to as the Red Sea) on dry land. When the Pharaoh's chariots pursue them the sea closes over them, drowning them all (Exod. 14).

Just prior to leaving Egypt, the Israelites declare their independence by establishing a definition of citizenship (or who is an *ezrakh*) and in a sense promulgating a declaration of independence (13:3–16), describing the Exodus and the reasons for it.[3]

> 3. And Moses said unto the people, Remember this day, in which ye came out from Egypt, out of the house of bondage; for by strength of hand the Lord brought you out from this place; there shall no leavened bread be eaten.
>
> 4. This day came ye out in the month Abib.
>
> 5. And it shall be when the Lord shall bring thee into the land of the Canaanites, and the Hittites, and the Amorites, and the Hivites, and the Jebusites, which he sware unto thy fathers to give thee, a land flowing with milk and honey, that thou shalt keep this service in this month.
>
> 6. Seven days thou shalt eat unleavened bread, and in the seventh day shall be a feast to the Lord.
>
> 7. Unleavened bread shall be eaten seven days; and there shall no leavened bread be seen with thee, neither shall there be leaven seen with thee in all thy quarters.
>
> 8. And thou shalt shew thy son in that day, saying, This is done because of that which the Lord did unto me when I came forth out of Egypt.
>
> 9. And it shall be for a sign unto thee upon thine hand, and for a memorial between thine eyes, that the Lord's law may be in thy mouth: for with a strong hand hath the Lord brought thee out of Egypt.
>
> 10. Thou shalt therefore keep this ordinance in his season from year to year.
>
> 11. And it shall be when the Lord shall bring thee into the land of the Canaanites, as he sware unto thee and to they fathers, and shall give it thee.
>
> 12. That thou shalt set apart unto the Lord all that openeth the matrix, and every firstling that cometh of a beast which thou hast; the males shall be the Lord's.
>
> 13. And every firstling of an ass thou shalt redeem with a lamb; and if thou wilt not redeem it, then thou shalt break his neck: and all the firstborn of man among thy children shalt thou redeem.
>
> 14. And it shall be when thy son asketh thee in time to come, saying, What is this? that thou shalt say unto him, By strength of hand the Lord brought us out from Egypt, from the house of bondage.
>
> 15. And it came to pass, when Pharaoh would hardly let us go, that the Lord slew all the firstborn in the land of Egypt, both the firstborn of man, and the firstborn of beast: therefore, I sacrifice to the Lord all that openeth the womb, being males; but all the firstborn of my children I redeem.
>
> 16. And it shall be for a token upon thine hand, and for frontlets between thine eyes: for by strength of hand the Lord brought us forth out of Egypt.

Moses leads his people out of Egypt and then must confront the task of turning them from a conglomeration of freed slaves into a nation. Once across the sea the Israelites are assembled at Marah where Moses, on God's command, changed bitter water into sweet so that people would have water to drink (Exod. 16:22–26), including the cryptic passage, "There He [God] made for them a statute and an ordinance and there He tested them" (v. 25).

Once out of Egypt and away from its jurisdiction, the Israelites are faced with the necessity of adopting a comprehensive civil law, not merely the kind of "ethnic" institutions that the Egyptians allowed them to preserve to facilitate their enslavement. Thus, in almost the very first act on the other side of the sea, after three days of wandering in the wilderness of Shur and a near rebellion against Moses for lack of water, God gave them *hok u'mishpat,* an interim basic legal system (Exod. 16:25), thereby setting the stage for Sinai.

The Bible sees God as having had to establish basic laws for the people prior to the full covenant so that they could live as an organized society once they were out from under the laws of Egypt. Medieval biblical commentators dwelt extensively on this phrase, some claiming that it reflected a natural law source in the Bible, others explaining which laws were so basic that they had to be given or reaffirmed before the Sinai covenant. Thus, the Israelites reached Sinai as a free people, functioning as humans within a framework of basic laws which provided them with sufficient order so that they could engage in covenanting freely and not out of desperation.

The climax comes shortly thereafter at the foot of Mt. Sinai, where Moses and all Israel—men, women, and children—assemble to encounter God:

And God spake all these words, saying,

2. I am the Lord thy God, which have brought thee out of the land of Egypt, out of the house of bondage.

3. Thou shalt have no other gods before me.

4. Thou shalt not make unto thee any graven image, or any likeness of any thing that is in heaven above, or that is in the earth beneath, or that is in the water under the earth.

5. Thou shalt not bow down thyself to them, nor serve them: for I the Lord thy God am a jealous God, visiting the iniquity of the fathers upon the children unto the third and fourth generation of them that hate me.

6. And showing mercy unto thousands of them that love me, and keep my commandments.

7. Thou shalt not take the name of the Lord thy God in vain; for the Lord will not hold him guiltless that taketh his name in vain.

8. Remember the sabbath day, to keep it holy.

9. Six days shalt thou labor, and do all thy work.

10. But the seventh day is the sabbath of the Lord thy God: in it thou shalt not do any work, thou, nor thy son, nor thy daughter, thy manservant, nor thy maidservant, nor thy cattle, nor thy stranger that is within thy gates.

11. For in six days the Lord made heaven and earth, the sea, and all that in them is, and rested the seventh day: wherefore the Lord blessed the sabbath day, and hallowed it.

12. Honor thy father and thy mother: that thy days may be long upon the land which the Lord thy God giveth thee.

13. Thou shalt not kill.

14. Thou shalt not commit adultery.

15. Thou shalt not steal.

16. Thou shalt not bear false witness against thy neighbor.

17. Thou shalt not covet thy neighbor's house, thou shalt not covet thy neighbor's wife, nor his manservant, nor his maidservant, nor his ox, nor his ass, nor anything that is thy neighbor's (Exod. 20:1-17).

It would be hard to exaggerate the place of the Decalogue in the Western political tradition. Believers in natural law have argued for it as a restatement of the essence of the natural law, while those emphasizing God's covenants with humans have seen it as the essence of the moral law of the covenant. Christians, because they do not see themselves bound by the whole law of the Torah, have treated the decalogue as separable from what follows. Jews on the other hand see the ten statements (commandments is a mistranslation, nor are they referred to as such at any place in the text—they are generally referred to as the tablets of the covenant [*lukhot habrit*]) as one of the most important elements of Torah but still part and parcel of the whole. In either case, its influence is hard to exaggerate.[4]

Various reasons have been given as to why there were two tablets. Perhaps the most widely accepted is that the first tablet deals with the proper relationships between God and man and the second proper relations among humans in the light of the first. But that is not the only explanation.[5] Hobbes, for example, argued that the first tablet included those commandments specifically applicable to the Jews and the second tablet included those that are universal.[6] Some modern biblical scholars have argued that the two tablets reflect the need for each party to the covenant to have a copy and that all the statements are on each of the tablets and simply repeated.[7]

Whatever may have been the original reason for the two tablets, the Bible refers to them consistently as the *lukhot habrit,* describes the ceremony of their dictation by God to Moses in the presence of the Israelites as a covenant making, and discusses the preservation of the tablets in the Tent of Assembly, frequently described as the Tent of the Testimony (*Edut*), a synonym for covenant (cf. Exod. 38:21). Subsequent interpretations by both Jewish and Christian commentators have erected a whole edifice of fundamental law on the contents of the tablets, suggesting that in essence nothing more is needed.

The question has frequently been raised as to whether the Sinai covenant required the Israelites' consent; that is to say, whether or not it was simply a unilateral act of God. In fact the argument here is predicated on the mutuality of true covenants including covenants between God and man. In the case of the Sinai covenant, the mutuality can be demonstrated, not only by the internal evidence of the text but also by contrasting it with the earlier incident, which is related in chapter 6 of the Book of Exodus, verses 2–9, where, through Moses, God attempts unilaterally to renew His earlier covenants with the three patriarchs as a working covenant with the Israelites in Egypt, without involving them in the process. God presents His side in the first eight verses, simply informing Moses of His earlier promise to Abraham and directing him to convey that information to the Israelites who are then still slaves in Egypt:

And the Lord said unto Moses: "Now shalt thou see what I will do to Pharaoh"; for by a strong hand shall he let them go, and by a strong hand shall he drive them out of his land. And God spoke unto Moses, and said unto him: "I am the Lord; and I appeared unto Abraham, unto Isaac, and unto Jacob, as God Almighty, but by My name YHWH I made Me not known to them. And I have also established My covenant with them, to give them the land of Canaan, the land of their sojournings, wherein they sojourned. And moreover I have heard the groaning of the children of Israel, whom the Egyptians keep in bondage; and I have remembered My covenant. Wherefore say unto the children of Israel: I am the Lord, and I will bring you out from under the burdens of the Egyptians, and I will deliver you from their bondage, and I will redeem you with an outstretched arm, and with great judgments; and I will take you to Me for a people, and I will be to you a God; and ye shall know that I am the Lord your God, who brought you out from under the burdens of the Egyptians. And I will bring you unto the land, concerning which I lifted up My hand to give it to Abraham, to Isaac, and to Jacob; and I will give it to you for a heritage: I am the Lord."

When Moses delivered the message to the Israelites, their response was to ignore him: "And Moses spoke so unto the children of Israel; but they hearkened not unto Moses for impatience of spirit, and for cruel bondage."

Despite all the references to the forefathers who are acknowledged by the Israelites in Egypt, and the promise of deliverance from bondage and transportation to their own land, the Israelites did not hearken to Moses. Because of their enslavement they are unable to see what is offered them; because they are humans who must consent, they cannot accept unilateral declarations. No consent, no covenant. Only when they are involved in the process at Sinai and consent to it is the covenant made. This is the only case in the Bible of a clearly unilateral effort on the part of God to impose a covenant. And in fact, even here there is some equivocation because, according to the biblical text, all God is trying to do is to renew a covenant that was established long since. Nevertheless, it does not work. God never again tries to impose a covenant without involving the partners who must consent to it.

Contrast the events at Sinai not long after (Exod. 19–24). In the third month after leaving Egypt, the Israelites camp at the foot of Mt. Sinai. Moses goes up to speak with God, initiating the encounter (19:3), and God instructs him in response (19:3-6):

> Thus shalt thou say to the house of Jacob, and tell the children of Israel; Ye have seen what I did unto the Egyptians, and how I bore you on eagles' wings, and brought you unto Myself. Now therefore, if ye will hearken unto My voice indeed, and keep My covenant, then ye shall be Mine own treasure from among all peoples; and for all the earth is Mine; and ye shall be unto Me a kingdom of priests, and a holy nation.

Every aspect of the terminology is significant. Israelites are referred to both as the "House of Jacob" and the "Children of Israel" (the term for the twelve tribes as a collectivity); in other words, as a family and as the beginnings of a nation. They are reminded of God's recent actions on their behalf and the power that those actions revealed. They are then told that if they hearken to God's voice and observe His covenant, He will make them a special or treasured people linked to Him in a way that no other people is linked. He has the power to do this because the earth is His, but they must consent before He will do so.

> These are the words which thou shalt speak unto the children of Israel. And Moses came and called for the elders of the people, and set before them all these words which the Lord commanded him. And all the people answered together, and said: "All that the Lord hath spoken we will do." And Moses reported the words of the

people unto the Lord. And the Lord said unto Moses: "Lo, I come unto thee in a thick cloud, that the people may hear when I speak with thee, and may also believe thee for ever." And Moses told the words of the people unto the Lord.

God instructs Moses to repeat these words exactly (v. 6). So Moses calls together the elders of the people, those chosen to govern them, and presents God's message just as God commands (19:7) and the whole people answers together, saying "All that God has spoken we will do." Then Moses reports the words of the people to God (19:8).

The negotiations completed, God then tells Moses that He will come to the people in a thick cloud so that they will be able to hear when He speaks to them. Up to now, Moses and God have communicated privately and the people have had to rely upon Moses's word that he has indeed communicated with Heaven. Now that the people have agreed to accept the covenant, they will, for a moment, hear God directly as part of the actual covenant making. God then gives explicit instructions as to how the people should prepare for His appearance, where they should stand, and how the encounter will be conducted (vv. 10-13).

The people carry out the instructions to the best of their ability. After preparing for the encounter, the people assemble as instructed.

And Moses went down from the mount unto the people, and sanctified the people; and they washed their garments. And he said unto the people: "Be ready against the third day; come not near a woman." And it came to pass on the third day, when it was morning, that there were thunders and lightnings and a thick cloud upon the mount, and the voice of a horn exceeding loud; and all the people that were in the camp trembled. And Moses brought forth the people out of the camp to meet God; and they stood at the nether part of the mount. Now Mount Sinai was altogether in smoke, because the Lord descended upon it in fire; and the smoke thereof ascended as the smoke of a furnace, and the whole mount quaked greatly. And when the voice of the horn waxed louder and louder, Moses spoke, and God answered him by a voice. And the Lord came down upon Mount Sinai, to the top of the mount; and the Lord called Moses to the top of the mount; and Moses went up. And the Lord said unto Moses: "Go down, charge the people, lest they break through unto the Lord to gaze, and many of them perish. And let the priests also, that come near to the Lord, sanctify themselves, lest the Lord break forth upon them." And Moses said unto the Lord: "The people cannot come up to Mount Sinai; for thou didst charge us, saying: Set bounds about the mount, and sanctify it." And the Lord said unto him: "Go, get thee down, and thou shalt come up, thou, and Aaron with thee; but let not the priests and the people break through to come up unto the Lord, lest He break forth upon them." So Moses went down unto the people, and told them.

The mountain is wreathed in smoke and fire, shaking and bellowing. Moses takes the next step by speaking to God, who answers him and calls him to the top of the mountain to which he, the Lord, has descended (vv. 18-20). Then follows an exchange between God and Moses regarding the further positioning of the people so that they do not come too close, which Moses descends to arrange (vv. 21-25). The only limit on the confrontation between God and the Israelites is the unwillingness of the latter to confront God "face-to-face," which necessitates that Moses play the role of intermediary.

God then proceeds to speak the Decalogue (20:1-14), which is presented in the pattern of a classic West Asian covenant covering matters of fundamental faith and law. The people are abjured to recognize God as their only God who directs their history and destiny, be careful in their references to him, observe the Sabbath, maintain proper family relations, refrain from committing murder, adultery, or theft, from bearing false witness, and from coveting their neighbors' possessions.

A description of the event resumes in verse 15.

> And all the people perceived the thunderings, and the lightnings, and the voice of the horn, and the mountain smoking; and when the people saw it, they trembled, and stood afar off. And they said unto Moses: "Speak thou with us, and we will hear; but let not God speak with us, lest we die." And Moses said unto the people: "Fear not; for God is come to prove you, and that His fear may be before you, that ye sin not." And the people stood afar off; but Moses drew near unto the thick darkness where God was. And the Lord said unto Moses: "Thus thou shalt say unto the children of Israel: 'Ye yourselves have seen that I have talked with you from heaven.'"

In subsequent Jewish tradition, there is a dispute as to whether or not the Israelites really had a choice, with one school holding that God threatened to bury them under the mountain if they did not accept His covenant. The other school, however, brings far stronger evidence that the covenant was truly mutual as the biblical text itself indicates.[8]

The account of the covenant making explicitly refers to Moses, God's minister, the 70 Elders of Israel, Aaron the High Priest, as the head of the priestly authority, the twelve tribes, and the whole people. These, then, are the partners to the covenant, the institutions capable of covenant making in the name of the people. Appropriately, they are partners with each other as well as with God in a federal act that requires that the *edah* be represented by different authorities—as a whole by Moses the Prophet, Aaron the High Priest, and the Elders as the Civil Authority, and also divided into their tribes. All are actively present at Sinai.

The manner of completion of the process is another indication of the importance of mutuality and consent. The people must consent again and again, to reaffirm their new constitutional status. Thus, even if God is the initiator (after all, someone must initiate the act), the act itself is mutual.

The theme of mutuality is expressed throughout the Bible even when covenanting is not directly involved. Scripture is pervaded by the covenantal process. After the Noahide covenant, God takes the initiative only at a few key points of transition. Otherwise God responds to His human covenant partners only when they make an initial move. Over and over again, the Bible says of God that He responds to the cry or call of the people (*tza'akatam*). God's intervention must be invoked in such a way that He will respond. His covenant partners have an especially good way to invoke him, by calling upon Him to exercise *hesed*, the loving obligation established by the covenant, which provides its dynamic dimension. Later generations of Jews were to term this as *gemilut hassadim*, the extension of *hesed* on the basis of mutuality, which properly defines what is involved. This kind of obligation is a political obligation in the highest sense. God's response is generally described as remembering the covenant (*vazakharti et briti*). God is not presented as a power that wanders the universe looking for things to do. His intervention is limited, precious and definitely not unilateral in most circumstances.

At the conclusion of the covenanting, the text repeats (20:15–18): "And all the people perceived the thunderings, and the lightnings, and the voice of the horn, and the mountain smoking; and when the people saw it, they trembled, and stood afar off" (v. 15). Their reaction was almost predictable (v. 16). They said to Moses: "Speak thou with us, and we will hear; but let not God speak with us, lest we die." In the end, "the people stood afar off; but Moses drew near unto the thick darkness where God was" (v. 17). Perhaps it was the people's inability to confront the reality of God that caused Him to repeat to Moses the prohibitions against graven images and the modes of worship associated with idolatry (20:19–23).

Notes

1. George Mendenhall, *Law and Covenant in Israel and the Ancient Near East* (Pittsburgh: Biblical Colloquim, 1955); Delbert Hillers, *Covenant: The History of a Biblical Idea* (Baltimore: John Hopkins Press, 1969); Moshe Weinfeld, *Covenant*

in the Old Testament and in the Ancient Near East (New Haven: Yale University Press, 1970).

2. Lincoln Steffens, "Moses in Red," in *The World of Lincoln Steffens,* ed. Ella Winter and Herbert Shapiro (New York: Hill and Wang, 1962); Michael Walzer, *Exodus and Revolution* (New York: Basic Books, 1985); Solomon Goldman, *The Book of Human Destiny, Vol. 3: From Slavery to Freedom* (London: Abelard-Schuman, 1958).

3. In *The Nursing Father* (Tuscaloosa: University of Alabama Press, 1984), Aaron Wildavsky examines the story of Moses's call, the struggle with the Pharaoh, and the Exodus. He looks at its political meaning and implications brilliantly. See also Walzer, *Exodus and Revolution.*

4. Johannes Althusius, the foremost political philosopher of the Protestant Reformation, devoted a considerable portion of his writings to discussing the political implications of the Decalogue, including a separate work on the subject, *The Decalogicae,* as well as treating it in his *Politica Methodicae Digestia.* Almost every medieval political philosopher considered the political implications of the decalogue as did the early modern ones.

5. U. Cassuto, *Commentary on Exodus* (Jerusalem: Magnes Press, 1967); Brevard S. Childs, *Exodus: A Commentary* (London: SCM Press, 1974).

6. Hobbes, *Leviathan* (London: J.M. Dent and Sons, 1947).

7. Mendenhall, *Law and Covenant*; Eduard Nielsen, *The Ten Commandments in New Perspective* (Chicago: Allenson, 1968); Johann J. Stamm with Maurice E. Andrew, *The Ten Commandments in Recent Research* (Chicago: Allenson, 1967).

8. Cf. Gerald Blidstein, "In the Shadow of the Mountain: Consent and Coercion at Sinai," *Jewish Political Studies Review* 4, no. 1 (Spring 1992).

9

The Mosaic Polity:
What Else Happened at Sinai?

The Covenant and the Book of the Covenant

The Sinai covenant consists of two parts. First is the Decalogue, the basic covenant, and the process of consenting to it in chapters 19–20. What follows from the very end of chapter 20 through chapter 23 is the Book of the Covenant, and the constitution that flows from it. The first establishes the first principles of Divine Law and human governance— what later would be termed the *political compact*—while the second translates those principles into a constitutional framework.

The Book of the Covenant deals with the basic civil and criminal law, basic religious obligations, and basic moral laws of the Israelite polity that supplement the Decalogue. The most direct political message has to do with the occupation of the land promised the Israelites. Because the Israelites already had adapted their tribal institutions to their new condition of freedom, all that was necessary was to affirm that the political structure established by Moses was in accord with the principles of the covenant. That is done through the process of receiving the Book of the Covenant (24:1–11).

While lacking the systematic consistency of the Greek and Roman constitutional documents, the internal logic of the Book of the Covenant can be uncovered by close reading. The constitution begins with a concern for liberty—the prohibition against the permanent enslavement of fellow Israelites. In other words, the reaffirmation of Israel as a free people with every man among them to be free except insofar as he renounces his freedom in a public ceremony designed to humiliate any who would do so. The same guarantee of freedom is applied to women, albeit in a different way. Rather than being automatically released at the

175

end of the seven-year bondage as in the case of men, they must be married into the family as free and equal persons or released (Exod. 21:2-11).

The second constitutional provision deals with the taking of life. It distinguishes between murder and manslaughter and establishes different categories of murder, singling out premeditated murder and parricide as the worst forms (21:12-15). It is followed by the other basic provisions of Israelite criminal law. Kidnapping and cursing one's parents are treated like murder (as in the Decalogue, no distinction is made between father and mother). Provisions are made for the punishment of assault, accidental injury caused by assault, injury as a result of negligence, theft, destruction of property as a result of negligence, arson, negligent arson, trespass, the obligations of guardianship and trusteeship, and the laws of restitution (21:16-22:13).

The fourth section is a short one dealing with offenses whose source is human appetites or fears, having serious social consequences, including the violation of an unbetrothed virgin (which affects her marriage possibilities), the prohibition against sorcery, and the prohibition against bestiality (22:15-18). In verse 19, sacrifices to gods other than the Lord are prohibited. The fifth section is devoted to embedding the basic principles of social justice within the constitution. Protection is provided for resident aliens, widows, fatherless children, and the poor (22:19-26).

Section six deals with obligations toward the governors of the *edah*, both Divine and human and those elements of social mutuality and mutual responsibility that are necessary for a society to maintain itself. Cursing God or the Nesiim (the magistrates selected out of the body of the people) is prohibited, coupled with the requirement of bringing offerings to God and to be holy by avoiding torn flesh (22:27-23:9). These are essentially repetitions of laws in the Noahide Covenant. These are followed by prohibitions against perjury, bribery, and showing favoritism in the administration of justice even for the poor. Participation in wrongful popular actions is specifically prohibited. A positive requirement to assist one's enemy as well as one's neighbor is included and linked with kindness to beasts of burden. The oppression of aliens is explicitly prohibited (23:1-9).

Section seven demarcates God's calendar for His people, beginning with the sabbatical laws, setting aside the seventh year as the sabbatical year and the seventh day as the Sabbath to demarcate the week (23:10-12). The three pilgrimage festivals are delineated to demarcate the year, indicating the character and content of the sacrificial offerings required (23:14-19). (The last phrase of v. 19 is the basis for the Jewish dietary laws.)

Verses 20-33, which conclude the Book of the Covenant, offer a clear statement of what God will do for the people in return for their hearkening to the Covenant and what will happen if they do not. The section concludes with the requirement that the Israelites drive out the Canaanites from the land they are to inherit, making no covenant with them or their gods, for only thus will God enable them to inherit the land.

Completing the Act of Covenanting

God having delivered this basic constitution to Moses, it then became Moses's responsibility to transmit it to the people (24:3-5):

> And Moses came and told the people all the words of the Lord, and all the ordinances; and all the people answered with one voice, and said: "All the words which the Lord hath spoken will we do." And Moses wrote all the words of the Lord, and rose up early in the morning, and builded an altar under the mount, and twelve pillars, according to the twelve tribes of Israel. And he sent the young men of the children of Israel, who offered burnt-offerings, and sacrificed peace-offerings of oxen unto the Lord.

Moses then "took the book of the covenant, and read in the hearing of the people; and they said: 'All that the Lord hath spoken will we do, and obey.' And Moses took the blood, and sprinkled it on the people, and said: 'Behold the blood of the covenant, which the Lord hath made with you in agreement with all these words'" (24:7-8), thereby completing the covenant ceremony by allowing the people two additional chances to consent or refuse to consent.

Moses is often described as Israel's version of the classic lawgiver, a Jewish Solon, as it were. From the perspective of the biblical sources and Jewish tradition, however, he is better described as a covenant mediator.[1] He does not give law; he simply communicates the Divine Torah as constitutional teaching to Israel, now a covenanted people obligated to learn it by virtue of their covenant with God.

"Covenant mediator" is a category unto itself, possible only within a covenantal system. In ancient Israel, it was a role principally associated with the *keter torah*. The prophets were classic covenant mediators, as were, in a real sense, the sages and rabbis. Whereas Moses and the prophets mediate directly between God and His covenanted people, the sages and rabbis mediate between the sacred constitutional texts and real life, making the kingdom of heaven simultaneously God's federal republic on earth, principally but not exclusively. The bearers of the other crowns, principals in their own domains, are also covenant mediators. Judges and kings and priests each play a mediating role according to the biblical record. Their role decreases as that of the prophets increases, and becomes further attenuated for judges and kings after the destruction of the First Commonwealth and the for priests after that of the Second Commonwealth.

If the purpose of the Sinai covenant was not to establish a specific political structure, what was it designed to do? The answer is clear. It was designed to transform a *goy*, a nation like all other nations, into an *am*, a people whose existence and identity rests upon their connection with a power greater than they. Then, it was to constitute that *am* as an *edah*, a polity, based upon the fixed and constitutionalized assembly of its citizenry—for covenantal purposes, all of them, men, women and children, and for constitutional purposes, all those recognized as bearing the full responsibilities of citizenship (in the Bible, the men who bore arms in time of war, the militias). In the fullest sense of the word, it establishes a regime; God's regime for the people He has chosen.

The Israeli historian Ben Zion Dinur describes the *edah* as follows:

> The distinctive social feature of early Israel is marked by its being an edah (congregation). A congregation is a social entity which comes into being and develops mainly as the result of a common will and not, like the family or tribe, by natural processes. Its members live in one place, but what distinguishes them is a common faith and common beliefs, a way of life, will; i.e., as in aspirations.[2]

This becomes even more clear when the Sinai experience is read in the larger biblical context. Between Exodus 12 and 23, we are given a step by step description of the process of the founding of the Israelite polity. At the beginning of chapter 12, God commands Moses and Aaron to initiate a new calendar for the Israelites, beginning with the spring month of Nissan (12:1-2). He then names the new polity *Adat Bnai Yisrael* (12:3) and sets down procedures for establishing citizenship in it through the sacrifice of the pascal lamb and the observance of Passover (12:3-28 and 43-51). As part of the process, Moses co-opts the existing elders into the new revolutionary regime (12:21ff.). The fact that these acts establish citizenship is confirmed at the very end of the chapter

(12:43ff.) when God makes this a *huka,* a constitutional statute specifying that only Israelites can eat of the pascal sacrifice while providing that bond servants and strangers can be inducted into the Jewish people, that is, given citizenship, so that they will be able to participate in this act if they so choose. (Note that in establishing this citizenship, God also specifies in v. 49 that other than in the case of the act of citizenship, there shall be one law for both citizens and aliens in Israel. With that, God takes the Israelites out of Egypt (v. 51).

The Sinai covenant is important for understanding the basic ties between the covenantal relationship and political structure. A political covenant does not mandate a particular structure so much as it mandates certain kinds of relationships. Needless to say, only certain structures are suitable for the maintenance of covenantal relationships but the range of options is real. Just prior to the chapters that describe the Sinai covenant the Bible tells of Moses consulting with his father-in-law, Jethro, a Midianite priest, not an Israelite, far removed from Divine authority, for suggestions on how to organize a national government for the Israelites (Exod. 18:13–26).

The interplay is more subtle than that, since the Book of the Covenant, which follows upon the giving of the tablets of the covenant (how much we obscure when we refer to them as the two tablets or, worse, the Ten Commandments) seems to be presented as God's response to Moses's delegation of power (Exod. 20:19–23:33). That is to say, as long as Moses himself was the sole judge and interpreter of God's commandments, they did not need to be set down. Specifics could be clarified through the direct and continuing discourse between Moses and God. However, once the power of judging, or interpreting and applying the commandments, is delegated, then a written collection of basic laws is necessary to provide the basis for those who are not privy to direct communications with the Almighty. The fact that this written collection was explicitly linked to the covenant should speak for itself.

Moses takes Jethro's ideas and applies them by weaving them into the covenantal situation in such a way as to be compatible with the relationships of mutuality and sharing that the covenantal relationship demands. The Bible makes clear that these arrangements for governance are not of Divine origin. This makes it possible for the Bible to chronicle later changes in the structures of government of the Jewish people without raising covenantal problems involving the changes *per se.* The only test imposed by the Bible is whether or not the changes were such that the covenantal relationship is maintained.

Israel went from the confederation of nomadic tribes under Moses to a government of settled tribes under Joshua; from the government of settled tribes on a confederal basis under the Judges to a federal basis under Samuel and Saul, to a federal monarchy under David and his successors. Subsequently, after the destruction of the first Commonwealth, Israel went from a monarchy to what has been called a "nomocracy" with no king established by Ezra and Nehemiah, and so on throughout Jewish history (see chap. 6).

These changes of political structure were possible because no single political regime is imposed by the covenant. On the contrary, the Bible makes it clear that there are options, such as whether or not to have a king. But each regime, each frame of government, is measured against the covenantal model to see whether the relationships are appropriate, whether they fit the model of theo-political relationships established by the covenant. This echoes again and again throughout the whole development of the covenant idea and its application in Western civilization. There is no set political structure for covenanted peoples although there is the expectation that their regimes will be republican in character, commonwealths in the original sense of *res publica*. To take the most simple example, if the Swiss have a plural executive and the Americans have a single executive, that is a matter of preference; the real question is the character of the relationship between the whole and its parts and the parts to each other. This is one of the major elements of the Sinai paradigm.

Explicating the Covenantal Text

Most of the remainder of the Book of Exodus and the bulk of Leviticus consists of elaboration of the original ten statements and the Book of the Covenant, all attributed directly to God, either spoken to Moses on Sinai or in the Tent of Assembly, the seat of government of the Israelite tribal federation in which the Ark of the Covenant was located. The entire section is concluded in Leviticus 26 and 27 where God reaffirms the character and conditions of the covenant.

In the fullest sense, then, the section of the Torah from Exodus 18 through the end of Leviticus is presented as the heart of the Sinai Cov-

FIGURE 9.1
The Israelite Covenants in the Torah with Their Constitutional Referents

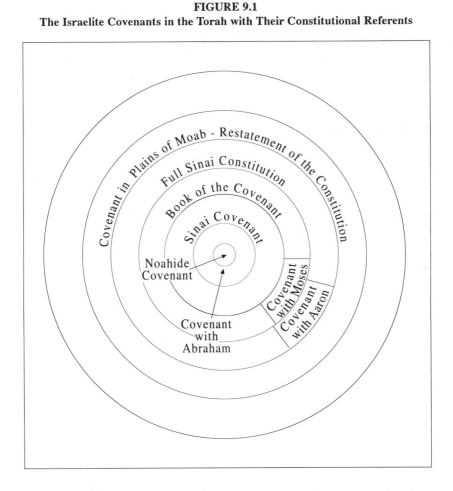

enant and its resultant constitution, with the covenant itself affirmed or reaffirmed in four places: Exodus 19, 24, and 34, and Leviticus 26. The whole consists of three basic elements that relate to each other concentrically in the classic manner of Hebrew thought rather than lineally, as in philosophic thought. At the very core is God's covenant with Noah. Surrounding it is the *Brit Ben HaBetarim,* the covenant with Abraham, and its reaffirmations with Isaac and Jacob. Then comes the Sinai covenant itself, especially that portion inscribed on the tablets of the covenant (Figure 9.1). Surrounding it in a first circle is the *Sefer HaBrit,* the

Book of the Covenant, which sets forth the basic operational meaning of the provisions stated in the Decalogue. Surrounding the *Sefer HaBrit* is a fuller elaboration of those provisions for operational purposes, encompassing the rest of the Book of Exodus and the entire Book of Leviticus, and concluding with an explicit restatement of the covenant and the relationship between covenant and constitution.

Leviticus is usually referred to by biblical critics as the "priestly code." It is assumed to be a text of almost exclusive interest to the priesthood. There is no question that Leviticus contains much that is primarily addressed to the *cohanim,* the priests or the *leviim,* their designated assistants, but it is much more. In describing the form and location of the sacrifices, in the end we have our series of elaborations on the Aaronide covenant, which, if addressed primarily to the priests, are also directed to the people as a whole.

It is widely accepted that the text that we have before us is among the older texts of the Bible. What is extraordinary is that in an age when priests were so powerful and what priests did among the nations of the world was to perform magical rites that could influence the actions of the gods, the priestly code for Israel was laid out for the members of the *edah* of whatever status to read and thereby to know that the prescribed rituals were not magic or even esoteric, that they were the property of the entire body of Israelites, fixed and formal and had to do with service to the *edah* as much as, if not more than, to God. It is clear that the priests are to perform no more than ministerial functions, that their presence does not add any magic to the sacrificial cult.

The sacrificial cult in general is portrayed in the Bible with the tone of "well, if you must have a sacrificial cult, here is the one you should follow." God does not seem to be all that interested in this mode of worship per se as the prophets are to emphasize later on. He authorizes it because of human needs.

While the book emphasizes the location, character, and procedure of the sacrifices, it also deals with other priestly matters such as healing certain diseases, at that time the province of priests. In describing the sacrificial cult, however, it emphasizes the role of the people and their leaders, presenting a reaffirmation of the Israelite tribal federation as legitimized through the form of the sacrifices to be brought by its leaders representing its constituent elements.

The book opens with the description of the sacrifices that the people owe individually and collectively (chaps. 1 through 7); it then provides for the consecration of Aaron and his descendants as priests pursuant to the covenant of priesthood God made with them (chaps. 8 through 10). The book then turns to the laws of prohibited and permitted foods (chap. 11). Chapter 12 begins the section on priestly medicine, which continues through chapter 15. Then follow two chapters (16 and 17) on purification by the priests of the people as a whole and of individual Israelites culminating in the repetition of the prohibition on drinking blood (an important aspect of purification).

Matters of purity lead to the purities and impurities of sexual relations (chap. 18). Social legislation is then tied into the matter of being pure (chap. 19). Chapter 20 turns to matters of purity in family relations, both sexual and interpersonal, and concludes with God's curse for violation of these sexual regulations in particular, namely expulsion from the promised land (chap. 21). Regulations are provided for dealing with death and prostitution, both sources of impurity. These are followed by regulations for the preservation of the purity of the priesthood (chap. 22).

The book continues by describing how time is to be consecrated. Chapter 23 deals with the consecration of time through God's annual appointed festivals or times of national assembly, culminating in chapter 24 in the observance of the Sabbath and the sacrifices required on that day, then the rules on the sabbatical year and the jubilee. The sabbatical and jubilee years are presented with their full social content of remission of debts and manumission of slaves, restoration of inheritances, and the entire corpus of land-related elements of social justice, ending with the legal structure for the mitigation of poverty and the prevention of permanent enslavement of Jews either to other human beings or to false gods (chaps. 25 and 26). Throughout all of this, matters of ethics and social morality are presented as issues of purity. He or she who violates the moral code essentially becomes impure. The end of the discussion involves a statement of covenantal blessings and cursings (chap. 26).

Chapter 27, the final chapter of Leviticus, is in the form of a fiscal appendix, dealing with the financial basis for maintaining those aspects of the *edah* of particular concern in Leviticus, a reminder of the biblical commitment to life with all of its necessary practicality.

Included in this elaboration of the constitution are the details regarding the construction of the Ark of the Covenant and the Tabernacle or Tent of Assembly in which it is to be kept and all the instruments to be used in the rituals of worship. The priestly office is established (by covenant with Aaron and his sons) and its uniform equipment and perquisites set forth, the sacrificial cult outlined and elaborated.

This constitution is interrupted only to deal with the episode of the Golden Calf (Exod. 32–33), a case of popular corruption and impurity initiated by the people themselves, to which Aaron, their leader, responds, ostensibly to mitigate its effects, which explains why the covenant must be reiterated and reaffirmed in chapter 34. The provisions regarding the construction and furnishing of the Tabernacle (Exod. 35:4–40:38), in essence, represent a discussion of the construction of the seat of Israelite government because that is where God the King, Sovereign of His people, resides to be in their midst. Hence, it is clearly part of the constitution, especially since the account concludes with the Lord entering the Tabernacle (Exod. 40:34–39).

In the end, the assembly of the Israelites consents to the entire covenant three times. The question can be raised as to whether this might have been the source for the common parliamentary practice of three readings of every piece of legislation, each of which requires the consent of the legislators. The biblical text presents the Sinai covenant as binding all generations of Jews, and Jewish tradition holds that every Jew, born or unborn, was present at Sinai. For Jews, that is not enough. The heart of subsequent Jewish ritual consists of continually reaffirming their consent to the Sinai and other covenants so as to leave no doubts as to their currently binding status on every Jewish individual and collectively on all Israel.

Numbers: The Application of the Sinai Covenant

The fourth book of the Torah, Numbers (in Hebrew, *BaMidbar,* literally: In the Desert), continues the constitutional corpus and is understood in the Jewish tradition to be an indivisible part of the original constitution. Numbers is an elaboration of aspects of the regime. It concentrates on the operational dimensions of the governance of the tribal confederation. The list of subjects included is revealing:

1. The national census by tribes and the federal means by which the census is taken (chap. 1);
2. The manner of forming the tribes around the Tent of Assembly (chap. 2);
3. The divisions of the tribe of Levi and their responsibilities in the Tabernacle (chaps. 3–4);

4. Operational rules for managing the camp (e.g., the removal of lepers and corpses (5:2-4) and rendering judgments (e.g., restitution for trespasses against the Lord—chaps. 5 and 6);
5. The order of tribal sacrifices (chap. 7);
6. Technical details for preparing the Levites for service in the Tabernacle (chap. 8);
7. The trumpet calls for public assembly (10:1-10);
8. Provisions for sacrificial offerings (15:1-3);
9. Implementation of the death penalty for Sabbath violation (15:32-36);
10. Commandment for all Israelites to fringe their garments as another sign of their covenantal obligations (15:37-41);
11. Prerogatives of the priestly families (chap. 18);
12. Purification rituals (chap. 19);
13. Provision for division of the land of Canaan once it is occupied by Israel (chaps. 26-27);
14. Provision for the succession after Moses (27:12-23, see also 11:16-17 and 24-30);
15. Seasonal, Sabbath, and festival offerings to the Lord (chaps. 28-29);
16. Adjudication of vows (chap. 30);
17. Division of the spoils of war (chap. 31);
18. Provision for the settlement of 2 1/2 tribes in territories east of the Jordan River in return for their commitment to assist the entire federation in conquering the west bank (chap. 32);
19. Rules for conquering the west bank (33:15-56);
20. The borders of the land of the twelve tribes (chap. 34);
21. An allocation for the Levites (35:1-5);
22. The establishment of cities of refuge and the rules relating to refuge in them (35:6-34);
23. Rules regarding the tribal lands inherited by women (chap. 36).

Interspersed with these addenda is a record of the Israelite tribes' wanderings for thirty-eight years in the desert, their aborted attempt to conquer Canaan after being frightened off by the scouts' report, their encounters with neighboring peoples, their conquest of the better part of the east bank of the Jordan, and the internal discontents and rebellions within the tribal federation.

This is a book filled with the day-to-day stuff of government and politics worth a political commentary in its own right. In that sense it is an excursus on the Book of the Covenant and the other constitutional laws of Exodus and Leviticus. If the Decalogue is the covenant and the Book of the Covenant is the basic constitution, Numbers provides several organic laws designed to implement the covenant and the constitution in the real world occupied by the Israelites both in the desert and in what was to become the historic land of the twelve tribes on both banks of the Jordan. In this sense it provides both the setting for and the bridge to Deuteronomy, the fifth book of the Pentateuch, which provides the constitution for the Israelites settled in their land.

A reading of the foregoing covenant and constitution exposes the biblical-covenantal view of human rights and obligations, which, while reading many of the same results as modern liberal democracy, begins from different premises. The Bible begins with the mutual obligations of humans and God resulting from their covenants. Thus, the Bible derives rights from the obligation of all humans to God as their creator, sovereign, and covenant partner.

The Mosaic Regime

If the present theories are correct, the period of Jewish history prior to the Exodus from Egypt encompassed between five hundred and seven hundred years, or approximately a span of two constitutional epochs. Indeed, the biblical accounts suggest that it can be divided into the epoch of the patriarchs and the epoch of the Egyptian sojourn. During the first epoch the patriarch was the sole repository of governing powers. He was governor and military leader and he conducted foreign relations. He also received instructions from God and made the covenants with Him that constituted the constitutional framework for the emergent Jewish people. In that context he prayed, sacrificed, built altars and monuments, and offered blessings.[3]

At the beginning of the second epoch of Jewish history, the families of the twelve sons of Jacob were well-ensconced in Egypt, living under a foreign rule that sooner or later reduced them to slavery. There were no more patriarchs. In their place were *zekenim* (elders) and *shoterim* (maintainers of the peace), officials who administered the customary law of the tribes, perhaps recalling in a latent way the patriarchal covenants.[4]

The first constitutional epoch after the Exodus stretches from the founding of the Israelite tribal confederacy, the Mosaic regime, to the establishment of the monarchy. The founding of the tribal confederacy immediately after the Exodus from Egypt comes simultaneously with the founding of the nation, or the transformation of the Hebrew tribes into a national entity. Since ancient times, Moses has been recognized as the founder of the nation and its constitution maker.[5]

The Mosaic constitution laid the foundations for the first Israelite polity, which was organized federally around a loose union of tribes, traditionally twelve in number. This union, perhaps the first true federal system in history, was bound together by a common constitution and law but maintained relatively rudimentary national institutions grafted onto more fully articulated tribal ones whose origins may have antedated the Exodus. This situation prevailed, in great part, because the constitution specified that God himself was to be considered the direct governor of the nation as a whole, assisted by a "servant" or prime minister (Hebrew: *Eved Adonai*) who would be His representative and who, in turn, would maintain a core of judges and civil servants to handle the transmission of his or, more correctly, God's instructions to the tribal and familial authorities. Depending on the importance of the issue in constitutional terms, the prime minister also interacted with the assembly of the children of Israel congregated as a whole—men, women, and children—the assembly of all men of military age, a national council representing the tribes, or ad hoc assemblies of tribal elders (*zekenim*) or delegates (*nesi'im*) for purposes of policy-making.

For the Israelites of the time, the general thrust of the Sinai covenant and its accompanying texts and actions was to bring the existing tribes with their primordial political structures based on kinship into the framework of a national constitution based on consent, comprehensive in character and designed to sanctify all dimensions of human life, in order to build the holy commonwealth. While, in light of our knowledge of the role of covenants and covenant ideas in West Asia at the time, we can assume that the Israelite tribes were culturally attuned to this turn of events, nevertheless, the covenantal process led to a new political invention, one that brought about a redesign of the political structure itself and created a basis for further redesign in later epochs of Jewish history, biblical and post-biblical.

An important aspect of this redesign was the use of covenants to divide powers within the *edah*. The initial division was between Moses and Aaron. God covenanted with Moses as His minister (in the political sense) responsible for relaying and interpreting God's teaching (Torah) and judging the people. These functions were immediately subdivided per God's instructions so that the seventy elders (as in a senate or board of aldermen) took on primary responsibilities for judging, meaning they functioned as one branch of government, while Moses himself retained

the responsibility for interpreting God's teaching. The separation between these two divisions was later to be institutionalized by the end of
the period of the Judges, with Samuel the last figure to attempt to straddle
both. God made a parallel covenant with Aaron and his sons, giving
them the priesthood with the authority to be the links between the people
and God in ritual and sacerdotal matters. The "executive" functions of
day-to-day governing were in the collective hands of the *nesiim* and
zekenim of the twelve tribes, who assembled together regularly. They
were the heirs of God's patriarchal covenant with Abraham. Thus, the
basis for a tripartite division of authority between prophetic, priestly,
and civil functions was set down through subsidiary covenants early in
the biblical account of the history of Israel as a polity.

Because the Jewish polity embraces a complete civilization, including its religious dimensions, even prior to the classic separation of powers into executive, legislative, and judicial, the *edah* separated domains
of authority. A millennium later, during the time of the Second Commonwealth, this tripartite division would be described in the Mishnah
(Avot 4) as the division into three *ketarim* (literally, crowns), the labels
they bear in the Jewish political tradition to this day. Those responsible
for relating and interpreting God's teaching are described as belonging
to the domain of *keter torah* (the crown of Torah). Those responsible for
the civil governance of the *edah* represent the domain of *keter malkhut*
(the crown of kingship or, better, civil rule), while those responsible for
the links between the people and God in ritual and sacredotal matters
are described as being in the domain of the *keter kehunah* (the crown of
priesthood). In biblical times, however, only the offices are named; no
generic terms for them are found. This tripartite system is restated in
Deuteronomy (see chap. 4); it became more fully articulated with the
introduction of the monarchy in the time of Samuel (who as judge and
prophet [his two official titles] continued in the line of Moses and Joshua
and straddled the constitutional divide between the Mosaic and Davidic
regimes [see below]), Saul, and David.

In the Bible, Torah was communicated to the *edah* first through the
Eved Adonai (God's chief minister, a title bestowed only on Moses and
Joshua), then through the *ro'eh* (seer) and the *neviim* (prophets—singular, *navi*). From a political perspective, the *keter kehunah* began with
the *kohen gadol* (high priest) having significant governance responsibilities in the *edah* as a co-adjudicator in matters affecting the tribes or

as a court of final appeal, as well as a channel to communicate with God through sacrifices, prayer, or whatever. Over time, that domain's political role diminished with the growing power of kings and prophets. This political role later became the task of the *soferim* ("Scribes") who developed the *ketaric* terminology.[6]

The oldest ketarim of them all is the *keter malkhut,* responsible for the tasks of normal governance. Its first separately articulated representatives were the *zekenim,* an institution that dates back at least to the Egyptian bondage, and their principal officers, the *nesiei haedah* (the magistrates). They had a dual function in that they headed the individual tribes and also participated in the governance of the nation as a whole.[7] An additional republican guarantee of this system was the fact that the Israelites had no standing army but relied for protection on the tribal militias consisting of every male age twenty or over. Nationally, the *keter malkhut* was later led by the *shofetim* (judges), and *melakhim* (kings). Each of these offices is recognized in the Bible.

This division of authority and powers is a direct product of the covenant tradition, both as a protection against overconcentration of power by dividing into potentially competing domains and as a manifestation of a worldview that sees cooperative relationships as essential for political and social harmony. We shall see that every political system worth its salt based on covenant also includes some form of division of authority and powers.

The entire body politic was known as *Adat B'nai Yisrael* from the time of the Exodus onward. *Edah* means congregation or assembly and reflects the popular and republican basis of the Israelite polity. Thus, from Sinai onward, constitutional decisions were taken by the entire *Edah*, men, women, and children, assembled together to give their consent, while major policy decisions such as declarations of war were made by the *Edah* in its more limited form of men of military age. Day-to-day governance was in the hands of the institutions mentioned above, which represented the *Edah*. It was the *Edah* that God led directly and to which He spoke through the *Eved Adonai*. Within the limits of God's constitution the *Edah* acted autonomously.[8]

Once the nation had been formed by Moses and settled in the land by Joshua, no single national leaders of this kind emerged until the very end of the first constitutional epoch. Instead, regional *shofetim* (judges)— also charismatic leaders—appeared from time to time, according to the biblical account at least one in each generation, to act as proto-national leaders, under God's direct sovereignty, primarily, though not exclusively, in the military realm. The term "judge," introduced in English Bibles as the translation to the Hebrew term, carries roughly the same meaning as the term originally did in Anglo-American political life—an executive office whose duties may include the settling of disputes but are essentially directed toward the authoritative execution of the law, as in the case of the traditional southern county judge who actually serves as the chief executive officer of the county.[9]

If the terminology used in the Pentateuch and the Book of Joshua is accurate, the use of the term *judges* to describe the post-Joshua leadership of the nation accurately reflects the less than nationwide scope of the judges' authority. The ministers of the Lord had in their governmental structures judges and officers, lesser figures responsible to them whose authority may have been parallel to that of the later judges, though limited by the existence of a national leader. Only after their departure did the judges acquire a leading role of their own.

The first constitutional epoch came to an end with the advent of the monarchy, which was instituted with some reluctance to cope with the Philistine threat to the very existence of Israel. The epoch's last stage was dominated by Samuel, the last of the judges and the first of the prophets, who brought the period to a close with his efforts to revive national unity in the traditional manner through a single nationwide leader with limited authority primarily in the military field. Pressed by the people of Israel in the wake of their conquest by the Philistines to designate a king "of flesh and blood" who will provide them with appropriate military leadership "like all the nations," he reluctantly grants such limited authority to Saul, whom he designated as high commissioner (*nagid*). This represented an effort to restore the kind of national institutions needed to promote energetic national unity that had existed in the days of Moses and Joshua.[10]

For Samuel, the Israelite constitution demanded that energetic government be limited government under God's continuing sovereignty. He emphasized the idea of dividing authority between the governor and the prophet, with the former holding executive powers limited by the latter's mediation of God's word. Samuel failed for a number of reasons, not the least of which was the fact that the successful implementation of such a political arrangement was not to occur for many centuries. In the end, he himself took the decisive steps necessary to create a more conventional monarchy, though one limited by the traditional constitution. Thus ended the Mosaic regime instituted at Sinai ten generations after its institution.

Notes

1. Meredith G. Kline, "Law Covenant," *Westminster Theological Journal* (n.d.): 1–20.
2. Ben Zion Dinur, "Jewish History—Its Uniqueness and Continuity," in H. H. Ben Sasson and S. Ettinger, *Jewish Society Through the Ages* (New York: Schocken Books, 1969), 17–18.
3. Cf. Daniel J. Elazar and Stuart A. Cohen, *The Jewish Polity* (Bloomington: Indiana University Press, 1987), Introduction and Epochs I and II. On the epoch of the patriarchs, see A. Malamat, "Origins and the Formative Period," in *A History of the Jewish People,* ed. H. H. Ben Sasson (Cambridge, MA: Harvard University Press, 1976), 3–87; B. Mazar, ed., "The Patriarchs," *The World History of the Jewish People,* vol. 1 (New Brunswick, NJ: Rutgers University Press, 1970); E. A. Speiser, ed., "Genesis," *The Anchor Bible, Vol. 1: Social Institutions* (New York, 1965), 3–15.
4. John Bright, *A History of Israel,* 3d ed. (Philadelphia: Westminster Press, 1982); G. E. Mendenhall, "Ancient Oriental and Biblical Law," *Biblical Archeologist* 17:2 (1954): 26–46; M. Weinfeld, "Berit-Covenant vs. Obligation," *Biblica* 56, no. 1 (1975): 109–28.
5. Aaron Wildavsky, *The Nursing Father: Moses as a Political Leader* (Tuscaloosa: University of Alabama Press, 1984); Leo Schwarz, *Great Ages and Ideas of the Jewish People* (New York: Holt, Rinehart and Winston, 1960), chap. 1; John Bright, "The Constitution and Faith of Early Israel," *A History of Israel,* part 2, chap. 4; Moshe Weinfeld, "The Transition from Tribal Rule to Monarchy and Its Impact on History," *Kinship and Consent,* ed. Daniel J. Elazar (Ramat Gan: Turtledove, 1981); A. Malamat, "Origins and the Formative Period"; Daniel J. Elazar, "The Book of Joshua as a Political Classic," *Jewish Political Studies Review* 1, nos. 1–2 (Spring 1989): 93–150; Martin Noth, "Israel as the Confederation of the Twelve Tribes," *The History of Israel,* part 1 (New York: Harper and Row, 1958); W. F. Albright, "Tribal Rule and Charismatic Leaders," *The Biblical Period from Abraham to Ezra* (New York: Harper Torchbooks, 1968), 35–52; R. G. Bowling and G. Ernest Wright, eds., "Joshua," *The Anchor Bible,* vol. 5 (New York, 1982); G. E. Mendenhall, *Law and Covenant in Israel and the Ancient Near East* (Pittsburgh: The Biblical Colloquium, 1955); *Studies in the Book of Joshua* (Jerusalem: Kiryat Sepher, 1960).
6. Moshe Weinfeld, "Judge and Officer in Ancient Israel and in the Ancient Near East," *Israel Oriental Studies* 7 (1977): 65–88; "Keter ve-Atarah," in *Encyclopedia Mikra'it,* vol. 4 (Jerusalem, 1962), columns 405–408; Stuart A. Cohen, *The Concept of the Three Ketarim: Its Place in Jewish Political Thought and Its Implications for a Study of Jewish Constitutional History,* Working Paper No. 18 (Jerusalem: Center for Jewish Community Studies, 1982), 1–40, and "Keter as a Jewish Political Symbol: Origins and Implications," *Jewish Political Studies Review* 1, nos. 1–2 (Spring 1989); C. Umhau Wolf, "Terminology of Israel's Tribal Organization," *Journal of Biblical Literature.*

7. E. A. Speiser, "Background and Functions of the Biblical Nasi," *Catholic Biblical Quarterly* 25 (1965): 111–17; Weinfeld, "Judge and Officer."

8. Moshe Weinfeld, "From God's Edah to the Chosen Dynasty: The Transition from the Tribal Federation to the Monarchy," in *Kinship and Consent*; R. Gordis, "Democratic Origins in Ancient Israel—the Biblical Edah," in *The Alexander Marx Jubilee Volume* (New York: Jewish Theological Seminary, 1950).

9. B. Lindars, "Gideon and the Kinship," *Journal of Theological Studies* 16 (1965): 315–26; R. G. Bowling and G. Ernest Wright, "Judges," *The Anchor Bible*, vol. 6 (New York, 1980); W. F. Albright, "Tribal Rule and Charismatic Leaders," *The Biblical Period from Abraham to Ezra* and *Samuel and the Beginnings of the Prophetic Movement in Israel* (Cincinnati: Hebrew Union College Press, 1961).

10. A. Alt, "The Formation of the Israelite State," *Essays on Old Testament History and Religion* (Oxford: Basil Blackwell and Mott, 1966); Daniel J. Elazar, "Dealing with Fundamental Regime Change: The Biblical Paradigm of the Transition from Tribal Federation to Federal Monarchy of David," in *From Ancient Israel to Modern Judaism,* vol. 1, ed. Jacob Neusner, Ernest S. Frerichs, and Nahum M. Sarna (Atlanta: Scholars Press, 1989), 97–129; Moshe Weinfeld, "From God's Edah to the Chosen Dynasty," 151–66; J. Levenson, "The Davidic Covenant and Its Modern Interpreters," *Catholic Bible Quarterly* 41, no. 2 (1979); W. A. Irwin, "Saul and the Rise of the Monarchy," *American Journal of Semitic Languages and Literature* 58 (1941): 113–38.

10

From Covenant to Constitution: Deuteronomy

The Book of Deuteronomy is a restatement of the entire constitution in a more systematic fashion, modified to provide for the *edah* in its new land. As such, it is a sixth concentric circle around the core. In a sense the first four books of the Pentateuch served as the constitution of the Mosaic polity in its classic period. The addition of its fifth, *Devarim* or Deuteronomy, reflects the change in regime with the addition of the monarchy and all that went with it.

The book is cast in the form of Moses's farewell address to his people camped in the plains of Moab just before his death. It includes a description of the recovenanting on the plains of Moab prior to the Israelite embarkation on the conquest of Canaan. Within the text itself, the book is referred to as *Divrei HaBrit,* the Words of the Covenant (29:8). Indeed, the entire book is presented as a constitution that embodies and restates the original covenant. A parallel example of this device is to be found in the Massachusetts Constitution of 1780, which begins with a restatement of the covenant/compact that forms the Massachusetts body politic and continues to present the fundamental law of the Commonwealth. The Deuteronomic constitution is presented as having been delivered before the assembly of Israel, the *edah,* all at one time.

Confronting an Ancient Constitution

It is not a new idea to suggest that the Book of Deuteronomy, known in Hebrew as *Devarim* (literally: words or utterances, here best translated as stated laws), is built to be a complete version of Israel's ancient constitution. If it is indeed of Mosaic authorship as it is presented to be, it is certainly the oldest complete constitution in our possession, dating from the thirteenth or fourteenth century B.C.E. Even if it is younger than

193

that, from as late as the time of Josiah (seventh century B.C.E.), it still is a most venerable document. Those theories that claim an even later origin for it still place it in the period of the classic Greek constitutions.[1] Thus, it, along with the Constitution of Athens, are the two oldest such documents available to students of government and politics.[2]

Deuteronomy is distinct among the Five Books of Moses in that it is not presented anonymously with the implicit claim of Divine authorship but is presented as a Mosaic work based upon the earlier Divine communications to him, the greatest of Israel's prophets. Deuteronomy is presented as an oration—a long and very grand farewell address by Moses summarizing all of his teaching. Knowing that he is about to die, Moses sets down his teaching in one final ordered form so that his people will have that teaching after he is gone.

This step can be understood as parallel to the earlier, similar situation in Exodus when Moses responded to his father-in-law Jethro's recommendations for governmental reorganization to share the burden of judging the Israelites and then feels constrained to write down the basic laws in the Book of the Covenant. Even great leaders like Moses are human and must die. For their leadership to succeed it must be embodied in a teaching and there must be teachers. For their teaching to succeed it must be written on the hearts of their followers (cf., e.g., 5:6) and in a constitution that will pass the teaching from generation to generation. This itself is a principal teaching of the Torah as constitution and of the Jewish covenantal tradition in general. Those who would be covenantal partners must have the opportunity to learn what they need to know to play that role. This is a critical emphasis of the Book of Deuteronomy.

Throughout the book, God is perceived as king, directly active in Israelite affairs. Nevertheless, the daily governance of the *edah* was in the hands of His prime minister and the other federal and republican institutions and officers of the polity.[3] Deuteronomy focuses more on the collective constitutional dimension than do earlier parts of the Torah, making it even more constitutional, as the idea of constitutionalism has come to be understood.

The Book of *Devarim* is presented as a covenant. The term itself is used in 11 of its 34 chapters and is implicitly present in virtually all of the others. Its structure follows the standard formula: (1) a historical prologue that explains the reasons for the covenant; (2) the covenant stipulations and, where it deems necessary, justifications for them; (3)

provision for mutual pledging; (4) enforcement clauses and punishments for noncompliance with its terms; and (5) a statement of blessings and curses, the former if the terms on constitutional provisions are hearkened to and the latter if they are not.[4] Moreover, it provides for a renewal of the covenant every seven years (31:10-13). The term *shamoa* is routinely used to describe the expected human response to God's commandments, statutes, and ordinances.

The changes or variants on the original statement of certain constitutional laws and principles in the other four books have suggested to many the theory that the book was actually compiled in the seventh century B.C.E. at the time of Josiah's reign in Judah, the surviving kingdom of biblical Israel, and that it is the text referred to in 2 Kings 22:8. There it is referred to as the Book of the Covenant (2 Kings 23:2) and is the basis for a covenant renewal in Judah (v. 3).

Others have suggested the book is somehow connected with the *mishpat hamelukhah* (law of the kingdom) promulgated by the prophet Samuel in God's name in the eleventh century B.C.E., when kingship was introduced into Israel against prophetic advice and it was necessary to provide a more precise constitutional framework for it.[5] Still others hold that at least the core of the book authentically dates back to the Mosaic period.[6]

From the internal evidence of the book it appears that the version we have before us has integrated several different texts. While the result is a coherent whole, there are some potential contradictions. Biblical scholars properly seek to identify these segments to understand how and when they were integrated. For our purposes, however, we can take the final product as a whole, for as such it was understood by those in subsequent generations who saw themselves as bound by it.

Was Deuteronomy Actually in Force?

It is hard to know precisely how Deuteronomy served as the constitution of ancient Israel, how it was interpreted and applied. The only source of information is the Bible itself, which discusses the composition and acceptance of the book in a covenantal ceremony on the plains of Moab towards the end of the generation of the Israelites' wandering on the desert and just before the death of Moses (28:69-30:20). The Bible also discusses the rediscovery of what seems to have been Deuteronomy in the days of Josiah and how Josiah, after reading the book, ordered that its provisions, at least with regard to the Jewish calendar and Jewish worship, be enforced. There may be some reference to the Deuteronomic constitution in the discussion of how King Hezekiah restored the central sanctuary for all Israel (2 Chron. 29), but that is directed more toward the issue of the reunification of the kingdom of Judah with the remnants of the Israelites from the shattered northern kingdom that had just been destroyed. Beyond that, we have no idea how the book was applied or interpreted, if at all, in biblical times.

In subsequent epochs, the directly political parts of Deuteronomy became the basis for discussions of what the ideal Jewish state should be like. These discussions formed the foundation of rabbinic and medieval Jewish political thought.[7] They continued to have influence in the modern and postmodern epochs as well.[8]

Constitutionally, they were important at two moments of Jewish history after the destruction of the Second Commonwealth. The first, in the second century of the common era, involved the constitution of the patriarchate in Eretz Israel and the exilarchate in Babylonia, as regimes that were organized in the spirit of the Deuteronomic political constitution.[9] The second came in the High Middle Ages, between the eleventh and fourteenth centuries, when a whole new constitutional architecture had to be erected to provide for the self-governing Jewish *kehillot* (communities) of Europe.[10] In both cases the constitutional debates and decisions insofar as we have them (and we have more for the latter period than we have for the former) involve frequent recurrence to Deuteronomic first principles dealing with the relationship of kingship to Torah and people and the tasks and roles of judges, officers, and elders.

At the beginning of the modern epoch there was a further recourse to the Book of Deuteronomy, but here strictly in the realm of political thought as emancipationist Jewish apologists sought to present the ideal Jewish polity of the Bible in terms that were acceptable to the new modern ideas of statehood and self-government. In the postmodern epoch, the reestablishment of the state of Israel led certain groups of religious Jewish thinkers to return to Deuteronomy in an effort to find guidance for a proper Jewish state, thus generating a new literature based on Deuteronomy as a political constitution.[11] Thus, what we have before us is a living tradition that, like any living tradition, has been filtered through different waves of interpretation, in this case going back perhaps 3,000 years. Here, however, it will be our task to try to recover the original structure of the constitution insofar as it is possible to do so.

Why was Deuteronomy Necessary?

Why is there a need for a restatement of the constitution previously presented in the first four books of the Pentateuch? Part of the reason is given in Deuteronomy itself: the restatement of the constitution as applied to the Jews in their land, Eretz Israel. The original constitution is designed to serve a nomadic people, a people formed in the desert and moving around without a permanent abode. Thus, it emphasizes portability in the political structure based upon households (*batei av*) and tribes (*shevatim*) assembled around the portable tabernacle (*mishkan*) and tent of meeting (*ohel moed*) where the portable Ark of the Covenant (*Aron HaBrit*) containing the portable tablets of the covenant (*Lukhot HaBrit*) are kept, rather than on permanent territorial divisions and a fixed, central shrine.

The other part has to do with the shift from the Mosaic to Davidic regime, that is, the introduction of a *nagid*-king. The problematics of that change are reflected in the book itself, which is ambiguous about whether a king is required or simply allowed. In any case, Deuteronomy is designed to serve a settled people.

The critical sections of the Deuteronomic constitutional restatement begin with some reference to the occupation and settlement of the land, usually phrased as follows:

4.1 Now, Israel, hearken to the statutes and to the ordinances which I teach you, to do them that you may live and go in and possess the land which the Lord, the God of your fathers, gives you.

6.1 Now this is the commandments, the statutes, and the ordinances which the Lord your God commanded to teach you, that you might do them in the land whither you go over to possess it.

7.1 When the Lord thy God shall bring thee into the land whither thou goest to possess it and shall cast out the many nations before thee....

8.1 All the commandments which I command thee this day shall be observed that you may live and multiply and go in and possess the land which the Lord swore unto your fathers.

By and large Deuteronomy only deals with those constitutional laws that are extensions or modifications of the constitutional laws presented in the first four books. It does not seem to repeat constitutional laws unnecessarily. Thus, in Deuteronomy's discussion of the land and its boundaries, the book does not repeat the division of the land presented in Numbers and in its discussion of governance does not repeat the basic structure of governance presented in Exodus. Rather it references both at the very beginning of the book.

The question may be raised as to whether all of the changes ostensibly needed to serve a settled population were indeed appropriate. One example stands out: the commandment to centralize sacrifices and public religious ceremonies at one central place, the Temple, built by Solomon (tenth century B.C.E) and restored several times, the last time by Josiah (seventh century B.C.E.). On the one hand, it could be argued that, if anything, it was during nomadic days when presumably everyone was moving together that sacrifice was more appropriately centralized, while once people were settled it was reasonable to enable them to build permanent places of sacrifice and public worship near their dwellings. On the other hand, Deuteronomy gives as its good reason that local sacrifices would be likely to be made at the holy places of the pagan idolaters and therefore lead to religious syncretism. For the Bible that is the same as idolatry. Indeed there is biblical and archeological evidence that this happened.

To complicate matters further there was also the real reason of the kings of the Davidic house attempting to consolidate their power by centralizing public worship under their wing in a central sanctuary. David, the founder of the dynasty, was the first to try to do this by bringing the Ark of the Covenant to his city, Jerusalem, and designating a particular family, the Zadokites, as the high priests, all under his protection. Apparently, he was not powerful enough vis-à-vis tribal and local interests to actually build the Temple in the face of what was no doubt great opposition to this aspect of royal centralization. It was left to his son Solomon to do so.

Even so, it is clear from the sources available to us that local sacrifice did continue, indeed with some of the negative results to which Deuteronomy referred, until the very end of the First Commonwealth in 586 B.C.E. Subsequently, a compromise was reached whereby the Temple was rebuilt and was given sole jurisdiction over animal sacrifices while normal public worship was detached from official and other ritual cults that could be shared by pagans and turned into prayer that could be performed in local houses of prayer that became known as synagogues, simultaneously with the Temple service.[12]

The institution of the kingship also reflects a shift from the earlier regime to a new one, presumably the federal monarchy introduced by Samuel, Saul, and David.[13] Here is greater ambiguity since, as later commentators forcefully noted, Deuteronomy does not clearly indicate whether the appointment of a king is mandatory or optional (17:14–20).[14] The rules for kingship can be read either way. The certain thing is that if a king is appointed, he is bound by the constitutional laws of kingship; he must be a constitutional monarch.

Another example of the change is that the judges and officers originally appointed to serve nonterritorialized tribal and familial units are now to be territorially based at the city gates (16:18).

The Structure and Contents of Deuteronomy

The book consists of lists of statutes (*hukim*) and ordinances (*mishpatim*) set in a historical and theological context. Here we will not examine the detail and character of most of the constitutional laws promulgated. That must await another occasion. Emphasis is placed on the historical context. Not only does the book begin with a recital of the significant history of the Bnei Israel, but segments of that history are repeated on different occasions where relevant to introduce particular statutes and ordinances. Moreover, history and theology are mixed.

Some scholars have referred to this as sacred history, but while that is a partially accurate description, here we have history designed to support the validity of the commanded legislation both from the general sense of why God's commands deserve to be observed by the people of Israel and the more specific sense, for example, in relationship to doing social justice because the Israelites were strangers in Egypt. The theology here is that of an omnipotent personal God who intervenes in history, indeed directs it, who has chosen Israel to be His people for His reasons, not because of Israel's merit, and who has covenanted with Israel to require them to hearken to and keep a certain constitution so as to achieve a certain way of life, that He will hold them and their descendants accountable for the fulfillment of their side of that covenant, that He is a God who loves, seeks and does justice, and expects His covenant partners to do the same.

There is much apparent repetition, especially in the historical-theological materials. Often it is just for emphasis. But in many cases the material has to be read very carefully to detect the nuances of difference that point to the purposes or new adaptations of the constitutional laws involved. This takes on added significance in those sections that are apparently repetitions of basic laws that appeared earlier in the other four books of the Pentateuch. In those cases, the difference of a word or two reflects an adaptation of a basic law established for a nomadic population for use by a settled population.

The repetition here must be understood in another context as well. Even if the text we have before us was written down early, the number of copies would have had to be very limited. Therefore, it was designed to be taught orally to people who did not have texts before them. Thus, the repetition of critical concepts is a teaching device, a mnemonic, that the Israelite public could follow. In a sense that style is testimony to the fact that, as advertised in the text itself (cf., inter alia, 30:11–14), this is a *public* constitution. It was designed to be heard, read, learned, understood by, and interpreted for all Israel. This is another sign of the constitutional character of the document and how it is designed to serve a covenanted people composed of fundamentally equal partners.

The people and their rulers had to know their constitution, had to learn and be familiar with its text and contents. One of the principal words for teaching, in Hebrew, is *lishanot,* to teach by repetition, and Deuteronomy was known from the first and is so referred to in the text (17:18) as *mishneh Torah,* that is to say, the repetition or restatement of the Torah, implicitly for learning purposes. This ties in to another dimension of Israelite constitutionalism. The style of the constitution is deliberately that of a teaching, not simply a code or a set of constitutional laws.

Teaching as *lishanot* is particularly appropriate to an oral tradition where repetition is critical to developing recognition if not memorization of texts. Not only that, but the repetition is done with formulas, so that the formulas themselves are mnemonic. Examples of such formulas can be found throughout the book. A few were presented earlier in connection with the land-related laws. The formulas are repeated as introductions to major sections of the constitution.

The first five verses of the book are an introduction indicating who is presenting the constitution, when and where, and in what context. In a sense it is outside the constitution but, in the manner of the Torah as teaching, needed to give us the appropriate framework.

Beginning with chapter 1, verse 6, and continuing until the end of chapter 3 we have a preamble, a summary of the history of the Israelites and an indication that it is time to take possession of the Promised Land. The areas that constitute the land are listed and God's historic promise of the land to Israel is reiterated. The preamble also includes a description of the established institutions of federal governance, the institutions of the tribal federation, and the requirement that judges provide equal justice. The preamble concludes with the information that Moses is to die outside the Promised Land and Joshua is reconfirmed as his successor who will lead the Israelites across the Jordan.

The body of the constitution, referred to as the *hukim* and *mishpatim* (statutes and ordinances), is presented in chapters 4 through 26, verse 15. It is followed by a section describing the enactment and promulgation of the constitution, first by presenting the covenant curses and blessings (21:16 to 28:68), then through a covenant renewal ceremony (28:69 to 30:20). The ceremony is concluded with a final word (30:11-20), emphasizing that the constitution is close to the people and not distant from them, that through it the people are given the choice between good and evil, and that heaven and earth are called upon to witness the covenant just made. The covenant ceremony is followed by an epilogue (chaps. 31-34) in which Moses transfers power to Joshua, summarizes his teaching in the Song of Moses, blesses the Bnai Israel, collectively and tribe by tribe, and then goes up Mt. Nebo to his death while Joshua assumes power.

The book describes how Moses assembled the people in the plains of Moab after they had conquered the east bank of the Jordan, to expound (*ba'er* 1:5) the Torah as constitution as a prelude to their occupying the land that God has designated as theirs (1:6-8). The constitution, then, is to apply to the Israelites in their land, first and foremost. The land is defined, albeit in the relatively vague way of the desert world, by listing the regions that constitute it (the Arava, the Har or hill country, the Shefela lowlands, the Negev southern dry land, the seashore, the land of the Canaanites, and Lebanon as far as the Euphrates). The Euphrates is the only actual boundary mentioned and even that is written rather vaguely. In an oasis culture, space perceptions are based upon the identification of core areas whose outer limits remain somewhat vague. Along with the geographic description, God's promise of the land to Israel through Abraham, Isaac, and Jacob and their descendants is reaffirmed (1:8).

The preamble (1:9–18) sets forth the governmental framework of the Israelites under the Mosaic Constitution, namely, that of a tribal federation:

> Get you, from each one of your tribes, wise men, and understanding, and full of knowledge, and I will make them heads over you. And ye answered me, and said: "The thing which thou hast spoken is good for us to do." So I took the heads of your tribes, wise men, and full of knowledge, and made them heads over you, captains of thousands, and captains of hundreds, and captains of fifties, and captains of tens, and officers, tribe by tribe. And I charged your judges at that time...the judgment is God's and the cause that is too hard for you, you shall bring unto Me and I will hear it. (13–17)

Moses reviews the history of Israel in terms of God's direct intervention on their behalf—militarily, demographically, and economically. He specifies the structure of government as originally proposed by Jethro, his father-in-law, but with a major difference. Whereas Jethro suggests that Moses appoint subordinate officers (Exod. 18), when Moses writes the appropriate clauses into Israel's constitution, he provides that the tribes shall themselves elect their officers (1:13). Moses appoints the judges only to administer justice through the Torah. He also reviews the Israelites' failures, all within the context of the functioning tribal federation. He culminates with the Israelite acquisition of the territories east of the Jordan and their allocation among the tribes.

Moses repeats the history of their journey, Israel's sins of rebellion against God and their punishment, and the first conquests in the transjordan (1:19–3:29), giving careful attention to the constitutional niceties. For example, in spying out the land: "I took twelve men of you, one man from each tribe" (23). He explains the long wandering and the reason for the Israelite occupation of the east bank, concluding this section with God's denial of certain east bank territories to Israel, having granted them to related nations, and the allocation of others to the tribes of Reuben, Gad, and half of Menasseh in return for their promise to participate in the conquest of the west bank.

In sum, the preamble sets forth the basic principles of the constitution, themselves paradigmatic of the covenantal polity:

1. That God is Israel's sovereign.
2. That Israel is to possess its promised land but no more than its promised land.

3.   That the Israelite polity is to be federal.
4.   That the Israelite polity is to be committed to equal justice.
The constitution that follows is organized around these four principles in that order.

Chapters 4 through 11:7 deal with the commandments to love, fear, worship, and hearken to God. Chapters 11:8 through 16:17 deal with the land and the commandments, statutes, and ordinances related to it. Chapters 16:18 through 21 deal with the system of government and domains of authority in the *edah*. Chapters 22 through 26:15 deal with the doing of justice. While there are some verses in these chapters that seem out of place, at this point in our analysis we cannot conclude whether they are indeed out of place or whether they require closer reading to understand why they are placed where they are.

The second section of the constitution, the restatement of the statutes (*hukim*) and ordinances (*mishpatim*), begins at the beginning of chapter 4. The traditional formula calling upon Israel to hearken (*shema Yisrael*) unto those statutes and ordinances is used. The constitution is presented as necessary to sustain the very life of the Israelites and their claim to the land that God has given them. The statutes and ordinances are presented as complete and permanent and the constitution itself commands the Israelites not to add or diminish them (4:2) since they are God's commandments (*mitzvot*). However, this provision is modified later by another allowing, even commanding, interpretation by the judges and authorities of each generation (17:10–11). There is an emphasis on teaching (verses 1 and 5) as an essential element of the constitutional system, in essence that a constitution is not merely a written document but something that is taught to the entire people. The statutes and ordinances are introduced as being those of a great nation and a wise and understanding people, that will be recognized as such by the other peoples of the world (4:6–8).

In chapter 4, Moses reminds them of the Sinai Covenant (consistently referring to Sinai by its other name, Horeb) with a full description of the theophany that took place there (v. 10ff.). He presents his description in the context of praise for the genius of the Israelite constitution and appropriate warnings with regard to the Israelite propensity to violate it. Here Moses emphasizes that God declared His covenant to them, commanded them, while at the same time demanding that he (Moses) "teach you (the Israelites) these statutes and ordinances." There is no discussion here of the elaborate negotiations and consent procedures described in the original description of the Sinai Covenant in Exodus.

This is the second great constitutional climax in the Torah, repeating as it does the Ten Commandments and, following them, the first paragraph of Sh'ma Yisrael. Let us recall that the commandments are referred to as *dibrot* (statements) and the book as a whole as *Devarim*. It is through *dibrot* that we reach *devarim*.

The Israelites are commanded to teach this constitution to their children. At this point Moses describes once again the covenant at Horeb/ Sinai, the first commandment of which is to reject all idolatry. This is presented as a teaching for all generations. It is also presented as one that will be violated, leading to exile from the land, a further punishment, followed by repentance and ultimate redemption. Then, as if to make a point about God's justice, Moses tends to a prosaic but vital detail of governing. He sets aside three cities of refuge east of the Jordan (4:41–43).

He then returns to the principal business at hand and restates the Ten Commandments. In describing the process of covenanting at Horeb/Sinai and explaining why it was the way it was, he summarizes the message in what Jews now use as the first paragraph of their most important confession of faith, the Sh'ma Yisrael (6:4–9)—literally, "Hearken Israel." The portion concludes by reiterating that the Israelites are an *am segula* (specially set aside, not chosen, people) who must know that their God is a faithful God, who maintains His covenant and its *hesed* (dynamic covenant love) for those who reciprocate by loving Him and observing His commandments unto the thousandth generation.[15]

Chapters 6–11 deal essentially with remaining faithful to God, especially after settling in the land, where the temptations will be great to worship other gods and thereby violate God's commandments. Moses goes into great detail with regard to the temptations and what would be considered the violations. The conclusion to this section, verses 10:21 through 11:7, recount how God manifested his power in Egypt in the course of the Exodus and throughout the forty years in the desert in a final reiteration of how Israel witnessed God's power to reinforce the previous statutes and ordinances.

The second section, beginning with chapter 11:8, deals with the land. It begins with a discussion of God's promise of the land to Israel. It describes the character and quality of the land, emphasizes the conditional element of the promise, and specifies the extent of the land promised. What follows thereon are the constitutional laws that are particularly related to the land including the commandment to establish a single place of sacrifice (chap. 12), the commandment to reject local land-related idolatrous customs (13:1–14:21), the commandment to tithe (14:22–29), the laws of the sabbatical year (15:1–18), and the observance of the pilgrimage festivals (16:1–17). Chapter 14 also sets forth the dietary laws, combining them with the laws of tithing to insure that the entire population is not only kosher but is fed.

The third section deals with government and domains of authority. It begins (16:18–17:13) with the establishment of civil government whose principal function is adjudication. The constitution specifies the basic rules of adjudication, its goal to achieve justice, the rules of judicial procedure, the rules of evidence, rules for capital punishment, the establishment of an appellate system, and provisions for interpreting the Torah in each generation.

The text then turns to the three domains (*ketarim*) into which the Torah divides authority. The Israelite polity was one of separated but shared powers. It was so built that power never could be concentrated in a single human authority. While the terminology of the *ketarim* is post-biblical, the division was present from the days of the desert. It is the basis of the discussion of governance in Deuteronomy, where it is taken for granted. Each of these *ketarim* is independent of the others, drawing its authority directly from Divine mandate, though both in theory and in practice the bearers of each *keter* must work with the others in order to govern the *edah*. The constitutional laws applicable to each of the domains are here presented with no comment, taking the division for granted.

Malkhut, the domain of civil rule, is the first to be discussed. Chapter 16 deals with judges and officers, the offices already in existence. In chapter 17 the discussion turns to the possibility of introducing a king into Israel. Chapter 17:14–20 specifies that a king can only be introduced by popular demand and indeed somewhat tainted demand at that since it would be a popular demand to be "like all the nations that are around Me" (v. 14). That is always considered a form of backsliding in the Bible. Nevertheless, permission is given to appoint a king, but that he must be chosen by God (v. 15) and he must be an Israelite, never a foreigner (v. 15).

This is followed by a list of restrictions, devoted principally to limiting the king's ability to accumulate wealth or to take many wives, which has a dual meaning, being both anti-hedonistic and anti-foreign alliances. As the Bible recounts subsequently and as we know from other sources, royal marriages were frequently part of the conclusion of alliances. The king is commanded to write out a copy of "this Mishneh Torah," presumably the whole Book of Deuteronomy, apparently in the presence of the priests and Levites, so that he will have no excuse for not knowing the law. The character of Israelite constitutionalism is no better illustrated than here:

> It shall be when he sitteth on the throne of his kingdom that he shall write a copy of this law in a book, out of that which is before the priests and the Levites. And it shall be with him and he shall read therein all the days of his life that he may learn to fear the Lord his God, to keep all the words of His Constitution and statutes to do them. That his heart be not lifted up above his brethren, that he not turn aside from the commandments to the right or to the left, so that he may prolong his days in the kingdom, he and his children, in the midst of Israel. (18–20)

It is clearly assumed that the tribal structure described earlier will continue to exist even if there is a king. Indeed, the only change made in it is that referred to in chapter 16 assigning judges and officers to territorial settlements rather than households and nomadic tribes.

The covenant with David and his house is not the first covenant of the *keter malkhut*. At the very least, the *mishpat hamelekh* in Deuteronomy is the constitutional law of that *keter*, though, in fact, the foundation goes back earlier to the patriarchs. What is important about *mishpat hamelekh* is that the covenant of *keter malkhut* is not made with the king but is made with the people, who are empowered to appoint a king if they so choose. Indeed, one can contrast the three covenants behind the three *ketarim*: the covenant for *keter torah* is made with the people through the mediation of the prophet Moses; the covenant with the priests is made with Aaron and his family and embraces the tribe of Levi in a subsidiary fashion; while the *keter malkhut* is made with the people without a king or equivalent leader being present. Only in a later epoch is an actual king introduced.

The issue of kingship is a controversial one in the Jewish political tradition. Does Deuteronomy mandate the appointment of a king once the *edah* is settled in its land or is it a discretionary matter? Biblical commentators and political thinkers from the Talmud to the present have divided on the issue. The text itself is ambiguous and can be read either way.

Aside from the ambiguous statement about placing a king at the head of the *keter malkhut,* the rest of the passage concerns itself with the constitutional restrictions to be imposed upon any such office should it be established. Later commentators juxtaposed this passage with 1 Samuel 8 where the Prophet Samuel warns the people of the arbitrary powers that a king is likely to take unto himself, most of which stand in violation of the Deuteronomic constitution. Some later commentators used 1 Samuel 8 as the basis for determining the scope of the king's powers, although the biblical text is plain. It is a warning against usurpations. Certainly it does not contradict the constitutional strictures of Deuteronomy 17.

From the positioning of the verses it is clear that *shofetim* (judges, in the sense of magistrates) and *shoterim* (civil officers) are more important than kings, or at least more basic. Indeed, when the sages of the Talmud divided the Torah into weekly portions they started the portions relating to the institutions of governance with the verse about *shofetim* and *shoterim.* Hence the portion is named "*Shofetim.*" Of course, *shofetim* and *shoterim*, while basic to any regime, represent the classic covenantal regime of the desert. Kingship, even federal kingship, is a step away from that classic regime to what became a contrasting classic model, but was not the original one.

Deuteronomy turns to the *keter kehunah* in chapter 18 where in verses 1-8 the status, place, and perquisites of priests and Levites once Israel is settled in its land are adapted to the new situation and reaffirmed. Here, too, the only matters dealt with are modifications of the basic constitutional laws of the first four books.

Verses 9-22 of chapter 18 deal with the *keter torah,* specifically prophets and prophecy. In a way this is a new institution and is presented as such, that God will raise up prophets to whom Israel should hearken, that prophets were introduced in place of requiring the people to meet God face to face, since the people had rejected that possibility at Horeb/Sinai out of discomfort with that confrontation. Punishment for false prophecy is indicated, as is a way to distinguish between true and false prophecy.

Chapters 19-26 contain the body of the constitutional laws dealing with civil and criminal matters, family relations, warfare, citizenship, and the like. This section begins by providing what is in effect a "bill of rights" for those accused of crimes (chap. 19 plus selections of chaps. 21 and 24) with appropriate judicial procedures and the laws of warfare (chap. 20) and family (25:5–10).

This "bill of rights" offers extensive protections for individuals, aliens as well as Israelites. Because of it and similar passages, the Bible has been properly celebrated as the founding cornerstone of the Western edifice of rights. At the same time it is an ancient rather than modern set of protections directed essentially to the people as a whole as a way to make them holy, rather than to individuals as a way to make them free. In other words, God commands the Israelites as a body and individually to behave with justice and fairness because that is the way for them to be holy, not because these are abstract individual or human rights. True, it is implicit that every human is entitled to such treatment because he or she is created in the image of God (Gen. 1:26–27). Nevertheless, the constitutional emphasis is on the holiness of the people obliged to conduct themselves in this manner. Indeed, for the Torah, rights are founded in the obligations that people have assumed through covenant. Clearly, for a holy people those obligations emphasize a certain standard of behavior toward other humans created in God's image.

The discussion of how the *edah* is to make war (20:1–9) is an excellent example of the formal procedures required by the constitution if the Jewish polity is to function in a constitutional manner. When the people assemble to go out to war, the priest, apparently the high priest, is to speak to them to remind them that God is with the people and will fight for them. Then, the civil officers (*shoterim*) are to speak to the members of the mobilized force or militia to formally proclaim the legitimate reasons for leaving the ranks specified in the constitution. Those who have just completed building a new house, planting a new vineyard, or taking a new wife and who have not yet had the opportunity of enjoying the fruits of their acts are excused from service. Also excused are the fearful and fainthearted. Each individual must declare himself to take advantage of these exemptions. Thus, the wise exemption of those distracted or psychologically unfit for a military campaign is modified by the necessity for each man seeking exemption to do so publicly before his fellows.

This is done before civil officers. Only after they have been offered the possibility to be exempted from service is the mobilized force turned over to army commanders who will then be appointed to command. In other words, most of the preparations are undertaken by civil authorities. Even where prophet and priests are not involved, civil officers are. The army is first prepared for battle psychologically before the army commanders are given authority, probably on the assumption that once the hierarchy of army command is established, whatever the rights people have are far more difficult to exercise in hierarchical systems.

The final section deals with the doing of justice, including commandments for neighborliness (*re'ut*), that is to say, how to show *hesed* (loving covenant obligation, the dynamic dimension of *brit*) to one's *re'im* or neighbors and to other living creatures, laws of marriage, personal hygiene, immoral sexual practices, commerce, support for the poor and needy. In two places the laws of *hesed* are extended to animals.

Provisions are made for the local administration of justice under the new territorial organization (25:1–5). While the constitution of Israel is comprehensive, the role of government is limited and, after the Israelites have settled in their land, primarily local. Thus, the local arena becomes the most important arena of governance and primarily self-government. Local elders, constituting a local council (*shaarei ha-ir*), handle day-to-day matters, primarily of adjudication, subordinate to the general assembly of the local citizenry (*ha-ir*). Here, *Devarim* gives this change due note.

With the body of the constitution before the people, the document concludes with the formal renewal of the covenant between God and Israel. The act begins with the presentation before the people by representatives of all three domains—Moses, the elders, and the priests and the Levites—of the curses and blessings associated with violating the constitutional covenant (curses) or keeping it (blessings) (26:16–28:68). Moses and the elders instruct the people to keep the commandments and to write the whole Torah on a public monument after entering the land so that it will be visibly accessible to all Israel. Then, Moses, the priests, and the Levites consecrate the people to God and require them to hearken to the commandments.

All this is in preparation for the covenant renewal ceremony on the plains of Moab (28:69–30:20). Covenant renewal takes place before the assembly of the entire *edah*—men, women, and children—and representatives of all three *ketarim*. The covenant reestablishes the people, affirms God as a partner to it, and requires the people to promise to be faithful partners on their part. The punishments for covenant violations, including exile from the land, are specified.

The conclusion of the covenant emphasizes that the constitution was openly given to the Israelites for them to live by. It is the opposite of those secret things that belong to God (29:28). At the conclusion of the covenant ceremony there is a final word reemphasizing that the constitution is close and not distant, that the people are given a choice between good and evil, and that heaven and earth have witnessed the covenant, to seal the matter.

In an appropriate conclusion for a covenant, chapter 27 provides for the writing down of the entire constitutional corpus once the Israelites are in their land and for a ceremony evoking curses on any violators of its provisions. The blessings and curses receive greater elaboration in chapter 28, which concludes (v. 69): "These are the words of the Covenant which the Lord commanded Moses to make with the Israelites in the land of Moab beside the Covenant he made with them at Horeb." Moses then makes a summation of the covenant with its promises and obligations (chaps. 29–31), concluding with the formal designation of Joshua as his successor, the writing of the constitution and its placement in the Ark of the Covenant, and the provision for a public ceremony to renew the covenant every seven years at the end of the sabbatical year during Succot (the Feast of Tabernacles):

> And Moses commanded them saying: "At the end of every seven years, in the set time of the year of release, the feast of tabernacles, when all of Israel is come to appear before the Lord thy God in the place which He shall choose, thou shalt read this law before all Israel in their hearing. Assemble the people, the men and the women and the little ones, and thy stranger that is within thy gates, that they may hear, and that they may learn, and fear the Lord your God, and observe to do all the words of this law; and that their children, who have not known, may hear, and learn to fear the Lord your God, as long as ye live in the land whither ye go over the Jordan to possess it." (31:10–13)

What follows in chapters 31 through 34 is in the way of an epilogue. Moses transfers power to Joshua quickly; he writes out the Torah and delivers it to priests, Levites, and elders; he establishes a covenant renewal ceremony to take place every seven years; God ratifies all this and the written Torah is placed in the Ark of the Covenant alongside of the commandments. Moses then presents his elaborate poem known as the Song of Moses, along with a final exhortation to the people to keep the commandments and to be faithful to their constitution (chap. 32). In chapter 33 he blesses the Bnei Israel before his death, collectively and tribe by tribe. In chapter 34 his death is described, as is Joshua's assumption of power. The book and the whole Pentateuch is closed with an evaluation of Moses's greatness and uniqueness as a prophet.

As he approaches death, God gives Moses a glimpse of the future retrogression of Israel and Moses delivers to them an eloquent poetic warning followed by his blessing, tribe by tribe, in a federal spirit, after which he goes up to Mount Nebo, dies, and is buried "where no man knoweth his sepulchre." In other words, the founder, prophet, statesman remains to guide his people only through the covenant he has obtained from God and the constitution he has written in accordance with it.

Conclusion

In the last analysis, the Pentateuch constitutes one comprehensive constitutional document in three parts. Genesis, the first book, establishes the setting for the emergence of Israel and its constitution with two sets of basic covenants with Abraham and the other patriarchs establishing Israel as a people. Exodus, Leviticus, and Numbers constitute the second part based on the exodus from Egypt and the covenant at Sinai, and its auxiliary additions, establishing *Adat Bnai Israel*. The third part, Deuteronomy, is a summarization and restatement of the second under the changed conditions of permanent settlement in the land of Israel. These three sections are profoundly the same and profoundly different. Together they present the foundations of the two classic regimes of the Jewish polity. The first is the classic *Adat Bnei Yisrael* (Assembly of the Children of Israel) instituted in the desert, a democratic federal republic directly governed by God through his *eved adonai* (the Lord's minister or prime minister). The second is the federal monarchy with a human king, albeit one chosen by God. In the first, sacrifices can, at least in principle, be performed in the tribes as well as before the common tabernacle. In the latter they are to be centralized at a common holy place.

On the other hand, these differences may not be as great as they seem at first blush. Under the constitution of the classic *edah,* was not God king? Was not the introduction of human kingship merely a part of the transfer of God's direct rule to human agency, not only to kings but also to elders, priests, and prophets? Was not there always a central place of sacrifice and worship, albeit a portable one in the days of the desert, so that the real change in Deuteronomy is the establishment of a fixed site now that Israel is in its own land, with certain precautions against idolatry in a land where every tree and rock could influence the superstitious? Moreover, there is no precise commandment to build the Temple, only to establish a central shrine.

Still, the actual consequences of the establishment of kingship and Temple went far beyond the original intent of the constitution to transform the "primitive" tribal democracy of ancient Israel into something else again. Subsequent generations of Jews have struggled with the problem of synthesizing various manifestations of these two regimes. The results have been at times more hierarchical and at others more egalitarian, at times more oligarchic and at others more democratic, at times more theocentric (in the original sense) and at others more civil. In any case, they have always been covenantal.

Appendix I: The Biblical Covenantal Chain

A. The Sequence of Covenants

0. Implicit Covenant with Adam (Gen. 2)
1. Covenant with Noah (Gen. 6, 9; establishes basic relationship between God and man)
2. Covenants with Abraham (Gen. 15, 17; establish new family with promised kith in promised land)
2a. Abrahamic Covenant Renewed with Jacob (Gen. 28; assures continuity of Abraham's line even though Jacob misunderstands it to be a contract)
2b. Abrahamic Covenant Renewed with Israelites in Egypt (Exod. 6; passes mantle of leadership to Moses and prepares for exodus from Egypt)
3. Covenant with Israelites at Sinai (Exod. 19; establishes permanent relationship between God and Israel)
3a. Sinai Covenant Completed After Presentation of Book of the Covenant (Exod. 24; establishes basic constitution of Israel)
3b. Sinai Covenant Reiterated at Writing of Second Set of Tablets (Exod. 34; established *keter Torah* through Moses)
3c. Sinai Covenant Reiterated at End of Second Constitutional Statement (Lev. 26; establishes validity of the added constitutional details)
3d. Covenant of Salt with Aaron and His House (Num. 18; establishes *keter kehunah* through Aaron)
3e. Covenant in Plains of Moab (Deut. 28:69–30:20; restatement of Torah-as-constitution with covenant included)

3f. Fulfillment of Covenant Terms at Shechem (Josh. 8; torah made operative constitution of Eretz Israel)

3g. Joshua's Covenant with God and Israel (Josh. 24; first tripartite covenant initiated by human design)

4. Establishment of the Federal Magistery or Monarchy (1 Sam. 8-12; describes process of reconstitution)

4a. Covenants with David (1 Sam. 16:1-13, 2 Sam. 2:1-4; 3; 5:1-3; 1 Chron. 11:1-3; network of intertribal covenants with minimum Divine intervention)

4b. David and the people acknowledge and reaffirm the covenant of the forefathers and God, in turn, establishes the Davidic dynasty (1 Chron. 16 and 17)

4c. Solomon and the Elders of Israel Incorporate the Temple into the Sinai covenant (1 Kings 8-19; 2 Chron. 5-7)

4d. Asa and the people renew the Sinai covenant (2 Chron. 15)

4e. Jehoiada the Priest restores the legitimate monarchy (2 Kings 11, 2 Chron. 23)

4f. Hezekiah renews the covenant with God in the name of all Israel through religious revival (2 Chron. 29; action in response to the fall of the northern kingdom)

4g. Josiah renews the covenant and restores the Book of the Covenant (2 Kings 22-23:29; 2 Chron. 34-35:19)

5. Ezra's covenant against foreign wives (Ezra 10)

5a. Reacceptance of Torah as constitution (Neh. 8-10)

B. Classification of the Covenants

	Character	Parties	Initiated by	How Concluded	Binds
1,1a	Personal	God and Ancestor	God	Privately	All Humanity
2,2a, 2b	Personal	God and Forefather	God	Privately	All Jews
3,3a, 3b,3c, 3e	Collective	God and Israel	God	Publicly	All Jews
3d	Collective	God and Aaronides	God	Privately	All descendants of Aaron and Jews
3f,3g	Collective	Israel and God	Joshua	Publicly	All Jews

	Character	Parties	Initiated by	How Concluded	Binds
4	Collective	Tribes of Israel	Israel	Publicly	All Israel
4a	Personal and Collective	Tribes of Israel, King and God	God and David, David and Tribes of Israel	Privately and Publicly	David and Israel
4b, 4c,4d 4f,4g	Collective	Israel, Rulers and God	King	Publicly	King and Israel
4e	Collective	God, King, and People	Priest	Publicly	King and Israel
5,5a	Collective	Israel and God	The People	Publicly	All Jews

Appendix II: Schematic of the Deuteronomic Constitution

Introduction	1:1-5	Presenter, time, place, and context.
Preamble	1:6-3-29	God recounts the institutional, spatial, and historical basis.
	1:6-8	Time to take possession of the promised land. List of promised areas west of the Jordan River. Reiteration of historic promise.
	1:9-18	Description of the establishment of the institutions of federal governance. Charge to judges to provide equal justice.
	1:19-46	Recounting of Israel's sin when spying out the land in the initial attempt to enter it, with due attention to federal niceties.
	2:1-23	Specification of the allocation of central and southern transjordan to the descendants of Esau and Lot.
	2:23-3:2	Description of the conquest of Gilead and Bashan (the Golan) and God's grant of those territories (from the valley of Horon to Mt. Hermon) to the tribes of Reuben, Gad, and half of Manasseh.
	3:21-29	Moses to die outside of the promised land; Joshua reconfirmed as his successor.

The Body of the Constitution: "Statutes and Ordinances" 4:1–26:15

God and Fundamental	4:1-40	Call to Israel to hearken to the statutes and ordinances as God has commanded them.

Principles

The statutes and ordinances are neither to be increased nor diminished (v. 2). Life comes to those who cleave to the Lord (vv. 3-4).

They are to be observed in Eretz Israel (v. 5).

This is a wise and understanding constitution that will win the admiration of all peoples (vv. 6-8).

It was commanded to the assembled people through the theophany and covenant at Horeb (Sinai) with the ten commandments (vv. 9-14).

No corporeality of God, hence no images to devote worship (vv. 15-24).

Punishments for violation of this prohibition: conquest and exile (vv. 25-28).

Possibility of repentance and promise of restoration—God's covenant and promise eternal (vv. 29-31).

The uniqueness of the theophany and God's choosing of Israel (vv. 32-39).

God's oneness, power, and favor by virtue of Israel's forefathers and the reciprocal necessity for Israel to keep His statutes and commandments (vv. 35-40).

4:41-43   Moses sets aside three cities of refuge east of the Jordan to provide protection of persons committing manslaughter from lynching or a blood feud.

4:44-49   Summary.

5:1-30   Restatement of the Ten Commandments (comp. Exod. 20:1-14).

5:1   Call to Israel to hearken.

5:2-5   Recalling Horeb/Sinai covenant.

5:6-18   Ten Commandments.

God identifies himself (v. 6).

Monotheism and prohibition of images (vv. 7-10).

Prohibition of taking the name of the Lord in vain (v. 11).

Command to observe the Sabbath (vv. 12-15).

Command to honor parents (v. 16).

Prohibition of murder (v. 17).

Prohibition of adultery (v. 17).

Prohibition of theft (v. 17).

Prohibition of false witness (v. 17).

Prohibition of coveting (v. 18).

5:19-20   Reference to assembly of people and their leaders by tribes at Sinai.

5:21-30   Explanation of why other commandments and teachings come through Moses because people feared direct contact with God.

6:1–25	Restatement of Sh'ma Yisrael (Israel's confession of faith): fearing God and teaching His commandments.
	Preamble: These statutes and ordinances are for Israel to do in the land they are to possess (v. 1).
	Subject: fearing the Lord and keeping His commandments (v. 2).
	Reward: long life and fertility in the land (v. 3).
	The confession—1st part (vv. 4–9).
	Loving God; teaching Torah to descendants; binding signs of loyalty to God.
6:10–25	Elaboration of vv. 4–9.
7:1–26	Commandments to eliminate the Canaanites and their idolatry upon conquering the land.
	Destruction of the seven Canaanite nations commanded (vv. 1–2).
	Prohibition of covenants or marriages with them (vv. 2–4).
	Destruction of all signs of idolatry commanded (v. 5).
	Israel's chosenness reaffirmed and explained (vv. 6–8).
	The generational basis of God's rewards and punishments (vv. 9–10).
	Israel's responsibility to keep the covenant (v. 11).
	Its reward for doing so (vv. 12–16).
	God will help (vv. 17–24).
	Summary: Israel's responsibility to eliminate all idolatrous signs and images (vv. 25–26).
8:1–20	All sustenance comes from God and will be provided only if His covenant is kept.
	The fertility and principal products of the land listed (important for the observance of other commandments) and the commandment to bless God for them (vv. 7–10).
	Remember that prosperity comes from God, not from human power (vv. 11–18).
	God's punishment if He is forsaken (v. 19).
9:1–29	Transfer of land to Israelites is because of wickedness of Canaanites, despite Israelite stiff-neckedness (vv. 1–6).
	Recounting examples of Israelite stiff-neckedness, esp. the Golden Calf (the other side of the Horeb/ Sinai theophany) (vv. 7–29).

Moses's successful interventions to save his people (vv. 18-20, 25-29).

10:1-11   The making of the two stone tablets and the ark to hold them, and the organization of their care by priests and Levites.

10:12-20   The fundamental principles of the constitution.

Loving the Lord and walking in His ways (vv. 12, 20).

Keeping His commandments (v. 13).

Recognizing that heaven and earth belong to the Lord (v. 14).

The chosenness of Israel (v. 15).

Israel should cease to be stiff-necked (v. 16).

God does equal justice, nor can he be bribed (v. 17).

God's justice includes widows, orphans, and strangers (aliens); therefore, yours should as well (vv. 18-19).

10:21-11:7 Conclusion to this section recounting how God manifested His power in Egypt, the Exodus, and the desert.

The Land   11:8-25   On the promise of the land.

The promise (vv. 8-9).

The character and quality of the land (vv. 10-12).

The conditional element in the promise (including the second paragraph of the Sh'ma (vv. 13-22).

The extent of the land promised (vv. 23-25).

11:26-32   The blessing and the curse set before the Israelites.

12:1-32   Commandment to establish a single place of sacrifice.

Local places of sacrifice forbidden (vv. 4, 13-14).

Central site to be chosen from tribal territories (v. 5).

Forms of sacrifice to be regulated (vv. 6-11).

Emphasis on change from system used in desert (vv. 8-11).

Separation of sacrifices and slaughtering for food (vv. 15-18, 20-28).

Exhortation to protect Levites who are disempowered (because they have no land and are not priests) (v.19).

Prohibition of infant sacrifice and other pagan abominations (vv. 29-32).

	13:1-19	Rejection of enticements to serve false gods and punishment for enticers: by false prophets (vv. 2-6); by relatives and friends (vv. 7-12); by demagogues or popular movements (vv. 13-19).
	14:1-2	Mutilation for purposes of mourning forbidden.
	14:3-21	Laws of kashrut (permitted and prohibited foods).
	14:22-29	Commandment to tithe.
		Tithe to be eaten at central place of sacrifice (vv. 23-26).
		Provision for continued support of Levites-in-residence (vv. 27-29).
		Tithe to be used for the needy (v. 29).
	15:1-18	Laws of the sabbatical year.
		Release of debts (vv. 2-6).
		Commandment to assist needy every year (vv. 7-11).
		Release of Hebrew slaves (vv. 12-18).
	15:19-23	Sanctification of the first-born to God.
	16:1-17	Commandments to observe the pilgrimage festivals.
		Pesach (vv. 1-8), including centralization of pascal sacrifice.
		Shavuoth (vv. 9-12).
		Sukkoth (vv. 13-15).
		Summary: requirement for pilgrimage thrice yearly (vv. 16-17).
Government	16:18-20	Organization of national judiciary.
and Domains	16:21-	Rules of judicial procedure.
of Authority	17:13	Prohibition of ritual abominations in worship (vv. 16:21-17:1).
		Punishment for idolatry (16:2-7).
		Rules of evidence (vv. 4-6).
		Rules of capital punishment (v. 7).
		Appeals (vv. 8-13).
Interpretation		Priests and Levites as appellate court (vv. 9-13).
of Constitution		Provision for constitutional interpretation in each generation (vv. 10-11).
Malkhut	17:14-20	Possible introduction of kingship.
		How introduced (v. 14).
		How chosen (v. 15).
		Must be an Israelite (v. 15).
		Restrictions on king (vv. 16-17).
		King must write out and keep with him a copy of this Torah (vv. 18-20).
Kehunah	18:1-8	Status and place of priests and Levites.
		Neither have territorial allocations (vv. 1-2).

		Both shall be supported by offerings to the Lord (vv. 1–8).
		Permanent grant of office to priests (v. 5).
		Responsibilities and rights of Levites (vv. 6–8).
Torah	18:9–22	On prophets and prophecy.
		Repetition of prohibitions on idolatrous behavior with addition of prohibition against sorcery and the like (vv. 9–14).
		God will raise up prophets to whom Israel should hearken (vv. 15–22).
		Prophets came in place of meeting God face-to-face which the people rejected at Sinai/Horeb (vv. 15–17).
		Punishment for false prophecy (v. 20).
		Distinguishing true and false prophecy (vv. 21–22).
Criminal Procedure and Bill of Rights (a) Laws of manslaughter and murder	19:1–13	Communal need to establish cities of refuge to solve the problems of the blood feud: three cities to serve three regions: (vv. 1–3).
		Law of manslaughter (vv. 4–10).
		Law of murder (vv. 11–13)
Criminal Procedure and Bill of Rights (b) Judicial procedures	19:14–21	Prohibition on removing boundary markers (v. 14).
		Requirement of at least two witnesses in capital crimes (v. 15).
		Punishment for false witness (vv. 16–20).
		Equal justice as measure for measure (v. 21).
	21:1–9,22 24:7,16	Determining responsibility for killing.
		Between local jurisdictions (21:1–9).
		Requirement to bury those executed on the same day (21:22).
		Laws against kidnapping (24:7).
		Every person punished only for his own crimes (24:16).
	20:1–19	Laws of warfare.
		Procedures for mobilization (vv. 1–9).
		Rules for conduct of warfare (vv. 10–19).
	21:10–22 25:5–10	Family law.
		Captured women (21:10–14).
		Inheritance in polygamous situations (24:15–17).
		Rebellious sons (21:18–21).
Covenant Obligations Beyond the Letter of the Law	22:1–4,8	Commandment to neighborliness.
		Restoration of lost property (22:1–3).
		Rendering assistance (22:4).
		Building safety requirements (22:8).

	23:20-21, 25-26	Prohibition of lending at interest to Israelites; permission to do so with foreigners (23:20-21). Laws regarding enjoying neighbor's farm produce (23:25-26).
	22:5-11	Maintenance of distinctions. Men and women commanded to dress differently (v. 5). Mixed sowing prohibited (v. 9). Mixed plowing prohibited (v. 10). Mixed weaving prohibited (v. 11).
	22:6-7	Taking bird and eggs forbidden.
	22:13-23	Marriage laws.
	23:1	Laws regarding virginity and marriage (22:13-24).
	24:1-5	Prohibition of relations between stepmother and stepson (23:1). Divorce laws (24:1-4). Laws regarding new marriages (24:5).
	23:2-9	Naturalization laws. Prohibitions on products of sexual violations being members of the polity (vv. 2-7). Possibility for third-generation Edomites and Egyptians to join polity (vv. 8-9).
	23:10-15 24:8-9	Personal hygiene laws. Disposal of human waste (23:10-15). Leprosy (24:8-9).
	23:16-17	Prohibition on returning fugitive slaves.
	23:18-19	Prohibition of harlotry and sodomy.
	23:22-24	Vows to the Lord to be paid.
	24:6,10-13 17-18	Laws of pledges: prohibition of taking necessities for collateral.
	24:14-15	Requirement of prompt payment of wages.
	24:19-22	Leftovers from harvest to be left for needy.
Local Government	25:1-3	Appointment of judges and officers in every township (v. 18). Basic rules for adjudication (v. 19). Goal of adjudication: justice (v. 20). Rules of corporal punishment.
	25:4	Kindness to animals: not to muzzle oxen when treading grain.
	25:5-10	Local responsibility for perpetration of family lines.
	25:11-12	Sexual modesty and domestic violence.
	25:13-16	Honest weights and measures.
Marking God's Commandments	25:17-19	Amalekites to be utterly destroyed.
	26:1-15	Worship services to be instituted upon settlement in the land. Offering of first fruits (vv. 1-11).

		On completion of tithing (vv. 12-15).
Covenant	26:16-	Enactment and promulgation of constitution.
Curses and	30:20	Conclusion of statutes and ordinances.
Blessings	26:16- 28:68	Moses and elders of Israel command people to keep commandments (27:1).
		Commandment to write the whole Torah as a public monument at Mt. Ebal (27:2-8).
		Moses, priests and Levites consecrate people to God and require them to hearken to commandments (27:9-10).
		Ceremony of curses for violating commandments (27:11-26).
		Blessings for observing them (28:1-14).
		More curses (28:15-68).
Covenant	28:69-	Moses summarizes God's good works for Israel (29:1-8).
Renewal on	30:20	
Plains of		Assembly of entire *edah* for covenanting in Moab (29:9-10).
Moab		
		Covenant established people (29:11-12).
		God a partner to the covenant (29:13-14).
		People called on to promise (29:15-17).
		God will not forgive those who reject Him (29:18-19).
		Punishments for covenant violations (29:20-22).
		Explanation of why the punishments (29:23-27).
		Final punishment is exile from land (29:27).
	29:28	This constitution openly given to Israelites for them to live by: the opposite of the secret things that belong to God.
	30:1-10	Promises of repentance and restoration.
		The greatness that God will do for Israel (30:3-10).
Final Word	30:11-20	Constitution is close, not distant (vv.11-14).
		People are given choice between good and evil (vv. 15-18).
		Heaven and earth called upon to witness covenant (vv. 19-20).
Epilogue	31:1-29	Moses transfers power to Joshua.
		People reassured that God will be with Joshua (vv. 3-6).
		Public transfer made (vv. 7-8).
		Moses writes out Torah and delivers it to priests, Levites and elders (v. 9).
		Establishment of covenant renewal ceremony every seven years (vv. 10-13).
		God appears to ratify all of the above (vv. 14-23).

Moses has newly written Torah placed in the ark of the covenant alongside the tablets (vv. 24-29).

32:1-43   The Song of Moses.

32:44-47   A final exhortation to the people to place the commandments in their hearts and keep the constitution.

32:48-52   God instructs Moses to go up Mt. Nebo to die because of his transgressions.

33:1-29   Moses blesses the Bnei Yisrael before his death, collectively and tribe by tribe.

34   Moses' death; Joshua assumes power; Moses evaluated.

Notes

1. On the authorship of Deuteronomy, see Richard J. Clifford, *Deuteronomy; with an Excursus on Covenant and Law* (Wilmington, DE: M. Glazier, 1982) and G. von Rad, *Studies in Deuteronomy* (English translation) (London: SCM Press, 1967).

   For the dating of Deuteronomy, see G. R. Berry, "Date of Deuteronomy," *Journal of Biblical Literature and Exegesis* 59 (1940): 133-39 and George Dahl, "The Currently Accepted Date of Deuteronomy," *Journal of Biblical Literature* 47 (1928): 358-79.

2. On the Constitution of Athens, see Ernest Barker, *Greek Political Theory: Plato and His Predecessors* (New York: Barnes and Noble, 1960); Aristotle, *The Athenian Constitution and the Eudemian Ethics,* trans. Harris Rackam (Cambridge, MA: Harvard University Press, 1981).

3. On the government of biblical Israel, see Daniel J. Elazar and Stuart A. Cohen, *The Jewish Polity: Jewish Political Organization from Biblical Times to the Present* (Bloomington: Indiana University Press, 1985), especially Epoch 3; and Daniel J. Elazar, "The Polity of Biblical Israel," in *Authority, Power and Leadership in the Jewish Polity: Cases and Issues,* ed. Daniel J. Elazar (Lanham, MD: Jerusalem Center for Public Affairs and University Press of America, 1990).

4. On ancient covenants, see Delbert Hillers, *Covenant: The History of a Biblical Idea* (Baltimore: John Hopkins Press, 1969); George Mendenhall, *Law and Covenant in Israel and in the Near East* (The Biblical Colloqium, 1955) and "Covenant Forms in Israelite Tradition," *Biblical Archeologist* 17 (1959): 50-76.

5. On *Mishpat HaMelukhah,* see Salo W. Baron, *A Social and Religious History of the Jews,* 2d ed., vol. 1 (Philadelphia: Jewish Publication Society, 1952), 63-101; Simon Federbush, *Mishpat HaMelukhah* (Jerusalem: Mossad HaRav Kook, 1973); *Encyclopedia Judaica,* vol. 12 (Jerusalem: Keter, 1971), 136-51. See also Daniel J. Elazar and Stuart A. Cohen, *The Jewish Polity,* part 1, epoch 4; George Mendenhall, "Ancient Oriental and Biblical Law," *The Biblical Archeologist* 17, no. 2 (1954): 26-46.

6. Cf. note 1 above.

7. On medieval discussions of the ideal Jewish polity, see Gerald Blidstein, *Political Concept in Maimonidean Halakhah* (Ramat Gan: Bar Ilan University Press, 1983) (Hebrew); Moses A. Maimonides, "Guide of the Perplexed," in *Medieval*

Political Philosophy, ed. Ralph Lerner and Muhsin Mahdi (Ithaca, NY: Cornell University Press, 1963); David Polish, *The Rabbinic Views on Kingship—A Study of Jewish Sovereignty* (New York: Ktav, 1989); Martin Sicker, *The Judaic State: A Study in Rabbinic Political Theory* (New York: Praeger, 1988); Leo Strauss and Joseph Cropsey, *History of Political Philosophy,* 2d ed. (Chicago: Rand McNally, 1963). See especially the chapters on Maimonides and Joseph Albo.

8. On modern and postmodern uses, see Moshe Hess, *Rome and Jerusalem: A Study in Jewish Nationalism,* trans. Meyer Waxman (New York: Bloch, 1943); Moses Mendelssohn, *Jerusalem* or *On Religious Power and Judaism,* trans. Allen Arkush (Hanover, NH: University Press of New England, 1983); Joseph Salvador, *Histoire des institutions de Moise et du peuple hebreu* (Paris: M. Levy, 1862); Mayer Saltzberger, *The Am ha-Aretz, the Ancient Hebrew Parliament, a Chapter in the Constitutional History of Ancient Israel* (Philadelphia: J. H. Greenstone, 1910); Baruch Spinoza, *Tractatus Theologico-Politicus* (Leiden: E. J. Brill, 1991).

9. Elazar and Cohen, *Jewish Polity,* epoch 9, pp. 137-45; Moshe Beer, *The Amoraim of Babylonia: Their Economic and Social Structure,* 2d ed. (Ramat Gan: Bar-Ilan University, 1982).

10. Menachem Elon, *Jewish Law: History, Sources, Principles, Vol. 1: Ha-Misphat ha-Ivri: Toldotav, Mekorotav, Ekronotav* (Jerusalem: Magnes Press, 1973); Elazar and Cohen, *Jewish Polity,* epoch 11, pp. 160-77.

11. Chaim Hershensohn, *Eleh Divrei HaBrit,* 3 vols. (Hoboken, NJ: 1918-1921) and *Malkhi BaKodesh,* 6 vols. (Hoboken, NJ: 1923-1928); R. Shaul Yisraeli, *Ha-Torah ve-Ha-Medinah* (New York: Rabbinic Council of Ha-Po'el Ha-Mizrachi, 1949, 1962).

12. This whole problem can be used as an aid in dating Deuteronomy and indeed the Pentateuch. The emphasis in the first four books on a polity and cult for the desert suggests a very early authorship for them or at least for the major portions of them. Most of the constitutional material within them becomes obsolete once Israel enters Canaan and must be reinterpreted by later generations to be relevant to, first, a settled people and then a nonpastoral one. The way in which these issues are put in Deuteronomy, on the other hand, also suggests a relatively early authorship for it. For example, the prescription for centralized worship refers to a place "out of thy tribes," which the Lord shall select. When the Temple was built, it was built in separate royal territory, Jerusalem, that had remained in the hands of the Jebusites after the original conquest and was only conquered by David as part of his rise to the kingship, and hence became his and never part of any tribal territory.

13. Cf. Daniel J. Elazar, "Dealing with Fundamental Regime Change: The Biblical Paradigm of the Transition from Tribal Federation to Federal Monarchy Under David," in the Marvin Fox festschrift entitled, *From Ancient Israel to Modern Judaism,* ed. Jacob Neusner et al. (Atlanta, GA: Scholars Press, 1989), 97-132.

14. For a discussion of whether or not kingship is mandatory, see David Polish, *The Rabbinic Views on Kingship—a Study of Jewish Sovereignty* (New York: Ktav, 1989).

15. The issue of "chosenness" is a major one in covenantal politics. Most peoples who see themselves as covenanted peoples believe that they have been "chosen" in some way. Thus, it is important to understand the original biblical understanding of what has come to be called "chosenness." The Bible presents God as constantly choosing and separating. The creation story is as much one of establishing distinctions as it is of the unity of creation. In other words, within that unity God

establishes firm distinctions, from the distinction between heaven and earth to that between humans and animals. Subsequently, God chooses Noah to perpetuate the human species and Abraham to generate a people that will be subject to the fullness of God's law. The Bible refers to that people, Bnai Israel, as his *am segula*, which means a people especially set aside, not chosen in the way that it is frequently used today. Clearly, to be set aside is to be chosen, but without the implications of being elevated. The Bible has other words for elevating. *Segula* suggests a special destiny rather than an elevated position. That is all that chosenness can mean for covenanted peoples, namely, that through the covenant they have accepted a special destiny.

Part III

The Classic Biblical Utopia

11

Joshua: God's Federal Republic

Deuteronomy completes the Five Books of Moses—the *Torah*—Israel's basic covenants and constitution. The second section of the Hebrew Bible—*Nevi'im,* the Prophets—is, along with the historical books of *Ketuvim*—the Writings—an account of Israel's effort to apply the Torah as constitution under different circumstances at different times. In a more narrowly political sense it chronicles and analyzes Israel's search for a workable political regime according to the spirit of the Torah. As such, it is a record of successes and failures, each of which features its own covenants and covenantal dynamics.

The Political Discussion in the Former Prophets

The Former Prophets include six books: Joshua, Judges, 1 Samuel, 2 Samuel, 1 Kings, and 2 Kings. A close reading suggests that among their other purposes each reflects and analyzes a particular form of regime as understood by the prophets, that is, the *keter-torah* of that time.

1. Joshua describes the classic polity envisaged in the Torah, headed by an *Eved Adonai* (God's prime minister), paralleled by a *Kohen Gadol* (high priest). The *Eved Adonai* is responsible for the civil rule of the *edah* (the classic Israelite federal republic—literally, assembly), what is later to become known as the function of the *keter malkhut* (the domain—literally, crown—of civil rule), and the *Kohen Gadol* is responsible for linking the people to God, what are later to become known as the function of the *keter kehunah* (the domain of priesthood). Both share the task of interpreting the Torah as constitution, the function of the *keter torah* (the domain of constitutional interpretation). Both leaders function within the framework of a very active tribal federation in which

227

the tribal leadership plays a vital role. The regime is presented as generally successful and classic in its form.

2. Judges presents the tribal federation in its minimalist state, what happens when the federation becomes a loose confederation and "every man does what is right in his own eyes." Power has reverted to the tribal elders, assisted by *shofetim* (judges, who lead the tribes in battle and administer justice as much as or more than they adjudicate disputes), who share the *keter malkhut*. The *keter kehunah* is also handled by local priests and Levites while the *keter torah* exists principally in the abstract as a fundamental law with no separate institutional mechanism. While tending to a negative evaluation, it offers a mixed picture, by no means all negative; for example, the rejection of monarchy is portrayed as good. On balance, however, confederal anarchism is rejected as a suitable regime.

3. Presented in 1 Samuel is a picture of a prophet-led regime, or at least an attempt to restore the tribal federation by eliminating confederal anarchy through institution of a prophet-led regime. It paints a very dynamic picture of a confederation whose principal federal office was a hereditary priesthood, which is deposed in the period under discussion, the rise of a prophet who was trained within the *keter kehunah* but shifts to the *keter torah,* and his introduction of a *nagid/melekh* (high commissioner/king) reluctantly and out of necessity to head the *keter malkhut,* but be subordinate to the prophet. The discussion documents the failure of this regime to stand up to foreign military pressure.

4. In describing David's reign, 2 Samuel presents the classic regime of kingship. The head of the *keter malkhut* becomes a king and not just a chief magistrate. He reaffirms the authority of the other two *ketarim,* but also subordinates them by bringing them into his court, and retains the form of a tribal federation while centralizing power through a standing army and bureaucracy. While this regime is portrayed as successful, its flaws are clearly pointed out as well.

5. Portrayed in 1 Kings is the regime of kingship in its ordinary or declining phases. In fact, it contrasts two forms of kingship—dynastic kingship in the regime of Judah and nondynastic kingship in the regime of Israel—showing the virtues and defects of both.

6. Finally, 2 Kings discusses ordinary dynastic kingship in a political union (rather than a federation), its strengths and weaknesses.

In addition, 1 and 2 Chronicles add texture to the historical discussion from the perspective of the *keter melkhut* of the time. They emphasize political and military affairs, government organization, and the problem of balancing powers and interests. In our examination of David and the establishment of kingship in Israel, it will be useful to keep these perspectives in mind.

The Mosaic Covenantal Paradigm in Action

The next step in the process initiated in the Pentateuch is to be found in the Book of Joshua, in which Joshua and Israel take the first steps in carrying out the provisions of the Torah as constitution in the newly conquered Eretz Israel. Joshua conquers and divides the land according to the Divine plan (with some modifications to reflect the reality of a situation in which Canaanites remain in parts of the land).

As a book, Joshua is constructed around three high points, each associated with a covenant renewal:

1. The renewal of the covenant with the two and a half tribes prior to crossing the Jordan and beginning the conquest (1:16ff.).

2. The covenant renewal at Shechem after most of the land is in Israelite hands followed by the division of the land according to the Torah's design (chap. 8).

3. The covenant renewal at the time of Joshua's farewell to the people as the final step in the normalization of Israelite life in the land (chaps. 23 and 24).

Each of these is treated as a central teaching of the book.

Beyond its place as a "historical" work, the Book of Joshua should be read as a classic of political thought, that can be and should be read as a coherent whole, in fact, as a major statement of the classic political worldview of the Bible and the regime it advocated. For political science, it is the first classic exposition of federal republicanism.[1] While the themes it emphasizes are derived from the Torah itself, the Torah combines them with other elements. In Joshua, the federal republican character of the Israelite *edah* under God is the central theme.[2]

This writer is fully aware of the theories that see the Book of Joshua as little more than a collection of ancient documents or written versions of different oral traditions, some say of questionable historical accuracy. Biblical critics argue on both sides of that question. Regardless of the degree of historical accuracy of those theories on one level, the result in hand is a classic, basically integrated work. Hence, it is also necessary to treat the book as we have it as a unified whole, a work that makes a coherent statement when taken as a whole.

In the largest sense, the Book of Joshua is concerned with matters far more significant than merely recounting the history of the conquest of the land of Canaan by the Israelite tribes, or even the reconstitution of that conquest within the moral framework of the Prophetic school.[3] It goes beyond both purposes to become the embodiment of a particular conception of what a good constitution and a good regime must be, in light of the moral framework of Prophetic thought. As such, it addresses the classic issues of constitutional design for Israel as a body politic. A full understanding of the book requires that it be studied utilizing the tools of political analysis.

The Former Prophets and Their Underlying Political Theme

The Book of Joshua is the sixth book of the Bible and the first book of the Former Prophets. It represents a continuation of the account of the history of the Israelite nation after the death of Moses and is devoted to the description of the conquest of the land of Canaan and its division among the tribes. Any consideration of the Book of Joshua must reckon with its place in the order of the biblical narrative and must consider its relationship to the Book of Deuteronomy, which precedes it, the Book of Judges, which immediately follows it, and the Books of Samuel (particularly 1 Sam.), which follow after that. Stylistically, the relationship between the first three of the aforementioned books is clear. Joshua has been characterized by linguist analysts as representing a transitional style from that of Deuteronomy to that of Judges.[4]

By common reckoning, there are eight "historical books" in the Bible. The term *historical books* is a misnomer. Even though the books covered under this designation do appear to relate the history of the Israelite nation from the time of Moses to their restoration to Eretz Israel after the Babylonian exile, their main purpose is not historical as such. That is to say, their recounting of the historical record is incidental to their major purpose, which is to develop the idea of the Lord's covenant with the Israelite tribes and the tribes' responsibility under it to create a holy commonwealth in their land.

An understanding of this characteristic of the Bible eliminates many difficulties. For one, it transforms the historiographic problem of apparent discrepancies, repetitions, and chronological gaps. Since the Bible attempts to be no more than roughly chronological in its sequences, it is not serious to the biblical authors if incidents are slightly out of chronological order. Since the Bible attempts to use cases to teach, it is not serious to the compiler if the same case is repeated in a slightly different version provided that each version teaches something special. Indeed, what one must look for, when one finds the same case repeated, is not the fact of the repetition per se but whether there was not some larger reason for the repetition in light of the Bible's purposes.

The Covenant Idea and Prophetic History

The central concern that binds all the historical books together is the Prophetic concern with the maintenance of God's covenant with Israel and the working out of the relationship between the Israelites, God, and other humans through the covenant. For example, the entire book is permeated with covenant vocabulary, a reflection of the way in which Hebrew rests upon a covenantal vocabulary in matters having to do with relationships.

Constitutional considerations are at least as important as the religious and ethical ones in the Bible and, indeed, are not separated from them. The books of Joshua, Judges, and 1 Samuel deal with constitutional questions primarily because the shape of the regime that was to govern the Israeli tribes was not yet fixed. The books that follow, beginning with 2 Samuel, continuing through Kings, and including Chronicles, are written about a period in which the regime is settled and a monarchy is firmly established. Therefore, the political questions considered are only constitutional ones at times of crisis, most often focusing on the manner in which the monarchy functions within the constitutional framework to serve the principles of the covenant.

Each book consists, in its substance, of a series of "cases" presented in roughly chronological sequence but not designed to form a historical narrative as such. (See, for example, the two accounts of the crossing of the Jordan in chaps. 3 and 4.) It includes a detailed presentation of the actual form of government to be used in the Israelite commonwealth (for example, chaps. 1 and 8).

In Joshua, the entire discussion is couched in rather precise technical political and geographic terminology. The narrative is centered around

Joshua, a classic statesman-general endowed with the Lord's charisma as the first minister (see, for example, chaps. 1, 4, 5, and 6).

Joshua is divided into three major sections, as follows:

1. The account of the conquest (chaps. 1-12).
2. The division of the Land (chaps. 12-21).
3. Joshua's farewell addresses and concluding covenant (chaps. 22-24).

Each of these sections deals with a major constitutional question and its resolution in the context of the Israelite polity.

For moderns, the Bible, like the American "Western," is cast in the form of a popular morality play. The story itself has the tone of a "Western" including "They went that-a-way" (2:5, in the story of Rahab and the two spies). The "Western," as the archetypical American morality play, follows the biblical pattern in its style and, to some extent, its purposes.

Major Problems in Reading the Book of Joshua

The very first problem of concern is the time of the conquest and its character, in other words, the validity of the biblical account. The traditional viewpoint takes the biblical account at face value. The critical viewpoints are varied but generally hold that the conquest was not a single movement but a long series of sporadic efforts (see, for example, the apparent contradictions between Joshua and the first chapter of Judges). Many also argue that not all the tribes came into the land at the same time. Some suggest that certain tribes were already in the land before the conquest and even before the main body of the people left Egypt. The critics cite the biblical text to show that the Canaanites were not all destroyed but that some were incorporated into the Israelite commonwealth. All suggest that the biblical account is a later patchwork of different versions.[5]

Others, principally Yehezkel Kaufmann, suggest that the biblical account is largely accurate. Kaufman argues that a large contiguous area was conquered in one fell swoop, but pockets of unconquered territory were left for later, as described in Judges. This also explains how the borders were extended by the individual tribes. Among Kaufman's arguments is that the Israelites invented their own form of government (the *edah*), unlike anything in Canaan, and that the division of the land was so complete that the Bible does not record any intertribal conflicts *over boundaries,* although it does mention intertribal problems in other spheres. It is not necessary to accept either view to appreciate the character of Joshua or to accept its place in the scheme of Israel's constitutional development as posited here.

It is generally agreed that the oldest portions of Joshua are original documents of the time. It is also held that the book was compiled by the same Prophetic school reflected in Deuteronomy. Joshua can be seen as their political commentary on the constitutional principles embodied in Deuteronomy. Biblical scholars estimate that this occurred no later than the seventh century B.C.E. This writer would suggest it occurred in the eleventh century B.C.E. in the course of the struggle over the monarchy, which will be discussed further below.

The Israelite migration, including the exodus from Egypt and conquest of Canaan, must be viewed as one of the great migrations of that era, which was an era of migrations and conquests in the eastern Mediterranean region. The four principal migrations and conquests involved:

1. The Israelites, who overwhelm Canaanite civilization.

2. The Dorians, who overwhelm Mycenaean civilization in Greece.

3. The Achaeans, Sardinians, and Lycoans, who overwhelm the Mediterranean islands.

4. The Philistines, who overwhelm the coastal peoples of Canaan.

Thus, whatever occurred in Canaan at that time was not only unique in its result—the Jewish people—but part of a larger human phenomenon that initiated a great leap forward in Western and ultimately world civilization.[6] The classic character of the Book of Joshua fits well into that classic epoch. Recovery of its teaching is part of the recovery of the foundations of the classic Western civilization of Israel and Hellas.

The Immediate Problems of the Israelite Tribal Confederacy

Our working hypothesis is that Joshua was first edited some time in the eleventh century B.C.E. at the height of the struggle between the Israelites and the Philistines. At the time of the book's appearance, the issue was probably still in doubt and, even more than that, it is likely that the Israelites had not yet found the leadership and organization necessary to win major victories against the well-organized and better armed Philistines. This was the period in which it had become apparent that the weak confederacy binding the tribes together was no longer adequate to the tasks of government at hand. Reliance on an impermanent national government of the period of the Judges had led to national disaster.[7]

The problem facing the Israelites, then, was how best to reform the confederacy's constitution. Joshua presents one solution to this problem. It is a progressive but essentially conservative solution, seeking not to change the Israelite constitution in new and untried ways but to restore what its authors believed to be its original form. It is an essentially republican solution designed to guarantee the continuation of limited, popular government along with renewed national energy, based upon the continued distribution of powers between the tribe, on the one hand, and the national authorities, on the other. Its republicanism is particularly marked since it was developed as an answer to the monarchists who argued that the only solution to the problem of effective government was a centralized monarchy. It is possible to theorize that the Prophet Samuel is speaking through this book since the ideal system proposed in it is much like the system that Samuel tried but failed to institute during his judgeship (1 Sam. 7-8).

Joshua makes its argument in a most indirect way, by describing a golden age of Israelite political and military successes at the beginning of Israel's dwelling in its land. It must do so because of the already sacred character of the texts in hand, that preserved record of the founding era. All the editors can do is arrange and slightly change (add to, modify) those texts so that they fit together. They feel compelled in their own minds to treat the texts with piety, as well as to preserve the credibility of their argument. Thus, the book implicitly evokes the great deeds of great ancestors in support of the editors' present claims, yet in a manner that allows those deeds to speak for themselves.

The book makes Joshua the hero because he was the last leader of a totally united federation for two centuries and, as such, a model for those who sought tribal unity later. The author/editor of this book wants to show that a successful tribal federation did exist once, that the system of government constituted by Moses is a feasible one even under conditions similar to those that have given rise to demands for a monarchy. According to the author, not only was the tribal federation successful in maintaining national unity, but it was successful in the face of the greatest national challenge—the conquest of the land. By implication, then, it could be successful in coping with the current challenge of the Philistines. It is precisely in the military field that the success of the federation must be demonstrated because of the military challenge confronting Israel in the author's day.

By demonstrating that the confederal system was once viable, the author is also trying to project an image of the best government for the future. This best government is a united Israelite federation, in which the tribes are strong, rooted in the land with an agrarian economic base, yet a government that possesses a federal authority built around a charismatic leader, chosen by the people before God (and/or vice versa), who has officers responsible to him (as the national authority) and thus direct channels to the people, at least for military or national purposes, and all operating under God's covenant.

It is to this end that Joshua is raised up as Moses's equal or near-equal in this book. He is, first and foremost, a statesman-prophet who, unlike Moses (the lawgiver-prophet) has spent his life in political and military roles and whose forte is in the political realm. The crossing and river-splitting sequences, the historical site project, the mention of the two and a half tribes, and the direct comparisons with Moses are all directed toward that end.

This is the essence of Joshua's direct encounters with God in chapters 3 and 4:1-14. There are two separate but interlocking "lessons," as it were, that had to be brought out to set the stage for the author's ideas. The apparent chronological confusion in these chapters can be accounted for once it is recognized that what is of interest to the author is not the history per se but its political implications.

The Larger Problem of the Good Commonwealth

Beyond the immediate political crisis, the book is concerned with larger questions of building the Holy Commonwealth on earth. Consequently, any solution the authors might try to design would have to conform to their ideas of what a proper constitution should be. The explicit details of the governmental structure they proposed were not necessarily considered by them to be ideal for all nations at all times. The biblical view, like that of the Greeks, is that different peoples need different constitutions (or forms of government) to meet their unique circumstances. Moreover, the Bible in general is more concerned with the relationship between governors and governed than with the form of regime.

But it probably means two things: (a) that this is the form of government best suited for Israel, and (b) that the essential principles of the constitution (i.e., sovereignty of God, federalism, republicanism, distribution of powers, and limited government) are necessary for any truly good commonwealth.

The very inclusion of the Book of Joshua in the Bible is one more bit of evidence to support this contention. If it had only been a political tract for the eleventh century, it would have gone the way of the majority of the other books current in Israel at its time. It is because of its larger political significance that it was raised to the stature of a special book deserving inclusion in the canon. The importance of Joshua in Jewish Rabbinic tradition is indicated in the fact that the book's first chapter is the *haftarah* (Prophetic portion, read every Sabbath morning at the conclusion of the Torah portion of the week) for Simchat Torah, the festival commemorating the completion of the annual Torah reading cycle and its beginning anew. This can be understood as symbolizing the continuity of Jewish history and Torah study, which, in political terms, is the study of Israel's constitution and its application.

General Principles

According to the Bible, forms of government are not Divinely ordained but human inventions, hence, the people of Israel are free to institute arrangements suitable to their situation at any particular time, provided that God's sovereignty and covenant with them is recognized as the source of their fundamental law and the Torah is maintained as their constitution. Thus, it is not the form of the regime that is crucial but the relationship between governors and governed. While the teaching in Joshua also rests upon this principle, it does propose one form of regime as the best, linking the two elements through the principle that it must be instituted through a covenant between the people, their rulers, and God (or in God's presence).

The Essential Problems of Government: A More Perfect Union, Domestic Tranquility, and a Common Defense

Joshua suggests that the problems of national unity, internal order, and national defense will be solved through a proper federal republic embracing the entire nation. What is needed is a united tribal federation governed under a republican form of government with national leaders chosen on the basis of their relationship to God but responsible to the people and, most important, to the law, and with tribal leaders retaining their essential roles under the new rule of law. Such a system is the basis for the ideal commonwealth in which power is shared by the national government and the tribes. Under such a system, God retains His sovereignty undiminished but governs through appropriate human leadership. God, the governors, and the people are united through a covenant subsidiary to and derived from the Sinai covenant. (Chapter 1 outlines the precise form of national political organization, and chapters 23 and 24 discuss its purposes.)

The Transcendent Question of "What Constitutes Political Morality?"

It is hard to say whether the discussion of this question within the confines of the Book of Joshua was purposive or not. In some cases (e.g., the discussion of what constitutes republican virtue) it gives every indication of being purposive. In others (e.g., the moral lesson of the spies), the issue is by no means clear. Still, a careful reading of the text reveals what can be understood to be a number of serious discussions of the great questions of political morality, perhaps placed purposely, perhaps simply unavoidable in any discussion of the great political questions confronting man.

Some examples of the book's concerns in this realm include:

1. The book emphasizes the idea of societies collapsing from within, out of moral weakness, that we encounter in Scripture as early as the Noah story (see the fall of Jericho, especially 2:9-10).

2. Honesty in maintaining the historic record is presented as a virtue (see Crossing the Jordan, 4:6-8; the battle of Ai, 7:26; 8:29).

3. There are limitations on waging war, even the most justifiable wars, namely, wars of national liberation.

4. Collective national responsibility is the key to political survival (see Josh. 7:1).

5. Government by covenant (7) under the law (8:32ff.) is a *sine qua non*.

Joshua's Authority is Established in the Keter Malkhut

The first chapter of the Book of Joshua is used to set the stage for the entire work. On the surface, it is devoted to telling the story of Joshua's accession to leadership of the tribal confederacy, his acquisition of a mandate from God, who renews His promise and restates the conditions that must be met by the Israelites for its fulfillment, His order to the tribes to begin preparations for crossing the Jordan, and the renewal of the promise of the two and a half transjordanian tribes to participate in the conquest. The manner of telling the story, however, indicates a meaning beyond the simple recounting of history.

Verses 1 through 9 serve as a general introduction to the entire work, covering God's charge to Joshua, effectively restating the terms of His covenant with Israel, including His repetition of the promise and its conditions, His statement and explication of the national motto, *hazak v'ematz*, (be strong and courageous), and His restatement of the centrality of the Torah in the life of Israel. Verses 10 and 11 show Joshua giving his first commands to the nation through his officials. Verses 12 through 18 cover Joshua's reminder to the tribes of Reuben, Gad, and Manasseh of their obligation to participate in the conquest, his instructions as to what they must do to prepare for their role, and their willing acquiescence based on their recognition of Joshua as Moses's legitimate successor.

The chapter introduces certain key political terms already used in the Torah. First among them is *Eved Adonai* (see also Exod. 14:31; Num. 12:7), used in the book's very first verse, as the title of the highest political and moral leader of the Israelite nation who serves God the King, "God's Prime Minister." The construction of the title implicitly recognizes the sovereignty of God and denies the legitimacy of vesting sovereignty in a human monarch. The *Eved Adonai* can be the head of the government of the Israelites, but only God can be the head of state.

In the Book of Joshua, the term is used 15 times, 13 times in connection with Moses and twice in connection with Joshua. In the rest of the Bible, it is used only five times and in only four books (Deut., Judg., 2 Kings, 2 Chron.). In all cases it is used as a modifier for either Moses or Joshua. In the other four books, it is used four times in connection with Moses and once in connection with Joshua. In Deuteronomy and Judges the term appears in immediate juxtaposition to the beginning and end of Joshua. In Joshua, where the emphasis is on identifying Joshua as Moses's legitimate and full successor, the term is used in connection with Moses (4, 12:6) until the very end of the book where, in the last chapters, it is explicitly applied to Joshua as it had been inferentially, earlier.

During the history of the tribal federation presented in Judges, the only term used for national political leaders is *Shofet*. Since the term *Eved Adonai* apparently did not enter common usage, one might ask whether it was accepted as an actual public title in the *edah*. Perhaps it never even had such connotations outside of the circle responsible for writing the Torah and the Book of Joshua. At the same time, the internal evidence provided by the Bible indicates that in the years between Joshua and the inauguration of the monarchy, the only person who could possibly have been considered for the title was Samuel, the only *Shofet* who was able to assert his leadership over the entire nation. It may be that awarding him this title is what is being implicitly suggested here.

Constitutionally, the term remains confined to the government of the classic *edah*. When kingship is introduced, it is not used for the king, apparently quite deliberately. Saul, clearly designated by Samuel to play a more limited role than the *Eved Adonai*, was given the title *Nagid*, best translated as High Commissioner. Even after David's ascension to the throne and consolidation of the kingship, the Prophets continue to refer to him and his heirs by the same term, *Nagid*. David's own court poets tried to introduce the title *Eved Elohim*, which has the same meaning as *Eved Adonai*, but uses a different term for God. They apply it to the new king in the Book of Psalms, but were unsuccessful, probably because of the historic associations of the formal Prophetic opposition. According to the Bible, only the people used the term *melekh* (king), which remained a colloquial title. Five centuries later, the prophet Ezekiel, in his description of the messianic days of restoration to come, endorses the Davidides' governmental role but carefully refers to the "king" as *nasi* (literally, someone raised up or elected, perhaps best translated as magistrate or chief magistrate). Thus, after the failure of Samuel's reform effort, God ceased to directly rule the *edah* so there was no further need for *Eved Adonai* as a technical term and it was abandoned.

A second major constitutional principle is that there is to be no hereditary leadership outside of the priesthood. Each new leader must be chosen by God and be endowed with charisma by him. Not even Moses can designate his heir alone. Though Joshua is the heir apparent, he is not the legitimate leader of the nation until God speaks to him directly and passes the responsibility to him (see vv. 1–2ff.). This strong reliance on the role of the Lord and the rejection of inherited leadership per se is part of the pattern often referred to by Puritan divines in the seventeenth century as the "republican virtue" of the Hebrew Bible. (See also Exod. 24:13, Num. 11:28.)

Joshua achieved leadership through his prior service to the nation. This is clear from the record in the Torah proper (see Exod. 17:9, Num. 27:19, and Deut. 1:28). The later sages apparently believed that this was to be a lesson for the people. In *BaMidbar Rabbah* 12:9, the Talmudic commentary on Numbers, it is related that Moses wanted his sons to succeed him, to make the leadership hereditary, but God chose Joshua on the grounds of his lifelong faithful service and demonstrated ability. This principle of leadership by election rather than inheritance outside of the *keter kehunah* has been the basis of rule for the Jewish polity for most of its history. Even when the Davidides sat on the throne in Jerusalem, the larger northern kingdom of Israel effectively rejected hereditary rule. Moreover, constitutionally, the people had a role. Even in the Davidic and Hasmonean dynasties, new kings went through at least a pro forma process of public acclamation and Prophetic or priestly anointment to signify the laying on of God's charisma.

In the Prophetic commonwealth all authority is from two sources, God and the people. Hence, Joshua has to have his authority affirmed by the people as well as by God. For the *edah* as a whole, that happens in the desert and is recounted in the Torah itself. However, because of the conquest of much of transjordan and the settlement of two and a half tribes in those lands under special conditions that required them to participate in the conquest of Canaan even after they settled, he must establish his authority as Moses's successor over these tribes and get them to reaffirm their commitment (v. 12ff.).

The two and a half tribes are described as accepting Joshua's authority in a confrontation reminiscent of a formal covenanting. Joshua gets his mandate from the Lord and then places it before the people (or a segment thereof), who pledge loyalty to him as long as the Lord is with him (i.e., he retains the Divine charisma). This is clearly a political covenant in the sense that it affirms or establishes (legitimizes) a power relationship by making it authoritative. As such, it is the first strictly political covenant of an internal character in the Bible, a renewal of the authority relationships established at Sinai.

The frequent mention of the two and a half tribes' role is designed to show the unity of the tribal federation in those days, as if to say, "See, even the two and a half tribes that settled east of the Jordan fulfilled their part of the agreement with Moses and sent men to help in the conquest of the Land." This can be read as another indication that the book was written in a period when tribal unity was a problem.

Once God's chief minister is entrusted with leadership—in the case of Joshua, by Moses before the latter's death—God is able to give him a direct mandate. God is explicit regarding the content of that mandate, including the task of conquering the land. Thus, a third constitutional principle having to do with the Israelites' right to Canaan is introduced. Already in verse 4 we have another review of the classic boundaries of the promise. Compare it to the promises in Genesis 15:18, Exodus 23:3-12, Numbers 24:3-12, and Deuteronomy 11:24.

God's mandate continues with regard to Joshua's relationship to Him (v. 5). He concludes by reaffirming the motto He has bestowed on the *edah* and its leadership (v. 6): "Strengthen your character and make yourself courageous," which is repeated three times in the course of this conversation. It is a statement of classic strength, which all of the ancients believed to be essential to the citizens of republics. Yet God never lets His people forget that they are bound by their Torah constitution and are under His judgment. He concludes His mandate to Joshua with a combined blessing-warning (vv. 7 and 8) with regard to learning the Torah as a constitutional teaching and living up to its requirements or else. Here is the opening of the Prophetic vision of why the full promise never came to pass—Israel's sin, the abandonment of Torah.

The term for a second office of the edah, *Shotrei Ha'am* (Officers of the People), is introduced in v. 10. The *shotrim* were the lesser officials of the national government, those entrusted with executing the policies of the *Eved Adonai* and the *Shofetim*. Note, however, that they are referred to as officers of the people (in modern terminology, public servants), not officials of the national government or its leadership.

The word *shoter* is from the terminological complex meaning "order," and is related to such terms as *mishtar* (political order or system) and *shtar* (contract). In modern Hebrew, the term means policeman, a recognition of its kinship with the English terminological complex meaning "order" in the same sense, as policy, political, and police in their original meaning of order. The term is one of the oldest in the Hebrew political lexicon. The Torah refers to *shotrim* as officers of the people during Egyptian bondage. Thus, the chapter concludes after having outlined the basis of the classic biblical polity, with its key terms and relationships in place.

Chapter 2, which deals with Rahab and the spies in Jericho, offers a stark and deliberate contrast to chapter 1. The whole chapter is presented in a simplified story form characteristic of such biblical narratives. Behind that story, however, is a contrast between the *edah* as a polity and the political systems of Canaan. This contrast is particularly important in light of the people's revolutionary demand in the eleventh century B.C.E. for a king "like all the nations."

Canaan was divided into city-states, each with its own ruler, referred to in the text as a *melekh* or king. Scholars argue as to the meaning of kingship in Canaan but, even if not a "king" in the sense of a powerful monarch, it is generally agreed that they were constitutional monarchs in the sense that they were responsible to or at least limited by local assemblies—either popular or notables or both. The biblical reference to all Canaanite rulers as "kings" may be considered a shorthand generalization, not a reflection of Israelite ignorance of the subtleties of the Canaanite political framework. Joshua actually identifies four forms of formal leadership among the nations with which Israel came in contact. The first is the *melech,* or king, common for Canaanite cities; the second, the *zekenim* of the Gibeonites (9:11); the third, the *seranim* (officers) of the Philistines (13:3); and the fourth the *nesiim* of the Midianites (13:21). Each term is used in a specific technical sense, reflecting as each does a different form of government.

Notes

1. I have elaborated on the theme of federal republicanism in the Bible in Daniel J. Elazar, ed., *Kinship and Consent: The Jewish Political Tradition and Its Contemporary Manifestations* (Lanham, MD: University Press of America and Center for Jewish Community Studies, 1983). See, especially, my article on "Covenant as the Basis of the Jewish Political Tradition" and Moshe Weinfeld, "The Transition from Tribal Republic to Monarchy in Ancient Israel and Its Impression on Jewish Political History," in *Kinship and Consent,* ed. Daniel J. Elazar (Ramat Gan: Turtledove, 1981). See also Martin Buber, *Kingship of God* (New York: Harper and Row, 1956); Daniel J. Elazar, *Covenant and Freedom in the Jewish Political Tradition* (Philadelphia: Gratz College, 1981); Daniel J. Elazar and Stuart A. Cohen, *The Jewish Polity* (Bloomington: Indiana University Press, 1985), Introduction and Epoch 3.
2. On the *edah* in this sense, see Robert Gordis, "Democratic Origins in Ancient Israel—the Biblical Edah," in *The Alexander Marx Jubilee Volume* (New York:

Jewish Theological Seminary, 1950), 373–88; C. Umhau Wolf, "Terminology of Israel's Tribal Organization," *Journal of Biblical Literature* 65 (1946), 45–48.

3. The principal scholarly works on Joshua include: Albrecht Alt, "The Settlement of the Israelites in Palestine," in Albrecht Alt, *Essays on Old Testament History and Religion* (Garden City, NY: Doubleday and Co., 1968), 173–222; John Bright, "The Constitution and Faith of Early Israel," in John Bright, *A History of Israel* (Philadelphia: Westminster Press, 1960); Z. Kallai, *The Tribes of Israel: A Study in the Historical Geography of the Bible* (Jerusalem: Bialik Institute, 1967); Yehezkel Kaufmann, *The Biblical Account of the Conquest of Palestine* (Jerusalem: Magnes Press, 1953) and *The Book of Joshua: A Commentary* (Jerusalem: Kiryat Sepher, 1963); Martin Noth, "Israel as the Confederation of the Twelve Tribes," in Martin Noth, *The History of Israel* (New York: Harper and Row, 1958); Benjamin Offenheimer, *Early Prophecy in Israel* (Jerusalem: Magnes Press, 1973) and *Studies in the Book of Joshua* (Jerusalem: Kiryat Sepher, 1960); and the publications of the Israel Society for Biblical Studies, volume 9.

4. For the place of Joshua in the Canon, see R. G. Bowling and J. Ernest Wright, eds., *Joshua, the Anchor Bible,* vol. 5 (New York: 1982).

5. For the various understandings of the Israelite occupation of Canaan, see Yehezkel Kaufmann, *The Biblical Account of the Conquest of Canaan,* 2d ed., trans. M. Dagut (Jerusalem: Magnes Press, 1985); Harry A. Orlinsky, *Ancient Israel* (Ithaca, NY: Cornell University Press, 1954).

6. On the migrations of the period of the Exodus and conquest of Canaan, see Albrecht Alt, "The Formation of the Israelite State," in *Essays on Old Testament History and Religion,* trans. R. A. Wilson (Garden City, NY: Doubleday and Co., 1968); W. J. Albright, *The Biblical Period from Abraham to Ezra: An Historical Survey* (New York: Harper, 1968). A coherent if problematic theory accounting for the events of this crucial period is to be found in the works of Immanuel Velikovsky. Cf. his *Worlds in Collision* (New York: Doubleday, 1950) and *Earth in Upheaval* (New York: Pocketbooks, 1980).

7. On the crisis of the eleventh century, see H. M. Orlinsky, "The Tribal System of Israel and Related Groups in the Period of the Judges," *Oriental Antiquities* 1 (1962): 11-20; Weinfeld, "The Transition from Tribal Republic to Monarchy"; H. Tadmor, "'The People and the Kingship in Ancient Israel: The Role of Political Institutions in the Biblical Period," *Journal of World History* (1968): 46-68.

12

Fostering Civic Virtue

Elements Fostering Civic Virtue: Historical Memory

In chapter 3, the description of the *edah* resumes, presented through the medium of the tale of crossing the Jordan River. If chapter 1 focused on the *keter malkhut* of the federation, this chapter focuses on the *keter kehunah,* the tribal role in the federal government, and the portable seat of that government. It begins with the latter, the Ark of the Covenant (*Aron HaBrit* in Hebrew). The Ark contained the tables of the covenant, the most holy material possession of the Israelite tribes. It was the focal point of the *edah,* testifying to the central role of the covenant in Jewish affairs. Elsewhere in the Bible and in Joshua the Ark is referred to as *Aron Ha'Edut,* the Ark of the Testimony or Witnessing (cf. 4:15). The term *'edut* is a synonym for covenant and reflects the process of promulgation of the covenant, which is done in front of the people, who are witnesses, as well as being indicative of the fact that this is God's testimony to His people.

The Ark is the focal point of the final assembly before crossing the Jordan, where God commands the Israelites to sanctify themselves. The conquest was not to be a pleasant task but a holy one. War, which necessitates killing, is at least partly neutralized in its effect on those doing the killing by hedging it with the procedures of sanctification. God is addressed here as "Lord of all the Earth." He is already universalized in the manner of the Prophetic literature. Each tribe sends its elected representative to participate in crossing the Ark (v. 12). The role of the tribes is an indication of the federal character of this national endeavor.

The commemoration of the crossing (4:3–10) by erecting a stone cairn reflects the sense of history that has been part and parcel of the Jewish approach to life since the very origins of the Jewish people. Here is the first "national historic site" of the Jewish people and perhaps in the history of the world. This is not a monument to a victory erected in a capital as kings in the ancient world were accustomed to erecting, and on which was recorded the historical record as the king wanted it remembered, not always with even approximate accuracy. This is an actual site marking, designed to make the event vivid to future generations, not through monuments erected elsewhere but through on-the-spot portrayal not subject to artificial distortion; though, of course, a traditional history of the crossing, not necessarily accurate to the last detail, clearly did develop. This account is based on it. This attitude is absolutely fundamental to popular government, which rests at least in part on a shared historical experience, based on the educational principle that history is only meaningful insofar as it is the common property of its heirs. Hence, verses 6-8 emphasize the retelling of the event: "ye shall say unto them...." The tradition is then presented in a form understandable to all—this is popular as distinct from "scientific" history. Hence, historical events have to be properly marked and understood.

The successful crossing provides the Israelites with experiential evidence reinforcing Joshua's charisma and right to succeed Moses as the God-appointed leader. The splitting of the Jordan story is part of this reinforcement of Joshua's position. Joshua, like Moses, splits flowing waters in the name of the Lord.

The tale of the ending of the crossing is repeated in verses 15-24 in what is the third section of the two chapters. It adds a more "religious," as distinct from political, tone. Here we see a typical biblical device, the multiple explanation. On the one hand, there is a sociological reason for the stone cairn and, on the other, a "higher" reason. Both are given since both are important. The reader seeking a sense of the whole book will see this not as a confusion of accounts, as many of the "higher-critics" would have it, but as a purposive educational device, no doubt used in full consciousness. The section forms a transition to the book's next concern, namely, the observance of the *mitzvot*—God's commandments—in the land, which is the subject of chapter 5.

The first four chapters, then, are not so much a continuous chronological narrative but a connection of relevant episodes in chronological order that form an epic record of sorts.

1:1-9   The passing of the mantle and the promise.
1:10-17 The assembly and the covenant.

2:1-24   The episode of the spies.
3:1-17   The crossing as a religious-covenantal event.
4:1-24   The crossing as a socio-political event.

Elements Fostering Civic Virtue:
Maintaining the Commandments

The fifth chapter focuses on actions in the land preparatory to the opening of the actual war of conquest.

5:1-9   The circumcision: fulfilling the personal covenant ritual and removing the last stain of the Egyptian bondage.
5:10-12   Passover observed: fulfilling the communal covenant ritual in the land for the first time by observing the harvest-freedom festival and beginning to live off the land itself.
5:13-15   The minister of the Lord's Host: renewal of God's grant of charisma to Joshua by a great experience, which, at the same time, raises God above the level of a mere God of battles.

Permeating the account are the historical explanation, the sense of intergenerational communal responsibility, and the sense of historical continuity. The order of the fulfillment of the first *mitzvot* in the land of Israel is important: mass circumcision as reaffirmation of the original covenant between God and Abraham (vv. 2-9); observance of Pesach by the newly circumcised citizens under the rules prescribed in the Book of Exodus to commemorate the Exodus, eating the produce of the land as the first Israel-related *mitzvah,* and then another reaffirmation of Joshua's status as *Eved Adonai.* The verses link the Exodus and the covenant, national liberation and the national calling, while cessation of the manna (v. 12) signifies that the Israelites have reached their home. Henceforth, they will live off the bounty (literally, "milk and honey") of the land, not depend upon God's miraculous beneficence. Taken together these events constitute a relegitimation of Israel as God's covenanted people.

The discussion in chapter 5 offers an opportunity for reflection on the generational rhythm of human affairs.[1] The reference to the fact that all the men of military age had died in the desert (v. 4) and a new generation has come of age suggests the passing of the generation of the desert and the coming of a new one. It also reflects the constitution of the *edah* whereby the adult males capable of bearing arms constitute its heart.

The matter is made explicit in v. 6 using the standard biblical phrase for a generation, that is, "forty years." The language of these verses is particularly important for establishing the technical terminology of the generational rhythm.

All three of the elements in this chapter are highly relevant as a prelude to the war of the conquest in which: (a) the personal responsibility required under the covenant could easily be forgotten in the heat of the conquest; (b) communal obligations under the covenant had to be transformed into land-based observances but, more than that, on the eve of such an enterprise, it was necessary to start by living the proper way in the land—earning one's food, remembering one's past, and observing the covenant; and (c) it would be easy to identify the Lord with Israel's cause rather than vice-versa, hence the reminder.

How a Covenanted People Wage War: Jericho and Ai

The Israelites' assault on Canaan begins with the stunning victory at Jericho that demoralizes the enemy and gives the attackers a psychological boost. A major Canaanite city of ancient vintage, a gateway to the land, yet one that tactically could have been bypassed, is dramatically destroyed. The conquest is the story of a decadent civilization that has long relied on others (mainly the Egyptians) for protection, in the process of declining and falling and is toppled by a wild, strong, almost "barbaric" people. There is a loss of nerve and paralysis of will in Jericho, as reflected in the feeling of individuals like Rahab that they must make their own "deals" for survival in the face of the advance of a disciplined group.

There is a moral problem in this entire story. On the one hand, the Israelites are to conquer Canaan by God's commandment, yet it is a conquest that is to be conducted within strict limitations. Conquest is bad enough without making it materially profitable, hence the idea of devoting all the stuff of the city to the Lord and eliminating personal profit. This is a very difficult restraint. Nomadic warfare was centered on loot. Thus, the abandonment of looting meant (a) the abandonment of an essential nomadic tradition and (b) the abandonment of nomadism for the settled life. The result either leads to maintenance of a sound idealism that curbs the excesses of conquest or a perverted one that justifies bloodshed because there is not immediate profit but a long-range good.

The vital importance of the restriction is the subject of the very next case study (chap. 7), which relates the story of how Achan violates the ban on looting, which amounts to no less than breaking the covenant (v. 15). This direct assault on the holiness that must be maintained by the Israelites in the process of the bloody conquest leads to the Israelites' unexpected setback that followed right on the heels of the extraordinary victory at Jericho. In the Bible's religio-moral terms of reference, the fact that Ai means ruins only adds to the impact of the repulse—mighty Jericho falls with ease and the pile of ruins east of Beth El is the site of an Israelite defeat. The difference is clear: God's active direction in the first case and His disapproval in the second.

Collective responsibility is a traditional canon of Jewish thought. Jews have always been jointly responsible for the actions of any of their people. Some think this is a trait that developed as a consequence of persecution in the exile because then accusations against one Jew were considered to be against all. However, we see in chapters 6 and 7 that the idea of collective responsibility is much older than that. It is part of the peculiar self-perception of the Jews as an extended family group that is also bound by covenant.

Like Moses, Joshua is human but still makes the system work, with the Lord's help, even to the point of carrying out the bloody but necessary execution of Achan for looting. Despite God's wrath, there is also a process of give and take, for in chapter 8, God slightly modifies his "no booty" commandment in light of the Achan episode. This is certainly a common phenomenon; the punishment of a lawbreaker for a violation that strikes at the fabric of the body politic and the subsequent modification of the law after a reassessment brought about by the affair. It is another reflection of the realistic character of the Bible and why it must be read so carefully.

The discussion of how to wage war reappears throughout the book as one of its main themes. Stated in shorthand, Israel wins victories through a combination of God's direct involvement, good generalship by the human commander, and precise responsive follow-through by the Israelite forces. All three are given equal emphasis here. In every military victory recorded in the Bible, all are present; conversely, in every military failure one or more are absent.

Renewing the Covenant at Shechem

After the Israelites' initial assault, Joshua assembles the tribes between Mount Gerizim and Mount Ebal (chap. 8) for the covenant renewal ceremony provided for in Deuteronomy 27:11–26. That ceremony can be seen as making the Torah the operative constitution of what is now *Eretz Yisrael,* of the land, as well as of *Am Yisrael,* the people. The covenant renewal describes the reaffirmation of covenant and constitution near Shechem. That constitution is referred to as Sefer Torat Moshe (the book of Moses's teaching), a title that becomes classic in Jewish constitutional terminology.

In verses 31 through 35, the text draws our attention to the practical requirements for good government. The first foundation of good government is Divine worship in the appropriate manner. The second foundation is knowledge of the constitution, especially on the part of the rulers. In verse 32, there is a restatement of the Deuteronomic principle that every chief of the Israelite confederacy must himself copy the constitution set forth in Moses's teaching as a demonstration of his being bound by that constitution and as a concrete way to make certain that he is familiar with it.

For the actual act of renewal, the whole people, specifically including women and children, citizens and resident aliens, along with their governors, are assembled between Mount Gerizim and Mount Ebal, which "face" each other across a valley (v. 33). This is a very holy place, specifically designated in the Torah as the place for reaffirming the covenant. Aside from the importance of the act itself, the assembled formation of the nation for the ceremony is a clear indication of the proper structure of Israelite polity.

Six kinds of government offices are mentioned here, in addition to the *Eved Adonai* mentioned in verse 31. They are:

Zekenim: Elders of the tribes
Nesi'im: Tribal magistrates
Shoterim: Officers of the national government
Shofetim: Judges of the national government
Cohenim: Priests
Leviim: Levites

The almost full repetition of the governing structure is appropriate to the occasion and a sign of its constitutional significance. The picture that emerges can be sketched in the following manner:

FIGURE 12.1

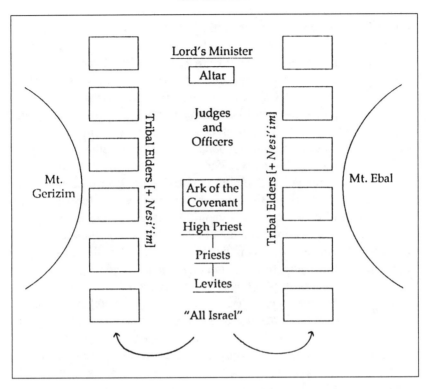

Reflected here are the two arenas of political organization, national and tribal, and the tripartite separation of domains *(ketarim)* in the national arena.

The ceremony itself is by Mosaic command; that is, it is part of the original political heritage of Israel, from the greatest prophet himself. Hence, the whole people is gathered here, as *kehal Yisrael*, the assembled polity (congregation) of Israel, before the "Ark of the Covenant of the Lord" (33). There is an inherent democracy in this action, a democracy that implies that all are obligated to consent to the constitution and to know the law, and have a right to know it. This classic scene is repeated, in miniature, in every synagogue every Sabbath.

An Unexpected Protectorate: The Covenant with the Gibeonites

Chapter 9 deals with the deception perpetrated by the Gibeonites and the treaty with them; it is a case study in the matter of honoring agreements. The Gibeonites obviously were aware that the Israelite conquest was a war of extermination and sought to protect themselves by deception rather than join the Canaanite alliance formed to fight the invaders. Understanding that they would not gain a treaty if they were recognized as locals, they presented themselves as coming from outside Canaan. The deception was sufficiently elaborate to fool the Israelites long enough to negotiate and seal the treaty, referred to as a covenant (v. 6).

This story is related to explain the Gibeonites' later presence in the land and also to illustrate the binding nature of treaties (covenants between man and man) in an age when treaties were frequently broken. Here we find man's commitments or actions exalted even above previous commitments to God when they involve the principle of *bein adam lehavero*, commitments between man and his neighbor.

The Gibeonites present themselves as having a form of government similar to that of the Israelites (v. 11), or elders (*zekenim*) and a popular assembly (*kol yoshvei artzenu*). It is quite likely that the Gibeonite system was the same; certainly it would have helped strengthen their case. The text provides us with some information on the treaty-making process (and maybe the legislative process as well) on both sides. For a matter so important, the Gibeonite elders can only recommend a course of action that must be ratified by the assembly. Then representatives are sent to do the actual negotiating and swearing. For the Israelites, the treaty is negotiated by Joshua and ratified by the *Nesi'ai HaEdah,* the representatives of the assembled people, (v. 15). Three covenantal terms—*shalom* (peace), *brit*, and *shevua* (oath)—are used in this one verse.

When the truth subsequently comes out, the *Nesi'im* feel honor-bound to maintain the covenant even though it was obtained by deception but the popular assembly (*edah*) responds negatively (vv. 18–22). The *Nesi'im* must present their position before the *edah* and secure its consent. A compromise emerges whereby the Gibeonites are allowed to live but in a subservient manner as "hewers of wood and drawers of water" for the entire *edah*.

The Gibeonites indicate that they are not unhappy with their fate, given the alternative. They are survivors, prepared to pay the price in order to survive. In chapter 10, they use their treaty status effectively by calling in the Israelites to protect them against a Jebusite-led coalition organized to attack and punish them for breaking ranks and becoming a protectorate of the Israelites, no doubt to discourage others from trying to do the same (10:3-5).

The Gibeonite relationship can be contrasted with that of Caleb ben Yefuneh, Joshua's companion in serving Moses in the wilderness and in spying out the land and, like him, last survivor of that generation, who claims Hebron, his promised inheritance. Caleb is not an Israelite in origin but a Kenizite who has joined with Israel and accepted the Lord as God (14:6-15). Caleb is to receive Hebron as a special inheritance by Mosaic instruction. When the division of the land begins, he is the first to receive his parcel. Caleb's speech is worth reading. It is touching in its simplicity and directness, giving us a picture of a bluff, straightforward warrior of simple faith. Caleb's claim is honored before the casting of the lots since it is based on a prior Divine promise.

The Completion of Joshua's Conquests

The war continues, Joshua destroys the Amorite coalition in the center of the country (chap. 10) and proceeds to conquer the hill country, the *shephelah* and the *negev,* and finally, the northern half of the country (chap. 11). The north was not conquered as fully, in any case, though it was conquered, as we see from subsequent history. Joshua's actions seem to have been more concerned with destroying the aggressive potential of the cities of the alliance than with anything else.

In a larger perspective, this is another example of the way the Bible explains how bad and even evil nations or individuals serve God's purposes without in any way mitigating their corruption. There exists in the biblical view of the world a dialectic of history. Good and bad (or the favored of the Lord versus their enemies) come into conflict to fulfill the Lord's plan on earth. The bad are placed in the way of the good to generate conflict and keep the good on the right path. It is through this dialectic of history that there will be achieved the preconditions necessary for the messianic age, when the Lord will consider it proper to intervene to bring *shalom*—peace and completeness in the world—when conflict will be ended. This will come only when the course of the conflict has reached a point when the people of the world are ready for it.

When that will be and under what conditions is the central subject matter of eschatology, not politics.

Joshua's last campaign is against the Philistines (14:21–23). As the Israelites were coming in from the east, the Philistines were coming in from the west, apparently from the island of Crete. The Philistines were proto-Greeks, with a high civilization which, like that of Israel, was probably reasonably humane for the age and their background. Both needed the land since neither had any other place to go, coming as emigrant peoples with their lines to their past residences cut. These two well-matched peoples were to clash over control of the land in what was to become the major conflict of the ensuing 200 years and was to decide the fate of the land and people of Israel for 3,000 years. The Philistine cities were Greek-style politea, aristocratic republics linked with each other in a confederacy, recognized in 13:3.

The whole struggle between the Israelites and Philistines, chronicled in Joshua, Judges, and Samuel, illustrates how outside pressures on a nation can force that nation to abandon aspects of its own ideals for the sake of survival. The Philistines left the land its Western name, Palestine, but were ultimately eliminated from history by the Jews. In the process, however, they also forced the Jews to establish a monarchy, with a court and bureaucracy and a stronger class system, to mobilize their national resources for victory. This, in turn, led to the demise of the tribal federation, the old republic with all that meant in terms of liberty and equality. This was a contributory factor to the tragic dimension in Jewish history, which was only partly reversed by the later triumph of the Prophetic movement represented in this book and throughout the Bible. The notion that permeates the Jewish religio-national myth that David's and Solomon's was a golden age reflects the tragic fact that Israel had to abandon its internal liberties to gain military security and even came to like it. The strength of those ideals in Israel can be measured by their subsequent reassertion, which could only be partial.

The Division of the Land

The division of the land is a constitutional act of the greatest import, which is treated at length and in detail as the heart of the book (chaps. 13–22).[2] The tribal allocations represent the basis for the economic, political, and religious organization of Israel. Hence, they are presented as permanent and inalienable, even in the end of days. The devotion of nearly half of the Book of Joshua to this issue is both a reflection of the importance of the topic and a sign of the constitutional character of the book.

Nahalah is the term used in every case to describe the tribal territories. This indicates the economic purpose of the conquest as much as anything else, as witnessed in verses 15 and 33 where the same term is used to describe the means of economic sustenance provided the Tribe of Levi through offerings to the Lord. The Bible never ignores the economic basis of human activity; rather it seeks to endow the right kind of economic life with holiness. Herein is found the root of the Jewish concern with social justice. The land is a religio-economic inheritance given to the people by the Lord, to be governed under a God-given constitution. It is sanctified in all these aspects; hence, economic misuse is as much a sin as is ritualistic religious violation. The economic basis and its importance is also explained in Numbers 32.

To be constitutionally complete, the account begins with reference to the transjordanian conquest and inheritances (vv. 9–24). They are given in detail because their boundaries are part of the ancient constitution of Israel as much as the other laws are. According to the Bible, they are to be restored at the end of days. Hence, they must be kept through accurate records (cf. Num. 32).

The constitutional division of the land west of the Jordan begins with chapter 14. The lands are divided by Joshua as chief executive, Elazar the high priest, and the heads of the tribes, *Rashei Avot,* (literally, the heads of the fathers of the tribes). A major constitutional act requires the action of all the holders of political authority in the tribal federation acting together. Here the High Priest clearly functions as head of a separate branch of government, one not charged with direct responsibilities for day to day government operations, who stands as arbiter in constitutional matters between the representatives of the tribes involved. The procedure for this action is outlined in the Torah itself, in Numbers 34, a chapter that gives the prospective boundaries and lists the participants and their positions by name. The same section of the Torah includes the clause making the tribal boundaries permanent and unalterable.

The initial division is by lot (*goral*), as prescribed in the Torah (Num. 34), to ensure a fair allocation, considering that the quality of the land in different regions is different and usable for different purposes. In the perception of the times, casting of lots was the way to let God decide since He determines the outcome of what to humans seems to be leaving matters to chance. Indeed the word *goral* is used for fate in Hebrew, the very opposite of chance.

The formula for recording the allotment for constitutional purposes begins with reference to the lot cast (v. 1). The formulary summary of the division refers first to the tribes and then to their families (*mishpahot*), not *mahlakot* (divisions) (v. 20), who received allocations of tribal lands. This is repeated in the case of every allocation.

Among the tribes, Judah (with Simon) is presented as the most important and receives its allotment first (chap. 15). The Joseph tribes, Ephraim and Manasseh (Joseph's two sons), are the next (chap. 16). The relationship and rivalry between Judah and the Joseph tribes is the biblical equivalent of the relationship between the American North and South. The Joseph tribes were to become the nucleus of the northern kingdom of Israel while the tribe of Judah became the nucleus of the southern kingdom of that name.

In the allocation, the "younger" tribe, Ephraim, takes precedence. Manasseh was another firstborn who was demoted. This is a common biblical phenomenon: Isaac in place of Ishmael, Jacob in place of Esau, Joseph over his brothers, Moses ahead of Aaron, and so on. The biblical teaching is that Divine merit precedes primogeniture, another element strengthening the covenantal against the organic basis of Jewish life.

There was also an appellate process, as this chapter shows in two places. Manasseh had five families with no male heirs. They appealed to the allocation committee on the basis of the ruling for the daughters of Tzelafhad in the Torah (cf. Num. 26:33–27:1ff.) permitting them to inherit. Hence, the tribe received allotments for the five male heirs and the five female heirs equally (vv. 5–6). The decision followed the precedent in the Torah and not only fulfilled Moses's commitment to the original parties but applied it to the other four cases as well, indicating that the original decision is generally binding and not an exceptional case. The decision was, of course, made according to the precedent of allocation by Elazar, the High Priest (mentioned first), Joshua, and the *Nesi'im*. Historically, the Manassalite family of Machir settled east of the Jordan and became a separate tribe for all intents and purposes. Its links with the parent tribe and the reason for its separation are mentioned in 17:1.

The tribal allotment is presented whole (vv. 7-10), combining borders, cities, and lands as demarcations, with one very specific boundary. Overall, the emphasis remains on nodes and their peripheries.[3] The term used here for town satellites is *b'noteha* (her daughters) (vv. 11-13), an appropriate description of a relationship between a larger settlement and its subsidiary settlements constituting a township.

The Joseph tribes are presented as complaining over the size of the inheritance (vv. 14-18). This suggests that there were clear principles of allocation determining how much each tribe should get. The Joseph tribes received the allotment as one because Joseph was one of the twelve sons of Jacob. Joshua's response is brusque and straightforward; they are given one allotment and license to conquer more territory promised but not yet granted, not dissimilar to the terms given the Calebites in Judah. This is another sign that, after the allocation, the task of completing the conquest would be left to each tribe or regional grouping of tribes.

After a digression to discuss the establishment of the seat of the tribal federation at Shiloh (see below), the rest of the territorial allotments are discussed in chapters 18 and 19. The allocation to the seven remaining tribes follows a slightly different procedure, proposed by Joshua (18:3). Joshua demands that they act and proposes a means for them to scout out the remaining available territory and then bring their requests before the allotments committee. In this case, three men are chosen from each tribe—again a federal procedure. Joshua instructs them to write down descriptions of the seven portions (18:6). The Israelites could write. After the tribal representatives of the seven tribes agreed among themselves as to how the seven portions would be divided, the commission was to cast the lots before the Lord to allocate them. Joshua's proposal is taken as an instruction and is done. The emphasis in the text is on writing the descriptions and on the "book" of descriptions of the remainder of the land (the descriptions were set down in a scroll or document). The descriptions were given by "cities" (or, better, townships), according to the perceptual framework described above.

At the very end of the process, Joshua, as national leader, received his allotment from the entire people but within his own tribal area (19:49-50). While Joshua received the *'ir* he requested, it is specified that the Israelites gave it to him per God's instruction. Joshua built Timnah-Serah as an *'ir* in Mt. Ephraim. This is the only reference to building a new permanent settlement in the book but should not be taken

as the only case in which this was done. Joshua was sufficiently important to warrant the mention; perhaps as a model.

The Levitical allotment completes the division of the land. The Levites
receive 48 cities scattered around the country, each with pasture lands to
2,000 cubits each (Num. 35). The inclusion of pasturage lands in the
grant is indicative of the basically rural character of the "cities" of Israel. An *ir* was any permanent settlement with its own government. One
that embraced 20 acres containing some 3,000 people was considered
large. A *hazar* was an unfortified cluster of dwellings within the orbit of
an *ir*. Together they comprised an organic unit, comparable to the Swiss
commune, the New England town, or the Latin American municipio. A
Canaanite *ir* was generally a politically independent entity. An Israelite
ir, on the other hand, was an integral part of the tribal government. It
maintained its own local government based on the assembly of resident
adult males. Day to day business was conducted by elders constituted at
the "city gate," that is, the council located at the city's gate where the
market was located so that it was more or less equally accessible to all
the inhabitants of the *ir* and its *hazerot*. In addition, there are *havot* (protected tent-camps) near permanent settlements put together for protection against marauders, like "forts" in the American West or the fortified
farms of contemporary Afghanistan.

The heads of the fathers of the Levites had to make their constitutional claim. They referred to their occupation as cattlemen and their
need for *'arim* with fields. In other words, they had to support themselves by their own labor and could not count on maintaining themselves through their ritual services. They were not a clergy living off the
labor of others. This is an old Jewish tradition, part of the approach to
civic life of the *edah*. While the constitution promises the Levites cities,
the tribal authorities had to do the actual allotting from their respective
inheritances (v. 3).

A Seat of Government: The Tent of Assembly at Shiloh

As part of the settlement of the land, the Israelite tribes established
Shiloh as the place of national assembly and seat of the federation by
locating the tent of assembly there (18:1). Shiloh appears here for the
first time on the pages of Jewish history as a concrete place, but it is well
to recall the cryptic reference in Jacob's final blessing of his sons, the

tribes of Israel (Gen. 49:10), *Lo yasur shevet meyehudah v'mehokek miben raglav ad ki-yavoh Shiloh v'lo yikhat 'amim,* which is interpreted by some to suggest that Judah (which could mean David's house) shall rule until the true ruler comes in the messianic age. In later Jewish literature, Shiloh acquired an association with the final redemption and the restoration of the original Israelite polity.

In essence, Shiloh was designated as the place where the tribal delegates convened to deal with national affairs. Not a capital like Jerusalem became later under David or like Paris or London today, but a seat of government, like Philadelphia for the United States between 1776 and 1790, or Brussels today for the European Community. Shiloh is referred to as a *mahaneh* (camp) (v. 9), in part simply because it was that, not a permanent settlement, but one suspects also because of the tradition brought out of the desert that the Lord's habitation cannot be fixed in a permanent settlement. This tradition had clear political implications and was to be an element in the constitutional controversy over the establishment of Jerusalem as the national capital after David's conquest of that city.

Shiloh remained the legitimate seat of the tribal federation throughout the existence of that regime, until it was destroyed by the Philistines, one of the acts that led to the people's willingness to entertain a constitutional change of great magnitude. When David moved the Ark of the Covenant to his new capital, it was a decisive sign of the shift in regimes.

The description of the inauguration of Shiloh as the federal seat is constructed with care to utilize the formal terms for political assembly, namely, *vayakahalu* (they assembled) related to *kahal* (congregation, assembly)—the term for formally congregating or assembling; *'Adath bnei yisrael,* literally, the assembly of the sons of Israel—the formal term for Israel as a body politic; *vayashkinu*—a formal term that implies setting something down, setting it up, and making it a fixture; *Ohel Mo'ed*—the tent of assembly where the business of the *edah* was done.

The Cities of Refuge

Another essential element in the Israelite polity was the provision of cities of refuge. They were set aside in the fulfillment of the Mosaic injunction (20:2) to give refuge from the blood feud to those who accidentally committed manslaughter. Six cities, each a major one in its region, were set aside as regional centers (20:7–9). This is also evidence that the land was considered divided into six principal regions. This provision indicates how it is possible to deal with tradition by dealing with it sideways, rather than attacking it head on. Little could have been accomplished by simply trying to abolish the feud system without a substitute. Here was a substitute that replaced it without harshly violating public sentiment.

In giving a description of the function of the cities of refuge, this chapter gives us a picture of some of the processes of government of *'Adat Bnei Yisrael,* especially local government and the judicial system. The perpetrator still had to stand trial before the *edah* (i.e., his peers) or he could wait until the incumbent High Priest died when there was a general amnesty. This account suggests five important points about Israelite judicial procedures:

1. Trial by the *edah* meant under the laws of the Torah, not tribal custom. The latter is simply the custom of the blood feud. It is superseded by the new positive legislation of the Torah for the whole nation.

2. Implicit here is some form of trial by one's peers, a major element in securing equity as well as justice.

3. The High Priest was the highest human judicial authority (in great part because he can cast lots indicating the Divine judgment).

4. There was a practice of general amnesty upon the death of the High Priest. This is another reflection of the separation of powers system in operation in the *edah.* In other polities, general amnesties usually were granted at the death of kings.

5. Resident aliens as well as citizens had the privilege of refuge and trial before the *edah,* as they had the privilege of Sabbath rest and other rights.

Notes

1. On the generational rhythm in the Bible, see Umberto Casutto, *From Adam to Noah* (Jerusalem: Magnes Press, 1978) and *From Noah to Abraham* (Jerusalem: Magnes Press, 1974); Daniel J. Elazar and Stuart Cohen, *The Jewish Polity* (Bloomington: Indiana University Press, 1985); and George Mendenhall, *The Tenth Generation: The Origins of the Biblical Tradition* (Baltimore: Johns Hopkins University Press, 1973).
2. The discussion is introduced by using the standard technical terminology (e.g., *nahalah,* inheritance; *shivtehem,* their tribes) with one exception, the use of the

term *mahlekotam* (their divisions). The term *mahlakah* is used forty-one times in the Bible, three times in Joshua, once each in Ezekiel and Nehemiah, and the thirty-six remaining times in 1 or 2 Chronicles, a royalist account of the history of the Jewish kingdoms of the First Commonwealth. Its use reflects the development of a strong national government with a bureaucracy that has divided the people into administrative units to manage the national government (if not in an effort to replace the tribes as the building blocks of the Israelite polity).

The system was introduced by David (1 Chron. 13–18) and reaffirmed by Solomon (2 Chron. 5 and 18). It is referred to subsequently as a Davidic ordinance and is treated as an important component of the constitution of Judah, mentioned in connection with Jehoyadah's restoration of the constitution by overthrowing Athaliah (2 Chron. 31) and Hezekiah's religious reform (2 Chron. 35). Ezekiel makes reference to it (48:29) in a manner similar to its usage here, as part of the restoration of the tribal system in the end of days. Thus, this coda is a gloss that either intentionally or unintentionally seeks to legitimize a later form of internal political organization, which would have been thoroughly rejected by the people in the time of Joshua, and initially was designed to replace the federal polity with a more centralized structure but which, over time, came to be viewed as an attempt to preserve the spirit of the old order within the new framework.

3. In reading the geographic descriptions in Joshua, it is useful to understand the way the Israelites conceptualized spacial organization. Space, for them, was not framed by fixed boundaries that were then given content within their boundaries, in the Anglo-American manner. The Israelite perspective is just the reverse: conceiving space as radiating outward from a core or node to some not always fully determined limits. This mode of thought is apparent in the discussion of the division of the land among the tribes. Thus, each of the nine areas mentioned is described by its central feature but its boundaries are not defined. This perspective also contributes to the confusion of accounts regarding the extent and process of settlement and conquest described in Joshua and Judges. No specific claim is made in Joshua to overt Israelite possession of the whole territory within each region, only general control over the country.

The nodal perspective is evident by the use of the term *gevulot* in connection with the earliest conquests. The term *gevul*, usually translated as border or boundary, really means borderlands, not a fixed line but a boundary region.

If there is any doubt regarding the consciousness of differences in geo-political organization in Joshua (v. 23) should resolve it. Geographers work with two major theories of regional spatial organization: linear and nodal. Joshua makes reference to both. A *nafah*, used in Joshua to describe predominantly rural regions or regions without a specific central point located in a core city, is a linear region and a *galil*, a circle, referred to in 13:1. This geographic sophistication becomes prominent in the subsequent discussion of the division of the land.

13

Joshua's Farewell Addresses

The final section of the Book of Joshua consists of the last three chapters of the book: 22, 23, and 24. In terms of the larger meaning of the book, they deal with two final problems, both of which were of vital importance at the time of Samuel. The first of these problems is that of national unity or, more particularly, intertribal unity, in the political sense. It is dealt with in chapter 22 through a tale involving the tribes that had been allotted land on the east bank of the Jordan. Again, what we have is a case study to illustrate a particular problem that confronted the tribal federation and to indicate a solution to that problem within the framework of the Israelite constitution.

The second problem is the larger question of the entire future of the Israelite tribal federation. This question is raised and discussed by Joshua, first in an address delivered to the leaders of the people and then in a covenant-making ceremony, to the people as a whole. These farewell addresses are great literary expressions as well as important political statements. They are fitting summations of a great political work and were no doubt intended to be eloquent and moving in their impact as well as important for their ideas.

National Unity Tested

Chapter 22 begins the concluding section of the book with the demobilization of the armies (vv. 1-6) and the story of a near-civil war (vv. 10-34). The campaign is over. Victory, though not altogether complete, has been substantial and the task so precariously initiated has been brought to a successful conclusion. For the moment, the wars are done. Now the tribal levies are disbanding, returning home to take up peaceful pursuits. As in all such cases, there is a mixture of happiness at being able to return home to family and civilian life; yet, at the same time, the rigors of the campaign are receding into the background and the joys of military comradeship and recollections of the excitements of battle prevail. Joshua, recognizing this, makes a short parting speech before the men leave for home, one whose purpose is, in the main, political and moral.

Joshua's farewell charges them to remain true to the covenant. It is the first of a long tradition of republican farewells. Those familiar with American history will recall George Washington bidding farewell to his troops at Newburgh, New York, and, in the process, reminding them of the ideals for which they had fought, discouraging them from their efforts to make him a monarch and forcing them to pledge themselves to maintain republican government; or, in a very different vein, Robert E. Lee's farewell to his troops after the surrender at Appomattox, when he gently suggested that they go home to pick up the remnants of their shattered lives in order to rebuild their beloved Southland within the Union. In the main, Joshua's farewell can be seen as a model for such conclusions not only in every classical history of a military campaign but for republican armies with great commanders whose last charge to their troops is to be faithful to the republic and its constitution.

The military forces of the tribes of Reuben, Gad, and that part of the tribe of Manasseh that had been allotted land on the east bank of the Jordan, assemble at Shiloh, are relieved of their duties in the conquest, and are demobilized to return home, with the thanks of Joshua speaking on behalf of the nation. Their demobilization is described in a scant six verses, yet one can feel the emotional aspects of the event clearly from the tone of Joshua's words.

> Then Joshua summoned the Reubenites, the Gadites, and the half-tribe of Manasseh, and said to them: "You have observed all that Moses the servant of the Lord commanded you, and have obeyed me in everything that I commanded you. You have not forsaken your kinsmen through the long years down to this day, but have faithfully observed the Instruction of the Lord your God. Now the Lord your God has given your kinsmen rest, as He promised them. Therefore turn and go to your homes, to the land of your holdings beyond the Jordan which Moses the servant of the Lord assigned to you. But be very careful to fulfill the Instruction and the Teaching that Moses the servant of the Lord enjoined upon you, to love the Lord your God and to walk in all His ways, and to keep His commandments and hold fast to Him, and to serve Him with all your heart and soul." Then Joshua blessed them and dismissed them, and they went to their homes. (22:1-6)

The style is such that the narration encapsulates a description of the behavior expected of all Israelites, no matter what tribe or what military situation. It restates the immediate obligation to serve the national cause and the larger obligation to maintain the Lord's commandments with *hesed* in war and peace.

There follows the story of a near civil war, which tells how a misunderstanding of the purposes of the eastern tribes in building an altar almost leads to internal conflict between the tribes (22:9–34). When the two and a half tribes returned to their own territories (*gelilot* [nodal regions] is the term used), they built a great altar, apparently at a central point along the Jordan. This was viewed by the Israelites on the west bank as a secessionist activity because, though couched in terms of religious observance, it really deals with a political question. The establishment of a new center of worship for that part of the nation living east of the Jordan could have involved shifting the center of their political loyalty as well (cf. 1 Kings 12:28–33—Jereboam's construction of new sanctuaries after the secession of the northern tribes).

Before engaging in precipitous action, however, the Israelites send a delegation to the eastern tribes to warn them of their sin and its consequences. This delegation is properly drawn under the terms of the Israelite constitution. It includes Pinchas ben Elazar, the son and heir of the nation's High Priest; an office, as we have seen before, that had an important function as arbiter of intertribal affairs and is apparently responsible for the maintenance of a more nationally oriented viewpoint on questions that touch the most important interests of the various divisions of the nation. He is accompanied by delegates (*nesiim*) from each of the ten west bank tribes. The account adds that the delegates in this case were the chief officers of the tribes, that is to say, the highest civil and military leadership, obviously because of the gravity of the issue.

The procedure itself seems to be a constitutional one: that is to say, the *edah* as a federal body warning tribes that are straying from God's constitution of the consequences of their actions before actually taking action against them, thus giving them the opportunity to turn from (repent) their erroneous ways. *Teshuvah* (repentance) is an essential feature of polities founded by covenant. The ability to turn back to the right way becomes part of the political process of Israel in other ways as well, such as the prophet's warning to the people and their kings in later centuries. Subsequently, it is incorporated into such covenantal polities as the Puritan colonies of New England as a regular device in which ministers issued warnings to governmental and religious bodies calling attention to the terms of the covenant and calling them back to those terms.

The mission from the main body of the nation delivers the warning and asks the two and a half tribes directly whether they are engaged in a rebellious act, forcefully reminding them of the precedents that would make them believe that building an altar was a rebellious action. They also indicate that the violation would lead to God's anger at the whole *edah*. They suggest a remedy if there is a real problem.

The two and a half tribes reply to the delegation through their leaders and deny any interest in rebelling against national authority. They were not secessionists but were seeking to find a way to communicate to their descendants the unity of the tribes on both sides of the river under the Lord's covenant. Through an oath-like formula, they affirm their belief in the Lord and that He knows they are not rebels, in the most emphatic possible manner. The oath uses all the names commonly used for God in one linked sentence, perhaps to indicate that they all believe in the same God, and that He is their God. Moreover, they deny that they built the altar principally for sacrifice but that it was built as a historical monument to remind their descendants of the connection between the Israelites on both banks of the river, and of their concern for that connection. Their statement is simple yet moving: "In time to come your children might speak unto our children saying, what have ye to do with the Lord, the God of Israel, the Lord hath made the Jordan a border between us and you; you children of Reuben and you children of Gad, you have no portion of the Lord, so might your children make our children cease from fearing the Lord." Finally, the two and a half tribes reaffirm their ties to the Tabernacle at Shiloh while the local altar is formally named as a witness that the east bank tribes accept the Lord as their God.

This explanation not only satisfies the delegation but pleases them. In the name of the delegation, Pinchas says, "This day we know the Lord is in the midst of us because you have not committed treachery against the Lord." The delegation returns, makes its report, the *edah* is satisfied, and the threat of civil war is ended. Only the action of the western tribes in sending a delegation to warn their confederates of their sin and the innocent reaction of the eastern tribes saves the day.

To what extent the case is historical, to what extent it is based on a reworking of a historical incident, is beyond our present competence and knowledge to ascertain. What is clear is that the author is trying to demonstrate once again how the nation could remain united and could solve the disagreements that could potentially lead to civil war under the constitution he advocated. The concern of the east bank tribes to remain united with their west bank brethren is strongly emphasized here. It is less a concern with their own descendants' connections to the west bank than with the attitudes of the descendants of the west bank tribes to those who might be on the east side of the river. Thus, it is suggested that it is the isolated tribes who desire unity most of all. Of course, this is an exact contradiction of the situation described in Judges where every incident involving intertribal rivalries is played up to indicate the necessity for a monarchic form of government in order to create national unity.

Why is this story included? It appears to be a final argument against the monarchists. The only argument left unanswered in the chronicler's effort to disprove the arguments of the monarchists that the federation as a political system could not solve its governmental problems is that of internal conflict. It has already made its case that when properly constitutional, the tribal federation could conquer the land, handle its division, and deal with Israel's external enemies. The question still remains whether, in time of peace, the tribes could be held together in spite of divisive tendencies among them. The monarchists argued that they could not. This story offers testimony that the federation could deal with internal conflict through the mechanisms of its political system (in this case, the assembly of the aggrieved tribes as the *edah*, the selection of a high level delegation, and the utilization of discussion and negotiation to clarify the issue and arrange a compromise), if they are fully in place and functioning. This final example of the tribal federation in action and of the mechanisms of its polity concludes the argument made in this most political of books. All that is left is Joshua's farewell address to the nation as a whole.

Joshua's Farewell Address to the Assembled Leadership

Chapter 23 is the first of two final chapters that comprise Joshua's farewell to the people. As in Deuteronomy, the final section is the leader's farewell in the form of a summary teaching and a renewal of the covenant. A comparison of chapters 23 and 24 indicates that the first is a preliminary message to the leaders of the people prior to a renewal of the covenant with the people as a whole in the second. The two chapters can be read as illustration of the difference between the mode of addressing leaders with their special responsibilities, and the mode of addressing the people as a whole in a democratic republic. Joshua first assembles the governing officials of the whole nation and addresses them. His message is directed to them as leaders or governors and emphasizes the problem they will confront of popular assimilation into Canaanite culture and how the success of Israelite settlement in the land depends upon faithfulness in maintaining Israel's covenant with God. Joshua formally continues to support driving out the Canaanite remnants from the land and warns the leadership of the potential consequences if that is not done.

From the context, it can be concluded that Joshua assembled all the holders of tribal and national offices in Israel (v. 2). The phrase *Khol Yisrael* (all Israel) refers not to the people but to the representatives of the people. The representatives assembled are mentioned explicitly by category, using the technical terms that are used throughout the book and in the Torah: *Zekenim* as heads of the families, *rashim* (heads) of the tribes, *shofetim* (judges), and *shoterim* (officers).

In reiterating God's promise to drive out the Canaanite remnants, inter alia, Joshua emphasizes the necessity for the people to maintain their moral character or the quality of virtue, especially in reference to the maintenance without deviation of the laws written in *Torat Moshe* (the Book of the Teachings of Moses); in other words, reaffirming the necessity for them to abide by the Israelite constitution. In fact, Joshua's emphasis on the integrity of the constitution is a prelude to its reinterpretation in this case (v. 7). He redefines the commandment to entirely drive out or exterminate the Canaanites to make it a requirement that the Israelites not associate with those remaining after the initial conquest. This constitutional change through interpretation is significant not only in itself but also for the model it offers of how a change is made, by first reaffirming that there can be no changes and then proceeding with the new interpretation as if it were not new. This model becomes the norm for constitutional change in Jewish tradition, reaching its fullest flowering in the days of the Pharisees and their sages, the Tannaim and Amoraim, and is reflected in their principal product, the Talmud.

The policy of cultural isolationism that Joshua advocates is characteristic of a covenantal people seeking to preserve its vocation in a hostile environment. The principle was to avoid other than the most casual contact with the nations around them and, in particular, to avoid such close dealings with them that would give cause to Israelites to have to swear in their courts, by their gods. This passage, which sounds like a simple religious prescription, carries substantial social and political overtones as well, because of this point. It is not simply the forbidding of idolatry for fear of the adoption of their neighbors' idolatrous customs, but it is virtually an interdiction of commercial and social intercourse with them.

The interdiction is continued and made more specific by reference to the problem of intermarriage (v. 12). Here we get to the root of the great social problem. Intermarriage in the ancient world could well mean that the wife would be obliged to raise the children in the religion of the husband, because she lived in the family fold of the husband. Consequently, intermarriage could be considered as a minor problem for the Israelite household as long as the male made the determination as to the children's way of life. At the same time, the Bible is profoundly aware that the problem is more than one of the formal linkages; rather, it is one of teaching practices, values, and spirit, that this task is bound to fall more closely on the mother than on the father and that the child's early exposure should be to a true Israelite, not to the superstitions or beliefs carried over from the pagan world that are likely to remain with the pagan wife, no matter how well she accepts her obligations to her husband.

Beyond the problems incurred within the household, however, there is the larger problem that marriage in the ancient world was a form of interfamilial alliance, bringing with it obligations between the two extended families involved, including mutual respect for household deities under certain circumstances, which would create additional unwholesome entanglements. The verse makes clear reference to this without being specific in detail because everyone would know what it meant. The national consequences of intermarriage are made clear; the remaining Canaanites will not be driven out of the land but will remain to trap the Israelites, disturb their way of life, and ultimately to weaken their attachment to their covenant and hasten their disappearance as a nation (v. 13). Sociologically this is a sound line of argument. Intermarriage will lead to ties between Israelite and non-Israelite families and will make it more difficult for the Israelites to avoid other forms of social intercourse and extremely difficult for them to drive the relatives of their wives out of the land. Thus, the latter are likely to remain, and since human beings tend to be weak and the demands of the Israelite covenant are difficult ones, it is likely that many Israelites will take the path of least resistance and succumb to the customs of the world around them, thus breaking the covenant and assimilating to the larger Canaanite society in which they are located. Needless to say, idolatry here refers not just to image worship but to the entire corpus of pagan custom and ritual that went with it such as infant sacrifice, ritual prostitution, and the like. Since the Israelite nation exists by virtue of its maintenance of the covenant rather than by virtue of particular ethnic ties, abandonment of the covenant will mean destruction of the nation.

Joshua completes his charge by reminding the leaders that, just as all the good things the Lord has promised have been fulfilled, so will all the bad things if they let the people depart from the covenant and its terms (vv. 14–16). He reminds them that Israel's inheritance of the land itself is contingent upon its maintenance of the covenant. Only for this reason was the land given to Israel and taken away from the sinful Canaanites. If Israel sins as well, it, too, will lose the land. The land, then, is holy and belongs to God who grants custody of it only to holy nations.

Joshua's message to the leaders, then, is one of advice and exhortation as to the problems they are likely to face in leading the people within the covenant framework in the future. He attempts to point out to them some of the specific problems that they are likely to encounter in maintaining the Israelite constitution and to warn them against neglecting those problems. In sum, it is the message of one leader to others.

The Renewal of the National Covenant and Constitution

In chapter 24, the people join with their leaders to renew the national covenant and the constitution derived from it, under Joshua's direction. The covenant-making recounted in this chapter differs from that recounted in chapter 8 in that there the people made a political covenant subsidiary to the great covenant at Sinai, to establish their polity in the land on firmly legitimate grounds. In that sense, while emphasizing Sinai, it is as much a renewal of the covenant with Abraham. Here Joshua has them renew the national covenant that constituted the *'am* and *edah* in the first place and its constitutional result. The emphasis is on "Abraham," that is to say, the story of the founding family, but the result parallels "Sinai." Joshua speaks to the nation as a whole.

> And Joshua gathered all the tribes of Israel to Shechem, and called for the elders of Israel, and for their heads, and for their judges, and for their officers.... So Joshua made a covenant with the people that day, and set them a statute and an ordinance (*hok u'mishpat*) in Shechem. (Josh. 24:1 and 25)

Consequently, his address differs in both style and approach from his earlier address to the leadership. In the first place, its language is much more elegant, as befits a covenant ceremony. In essence, it is a full description of the making of a covenant in ancient Israel.

The text explicitly states that all the tribes of Israel and their leaders were assembled at Shechem (v. 1). The phrasing suggests that a ceremony is involved. Indeed, the nation will be asked to reaffirm their covenant once again. The same offices are mentioned, restating the organization of the polity.

Joshua starts the ceremony by reviewing in a few eloquent sentences the history of the Hebrew people from earliest times (vv. 2-13), reaffirming that the sense of historical origins was already important in the Israelite worldview. The events that Joshua mentions in his historical summary are worthy of note for what they tell us of the Israelites' historical self-perception:

1. The pre-Israelite ancestors of the Israelites and their origins in Mesopotamia, and their previous idol worshipping ways to remind them that they have no claim to perfection by virtue of their ancestry or kinship, only by their own actions in consenting to God's authority.

2. The order of the patriarchs, their movement into the land of Israel, and God's promise of the land as the historical justification for their being in Canaan.

3. The descent to Egypt, which, though it contains no formal mention of slavery, implies slavery as part of the telling to explain why they had to reconquer the land.

4. The passage of the mantle of leadership to Moses and Aaron, to indicate the beginning of the formal existence of Israel as a nation as distinct from its previous existence as a family, and the beginning of the line of legitimate national leaders.

5. The plagues in Egypt, the Exodus, the Egyptian pursuit, and the miracle of the Red Sea, all of which serve as testimony to the Lord's power and the favor He has granted Israel.

6. The wilderness wandering (though there is no mention of the Sinai covenant per se).

7. The meeting with Baalam to indicate how the Lord even requires the nations around Israel to recognize the latter's special providence.

8. The invasion of the land and its deliverance into the hands of the Israelites intact with its fertility unimpaired—another illustration of the extraordinary goodness of the Lord (beyond the call of the covenant, as it were).

9. The offering of a once-and-for-all choice between the Lord and foreign gods, which is the climax of the narrative. Joshua refers to the contemporary generation as witness to all of the foregoing. This view that all generations were present at the Exodus is a traditional one.

There is no mention of the Sinai covenant here, perhaps because the purpose of the assembly was to freely enter into a covenant accepting their obligations to God, presumably without prejudicing the issue.[3]

Joshua's review is a preamble to the covenant to be made. The text explicitly mentions that it is directed to the people to remind them of their origins and founding. The message is delivered in the name of God and in the first person, emphasizing God's actions as the basis for the founding and redemption of Israel. Each critical event is mentioned in turn, leaving no doubt as to who was responsible for it.

Joshua concludes this section by offering the people the choice that day between serving the Lord or serving other gods: "either the gods your fathers served before you or the gods you will take up in the land of Canaan" (vv. 14-15). He ends, very eloquently, with the statement that whatever their choice, he and his household are committed to the service of the Lord. It is evident that this is not designed to be a neutral appeal, but one that will call the public to reaffirm their covenant with God following Joshua's example.

The people's reply is presented in so stylized a fashion (vv. 16-18) that it seems to be part of a formula in which the answer was foreordained. They give as their reasons (vv. 17-18) the very ones that Joshua presented to them as being worthy of their consideration in the first place, albeit in short form and beginning with the Exodus.

The impression that the whole ceremony is stylized and follows a formula is strengthened in verse 19ff. Joshua raises the question again, reiterating it but also adding a new dimension, that it is difficult to serve the Lord, that He is specially set apart, especially jealous of His prerogatives and specially unforgiving of transgressions against His law. In others words, Joshua puts the hardest possible face on the decision and its consequences. This is a formula designed to secure the fullest possible ratification of the covenant even after second thoughts. That is to say, in important actions involving the very consensus upon which political societies are built, people should not be forced into quick decisions. In modern terms, the plebiscite method often used to create the aura of "democratic" acceptance of totalitarian regimes is rejected in favor of a method that allows the people to reconsider their decision and by reaffirming it, strengthen it beyond the limits that a decision based on immediate reactions would normally be considered to have.

The people, replying either spontaneously or according to formula, reiterate their commitment (v. 21). Joshua then tells the people (v. 22) that by giving their consent a second time, they are witnesses against themselves to their decision; that is to say, it can be used against them and their descendants if their descendants backslide. This, in essence, is a third statement of the question to which the people are invited to respond, saying, "we are witnesses." Repeated reaffirmation adds to the binding and sacred character of the whole.

After this thrice questioning and thrice answering (as at Sinai), Joshua summarizes the key element of the covenant, that they must put away their strange gods and incline their hearts toward the Lord, the God of Israel. The people accordingly reply, "The Lord our God we will serve and unto His voice we will hearken." The three oral affirmations are then ratified by a written covenant (vv. 25–26). This written covenant becomes the basis of the constitutional law (*hok u'mishpat*) of the people or, as it is called in verse 26, the Book of the Teaching of God, and the place where the covenant is formulated and agreed to is marked by a monument, a great stone.

Here we have the conclusion of the ceremony, which marks the essence of republican constitutional government. The people here consent to the covenant, which redefines them. In doing so, they reformulate the consensus undergirding their society. The democratic element is founded on the original power of the people to determine the consensus, ratify the constitution that embodies that consensus, and participate in political decision making under that constitution in appropriately institutionalized ways. For ordinary matters they have leaders, as indicated in chapter 23. What they must do is legitimize those leaders by giving them authority and, more important than that, they must set the boundaries, the framework, the consensus within which those leaders must work.

As the final step in the covenant ceremony (vv. 27–28), Joshua explains the stone as witness to the covenant making, that it will be a witness against them to the effect that they have heard all the words of the Lord that Joshua has put before them and have agreed to accept the Lord's constitution. The scene ends appropriately, with the people dispersing—as the Bible says, "every man unto his inheritance."

The Future World Order and the Right of Every Nation to the Land Assigned It by God

Chapter 24, verse 4 reaffirms the assignment of the mountain land of Seir to Esau. The Bible is opposed to Israelite imperialism or territorial expansion beyond the allotted boundaries and makes its point in this oblique manner. There is an implicit conception in the Bible, reaffirmed again and again in specific statements, that each nation has a right to exist unless and until God decides otherwise (e.g., in the case of the Canaanites).

The Jews have maintained this position ever since. It lies at the root of the Zionist idea; more than that, it is a basic aspect of the Jewish worldview. Universal peace and the messianic age are not obtained by eliminating nations but by seeing to it that all nations are located in their proper lands. The messianic era, then, is not one of a single world state in which national differences are leveled but a product of the sum of the nations peacefully located in their own lands and cultivating their diverse integrities. These nations will be bound together (federated) by a common covenant with God and each other without losing their identities. So long as the nations will be bound in harmony and peace by covenant, this is no less a universalistic view than the other.

The biblical view is that national attachment or patriotism is not an atavistic evil to be eliminated at the end of time but, provided that it can be brought into harmony with the universal moral order as set forth by God, love of nation and country can be a positive good. The Bible goes further. If a country is allotted to a particular people by Divine decree, that people can honestly fight for it and even seek to conquer it. Of course, many others aside from the Jews claim the same kind of Divine promise. The fact that some of these claims are patently false does not eliminate the possibility that others may be justified. The problem is always to distinguish the true claims from the false, but this problem is not unique to claims of Divine favor.

The End of an Era

The last section of chapter 24 (vv. 29-33) deals with the passing of the last leaders of the generation of the wilderness and their burial in the land of their fathers, and hints at what the future will bring. Joshua is buried in his inheritance in Ephraim. Joseph's remains are reburied near Shechem in the lot purchased by his father Jacob, and Elazar the High Priest is also buried in Ephraim. In the meantime, the statement that Israel served the Lord until the last of the elders who knew Joshua (that is to say, those who experienced the generation of the conquest) had passed away suggests that there was a later lapse into idolatry, something that the narrator would undoubtedly know about, since he himself was a product of the later era. The human truth of the impact of the founders on their sons and its subsequent diminution is part of the biblical teaching about the importance of generations in history while the reference to elders as custodians of the nation's steadfastness is part of the biblical teaching on the importance of proper leadership. This is an opening to dealing with the later lapses of Israel from the antimonarchical perspective. Those lapses were not a result of republicanism per se, but of corrupted republicanism, which is the essence of the message of the Book of Joshua.

Note

1. There is a thesis that has broad support among biblical scholars, that not all the Israelites were in bondage in Egypt and therefore left in the Exodus but that a portion of the people remained in Eretz Israel. This account could be read as one in which Joshua reunified the whole people, as distinct from the first Shechem assembly of the newcomers alone, hence the emphasis at first on the common ancestors and events in Israelite history and then the relation of the subsequent events in such a way as to indicate that even those not present have a share in them. While this writer does not accept this thesis, it does not alter in any way the basic political thrust of the book.

   Chapter 24 is often treated as presenting a major textual problem that may imply that Joshua's covenant was the first national covenant of the Israelites. In verse 25, the narrative describes how Joshua writes down the agreement of the people in the Book of the Teaching of God, not as previously stated in other parts of the Book of Joshua, which refers to the Book of the Teaching of Moses. The whole chapter has been considered by some to be a separate account of a covenant between the Lord and Israel initiated after the conquest by Joshua rather than after the Exodus by Moses, at Shechem rather than at Sinai.

Biblical critics have seized upon this and made much of it. There are several possible explanations here. One is that the text is slightly distorted and that it really was a reaffirmation of the Mosaic covenant, not a new one. This, of course, is the most traditional explanation. The second is that the whole story was developed after the ten northern tribes separated themselves from Davidic monarchy, developed their own shrines, and needed a justification for doing so. This is the most radical explanation and does the most violence to the theory presented here since it would imply a much later authorship of the Book of Joshua, one that was somewhat (but still not entirely unlikely) to be responsible for an anti-monarchist tract. A third explanation is that since the text is a full account of a covenant ceremony, it is natural that it ignores the problem it seems to present at first glance.

14

Judges: The Reality?

The Regime of the Judges

If Joshua presents a picture of the classic Mosaic regime in its ideal manifestation, the Book of Judges presents a picture of a far different reality. By that reality, Israel shifts from being a reasonably strong federation to a weak confederation, operationally hardly more than a league at times. Its prolonged problems as a result of that weakness ultimately lead to a change in regime of major proportions, a change that undermined the very character of the covenant in its pristine form.

According to the Bible, *Adat Bnai Yisrael* took a new turn after the end of "the polity settled by Moses" (in the words of Josephus) that came with the death of Joshua. Formally, that polity or regime was still in place. God ruled Israel directly, the nation was unified through the Torah and governed through the tribal federation, but Joshua left no successor as *Eved Adonai*. According to the biblical text, between Joshua and Samuel there was no nationwide federal leader. The conquest had gone as far as it would go except for border adjustments and the conquest of holdout Canaanite cities. The newly settled Israelites became agriculturalists—both farmers and herders of cattle, sheep, and goats— and artisans (weavers, dyers, tanners, smiths, potters, and other crafts). Class divisions were still insignificant. This was the ideal age in that respect.[1]

While the tribes were still linked by covenant, the Israelites shifted to less institutionalized national government, rooted more in tribal and local custom, modified only by the emergence of charismatic judges in times of crisis who emerge as civil and military leaders as needed, generally on a regional basis.[2] The only standing national institutions were the priestly servants of the Ark of the Covenant at the central sanctuary and the Levites, scattered throughout the land, who are described as both private entrepreneurs and representatives of the cult. The tribal government itself, led by elders, is a constant; its local government based on a system of townships, each with its own township assembly based on all males eligible and obligated to serve in the local militia (in Hebrew: *ha'ir*) and a court of local elders that meets at the city gates (in Hebrew: *shaarei ha'ir*).[3]

The term *shofet* is not exclusive to ancient Israel. The Phoenicians and their Carthaginian offshoot used the term to describe their civil rulers. Moreover, in Targum Yonatan to the Bible, *shofet* is presented as being the equal of *nagid* or God's high commissioner. In the Pentateuch, the *shofetim* had been second-level officials, combining executive and judicial functions in the tribal federation, responsible to the *Eved Adonai*.

The Bible is ambivalent about this period and its regime. On the one hand, it was seen as an attempt to implement the classic version of the polity in which God alone would be the supreme national ruler with no permanent human leader except for local purposes or in times of national emergency. As a system of government it failed because it was too weak to meet the challenges that the Israelites faced. Beyond that, it also failed to prevent Israelite lapses into paganism or syncretism ("idolatry"), which are of prime concern in the Bible. It is not clear from the text whether these lapses were part of the overall dynamics of Israelite life or preventable sins.

Governmentally, the national political system came close to being a true anarchy.[4] This had consequences in Israel's internal affairs, including problems in the maintenance of the covenant among the tribes as well in its external affairs, in dealing with "barbarian" invasions, wars with local Canaanites, and, in the end, the Philistine menace. Gideon, Jeptha, and Samson were the most famous military heroes with varying degrees of peacetime authority.

The book mentions twelve judges but it seems that there were more. Again, the biblical chronicler is not concerned with relating the history of the period but in using historical materials to develop moral issues and points. The climax of the period as presented is when Gideon responds to God's call, brilliantly defeats the Midianites through a combination of reliance on men's faith in God and clever military tactics, and then refuses the kingship. Gideon came closest to being a national leader. He is presented as a faithful servant of God, portrayed as believing in the Mosaic regime and refusing a popular offer to make him king.

Deborah played a civil role in a military situation. She and one other anonymous figure at the time of Gideon are referred to as prophets. The distinction is clearly *ketaric*. Judges were raised up to lead the people civilly and militarily. Deborah and the anonymous prophet, on the other hand, pass on God's communications to the people and are designated by the appropriate *ketaric* name. The priests were the custodians of the central shrine, principally located at Shiloh, suggesting that all that was left in the form of national organization is what the Greeks referred to as an *amphictyony,* a collection of bodies politic united for religious reasons around a central shrine.[5]

The principal regional divisions were along northern and southern lines. The northern tribes, located in a topographically more open part of the country, were harassed by invaders and marauders during most of the period. They also had more Canaanite enclaves in their midst and were exposed to greater pagan pressure. The material in the book deals mostly with them.

The southern tribes lived relatively undisturbed until the very end of the period when the Philistines on their western border invaded their land. At first the tribe of Dan served as a buffer and absorbed most of the Philistine's blows as indicated in the story of Samson, a Danite whose role in the Divine scheme of things was to fight the Philistines. Then they tired of the responsibility and migrated to the far north of the country, exposing Judah's flank, which changed the history of Israel.

The book before us has the usual problems of authorship. It is rather obviously based on several sources, at the very least a compilation of ancient texts (the Song of Deborah has been recognized as one of the very oldest passages in the Bible, apparently dating from the period claimed). It is generally agreed that these texts and sources were compiled by an editor from the prophetic school who gave the book its tone and direction. It is equally clear that some of the events recounted in the book occurred simultaneously. Because this is not a history, chronology is not of the essence to the author. At the same time, the language and style of the book are consistent with the other books of the former prophets and of the Torah. One source has identified 108 parallelisms with the Pentateuch and running parallelism with Joshua and the other prophetic books.[6]

The book's major contradiction of previous material is in its suggestion that the Israelite conquest of the land did not take place in one fell swoop as is suggested in Joshua but took place slowly. Without trying to resolve the problem, in fact the two are not that contradictory, since Joshua describes the conquest as a sweep, leaving behind pockets, and Judges refers to the reduction of the pockets. While Joshua emphasizes the Joseph tribes, Judges begins the shift of emphasis to Judah, as the book's beginning indicates.

The pattern of the book is the Israelites' lapse into idolatry, their defeat by a foreign enemy, their *tza'akah* (formalized crying out) to God, the raising of a *shofet* by God, salvation by the Lord's mercy, the Israelites' temporary repentance, the death of the *shofet,* again the Israelites' relapse, and the cycle starts anew, until by the end of the period covering the book, God is entirely disgusted and refuses to help, leaving the Israelites to the domination of the Philistines. This pattern suggests why the ideal commonwealth failed. The refusal of the Israelites to follow the "way of the Lord" made them more like all other peoples and finally made kingship necessary. The book suggests that kingship was their first punishment (the Prophets as a whole suggest that when this was not enough, the long suffering Lord inflicted a more drastic punishment—exile).

The Character of the Book

Judges is a difficult book to read alone. It is so much embedded in the context of its predecessor, Joshua, and its successor, 1 Samuel. It begins as a continuation of Joshua, reflecting the slow but continuing process of the Israelite conquest of Canaan. It continues to deal with the Israelites' religious backsliding after they have settled in. It concludes with what is, in part, a harsh indictment of the Israelite tribal federation under the Judges for its inability to maintain Israel's security and even its internal order without a king. In this respect, as a book Judges is ambivalent about the existing regime.

Nevertheless, at the beginning, the book seems very accepting of the regime. Even the rhythm of backsliding and redemption seems to be part of the regular rhythms of life: peace and prosperity, religious backsliding, the emergence of a charismatic judge to lead the people to redemption in security matters by returning them to the true ways of God fearing, thus bringing a generation of peace before the process starts all over again. The more condemnatory tone develops only in the latter chapters of the book (chaps. 17–21).

If one emphasizes the documentary hypothesis of biblical criticism in its pure form, which does not seek coherence in the Bible and indeed rejects it, then this is easily explained. If, however, one believes that, however formed, the Bible as we have it is a coherent work, then the shift three-quarters of the way through the book must be accounted for in some reasonable way. Michael Walzer has suggested recently that the Bible has to be read as a dialogue between different viewpoints, much as later Jewish sacred literature, such as the Talmud. Judges would certainly fit his thesis.

The book is written in the spirit of covenantal religion in the covenantal polity, although the only direct references to covenant are at the beginning. The first is chapter 2:1–5, where a messenger of the Lord appears to the Israelites to accuse them of breaking God's covenant with them by entering into covenants with the inhabitants of Canaan, which have allowed idolatry to persist in the land. In the end, as a punishment, God will not drive out the rest of the Canaanites. Upon hearing this the Israelites wept and named the site of the visitation *Bochim,* which means "They cried." It is this visitation that sets the stage for what happens in the rest of the book. Judges, then, is the first book of the Bible based upon the playing out of the theme of the broken covenant.

At two other points in the book there are special references to what would have been understood by the readers of the time as covenantal: in chapter 8:22–23, where Gideon defers the kingship proffered him by the Israelites on the grounds that according to the Israelite constitution only the Lord is to rule Israel as king; and then again in chapter 21, where the Israelites find a way to restore the tribe of Benjamin after its punishment for the gross incident of the murdered concubine. On the other hand, the pattern of backsliding and foreign invasion as punishment, repentance and redemption by a judge who mobilizes the people, is in itself the repetition of a covenantal pattern, but recognizes the reality of human weakness.

An Outline of the Book

Judges begins the biblical shift of focus from the Joseph tribes to Judah, with its sister tribe, Simeon, that seems later to have disappeared within it. In chapter 1, Judah, with Simeon, takes the lead in extending the conquest, led by Joshua's co-survivor from the desert, Caleb ben Yefuneh, a Kenite. While the focus is on Judah, the chapter also deals with the conquests of the Joseph tribes, Zebulun, Asher, Naftali, and Dan, and their tribal limits, to bring us up to date on the progress of the conquest along the borders of Israel. These provide a setting for the book. All this is presented as happening immediately following the death of Joshua.

In chapter 2, we have the incident at Bochim where God's messenger conveys to the Israelites the consequences of violating God's covenant. In a sense we are presented with a dilemma. Realistically, there were limits to the Israelites' ability to conquer fortified cities, but equally realistically, by having the Canaanite peoples in their midst they were constantly tempted by pagan local custom with its idolatrous consequences.

The incident is followed (2:6–10) with a description of how the Israelites remained faithful to the Lord "all the days of Joshua, and all the days of the elders that outlived Joshua who have seen all the great work of the Lord" (v. 7), in other words, as long as there was human witness alive that had been present at the great events testifying to God's role on behalf of Israel. Later, after "all that generation were gathered unto their fathers and there arose another generation after them that knew not the Lord nor the work that he had wrought for Israel," the backsliding began (v. 10).

The rest of the chapter is essentially a generalization of the historical pattern to come, thereby strengthening the Lord's resolve not to drive the remaining Canaanites from the land, even if He intervenes from time to time to send a judge to redeem His people, because the people are faithful only so long as that judge is alive. The specifics begin in chapter 3:7, where intermarriage and idolatry bring God to give the Israelites into the hands of Aram-Naharayim, the Syria of today, for eight years. Following the covenant formula, the Israelites cry out to the Lord, who sends them Othniel ben Kenaz, another Kenite (Kennizite) and son of Caleb's younger brother, as their judge and savior, to throw out the Arameans and establish a generation of peace until his death.

Next it was the Moabites' turn when again the Israelites lapsed into idolatry. Assisted by Ammon and Amalek, the Moabites imposed tribute on Israel for eighteen years until they again cried unto the Lord in the formulary manner. God responds to them by providing them with Ehud ben Gera, a Benjaminite, who by strategem, while presenting the tribute to Eglon, the king of Moab, also stabbed him to death with his sword.

This stimulated an uprising that freed Israel and brought two generations of peace, according to the biblical account. Ehud had a successor, Shamgar ben Anat, who did not have to restore Israelite independence but to preserve it by fighting with the Philistines. From the context, he seems to have been either of the tribe of Judah or Simeon.

Once again, there is a backsliding (chap. 4). Jabin, the Canaanite king of Hatzor, aided by his military commander, Sisera, subdued the Israelites for twenty years. Once again, the Israelites cried unto the Lord who sent them Deborah, apparently an Ephraimite, a prophetess who judged Israel. She mobilized Barak ben Avinoam from the tribe of Naftali, who mobilized his fellow tribesmen and the Zebulunites. They destroy Sisera's chariot force by intelligently forcing the enemy to come to them where their infantry had the advantage of the high ground.

Once again, the Kenites play an important role, in this case through Yael, the wife of Heber, who lives in the north. The prominent role of the Kenites in Judges may be another sign pointing to the prophetic view of the importance of maintaining whatever possible of the nomadic life of the desert rather than being corrupted by the sedentary life of the Fertile Crescent. The Kenites are portrayed in the Bible as a tribe who have joined the Israelites as God fearers without merging with them, who have refused to end their nomadic existence after reaching the Promised Land, but rather continue to live in tents in the manner of the original wandering Israelites. The implicit argument is that because they do not live in settled towns, they do not become involved with the Canaanite city dwellers and are not turned by them into idolators. The Song of Deborah, recognized as one of the oldest documents in the Bible, is presented. Once again, peace came to the land for a generation.

By chapter 6 the Israelites were backsliding again, so "the Lord delivered them into the hands of Midian for seven years" (6:1). Being subdued in this period meant being forced to pay tribute to the subduing power. The Midianites, however, were nomadic tribes, not settled kingdoms, so they and their Amalekite allies simply raided Israel whenever the harvest was ready, taking not only organized tribute, but worse, taking whatever there was. Thus, God had escalated the Israelites' punishment.

This time when the Israelites cried unto the Lord, God sent an anonymous prophet and a messenger who chose Gideon ben Joash to judge and redeem Israel. Gideon was of the tribe of Menasseh. The story of his victory and the subsequent refusal to accept the kingship of Israel in violation of God's commandment is the climax of the Book of Judges. The story is told in much greater detail than in the case of the previous judges.

As is often the case, God is presented as having chosen an unlikely candidate, a man from the poorest household in Menasseh. Gideon goes through a test with the messenger of God, which ends with his assault on and destruction of the idolatrous altars. Gideon uses, in his defense as to how he could do such a thing, the classic Jewish argument that if the gods could not save themselves, why should anybody else be angry (6:27-32). Significantly, the story reveals that Gideon had another name, Jerubaal, one that clearly reflected *baal* worship or the kind of syncretism that was a product of Israelite assimilationism. We do not know from the story whether his name was Jerubaal before it became Gideon or whether he bore two names as most Jews in the diaspora do today.

There follows the rather complete story of Gideon's successful war against the Midianites, where, once again, it is the Lord's favor combined with good tactics that win the day. Gideon's tactics are portrayed as being dictated by God down to the last detail. Gideon is presented as having all the experiences of a true charismatic leader of the Lord: an encounter with God's angel messenger, Divine dreams, God's promises through them, taking a strong and public stand against idolatry, and demonstrating great faith in God's highly unconventional military tactics.

Gideon not only liberated the Israelites at home but, to make his victory complete, he pursued the Midianite enemy across the Jordan and inflicted a major defeat upon them. In the process Gideon is portrayed as having some problems with his fellow Israelites from other tribes. After resolving those problems Gideon is offered the kingship by the Israelites (8:22). In what is clearly presented as his finest hour, he turns down the offer, rejecting the very idea of kingship for Israel.

Gideon remained as Judge for the remainder of his life. While he brought a generation of peace to the land, he also reflected the syncretism of the time by erecting an ephod to the Lord, which in due course is turned to idolatrous purposes, to the worship of the *baalim,* especially *baal brit,* a *baal* about which we know little but who has a significantly covenantal name.

Gideon may have turned down the kingship but he lived like a king. He is presented as having many wives and sons. One of his sons by a concubine, Abimelech, settled in Shechem and sought to establish monarchic rule over Shechem and the adjacent Israelites (chap. 9). Abimelech secures the support of the men of Shechem in the traditional way. First he proves his prowess as a warrior, in this case by killing the other eighty sons of Gideon, all except the youngest, Jotham. After this feat, the Shechemites assembled and proclaimed him king. At the assembly he is challenged by Jotham through the parable of the trees, one of the great democratic and anti-monarchic parables in Western literature (9:7–15):

> When they told it to Jotham, he went and stood at the top of Mount Gerizim and raised his voice and cried out to them, "Hearken unto me, you men of Shechem, that God may hearken unto you. The trees went forth at one time to anoint a king over them and they said unto the olive tree, 'reign over us.' But the olive tree said to them, 'should I leave my fatness, seeing that beyond they honor God and man, and go to hold sway over the trees?' And the trees said to the fig tree, 'Come thou and reign over us.' But the fig tree said to them, 'Should I leave my sweetness and my good fruitage and go to hold sway over the trees?' And the trees said to the vine, 'Come thou and reign over us.' And the vine said unto them, 'Should I leave my wine which cheers God and man, and go to hold sway over the trees?' Then all the trees said to the bramble, 'Come thou and reign over us.' And the bramble said unto the trees, 'If in truth you anoint me king over you, then come and take refuge in my shadow, and if not, let fire come out of the bramble and devour the cedars of Lebanon.'"

Nevertheless, Abimelech held sway over Israel, apparently through Shechem, for three years. Then there was a falling out between him and the Shechemites. Taking advantage of Abimelech's absence, they revolted. While in the process of successfully subduing the Shechemites and those who joined in rebellion against him, Abimelech was mortally wounded in battle, thereby ending the episode of the maverick who claimed to be king.

After Abimelech, Tola ben Pua of Issachar judged Israel (10:1–2). He was followed by Yair the Geriotite, both of whom could function as civil judges since the land was at peace (10:3–5). Then the Israelites backslid again and were conquered by both the Philistines from the west and the Ammonites from the east. Once again the Israelites cried out and repented.

The Israelites mobilized on the east against Ammon led by the people of Gilead who chose Jephthah as their military leader. His is the interesting story of a social outcast who was a natural leader called upon to save his people. He does so but he destroys himself by a thoughtless vow that leads him to sacrifice his daughter in one of the dramatic and poignant stories of the Bible. For accepting the call of his Gileadite brethren to help them, he insisted on being appointed the head of the Gileadites and made a pact with the Gileadite elders to that effect (11:6-11).

Jephthah is then presented as sending a message to the Ammonite king in which he summarizes the history of Israel's experience with the peoples east of the Jordan on their way to the Promised Land after the Exodus. The account suggests that even a ruffian outcast was expected to know the history of his people (11:12-27). Jephthah wins a great victory, which leads to the horror of his having to sacrifice his daughter to fulfill an ill-considered vow. He then got involved with a brief civil war with Ephraim, judged in Gilead for six years, and died young.

Jephthah was followed by Ibzad of Bethlehem (Judah), Elon the Zebulunite, and Adon of Ephraim. All three were essentially civil rulers who were not confronted with military conflict. Following those three, the Israelites again turned away from God and were oppressed by the Philistines for a generation, bringing us to the story of Samson. Even more than any of the other judges, Samson is purely a warrior. He is presented as having few if any qualities needed to hold public office other than great strength and courage, good for leading people into battle. In a sense, the book portrays a decline in public virtue from Gideon to Jephthah to Samson, thereby setting the stage for the need to change the regime from one resting upon the public spiritedness and diffused talent required in a democratic republic to a system of hereditary kingship where at least one family is chosen because of its founding father and subsequently is expected to be educated into public leadership.

Samson, of the tribe of Dan, is portrayed as having been born through God's intervention and bound to preserve his Nazerite status by letting his hair grow and abstaining from wine. He is portrayed as being clever (e.g., his riddles) and extraordinarily strong. He gets involved with Philistine women who prove to be his downfall. Even his motives for helping his people are personal. He is seeking revenge on the Philistines for taking away his Philistine wife and otherwise slighting him. He is never portrayed as having any public-spirited interest except, perhaps, at the very end of his life where, a prisoner blinded by his Philistine captors, he brings down the Temple of Dagon on their heads and his, utilizing his extraordinary strength. While he is numbered among the judges, he is not like any of his predecessors so labeled since his public role is a very limited one.

After Samson's death, the book portrays an Israel in decline, beginning in chapter 17 with the story of Micah and his molten image dedicated to the Lord. Another example of the syncretism of Israelite religion, Micah worships the Lord but he does so through building a graven image and consecrating a Levite as a priest to serve it. It is in this chapter that we first come across the formula: "In those days there was no king in Israel. Every man did that which was right in his own eyes" (17:6). Here we have a story of an entirely private act not associated with governance in any way but reflecting the decline of virtue in Israel.

In chapter 18 the story is continued and connected with intertribal conflict. The migrating Danites seize Micah's graven image and his Levite to take with them to their new northern home, thereby making Micah's private lapse into a public sin, not only because of the image but because of establishing an alternate shrine when "all the time... the House of God was in Shiloh" (18:31). Chapter 18 includes the "no king in Israel" formula.

So does chapter 19, which begins the horrible story of the mass rape-murder of the concubine at Gibeah. According to this story, the base men of Benjamin assault an Israelite passing through from Judah to Ephraim and have their way with his concubine until she is dead. The wronged Israelite summons men from the other tribes to punish Benjamin.

Here for the first time since the days of Joshua all of Israel from Dan to Beersheva and from both sides of the Jordan is presented as assembling at Mizpeh to punish the Benjaminites. The processes of federal governance described in chapters 20 and 21 to close the book are of special interest, giving us a glimpse of the tribal federation in action in that epoch, first to respond to a case of wantonness and wickedness and then to preserve the intertribal dimensions of the *edah*.

After three days of battle against the obviously powerful Benjaminites, the other tribes prevail against them, winning by strategem, destroying the tribe's settlements, and killing most of the Benjaminite men. Then, realizing that the long-term consequences of this action (chap. 21) would be to eliminate Benjamin as one of the tribes, they set about to prevent that consequence. Having bound themselves by oath not to give their women in marriage to the Benjaminites because of Benjaminite wantonness in the previous episode, they arrange for the surviving Benjaminites to "kidnap" the womenfolk they need with the implicit consent of the other tribes. The deed is done and Benjamin is restored.

The whole story suggests how the tribal federation could function to maintain the law throughout the land while at the same time assuring that even in the case of civil war no tribe should be eliminated from the federation. The story concludes with the formula: "In those days there was no king in Israel. Every man did that which was right in his own eyes" (21:25).

What Does the Book of Judges Teach Us?

While this story is presented at the end of Judges, from the context of the story, where the High Priest is Pinchas ben Elazar, Aaron's grandson, it must have taken place much earlier in the period of the judges when the tribal federation was still constitutionally capable of acting together. The problem of chronology is not an insignificant one in Judges While the figures presented as "judges" are presented as if they follow one another chronologically, there is no certainty that this is the case. First of all, while the matter is not entirely clear, the judges mentioned came from eleven of the twelve tribes, omitting only Asher and of course the Levites, who have an entirely different role. This may mean that judging was rotated among the tribes, or it may describe historically parallel developments.

Representatives of all three of the *ketarim* are mentioned in the course of the book. The High Priests, Elazar and Pinchas, play their allotted roles, plus two unnamed Levites who are turned to other purposes. There are two prophets from the *keter torah*. One, Deborah, plays a leading role in delivering her people and is shown to have had influence over a substantial portion of Israel. In addition there were the anonymous prophets who appeared in connection with Gideon, suggesting that there were prophets active throughout this entire period.

The other figures mentioned are all of the *keter malkhut,* most designated judges. Five—Tola, Yair, Ibzan, Elon, and Abdan—are presented as civil judges with no military involvement. Three—Ehud, Shamgar, and Samson, plus Barak who is not designated a judge—had purely military functions, while three—Othniel, Gideon, and Jephthah—are presented as combining civil and military functions.

The choosing of the judges is generally presented as an act of God's charisma, as in the case of Gideon and Samson. But Jephthah is made a judge by covenant with the elders of Gilead. Only then does the spirit of the Lord come over him (11:29); while Abimelech, a deviant case, is the only one who seems to have attempted to impose a hierarchical regime and he has his major source of support in Shechem, a very non-Israelite city. Even he, however, is unable to do so, and indeed provokes a successful revolt against him as a result of his trying.

While the term *brit* is used only twice, at the beginning of the book, covenanting is pervasive throughout. Jephthah makes a pact with the elders of Gilead, the Israelites who assembled against Benjamin take oaths; Gideon and even Abimelech are offered power as rulers by popular assemblies. The spirit of the age is summarized in the fable of the trees told by Gideon's surviving son, Jotham.

Tribal government in Israel is still in the hands of elders, but *sarim* are also mentioned. Here they seem to be permanent tribal officers. Othniel (and his uncle Caleb before him) are Kenite/Kennezites from a people that has thrown its lot in with Israel, serving the Lord in a way that tries to maintain republican virtue through preserving the nomadic way of life. Yair and Jephthah are from Gilead; that is to say, they are identified with a territorial rather than a tribal division that has come in place of the tribal designation, reflecting another theme in the Book of Judges, namely, the transition from ideological to territorial democracy, a theme common to all new societies.

From Ideological to Territorial Democracy

If Joshua describes the fulfillment of the Mosaic promise that Israel will be rewarded by the Lord with a land flowing with milk and honey, then Judges, inter alia, reflects the transition of a new society from one held together by its ideology to one rooted in a particular territory where its original ideology has to struggle to maintain itself in its pure form. Part of that struggle is, of course, the struggle over periodic Israelite backsliding into idolatry and its return to the ways of the Lord. The pattern is relatively straightforward. A new people is formed around some great idea and a way of life attached to it. This motivates them to migrate from their place of origin to a new land where they are able to establish that way of life with relative freedom and with a maximum of detachment from the cultural baggage of their previous lives.

Over the course of time new generations are born whose primary commitment is once again to family and neighbors rather than to ideological motivations. They are members of the new society by accident, as it were, not by choice. Ironically, they represent both the success of the new ideology and sow the seeds for its failure to ultimately change the world in the ways it seeks.

Much has been written about how New England was transformed from the Puritan effort to build a city upon a hill into a Yankee society pursuing both higher and lower ends.[7] Biblical Israel represents the first such case in recorded history. The process is reflected in the Book of Judges, both in the references shifting away from identifying people purely on tribal lines to also identifying them on territorial ones, as, for example, the people of Gilead, or judges as first and foremost coming from particular townships within tribes.

Increasingly, the security struggles also revolve around protecting particular territories from foreign incursion, and the involvements of the various tribes depend upon their geographic positions. Unless the issue is an ideological one, as in the case of the concubine in Gibeah, the military involvement is by tribes or region and is clearly geographically motivated. Then, too, the tribal leaders themselves, judges, and even prophets are leaders in specific geographic areas rather than comprehensive leaders of the entire federation, so much so that while the first figure in the book, Caleb, is still fighting to conquer the land in the name of the Mosaic ideology, the last, Samson, has only personal territorial interests in what he does to advance his interests or to protect his fellow Danites.

The Decline of Republican Virtue

Overall, the book seems to be about the decline of civic virtue. While subsequent generations have read it as if it were presented to describe that the tribal federation without a king could not handle Israelite backsliding, this does not seem to be the major issue in the book. A close reading suggests that, at least at the beginning, the pattern of backsliding, return, and deliverance is the predicted normal course of human events, which God Himself has forecast and which is entirely compatible with the regime of the twelve tribes, as long as the regime has the capacity to produce virtuous ("righteous") judges. The real problem is that after Gideon, Judges portrays a decline in the republican virtue of the Israelite leadership. Gideon, the climactic character in the book, is the epitome of the virtuous republican leader as portrayed in the Bible. Jephthah is already a step downward and Samson does not even have the minimum requirements of republican virtue, only personal strength and courage.

Under these circumstances the provisions of the classic regime for responding to the ordinary dynamics of life and the realities of human frailty no longer are sufficient, hence a constitutional change must be introduced. The conclusion of the book seems to suggest that republican virtue must first repose in the people (who at least earlier in the period did possess it) if their leaders are to have it. By the time we reach the end of the Book of Judges we have already been given at least a broad hint that the tribal federation can be saved, but only by a proper revival of, by then, degenerated republican virtue. If not, there will be a regime change, for good or for ill.

Civic or republican virtue is not an insignificant theme in the Bible. Indeed, the Bible tries to present its own understanding of what constitutes republican virtue within the context of *yirat shamayim* (God fearingness). While certainly not the only books to dwell on this, Joshua and Judges together present us with a fairly comprehensive picture of the biblical understanding of republican virtue:

First of all, republican virtue, like all biblical virtue, begins with fear of the Lord as manifested by hearkening to God's Torah. (Contrast this with the foundation of classical virtue that involves having the requisite talents for the particular task at hand.) Second, it involves public spiritedness. Third, it requires a respect for the Israelite constitution and its limitations. Fourth, it emphasizes courage in the pursuit of public purposes. Fifth, it demands faithfulness to the tradition. Sixth, it expects a sense of the equality of all Israelites and public behavior reflecting that sense.

This republican virtue is grounded in a combination of what Martin Diamond described in connection with the American regime of the low but solid virtues of the middle class and the high and enobling virtues of the Torah as embodied in God's covenant with Israel.[8] These virtues are found in abundance in the Book of Joshua and continue to animate the Israelites after they have settled in their land until the prosperity and ease that come with permanent settlement begin to erode those virtues, as portrayed in Judges. This will lead to a civic and constitutional crisis in 1 Samuel that will bring about a change in regime to one that has less expectations of the broad body of the people but in return limits their freedom and the closeness of their connection to God.

Notes

1. The following offer a range of views of the period: William Foxwell Albright, *The Biblical Period from Abraham to Ezra* (New York: Harper and Row, 1963); Albrecht Alt, *Essays on Old Testament History and Religion* (Sheffield: JSOT Press, 1989); Martin Noth, *The Old Testament World* (Philadelphia: Fortress Press, 1960); Harry Orlinsky, *Ancient Israel* (Westport, CT: Greenwood Press, 1981); Roland de Vaux, *Ancient Israel*, 2 vols. (New York: McGraw Hill, 1965). It should be noted that the German and French scholars in particular do not see the *amphictyony* as a polity and date the rise of the Israelite "state" from David, while Americans see the earlier regime as serving a polity as well. The difference has to do with differing conceptions of what constitutes a state or a polity of contemporary continental Europeans and contemporary Americans and is itself an interesting footnote to modern intellectual history.
2. Cf. Delbert R. Hillers, *Covenant: The History of a Biblical Idea* (Baltimore: Johns Hopkins Press, 1969), 171.
3. E. A. Speiser, "The City" and the "Gates of the City," in *Oriental and Biblical Studies: Collected Writings of E.A. Speiser,* ed. J. J. Finkelstein and Moshe Greenberg (Philadelphia: University of Pennsylvania Press, 1967).
4. Martin Buber writes of this period and its regime positively in *Kingship of God,* 3d ed. (Atlantic Highlands, NJ: Humanities Press International, 1990) where he argues for this anarcho-federalism as the best regime. See also Bernard Susser, "The Anarcho-Federalism of Martin Buber," *Publius* 9, no. 4 (Fall 1979).
5. Cf. Albrecht Alt and Martin Noth, in *Oriental and Biblical Studies,* ed. Finkelstein and Greenberg.
6. *The Book of Judges,* interpreted by Yehudah Elitzur (Jerusalem: Mossad HaRav Kook, 1989) (Hebrew).
7. Perry Miller, *The New England Mind, Vol. 1: The Seventeenth Century* and *The New England Mind, Vol. 2: From Colony to Province* (Boston: Beacon Press, 1939, 1953), esp. Vol. 2, Book 1; Daniel J. Elazar, *Cities of the Prairie* (New York: Basic Books, 1970), chaps. 1 and 2, and *Israel: Building a New Society* (Bloomington: Indiana University Press, 1986), chaps. 1 and 2.
8. Martin Diamond, *As Far as Republican Principles Will Admit,* ed. William Schambra (Washington, DC: American Enterprise Institute, 1992).

Part IV

The Alternate Model

15

Covenant and Kingdom: Dealing with Fundamental Regime Change

The biblical account of David's rise and reign and its consequences for subsequent Jewish history offers a paradigm of regime transition and the successful imposition of a new regime on a reluctant or ambivalent body politic. It describes and analyzes the struggle for succession, the steps taken by David to consolidate his power by gaining control of the several domains of authority operative in Israel, while at the same time preserving their forms so as to avoid excessive conflict with traditionalists. It examines David's establishment of Jerusalem as his capital on territory independent of any tribe; his transfer of Israel's major religious symbol to his capital as a first step toward centralizing worship under the aegis of the king; his establishment of a professional military force, a court, and a bureaucracy dependent upon and responsible to him.

The contrast between the models of the polity settled by Moses and that settled by David, the two classic polities of the Jewish people, has reappeared throughout Jewish intellectual history, often very directly and if not, in one guise or another. Maimonides and Abravanel draw that contrast, but so, too, did biblical commentators like Sforno (Obadiah Sforno), who explicitly contrasted the regime model of the judges with the regime model of the monarchy.

David's politics were the key to his success: his use of personal charm, his claim to God's charisma, his appeals to the people over the heads of the established tribal leaders, and his personal image building were his tools in his successful effort to consolidate power. David dealt with the opposition to him, both tribal and prophetic, through co-optation where possible and confrontation where necessary. All this is conveyed in an account of epic proportions—what has been referred to as Israel's equivalent of the *Iliad, The Peloponnesian Wars,* or *The Anabasis.*

With this account, the Bible turns, as it were, to the "flesh and blood" of human history, devoid of most of the fabulous dimensions of the earlier books, applying the covenantal approach to politics in the most concrete ways. The Davidic paradigm is one of two competing paradigms of the classic regime in the Jewish political tradition, along with the previous Mosaic regime. Not only have the two become competing models of the ideal polity in the Jewish political tradition, but also in the European political tradition prior to the modern epoch, when it was customary to turn to biblical paradigms for justification of current or proposed regimes.

While much can be learned from the biblical account from a strictly behavioral perspective, the Bible, as always, addresses the issues from a normative stance, emphasizing that regime legitimacy must be anchored in God's covenant with Israel. Beyond that, covenantal politics is emphasized at every turn, expressing both an understanding of Israelite political culture and a set of normative political expectations which place political actors and actions under judgment. The emphasis here is on the interworking of behavioral and normative themes within the covenantal tradition.

The End of the Tribal Federation

By the end of the first epoch of the history of the twelve tribes of Israel, the general thrust of events was to bring the existing tribal system with its political structure into the framework of a national polity, comprehensive in character and designed to establish a regime capable of defending Israel against its enemies, especially the Philistines who had overrun the Israelite tribes and subjugated them.[1]

The Bible itself offers contradictory assessments as to the success of the tribal federation as a polity. What is clear, however, is that its collapse was a result of external forces rather than internal weaknesses per se. A noncentralized polity based on a loose federation of tribes could not stand up to the assaults of the Philistines. In the process of responding to those assaults, Israel created its own particular brand of what is formally termed a monarchy, but which, in the strict meaning of the term—rule by one—was not that at all because it was limited by specific covenants and the covenant idea generally. According to the biblical account, a limited constitutional monarchy was established and periodically reaffirmed through a covenant between king, people, and God. While under the monarchy a much stronger center of power was created in the polity, other centers and institutions retained real powers as well and at least one, the institution of the prophets, was actually strengthened to counterbalance the king.

In fact, the very name of the regime was in some dispute for the prophets and hence the people referred to their leader as a king and more or less recognized a hereditary monarchy. For the prophets, on the other hand, speaking in the name of God, Israel did not have a king but a *nagid*, a high commissioner appointed by God to rule in his stead. And while God might look favorably on hereditary succession, each *nagid* had to be appointed by Him through prophetic designation and *meshikha* (anointment).

The Philistines, a sea people, assumed by scholars to be from the Greek isles (Crete?), had landed on the southern coast of Canaan at approximately the same time that the Israelites had entered the hill country from the east. Possessing an iron technology and sophisticated political organization, with a well-developed military component, the Philistines captured the lowlands of Eretz Israel (the new Israelite name for Canaan), and established five cities—Gaza, Ashkelon, Ashdod, Ekron, and Gath. In the eleventh century, they began to invade the highlands, actually capturing the Ark of the Covenant (1 Sam. 4-6) at one point. The generally disorganized Israelite tribes were unable to concentrate sufficient power to restrain the invaders, hence their decision to seek a king to lead them to military victory over their powerful new foe.

Israel's fortunes had indeed been laid low. Not only were they soundly beaten at the battle of Aphek (ca. 1050 B.C.E.) and the Ark of the Covenant captured, but the Philistines proceeded to occupy the whole country and destroy Shiloh, the seat of the tribal confederation. The leader of the tribal confederation, Samuel, the twelfth and last of the judges, was faced with an extremely difficult situation. The old confederation had virtually disintegrated. Shiloh, once destroyed, was never revived. The old regime, whose major national leaders were the priestly guardians of Shiloh and the judge of the time, was discredited. The family of Eli, the chief priest at Shiloh, was, for all intents and purposes, destroyed. Eli's sons, Hophni and Phinehas, were killed while bearing the Ark in battle and Eli died of shock after learning of the defeat. Since his family was already portrayed as corrupted, no heirs emerged to assume the high priesthood until David appointed Abiathar and Zadok two generations later. (Indeed, the vacuum in the priesthood was to help David to consolidate his power in Jerusalem.)

Samuel, who was a prophet as well as a judge, was not a military leader. Nevertheless, he attempted to restore the administration of covenant law and to reestablish the shrine of the federation at Mitzpah. He moved from Shiloh to his ancestral home at Ramah from where he traveled on a regular circuit between Mitzpah, Gilgal, and Beth El, three towns with sacred and historic associations. While the Israelites thus maintained a degree of autonomy and may even have remained independent in parts of the Galilee or transjordan, as long as the Philistines continued to have a monopoly of iron, they were able to keep military control over the country. Nevertheless the Israelite will to resist remained strong, if ineffective.

Seeing that the old regime was ineffective if not dead, Samuel attempted to institute a constitutional reform of his own, one that would have strengthened the civil institutions of the old federation to give the regime sufficient authority, power, and leadership to overthrow the Philistines and regain Israelite independence. It has already been suggested that the Book of Joshua as canonized in the Bible is the presentation of Samuel's ideal regime for the tribal federation, built around the argument that if that regime, properly constructed, was strong enough to conquer the country, it would be strong enough to repel all enemies.[2]

For reasons not explicitly conveyed in the Bible, Samuel failed. According to the biblical account, as Samuel aged and his sons proved unworthy as his potential successors, the people demanded a king; Samuel opposed their demands, formally on the grounds that this was a rejection of God's kingship, the classic feature of the regime of the tribal federation whereby Moses and Joshua as God's prime ministers (*eved adonai*) and the subsequent twelve judges (*shofetim*) were simply his deputies, chosen charismatically to lead the people. God intervened to indicate that the people's request was to be met, at least in a limited way. Reading between the lines, it seems that Samuel's own personality played no small role in the failure of his plan. From the tone of the text it also seems that Samuel was personally jealous of a new and more powerful political leader. Larger political forces were also involved.

In an act of charismatic transfer, Samuel was forced to find an appropriate candidate for the kingship, give him God's blessing, and then bring him before the people to be elected. Samuel fixed upon Saul, a decent, simple young man of great strength and courage, no doubt because he thought that Saul was suitable to be a military leader but would remain politically subordinate to him as prophet.

In an effort to preserve the spirit of the old regime, albeit with a new institutional framework, Samuel exercised his primordial constitutional function to designate the first incumbent of the office as *nagid* (best translated as high commissioner), rather than *melekh* (king) (1 Sam. 10:1). For the rest of the history of the monarchy the two terms appear parallel to one another, with God and His prophets referring to the rulers as *nagid,* or God's high commissioner, and the people referring to them as *melekh.* He also established a constitutional framework within which the *nagid* is required to function (1 Sam. 10:25), specifying that Saul's principal function as *nagid* was to lead the *edah* in war. However, the people still had to elect Saul, which they did (1 Sam. 11:15), and they proclaimed him *melekh.*

Saul is presented as a charismatic leader: "The spirit of God came mightily upon him" (1 Sam. 11:6). His choice also had an internal political advantage since he was a Benjaminite, from one of the smallest tribes, located geographically between powerful Judah and equally powerful Ephraim. At the beginning, Saul performs as expected, but, a serious man, he takes his responsibilities as king seriously, too seriously for Samuel's taste. The two clash in a power struggle and Samuel publicly rejects Saul. Moreover, the complex responsibilities of kingship are too much for the bluff, unsophisticated Saul and he begins to deteriorate mentally, first as a result of Samuel's rejection and then in response to politics and intrigues in his developing court, which are exacerbated by the appearance of David as a fair-haired young hero whose popularity rapidly comes to outshine that of Saul. Nevertheless, as long as Samuel remains alive it appears that Saul stays more or less within the limited framework of a *nagid* and only after the death of the prophet does an institutionalized kingship begin to emerge, limited primarily by Saul's limitations. In the end those limitations are to destroy him and his chances for establishing a dynasty.

Saul's final defeat and death on Mt. Gilboa are as much a result of his psychological state, according to the Bible, as to the continued strength of the Philistines. Militarily, Saul and his son Jonathan continued their successful tactic that had brought them earlier victories, of luring the Philistines into the mountains where the terrain favored the Israelites. But this time Saul is convinced that he will be defeated because God has rejected him. And so it comes to pass.

The Constitutional Process of Regime Change

The Bible presents us with two parallel accounts of the establishment of the monarchy. One (1 Sam. 8, 12) is bitterly hostile to the very idea, and the other (1 Sam. 9-10) tacitly accepts it. Together these are among the important political statements in the Bible, whose impact has echoed through the generations. (The Book of Chronicles, on the other hand, ignores the process of instituting the monarchy, merely mentioning the death of Saul as a prelude to the enthronement of David. In general it seems to be a book designed to strengthen the claims of David and his house to the kingship, which is discussed further below.) The importance of the regime change is reflected in the fact that the whole Book of Samuel, which has come down to us as two books, is devoted to the transition, covering a period of three generations, chronologically slightly over a century, from ca. 1070 to 950 B.C.E., the first book concentrating on the period from the military failure of the old confederation, Samuel's judgeship, the appointment and rule of Saul, down through Saul's death, and the second dealing with David's reign.

Constitutionally, the appointment of Saul seems to have followed a threefold process. First the tribal elders traveled to Ramah and, in an informal meeting, called upon Samuel to change the constitution and institute kingship. After trying to resist them and warning them of the price of kingship, Samuel acquiesced—following God's instructions according to the biblical account—but not before he had warned them of the likely political and social consequences of introducing kingship, all of which were in the direction of drastically reducing Israelite liberties. Samuel then proceeded to find a candidate for the position he advocated, that of *nagid,* which did not carry the powers or the hereditary element of kingship; and, choosing Saul, anointed him in the name of God.

Following that, Samuel formally called the people together as a constituent assembly at Mitzpah, the new shrine, in the manner of the old constitutional assemblies of the *edah,* and formally presented the new constitution and the new *nagid* to them for their approval. The people then elected Saul their king, using the term *melekh* (king) in preference to *nagid.* Samuel concluded by promulgating the *mishpat hamelukhah* (the law of the kingdom). He wrote down the civil constitution of the new regime within the framework of the Torah, which continued to be the general constitution of the Israelite polity, after which everyone including Saul returned home.[3]

Thus, the covenant with David and his house is not the first covenant of the *keter malkhut.* At the very least, the *mishpat hamelekh* in Samuel is the foundation of the kingship, though, in fact, the foundation of the *keter malkhut* goes back earlier to the patriarchs. What is important about *mishpat hamelekh* is that the covenant of *keter malkhut* is not made with the king but is made with the people, who are empowered to appoint a king if they so choose. Indeed, one can contrast the three covenants behind the three *ketarim*: the covenant for *keter torah* is made with the people through the mediation of the prophet Moses; the covenant with the priests is made with Aaron and his family and embraces the tribe of Levi in a subsidiary fashion; while the covenant of the *keter malkhut* is made with the people without a king or equivalent leader being present. Only later is an actual king introduced.

In light of our knowledge of the role of covenants and covenant ideas in West Asia at the time, we can assume that the Israelite tribes were culturally attuned to this means of reconstitution. The civil covenantal process introduced by Samuel brought about a certain redesign of the political structure and created a basis for further redesign in later epochs of Jewish history, biblical and post-biblical. This was to be the limit of Samuel's political success as a constitutional reformer.[4] In retrospect, the most important aspect of this redesign was the reaffirmation and strengthening of the division of powers within the *edah*'s leadership, a division established by a special set of covenants.

This tripartite system became more fully articulated with the introduction of the kingship. Prior to the regime change, Samuel as judge and prophet (his two official titles) continued in the line of Moses and Joshua and straddled the constitutional and civil authority. Moreover, because he was raised at Shiloh, the central shrine of the tribal federation, within the priestly family of Eli, he had close connections with the priesthood as well. There are hints in the biblical text that, in his efforts to restore more effective framing institutions for the *edah* after so many generations of national weakness, he tried to encompass all three domains of authority within his own office. This was decisively rejected by the people and, apparently, by God as well, and is one of the precipitating causes for his failure to reform the old constitution on its own terms and the introduction of kingship as such.

Saul then proceeded to fall into the same trap that was the undoing of Samuel by seeking to encompass in his office the functions of all three domains. For that he was punished and his family was denied dynastic inheritance. In 1 Samuel 13:8-13, we find Saul usurping priestly functions, such as offering sacrifices; and in 15:7-9, he usurps prophetic functions of constitutional interpretation by allowing his army to retain certain spoils from a captured Canaanite city, against the proscriptions of the Torah. Thus, the principle of tripartite division is firmly established and is made part of God's covenant with David, which is then ratified by the people.

David, with all his power and his success at centralizing the powers of government in his court, did not attempt to abolish this tripartite division, only to bring it under his control. So, he brought the tabernacle to Jerusalem and appointed a new priestly family to tend it, one that would be beholden to him, but in so doing reaffirmed their priestly power. He brought the prophets into his court, reaffirming their powers, even allowing them to denounce him for transgressions, but again keeping them within his purview. In short, David's genius was to formally maintain the constitution while altering the distribution of powers within it. David's wisdom was to recognize that, once constitutionalized by covenant, the basic lines of authority had to be maintained but could be manipulated to serve his ends.

David Begins to Advance

David appears on the scene as a somewhat innocent young shepherd boy from Bethlehem; "somewhat innocent" because even the laudatory biblical account that we have suggests a more complex figure than subsequent legend has it. David first appears in three accounts contained in 1 Samuel 16 and 17. In the first, Samuel seeks out David the young shepherd under God's instructions to anoint him as king to replace Saul. In the second version Saul, plagued by the psychological terrors that are to be his undoing, seeks relief in music; a member of Saul's entourage remembers David as a young harpist, and Saul invites him to court where David's playing provides temporary relief. In the third version, David, as the youngest son of Jesse, is not yet mobilized in the tribal militia levees confronting the Philistines in the Valley of Elah, but he does go back and forth, bringing food to his mobilized brothers, until he seizes the opportunity to distinguish himself by fighting Goliath.

These three accounts are not contradictory; their sequential placement even may be accurate. What is important is that we see before us a young man, appropriately modest in his overt behavior, yet handsome and talented and capable of winning over powerful people and garnering their support; a young man of original ideas, good bearing, and military prowess. All these are characteristics that will stay with David as he acquires political power. They will be used by him to gain and secure that power.

David's first signal triumph is to become part of Saul's entourage. In other words, he begins to move upward from within the "court" where he is able to acquire knowledge and experience in politics, and perhaps also in governing. Since he enters the entourage as a popular hero, he also has a public dimension, which gets him into trouble with Saul but also enables him to survive exile from the court.

Whether precisely accurate or not, the paradigm of a potential leader successfully pursuing power is complete. It is entirely possible, indeed likely, that David was a gifted musician and poet. The Goliath story, on the other hand, raises some questions. Elsewhere in the text there is a cryptic reference to Elhanan as the slayer of Goliath. Did David appropriate this story of mythic proportions? If so, when? If not, what is the textual reference? Did Elhanan adopt the throne name of David upon becoming king? This hint of something amiss is characteristic of the Bible, which, whatever its literal truth in some matters, is not a book of myths but what we might call moral science, using history as its raw material. Written as it is for the broadest public, its general tone must be and is popular; but, for the careful reader, it often drops important hints of this kind.

Since the Bible is not a book of myths, it does not have David automatically ascend to the throne. Instead he has to pass through a period of trials that sharpen his already substantial leadership skills and test his moral qualities. During that period he displays a wide range of human qualities: generosity, and opportunism, love and cunning, loyalty and treason, forthrightness and deviousness.

David's troubles begin with his popularity, which exceeds that of the king (1 Sam. 18:7). Nor is David an innocent victim here. He encourages public adulation. In an effort to be sly, Saul attempts to have David killed in battle by requiring him to deliver 100 Philistine foreskins as the bride price for Michal, Saul's daughter, whom David seeks to wed. But poor Saul is never successful at slyness and David, instead of getting himself killed, brings back the 100 foreskins and the couple are married (1 Sam. 18:17-29). Now David is not only of the court, but married into the royal family—another bond strengthening any future claim to the kingship he might advance. The marriage to Michal is to go badly and when David flees, Saul gives her to another, but David retrieves her after Saul's death and keeps her with him until he has consolidated his hold on the throne. (Michal is Saul's second daughter, younger than Merab who was originally promised to David but given to another. Michal is presented as loving David and supporting him against her father. Did she hope to rise to the top through her husband rather than simply be a second daughter? Is her later disgust with David over his populism a reflection of her pretensions?)

David also develops a very special relationship with Jonathan, Saul's oldest son and heir apparent. Jonathan is the biblical model of the singularly noble man who sacrifices his own interests for his friend. The friendship is portrayed through a series of increasingly sad vignettes. David appears to be a good and magnanimous friend, but his friendship never gets in the way of his ambition; while Jonathan, a far more noble character, is forced to choose between filial loyalty to his increasingly mad father and the throne, on one hand, and David, on the other. When he makes his choice and it is described in the usual spare biblical style, we can palpably feel Jonathan's consciousness of what he is doing and the nobility attached to the act (1 Sam. 20-21:1).

From Outlaw to King

David is forced to flee from Saul's court. He becomes a political refugee, drawing about him a band of outlaws who have nothing to lose in being with him, but who give him strength because of the kind of characters they are—"natural men," described by one biblical scholar as having "contempt for authority and settled communities." They are to stay with him as his most trusted men for the rest of his life. Meanwhile, David's own kin stayed away from him.

David and his followers are given modest help by the priests of Nob, perhaps because the latter were descended from Eli and the priestly family that had officiated at Shiloh and had been dispossessed with the introduction of the new regime. Whatever the reason, Saul has them massacred (1 Sam. 22:11-19), leading to the alienation of other priests from Saul's rule, one of whom, Abiathar, joins David's growing band, bringing with him religious objects that endow David with the beginnings of legitimacy.

One can assume that it was in this period that David's understanding of the importance of legitimacy, already evident from the very first moment that he appears on the scene, is strengthened. When he ascends to the throne, David is to resurrect the national priesthood, which had fallen into desuetude for two generations. He reestablishes the office of high priest, raising it to an honored position in Jerusalem where it is associated with the new central shrine, while at the same time assuring that his appointees, Abiathar and Zadok, and their families, are tied to the court.

It is at this point that David's military strength grows sufficiently to give him and his force a semi-legitimate mission within Israel, namely, to serve as an irregular border guard that acts to protect villages and herds against the Philistines and other raiders (23:1-5, 25:1-42). David makes other efforts to strengthen his hand by making marriage alliances with leading families in the borderlands (25:42-43). Nevertheless, Saul's pressure against him continues undiminished and David is finally forced to seek refuge with the Philistine king Achish of Gath (the two versions of this event are found in 21:10-15 and 27:2-12). He settles in Ziklag as a Philistine vassal who engages in near-treasonous acts against Israel.

The Philistines then go out for the major assault on Saul and the Israelites, which ends in Saul's defeat and death (996-995 B.C.E.). Either deliberately or fortunately, David and his men are not called upon to join in the campaign and remain behind. David is able to memorialize Saul and Jonathan in perhaps the greatest of his poems, which seems to reflect true emotion but also establishes his magnanimity and his claim to leadership of Israel.

The story of David's ascension to the kingship and reign are told in 2 Samuel, which opens with David's elegy. Taking advantage of the vacuum created by Saul's death, David moves to Hebron, the seat of the government of the tribe of Judah and its religious center. According to the Bible, he does so after asking God whether he should and receiving an affirmative answer. There the men of Judah anoint David king over "the house of Judah" (2 Sam. 2:1–4). David was to be king of the house of Judah alone for seven years and six months.

In the meantime, Abner, the commander of Saul's army, who survived the battle, took Saul's surviving son (Ishbosheth in the Bible, apparently because his real name was the pagan Ishbaal) and made him king over all the other Israelite tribes, north of Judah. David tried to undermine the appointment by diplomacy and apparently by limited conflict. The decisive clash is at Gibeon where Abner and other members of Ishbosheth's court meet with Joab, the commander of David's army and others of David's court. In the ensuing battle, Abner kills Joab's brother Asahel and he and the Israelites are forced to flee.

The long war leads to dissension between Ishbaal and Abner, according to the Bible over one of Saul's concubines. Abner determines to abandon Ishbaal and make a deal with David. As a prelude to any arrangement, David insists on having Michal returned to him. Abner arranges it, after which David and Abner meet and agree on a settlement, making David king over all Israel. Abner departs, only to be pursued by Joab and his men and killed in revenge for Abner's killing of Joab's brother. David treats the killing as if it were against his orders, but unquestionably it aided him by eliminating a potential source of opposition.

With Abner dead, Ishbosheth's court falls apart. Saul's son is killed by his own courtiers, who hope to win favor with David by bringing him the head of his rival. David's response is to punish the murderers with death; but again, since his rival is removed from the field, the last real obstacle was removed to his being chosen as king of all of Israel (chap. 5). All the tribes of Israel came to David in Hebron and, emphasizing the blood relationship among the tribes, covenant with David and make him king over Israel (c. 988 B.C.E.). The formula they use is important. First they indicate that they know that God has appointed him *nagid* in place of Saul. Then they anoint him *melekh*, thus preserving the dual constitutional formula of the *melekh* of the people being God's *nagid*.

David's New Regime

Now king over all Israel, the 30-year-old David was to reign 33 years in addition to the 7 1/2 years he reigned over Judah. He moved swiftly to consolidate his rule by attacking the Jebusites in Jerusalem, capturing the city and making it his capital. This had the dual effect of removing a Canaanite city-state that had divided Judah and Israel geographically and giving the new federal monarchy a capital outside of the territory of any of the individual tribes, a federal district as it were. Officially the personal property of David, it became known as the City of David and literally was that.

There David established his court and began to build an appropriate capital city, building himself a grand "house" with imported cedar from Tyre, constructed by Tyrean carpenters and masons. There he settled his family and from there he marched against the Philistines, who responded to David's growing strength by sending a force to reimpose their rule on a vassal state that they saw was growing too strong. In two battles at Baal Perazim and the Valley of Refaim, the Philistines are defeated by David.

With the Philistine threat substantially reduced, David assembles the tribal militias to bring the Ark of the Covenant to Jerusalem. His first effort is stopped by a tragic accident when the Ark almost falls off of the cart upon which it was placed and Uzza, the man who saves it, drops dead. But several months later the task is completed. Amid joyous ceremonies the Ark is ensconced in Jerusalem, thereby further consolidating David's power by making his city the principal cultic center.

The story of the interrupted journey of the Ark of the Covenant as told in 1 Chronicles 14–15 suggests that a constitutional issue was involved here as well. David's first effort to bring up the Ark has the people of his army hauling it. After the death of Uzza, David concludes that none ought to carry the Ark of God but the Levites (15:2) who were entrusted with that responsibility by God and Moses in the Torah, so the second time he brings it up he entrusts the Ark to the custody of the Levites, making that custody permanent, thereby consolidating their support as he has consolidated that of the priests and the Prophets. The culmination of the transfer of the Ark is described in Chronicles 16:4ff. where David appoints certain of the Levites to permanently minister before the Ark of the Lord.

By this time David also has brought Nathan, the leading prophet of his generation, into his court as a personal consultant (2 Sam. 7). Wanting to build a proper house for the Ark, David asks Nathan for God's permission to do so and Nathan's immediate response is to grant it. But, according to the Bible, the word of the Lord comes to Nathan that night to indicate that David should not build such a house on the grounds that God does not need a house and, indeed, that it is a violation of the spirit of the Israelite religion to violate the simplicity of the tent of meeting. Nathan is instructed to bring this message to David but also to indicate to him that he and his descendants are to be God's *negidim,* God will assure the rule of his dynasty, and that later in the history of the dynasty his son will build the house.

This dream is the principal source of God's promise of permanent dominion to David and his heirs. The fact that it is communicated to Nathan the prophet (*keter torah*) lends it constitutional credibility. David's response in a prayer to God directly makes it a mutual promise or covenant. In his response, David fully assumes the posture of spokesman for his people.[5] While David was unable to build the Temple himself, he did choose the site that Solomon was later to use, purchased the land, had plans for the Temple drawn up and materials assembled before his death (1 Chron. 21:18–22). In addition to recording and publicizing God's promise via Nathan, David left few if any stones unturned to establish his legitimacy. He kept Saul's daughter, Michal, as his wife, even after she rejected him and brought Jonathan's son Mephibosheth (Mephibaal) to his court to "eat bread at David's table."

David accepts God's will with all humility and proceeds with the business of building his kingdom. Now it is his turn to attack the Philistines (2 Sam. 8) and he reduces them to vassals although he does not annex their territory. The Canaanite enclaves in Israel's territory are reduced and annexed. He then turns to conquer Ammon and Moab, which also become vassal states. Turning northward he conquers Zobah and Aram, extending his rule over the two states as far as the Euphrates. Amalek and Edom also come under his rule and on the south his kingdom is extended to below Etzion Geber on the Red Sea. Taking advantage of the weakness of both Egypt and Assyria, David creates a small but strong empire and his rule is acknowledged by his neighbors. Only Phoenicia, whose king Hiram had entered into an alliance with David, remains unconquered.

David's military successes enable him to begin the construction of a state of the kind that the Israelites had not previously known. The Bible describes this step in Samuel 8:15–17, immediately following the record of David's military conquests, listing David's principal officers in the

FIGURE 15.1
The *Edah* as a United Kingdom

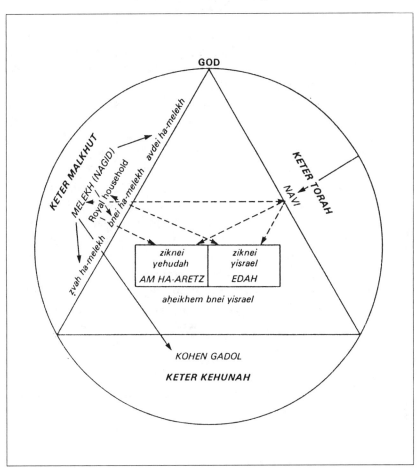

following order: his military commander, Joab, son of Zeruiah; *mazkir* (usually translated "recorder" but apparently more like its present use in the sense of "appointed manager") Jehosephat, son of Ahilud; two priests, Zadok, the son of Ahitub, and Ahimelekh, the son of Abiathar; *sofer* or secretary in the sense of keeper of the records, Seraiah; commander of the mercenaries, Beniaiah, son of Jehoiadaa; and David's loyal supporters (referred to as "sons of David"), heads of the various ministries.

Thus, we have a court and a cabinet, as well as the concentration of the three domains in David's court. Figure 15.1 describes the new state structure.

Perhaps the most significant development here was the organization of a mercenary force loyal to the king himself. While wars were still conducted primarily through the tribal militias, organized in the traditional twelve divisions (1 Chron. 27:2–15), they normally remained under tribal leadership as reserves who were fully mobilized only in time of war. David's power position was secured by his mercenaries, a standing army loyal only to him who were to prove decisive in the various revolts against his rule, particularly in the great revolt of Absalom, which came closest of any of them to succeeding.

The full scale of David's organizational effort is described in 1 Chronicles 23ff. The description has several elements. First of all, the bureaucracy provides offices for David's loyal supporters, his courtiers, and their families, so as to consolidate their support for the throne. The priests and Levites are provided with full employment and the tribal levees are reorganized so that while they remain tribal, they can be easily mobilized into David's service.[6] While the changes introduced by David brought the country peace and prosperity, they also completed the destruction of the old regime, but not entirely. David realized, either out of choice or out of necessity, that Israel had to remain a federation in which the tribal institutions retained considerable political power; hence, what emerged from his reconstitution was a federal monarchy with the tribes in place, but the overall thrust was toward centralization. This led to several tribal revolts, often helped along by David's own sons who, because of interfamilial quarrels or sheer impatience to gain their father's throne, appealed to the "state's rights" concerns of the tribes.

From the biblical description of the characters and individuals involved, it is hardly likely that this was more than a political ploy on their part that would have disappeared as soon as they had used tribal support to gain the throne. If anything, David was probably more sensitive to the virtues of the old constitution than his sons, who had already been raised, if not born, into royalty. Certainly the subsequent history of the Judean monarchy suggests that was the case.

The greatest revolt was that of Absalom eleven years before David's death (2 Sam. 15). Absalom had built up the revolt by appealing to the tribal elders on "state's rights" grounds. He actually succeeded in capturing Jerusalem and causing David to flee. David defeated Absalom's tribal levees with his professional soldiers. Absalom was killed (officially against David's instructions) and David returned to Jerusalem with the nation rallying around him once again. A second revolt by an Israelite named Sheba ben Bichri was an effort to divide the kingdom through the secession of the northern tribes. David put this down as well and had Sheba killed (2 Sam. 20).

Seven chapters (13–19) of 2 Samuel are devoted to Absalom and David, beginning with the personal conflict between Absalom and Amnon, another of David's sons, over Tamar, their sister, as a result of Amnon's rape of Tamar and his subsequent murder by Absalom, Joab's role in restoring Absalom to the court, Absalom's revolt and its repercussions, and David's restoration and its repercussions. In the story we see the power struggle among the king's sons, the crucial role of Joab in keeping David on the throne and his family and court together, the side intrigues of the various people in the court such as Mephibosheth's servant Ziba, who tries to curry favor with David and betray Mephibosheth, and various others. Finally, after David's victory, there are the efforts of the leaders of the tribe of Judah and the tribes of Israel to get back on David's bandwagon.

One of the by-products of Absalom's revolt was a stirring among the family and tribe of Saul, a testing of the waters to see if David's weakness could lead to their restoration to the throne. Mephibosheth may or may not have been linked to the conspiracy but he had to make an effort to get back into David's good graces after the latter's triumph. David bides his time and once the revolts of Absalom and Sheba are put down, he uses the pretexts of compensating the Gibeonites for Saul's massacre of them years before to hand over most of the remaining descendants of Saul's family (not including Mephibosheth to whom he had promised permanent protection) for execution, thereby substantially reducing if not ending that threat. At the same time David has the bones of Saul and Jonathan reburied in their native soil of the tribe of Benjamin so as to distance himself from the execution.

David the King

One of the greatest characteristics of the Bible is that it portrays David "warts and all." His worst transgression in the eyes of the Bible was sending Uriah the Hittite to his death in the war against Ammon in order to take his wife Bathsheba. Considerable space is devoted to the incident (2 Sam. 11-12), to the story itself and to its prelude (2 Sam. 10). In part, this is because the second product of the union of David and Bathsheba, Solomon, is to inherit David's throne and establish the dynastic principle. In part, it is part of the biblical teaching that even kings are under the judgment of God and his prophets. From another perspective, it shows how David has consolidated his power by bringing the prophet into his court, but at the same time the price he must pay, namely, within the framework of the court the prophet must be free to chastise him when necessary. The story also reveals David's character, how he could succumb to his passions, how his own sensitivities developed, and how his rational faculties never departed from him. David was not the only one prey to human weaknesses. The biblical account tells of the court intrigues, especially among his children, giving us a taste of what is to come as the result of kingship.

David's last days are described in chapters 1-2 of 1 Kings and 23-24 of 1 Chronicles. As his end grew near, the dynastic principle had still not been established and his son Adonijah attempted to seize the throne. Adonijah managed to secure the support of Joab and Aviatar, but Zadok the high priest, Beniaiah head of the court bureaucracy, and Nathan the prophet lined up behind Solomon. Nathan became the decisive factor, mobilizing Bathsheba to intervene with the king to have him designate Solomon as his successor. In what is obviously an orchestrated move, Nathan joins Bathsheba in the presence of the king. Both make the point that if Adonijah is to become king, then their lives will be forfeit. This essentially forces David to designate Solomon as his heir.

In the process we have a new form of anointment instituted, whereby priest and prophet join together to proclaim which of David's sons is to be his heir to the throne, a proclamation that is then executed by one of the senior court officials. Again, all three *ketarim* are represented. Here, too, the formula used is both *melekh* and *nagid*. The proclamation must be public because the people must respond to it and assent.

David then personally and privately charges Solomon to maintain Israel's constitution as king, using the classic formula of the Torah, *hukotav, mitzvotav, umishpatav* (his statutes, his commandments, and his ordinances) *ve'edotav kakatuv b'torat Moshe* (his covenant witnesses as written in the Torah of Moses). After that constitutional charge, he turns to more practical matters, directing Solomon to make sure that Joab is assassinated so that he cannot intrigue against David's chosen successor and that Shimi ben Gera of Saul's family, who had cursed David when he fled Jerusalem during Absalom's revolt, also be killed so as to keep the mystique of the monarchy intact and end any efforts on the part of the supporters of Saul to seize the throne. With that, David died.

According to 1 Chronicles 28–29, David himself assembled all the relevant actors to inform them of his designation of Solomon as his heir in a formal assembly (*vayakhel,* 1 Chron. 28:1). These included, in order and by their titles listed: the ministers of Israel, the chief ministers of the tribes, the ministers of the departments that served the king, the officers of the regiments and companies, the officers responsible for the king's possessions, and David's personal bodyguard. In front of them he went through the appropriate constitutional litany with the addition of the promise to build a temple, and required all of them to pledge allegiance to Solomon.

The Role of Covenanting in a Constitutional Monarchy

The covenant with David and his house was not the first covenant of the *keter malkhut*. At the very least, the Bible presents *mishpat hamelekh* (civil constitution) in Deuteronomy as the foundation of that *keter,* though, in fact, the foundation goes back earlier to the patriarchs and the people.

During the six centuries following the conquest of the land, the Israelite tribes attempted to build or rebuild their commonwealth through various internal political covenants based upon the overarching covenants with God established earlier. It has already been suggested that the Book of Joshua is the account of the initial effort in that direction. When the original tribal federation collapsed under external military pressure from the Philistines, Israel created a limited constitutional monarchy, bounded by the *mishpat hamelekh,* the covenant of civil rule, which was periodically reaffirmed through specific covenants between kings, the people, and God. The establishment of the office of *nagid/ melekh* under Samuel with Saul as the first incumbent, is described as a covenanting (1 Sam. 9). The next major example, that of David, involves both bilateral and tripartite covenanting. First a relationship is established between God and David, which gives David a theo-political status (1 Sam. 16). Then that relationship is transformed into covenants between David and the people, with God acting as the guarantor (2 Sam. 5:1-3):

> Then came all the tribes of Israel to David unto Hebron, and spoke, saying: "Behold, we are thy bone and thy flesh. In times past, when Saul was king over us, it was thou that didst lead out and bring in Israel; and the Lord said to thee: 'Thou shalt feed My people Israel, and thou shalt be prince over Israel.'" So all the elders of Israel came to Hebron; and King David made a covenant with them in Hebron before the Lord; and they anointed David king over Israel."

It seems that, despite the hereditary element introduced by David, his heirs had to be confirmed through covenants with the representatives of the people. Thus, Solomon (965-928 B.C.E.) and the people covenanted with one another before God at the time of the transferring of the Ark of the Covenant to the Temple (1 Kings 8). At least this was so after crises involving a previously reigning monarch who had violated the covenant and thereby cast doubt on the legitimacy of the Davidic house, as in the cases of Asa (908-867 B.C.E.), Joash (836-798 B.C.E.), Hezekiah (727-698 B.C.E.), and Josiah (639-609 B.C.E.).

What was characteristic of the new regime was the combination of monarchic and tribal (or federal) institutions. David was elevated to the kingship by the tribal leadership speaking in the name of the people, Solomon was reaffirmed by that leadership, and Rehoboam was denied the kingship by ten of the tribes acting in concert when he went to them to establish a similar pact at the beginning of his reign (1 Kings 12; 2 Chron. 10). Considering his arrogant attitude toward the tribal leadership, it is clear that he was required to go before them by the constitution and did not do so of his own free will. Subsequently, while multi-tribal institutions disappeared from the southern kingdom because of the dominance of Judah (with the original federal institutions surviving only in the realm of local government), the northern kingdom maintained them until the very end of its existence.

The establishment of the federal monarchy under David required a complex network of covenants. The Bible states that God chose David to be his anointed one in a private conversation with Samuel, who proceeded to anoint David secretly (1 Sam. 16:1-13). This made it possible for David to be chosen king by the people through their elders in a manner consistent with covenant tradition, a necessary second step. The people and elders of Judah did so (without any reference to God's earlier intervention) immediately upon the death of Saul (2 Sam. 2:1–4) but the other tribes of Israel followed suit only after a civil war and protracted negotiations between Abner, the commander of the Israelite forces and real power in that regime (2 Sam. 3:6), and David (3:12–21). The issue was complicated by Abner's murder at the hands of Joab, David's military commander (3:27–39) and the intrigues at the court of Ish-Bosheth, Saul's heir (3:6–11 and 4). Finally, the elders of Israel went to Hebron, the seat of David's government, and covenanted with the new ruler (2 Sam. 5:1–3 and 1 Chron. 11:1–3). This covenantal "package" includes several examples of different kinds of covenantal usages: for political alliances (Abner and David), for defining the relationship between rulers and ruled (David and the tribes of Israel), and for establishing dynastic legitimacy (David and God), all of which find later echoes in Western political thought and behavior.

The establishment of the Davidic dynasty came only in the wake of the removal of the Ark of the Covenant to Jerusalem and the reaffirmation of the national covenant by David and the people at the time (2 Sam. 6, 1 Chron. 16 and 17). David was careful to make the transfer of the Ark a constitutional event since it was designed to recognize Jerusalem as Israel's capital and seat of God's providence as well as David's government. He carefully followed the right procedures (1 Chron. 13:1–7). After the Ark was settled in Jerusalem, Nathan, the first of the court-connected prophets (whose office emerges as a check on the new centralized executive), brought God's promise of dynastic succession to David (2 Sam. 7, 1 Chron. 18).

Implementation of the right of succession would come only when David's wife Bathsheba, Nathan, Zadok the High Priest, and various court figures engineered the appointment of Solomon to the throne by David in the latter's waning years, outmaneuvering Adonijah and David's other sons (1 Kings 1). Upon Nathan's recommendation, David promised the succession to Solomon and ordered his decision proclaimed by the chief representatives of the three branches of the Israelite national government: the high priest, the prophet, and the steward of the royal court (1:32–37). This was done in a public ceremony to which the people responded by proclaiming Solomon king (1:38–40). The parallel account in 1 Chronicles 28 and 29 has David assembling the representatives of the people before the Ark of the Covenant to anoint and proclaim Solomon as God's chief magistrate.

Solomon himself reaffirms the covenant, along with the representatives of Israel's tribes, at the dedication of the Temple, in a manner parallel to David's reaffirmation on the occasion of the transfer of the Ark of the Covenant to Jerusalem (1 Kings 8, 2 Chron. 5). But David's son goes beyond his father to initiate what is, for all intents and purposes, a supplementary covenant with God designed to ground the Temple within the Israelite covenantal system. Since, by tradition, pacts between God and man must be initiated by God, Solomon presents his initiative in the form of a public prayer, which he delivers at the dedication ceremony before the appropriate popular witnesses (8:1), "[t]he elders of Israel, all the heads of the tribes, representatives of the households of Israel" who are referred to collectively as *Kahal Yisrael,* the Congregation of Israel in (8:22).

The essence of Solomon's prayer consists of a series of practical proposals for including the Temple in the religio-legal-constitutional system of the nation. They are necessary because of the revolutionary implications of the Temple as a geographically fixed earthly locus for the Divine presence. Under the tribal federation, God explicitly abjured such a fixed dwelling place. God was free to locate and relocate His earthly presence. While He had commanded Israel to prepare the Ark of the Covenant and the Tent of Assembly, they were deliberately portable. This portability became a central element in ancient Israel's original theo-political ideology.

Solomon had the task of transforming that ideology into one that justified a permanent central worship site in Jerusalem, the city associated with the Davidides. His proposed covenant modification was a major step in that direction, one that followed upon his father's actions to constitutionalize the Davidic monarchy and preceded efforts of his heirs that continued for the duration of the kingdom. The Bible reflects Solomon's case; in 1 Kings 9:1-9 and 2 Chronicles 7:12-22, God is portrayed as responding favorably to Solomon's prayer, albeit to Solomon in private, in a dream, and with a clear warning that if he or his heirs should violate the original constitution, the Temple and the land shall be destroyed.

Throughout the years of the united kingdom, the strength of the tribes as constituents of the federation is clear. Despite the very real centralization that takes place under David and Solomon, the tribal institutions maintain much of their power and a serious role in the governance of the polity, a sure sign that the political covenant that united them under the monarchy remained a vital part of the Israelite constitution. Indeed, the Bible portrays the various revolts that punctured the period as reflecting conflicts over the federal character of the regime (e.g., 2 Sam. 15-19, 2 Sam. 20, 1 Kings 11).

Notes

1. For a history of this period see Martin Noth, *The History of Israel* (New York: Harper and Row, 1958); W. F. Albright, "Tribal Rule and Charismatic Leaders," in W. F. Albright, *The Biblical Period from Abraham to Ezra* (New York: Harper Torchbooks, 1968), 35-52
2. Daniel J. Elazar, "The Book of Joshua as a Political Classic," *Jewish Political Studies* 1, no. 1 (forthcoming).
3. B. Halpern, *The Constitution of the Monarchy in Israel* (Harvard Semitic Monographs No. 25, 1981). The idea that the Torah should be understood as the constitution of the Jewish people is an old and oft-recurring one, expressed by traditional and modern thinkers, as diverse as Spinoza, who understood the Torah as a political constitution first and foremost, and Mendelssohn, who viewed the political dimension as utterly dispensable. See Benedict Spinoza, *Politico-Theologico Tractate*; Moses Mendelssohn, *Jerusalem,* and Eliezer Schweid, "The Attitude Toward the State in Modern Jewish Thought Before Zionism," in *Kinship and Consent,* ed. Daniel J. Elazar (Ramat Gan: Turtledove, 1981).
4. Moshe Weinfeld, "From God's Edah to the Chosen Dynasty: The Transition from the Tribal Federation to the Monarchy," in *Kinship and Consent, The Jewish Political Tradition and Its Contemporary Manifestations,* ed. Daniel J. Elazar (Ramat-Gan: Turtledove Publishing, 1981); Hayim Tadmor, "The People and the Kingship in Ancient Israel: The Role of Political Institutions in the Biblical Period," *Journal of World History* (1968): 46-68.
5. J. Levenson, "The Davidic Covenant and Its Modern Interpreters," *Catholic Bible Quarterly* 41, no. 2 (1979): 205-19. God's covenant with David is emphasized in the Psalms (e.g., Psalms 89, 132), many of which are court poems designed to praise the king. Its first important prophetic endorsement is by Jeremiah (Jer. 33). See also S. Talmon, "Kingship and Ideology of the State, in *The World History of Jewish People,* vol. 4, part 2 (Jerusalem, 1979), 3-26.
6. A. Malamat, "Organs of Statecraft in the Israelite Monarchy," *The Biblical Archeologist* 28, no. 2 (19656): 34-50; Roland de Vaux, "The Administration of the Kingdom," in Roland de Vaux, *Ancient Israel,* vol. 1 (New York: McGraw Hill 1965), 133-42.

16

The Institutionalized Federal Monarchy

A final demonstration of the importance of the political covenant came with the rupture of the kingdom after the death of Solomon. Despite the dynastic element that had been introduced into the constitution, every ascendant to the throne had to be accepted by the assembled people as represented by their tribal leaders. Rehoboam, Solomon's son, presented himself to the assembly as one who would increase the centralization of the kingdom (1 Kings 12, 2 Chron. 10). Already smarting under the royal court's encroachment on tribal liberties, the leaders of ten of the tribes proclaimed their secession by refusing to reaffirm their original pact with David. Thus, the kingdom was divided into two states and remained divided for nearly 250 years until the Assyrian invaders destroyed one of them.

While the ten seceding tribes also organized themselves as a federal monarchy, keeping the name Israel, the dynastic principle never really took hold among them. At first, the assembly of tribal representatives elevated and deposed chief magistrates. Later, as Israel's polity degenerated, the changes were initiated through court intrigues or military coups but the basic principles were honored at least *pro forma* until the end.

Meanwhile, back in Judah, the southern kingdom, the House of David continued to reign on the basis of their founder's covenants at Hebron and Jerusalem for over 500 years, through the Babylonian exile until the Persians deposed the last of them. Those covenants were formally renewed at least three times, on each occasion as a response to a serious threat to the legitimacy of the Davidic house. Not every monarchic succession required recovenanting. For the most part, they remained within the same constitutional framework, with each new king subject to affir-

319

mation of his legitimacy because the covenantal relationship required public acceptance of each new ruler.

Only after rulers had usurped power or done something to break the normal constitutional relationship between governors and governed was it necessary to go through some formal covenantal act in order to reestablish the principles upon which the relationship was built. Thus, after Athaliah, the queen mother, usurped the Judean throne in 842 B.C.E. and murdered most of the royal family, responsibility for restoring the Davidic house fell to Jehoiada the Priest (2 Kings 11 and 2 Chron. 23). He proceeded to organize a rebellion against her (885 B.C.E.), mobilizing the people and using part of the palace guard to restore the throne to its legitimate heir, Jehoash. The process by which he did so was significant. He simultaneously mobilized a segment of the palace guard and covenanted with them (11:4), and mobilized the people through traditional institutions, simultaneously making a covenant with them (2 Chron. 23:2 and 3).

With this combination of popular support and military power within the palace, he succeeded in overthrowing the Queen Mother, capturing her, and restoring a surviving member of the Davidide family, Jehoash, to the throne. To assure the legitimacy of his act, he initiated a tripartite covenant between God, the new king, and the people (2 Kings 11:17; 2 Chron. 23:16). Significantly, the task fell to a priest, who mobilized his fellow priests and Levites along with the people. Both bodies joined to use the symbols of monarchic legitimacy to anoint Jehoash king even before Athalia was overthrown. Other cases include Hezekiah's extension of his authority over the remnants of the northern kingdom and Josiah's theo-political reform. In addition, Asa brought the people of all or parts of five tribes together in Jerusalem to renew the Sinai covenant (2 Chron. 15).

Of these, Hezekiah's covenant renewal marked both the restoration of the supremacy of the Davidides in all Israel, by default as it were, and the transition to a new epoch in Jewish political history. The Bible hails him as the most pious of all the kings who was rewarded by God accordingly. He saved Judah and Benjamin from Assyria and reunified what remained of the people, north and south (2 Chron. 30). His alliance with Isaiah (e.g., 2 Kings 19:20–26) restored the relationship between king and prophet, which had been a feature of David's reign. On the other hand, he was the first to preside over an Israelite polity not constituted on a tribal basis (e.g., 2 Chron. 29:20–30, 30:2). The tribes continued to exist, at least as sociological entities—the Bible mentions seven by name in connection with Hezekiah's reign (2 Chron. 30, 31)—and perhaps as local governing units as well, but they are not mentioned as participating in the national government.

The disappearance of the tribal federation as a reality after the fall of the northern kingdom in 722 B.C.E. can be said to mark the end of the original monarchic epoch in Jewish constitutional history, leading to a search for new political arrangements that culminated in the days of King Josiah when the Book of Deuteronomy became the constitutional basis for the regime (2 Kings 22 and 23). The Josianic reform involved the Book of Deuteronomy itself (referred to as *Sefer HaBrit,* the Book of the Covenant), which is reported as rediscovered hidden in the Temple in Jerusalem early in the rule of Josiah, King of Judah (622 B.C.E.), and is reaffirmed as the national constitution (2 Kings 22 and 23).

The accession of Josiah to the throne came after his grandfather Manasseh and his father Amon had suspended the constitution. Amon was actually murdered by his courtiers in a palace uprising. Josiah was the legitimate heir to the throne; his problem was to restore the observance of the constitution. This he did when he became of age, first by restoring the Temple, during which time the *Sefer HaBrit* was discovered, and the constitutional laws within it became the basis for a covenant renewal. The king consulted with Hilkaihu, the High Priest, Hulda the prophetess, and Shafan the Scribe, who indicate that he must restore the book of the Torah to its proper constitutional place. His actions are described in 2 Kings 23 and 2 Chronicles 34:29. He gathered the representatives of the people, the elders of Judah, in Jerusalem, as much of the population as could gather with them, the priests and the prophets, before whom he made the covenant to which they assented.

> And the king sent, and they gathered unto him all the elders of Judah and of Jerusalem. And the king went up to the house of the Lord, and all the men of Judah and all the inhabitants of Jerusalem with him, and the priests, and the prophets, and all the people, both small and great; and he read in their ears all the words of the book of the covenant which was found in the house of the Lord. And the king stood on the platform, and made a covenant before the Lord, to walk after the Lord, and to keep His commandments, and His testimonies, and His statutes, with all his heart, and all his soul, to confirm the words of this covenant that were written in this book; and all the people stood to the covenant (23:1-3).

As in the case of the previous covenants of this kind, the formal declaration of acceptance of the covenant was followed by a celebration of the Passover, the most important celebration of citizenship in ancient

Israel because participation in the paschal sacrifice was confined to citizens and, indeed, was used as a basis for defining citizenship—this in a system that otherwise explicitly treated resident aliens and strangers as virtual equals in most areas of concern.

The Josianic reform restored the idea that the Israelite polity was based on a tripartite covenant between God, Israel, and the king, with God as sovereign and lawgiver represented in day-to-day matters by his prophets (2 Chron. 23:1–2,21 and 34:29–32). Coming as it did after the reconstitution of the Israelite regime on a nontribal basis, the reform reaffirmed the essentially covenantal basis of the Israelite polity, just in time to strengthen the Jewish will to survive after the destruction of the first Temple (586 B.C.E.).

Israel: Monarchy or Theocracy?

All told, the Bible is quite ambivalent about the entire idea of monarchy and whether or not a monarchic regime is consistent with a covenantal system.[1] God's authorization of kingship in the Torah (Deut. 17:14–20) is so ambiguous that traditional commentators and biblical critics alike to this day argue over its meaning. Is the appointment of a king mandatory or a matter of human choice? To this writer, the text seems to take the latter position. What is clear is that the king must be subordinate to and bound by covenant (*brit*) and constitution (*Torah*) both. This is iterated and reiterated in the text from that first passage of authorization until the disappearance of the monarchy.

Throughout the period of the Judges, monarchy is rejected as a form of government consistent with God's covenant—by Gideon as the climactic figure among the Judges (Judg. 8:22–23) who restates the classic theory that only God rules over Israel and by the text in connection with usurpers (e.g., Abimelech in Judg. 9). The actual adoption of a monarchy is portrayed in very negative terms (1 Sam. 8). Samuel resists the change until God instructs him to capitulate to popular demand, telling him "they have not rejected thee, but they have rejected me that I should not be king over them" (8:7). Samuel's subsequent acquiescence is accompanied by dire warnings as to the consequences of a monarchical regime and, indeed, he spends the rest of his life trying to contain the new institution within an appropriate constitutional framework, including a special *mishpat hamelukhah* (law of the kingdom) and appropriate checks and balances.

In the last analysis, the text justifies human kingship only as a response to necessity—the deteriorated security situation of the tribal federation that is surrounded by powerful enemies and the deteriorated domestic situation as a result of the corruption of the priest Eli's and the prophet Samuel's sons. The federation needs stronger leadership to confront the first, while the collapse of its established institutions makes the change possible. The Bible is even reluctant to use the term *melekh,* or king, to describe the incumbents of the new institution, preferring the term *nagid,* best translated as high commissioner (of God) or chief magistrate.

The introduction of the major features of the monarchy are portrayed in the Bible as being of strictly human agency or as a result of God's private promises to the king. In the first category are the military and administrative innovations of David and Solomon, which lead to the establishment of Jerusalem, the private preserve of the Davidic house, as capital of Israel, the development of a standing army of non-Jewish mercenaries, and the emergence of a royal court with substantial administrative functions nationwide. In the second category is God's granting to David's family dynastic succession and Solomon's Temple in Jerusalem special status in the Jewish religious system. Both grants are made privately in dreams by the principal beneficiaries, unlike all other Divine covenants and dispensations after the age of the Patriarchs, which are made publicly and, indeed, are pointedly public in character. Is the Bible asking us to read between the lines in connection with David and Solomon?

The reorganization of the priesthood, the transfer of the Ark of the Covenant to Jerusalem, and the building of the Temple partake of both human agency and Divine ratification on a private basis. All three involve major redistributions of power within the polity, leading to greater centralization of power in Jerusalem and a dominant role for the royal court. While all three are undertaken by David and Solomon, in fact the Bible indicates a continuing struggle over the full implementation of the intended goals throughout the history of the monarchy, which ultimately ends in a compromise that preserves a polycentric system but integrates Jerusalem and the Temple within it.

The Federal Monarchy: A Case Study in Covenantal Adaptation

In a sense the biblical history of the monarchy is a history of how covenantal principles often must be adapted to necessity. While there are ambiguities involved, it is not unfair to suggest that the Bible portrays kingship as a second-best alternative, necessary because of external circumstances and internal corruptions whereby the success of external enemies brings people to lose faith in the classic regime of the tribal confederacy and exacerbates the Israelites' desire to be like all the other nations. The ultimate biblical confirmation of the Davidic house as a permanent dynasty does not contradict this since the Bible simply recognizes that the necessity also is likely to be long-lived. The way subsequent Jewish tradition elevates the Davidic house to messianic status, thereby eliminating the need to have living Davidides in kingly positions on earth, at least prior to the messianic age (and who knows when that will come) reflects the tenuousness of the tradition of kingship in the *edah*.

The problem was how to establish a legitimate monarchy within the covenant tradition. We have seen how that was resolved formally through covenants of kingship that had to be renewed even where the dynastic principle was observed. Three elements can be identified as part of that effort, all connected with the separation of powers into the three domains and all learned at the expense of Samuel's initiative with Saul.

First, the prophets are given a role as king makers and critics but do not seek to rule.[2] Second, kings can only rule by popular consent, meaning, at the very least, the consent of the tribal leaders. Third, while the people may refer to their civil rulers as kings, the kings themselves are repeatedly reminded by the prophets that from God's point of view they are only *negidim* or high commissioners. This *nagid* tradition functions as a limiting factor on monarchic self-aggrandizement. Because of the separation of powers, within a relatively short time the high priest, although of the family originally installed by David, also acquires an active role in the process. Thus, the king is tied to the constitution in three ways: (1) through the separation of powers into the three domains; (2) by having to have the confidence of the citizenry; and (3) through the limits of the constitutional tradition of God as Israel's real and only sovereign.

From the first there were differences between the ten northern tribes that became the Kingdom of Israel and the tribe of Judah with regard to dynastic succession, which succeeded so well in the Kingdom of Judah but never took root in Israel.[3] Nevertheless, it seems that the prophets threw their weight behind dynastic succession in the southern kingdom, probably because they discovered that while any dynasty or kingship is likely to be corrupted, ordered continuity is a necessity for stable government and peace, so that ordered continuity coupled with checks and balances to control the king was the lesser evil, again in an adaptation of a grand ideal to reality.[4]

The prophetic role becomes threefold. The prophets serve as king makers, as critics, and, if necessary, as king removers; they also serve as definers of the ideal exercise of the rule (cf. Jer. 22:13-17, where the prophet denounces Jehoiakin on the grounds that the king must be implementer of justice and human rights).

The tribes play much the same role as the prophets, in tandem with them, joining the prophets as king makers and king removers, but playing less of a role as critics or definers of the royal ideal. This is evidenced in the various covenants between kings and people, as in 2 Samuel 3, 5; 1 Kings 12; 2 Chronicles 23—all based on Deuteronomy 33:5.

The Use of Psalms to Legitimate Covenant as Relationship

The Psalms echo this system of checks and balances from the perspective of the *keter malkhut*. For example, Psalm 89 emphasizes the three-way covenant and Psalm 101, the king's covenant pledge. It seems that David's ascension to the kingship inaugurated a new form of scriptural literature associated with the *keter malkhut*. Biblical scholars have commented on how much of the *Torah* is associated with priestly matters—detailed descriptions of sacrifices, the role and function of priests and Levites. Indeed it has been suggested that the Torah was originally in the custody of the priests and hence was a national constitution skewed in the direction of priestly interests. According to the best scholarship, *Neviiim*, the prophetic sections of the Bible, date back at least to the time of Samuel and, while they represent a commentary on the kings, they have their own thrust connected with the *keter torah* in its prophetic form.

Extrapolating from the text and Jewish tradition, David as king is seen as beginning the process of developing a literature associated with the *keter malkhut,* which we have before us principally in the Psalms and the Book of Chronicles. Covering the history of David's reign, 1 Chronicles is essentially a military and political history. Solomon is viewed as carrying on the tradition in Proverbs, Song of Songs, and Ecclesiastes. Other books that should be identified with this domain include Job, which describes the tribulations of an elder in some fictitious land; Ruth, which both glorifies life in the days of the tribal federation and also refers to David's ancestry; Esther, Daniel, and Nehemiah, which deal with the bearers of this *keter* after the destruction of the First Commonwealth. All of these books are places in the third section of the *Tanach,* the Hebrew Scriptures, known as *ketuvim.*

Psalms is a religio-political document designed to strengthen the kingship as a religious value and source of religious inspiration. One hundred and fifty Psalms are collected in the Book of Psalms. (There are some others found in other books including the long Psalm of David in 1 Samuel 2:1-10 and 2 Samuel 22:1-23:7.) The Psalms attributed to David include 3-32, 34-41, 51-65, 68-70, 86, 108-10, and 138-45. Psalms 71 and 72 are otherwise identified as Davidic. Indeed at the end of 72 it states, "the prayers of David, the son of Jesse, are ended," suggesting that this is where the Book of Psalms originally ended. All told, 73 of the 150 Psalms are directly attributed to David by the oldest tradition.

What is important, however, is not the authorship but the function of the Psalms, which emphasize national, monarchic, and messianic themes, tying them together to establish or strengthen the links between the king and national religious aspirations. This is the overall thrust of the entire collection, which seems to be divided into five books. The Midrash points out the parallel between this division and the Torah itself, stating that Moses wrote the five books of the Torah and David wrote the five books of the Psalms. While the statement represents tradition rather than historic fact, the parallelism suggested by the representatives of the *keter torah* is instructive.

We can surmise that the combination of David's artistic talents and the need for establishing the role of the king within the framework of Israelite religion combined to produce the Psalms and the religious poetic tradition they represent. The Psalms restate the covenantal dynamic, *habrit vehahesed* (the covenant with its loving obligations), in connection with such aspects of civil rule as *mishpat* (covenant law,) and *shofet* (the judge engaged in judgment, often a reference to the king as the continuer of the role of the shofet in the previous regime), often together as in Psalm 89. All this is embedded in literature of the highest order. The Psalms also offer explanations of the events chronicled elsewhere in the Bible, presented in poetic form to invoke a sense of God's greatness in the minds of the reader or listener and to identify Him with the king. Of the 150 Psalms collected in the book of Psalms, 75 contain directly covenantal references, half again (37) in relation to King David. Those references range from reflections on nature as a covenantal phenomenon to explanations of the shifts of political power within the Jewish polity *Adat B'nei Yisrael* to a probing of personal covenants linking individuals.

What is striking in reading the Psalms is the extensive and intensive use of political terminology. There is hardly a Psalm that does not use political metaphors even if it is not referring directly to political matters. These, along with the attribution of the Book of Psalms to King David and the fact that so many of the Psalms are labeled as his or written for him, make it reasonable to view the Book of Psalms as the voice of the *keter malkhut*. Hence, the heavy emphasis on covenant and covenantal dynamics is doubly significant. Its theme is that God's covenant and pledge to His people is a reflection of the fact that we are all living within His kingdom under His sovereignty and judgment, that his judgment is based on righteousness and *hesed*. The latter in particular reflects the ways in which God shows favor to the one he has selected to bear the *keter malkhut* or the burdens of civil rule. The Psalms are the anthems of the kingdom of God designed to celebrate His justice and praise His covenant love.

The Psalm with the most extensive and comprehensive covenantal vocabulary is Psalm 89, ascribed to Ethan the Ezrachi (*ezrach* equaling citizen). It begins with a commitment to praise God's *hesed* over time and space (*olam* equaling space and time) from generation to generation because the universe is built on *hesed* and the heavens on covenant faithfulness. On this basis God has established His covenant with David and his heirs forever. The Psalm continues (v. 6ff.), describing how the heavenly hosts praise God who is their infinite superior. The former are described as the assembly of the holy ones and the council of the holy ones while God is described as the Lord of hosts.

Verse 10 begins a description of God's rule on earth, describing His rule over the primordial seas and how He crushed the mythical sea monster. In verse 12 the heavens and earth are described as God's possession because He founded and created them. Furthermore, His throne is founded on four principals: justice, law, loving covenant obligation, and truth (*tzedek u'mishpat, hesed v'emet*).

In verse 16 the Psalmist turns to describe how fortunate is the people that knows God's call and walks in the light of His countenance. By rejoicing constantly in His name, they are exalted by His justice. In verse 18 this is applied to Israel and in verse 19 the Psalmist proclaims God to be Israel's king. The next ten verses describe God's mandate to David, His anointed one, how He will strengthen him through his faithfulness in covenant love. The latter will be forever, along with His covenant, so long as the Davidides do not foresake God's Torah, laws, statutes, and commandments. If they do foresake those commandments, they will be punished but the covenant will not be broken.

From verses 39 through to the end, the Psalmist apparently is writing after the transgression has occurred and the punishment is in progress. In those verses he addresses God, summarizing the punishment that has been meted out, asking God to end His wrath and restore his *hesed* toward the faithful. In short this Psalm integrates time and eternity, heaven and earth, nature and man, the nations and Israel, God's justice and wrath, punishment and redemption, all within the covenantal framework. This is the recurrent theme of the Psalms.

Psalms: Covenant as Relationship

Hesed is the key covenantal term in Psalms, reflecting the Psalms' emphasis on relationships. While the term *brit* appears in only 13 psalms, *hesed* appears in 64; in Psalm 136, it appears 26 times. This modest quantitative measure suggests what a close reading of the Psalms reveals, namely that they are particularly concerned with covenantal dynamics, emphasizing God's sovereignty and kingdom, justice and judgment bound together by *brit* and *hesed*.

This mode of expression in Psalms takes one of several forms. Most prevalent is a human describing how God functions in a covenant relationship, as in Psalm 25, verses 9–10: "Good and upright is the Lord, therefore does He instruct sinners in the way. He guides the humble in justice and He teaches the humble in His way. All the paths of the Lord are covenant love and truth unto those who keep His covenant and His testimonies." This can also be seen in Psalm 85, verses 2-4: "Lord Thou hast been favorable unto Thy land. Thou hast turned the captivity of Jacob. Thou hast forgiven the iniquity of Thy people. Thou hast pardoned all their sin." It continues (v. 11), "Covenant love and truth meet; justice and peace kiss." Another example can be found in Psalm 98, verse 9: "For He has come to judge [rule] the earth. He will judge the world with righteousness and the peoples with equity."

In others it is the people who aspire to follow in the Lord's footsteps as in 101:

Of David, a psalm I will sing of covenant love and justice;
Unto Thee, O Lord, will I sing praises.
I will give heed unto the way of integrity;
Oh when wilt Thou come unto me?
I will walk within my house in the integrity of my heart.
I will set no base thing before mine eyes;
I hate the doing of things crooked;
It shall not cleave unto me.
A perverse heart shall depart from me;
I will know no evil thing.
Whoso slandereth his neighbor in secret, him will I destroy;
Whoso is haughty of eye and proud of heart, him will I not suffer.
Mine eyes are upon the faithful of the land, that they may dwell with me;
He that walketh in a way of integrity, he shall minister unto me.
He that worketh deceit shall not dwell within my house;
He that speaketh falsehood shall not be established before mine eyes.
Morning by morning will I destroy all the wicked of the land;
To cut off all the workers of iniquity from the city of the Lord.

Other exemplary expressions of that theme include:

Psalm 44, where the Psalmist attributes the allocation of lands among the nations to the handiwork of God and asks that the Jews be restored to their land because they have not been "false to Thy covenant" (v. 19).

Psalm 54, verse 21, *Shalah yadav bishlomav hilel brito*—He raised his hand against his covenant partners and profaned his covenant, (illustrating the link between *shalom* and *brit* as covenant terms).

Psalm 74, in which the Psalmist calls for a restoration of the *edah* after the destruction of its territorial base, described here as the destruction of the Temple in Jerusalem (v. 7) and the places of religious assembly throughout the land (v. 8) and the disappearance of prophets (v. 9).

God is hailed by the Psalmist as King (v. 12), as well as King of the universe (v. 13–17). He is asked to recognize the covenant and restore it to overcome *hamas* or the senseless violence that pervades the dark places of the land (v. 20), on behalf of the poor (v. 19) and the oppressed (v. 21). Their cause is presented as His (v. 22).

Psalm 78, which explains why political power has been transferred from Ephraim or the Northern Kingdom of Israel to Judah and the Davidic monarchy by the Ephraimites' violation of God's covenant (v. 10, v. 37) and the synonymous testimonies (v. 5, v. 56). The psalm recounts the history of the tribes of Israel in poetic form with frequent use of the classic biblical theo-political terminology.

The Regime Instituted by David

The establishment of the kingship opened a new constitutional epoch in Israelite history, one marked by the institutionalization of a limited monarchy and the struggle over the means to insure its limitation.[5] David can be considered the first true king of Israel, with Saul a transitional figure who was really part of the older federal republican tradition. At the same time, the struggle between Samuel and Saul did set the stage for the character of the political struggle in the monarchic period. As Saul was endowed with increasingly kingly powers, Samuel transformed his own role from that of judge to that of *navi,* or prophet, whose main task was to keep the monarch within the limits of the constitution. To that end, he introduced the *mishpat hamelukhah* (the law of the kingdom) as the framework for the limited kingship. This tension between king and prophet was to be the primary constitutional feature of the second constitutional epoch. During most of that period, the prophets functioned to critique, direct, and restrict kingly action and powers.

David was the first to formally assume the mantle of kingship. Like Saul, he did so through a combination of Divine designation (anointment by a prophet) and popular consent (covenants with the elders of Judah and Israel). He established most of the fundamental powers of the king during his long reign, including the power of hereditary succession within his "house." He did so by grafting the kingship and institutions designed to support it upon the governing base of the old tribal federation, preserving most of the institutions of the federation otherwise intact but increasingly subordinate to the king and court. David accomplished this by utilizing military necessity as the basis for development of a ruling class and a standing army whose powers came from their military role rather than from traditional sources and who were consequently tied to the king first and foremost.

Brilliantly, he captured Jerusalem and made it his city, the functional equivalent of a federal district in our time, outside of the jurisdiction of any individual tribe, and then proceeded to build his court there. He further strengthened the *keter malkhut* by developing a royal bureaucracy and a small professional army. Through the transfer of the Ark of the Covenant and the designation of the Zadokites as the priestly guardians of the Ark, David both strengthened the *keter kehunah* and gained control over it. He showed similar wisdom in dealing with the *keter Torah* as represented by the prophets, encouraging the leading prophets to take up residence at his court by giving them free rein to criticize him without penalty, but by the same token subtly tying them to the king as their protector. In sum, rather than seek to exert control by destroying the traditional institutions of the Israelite polity, he co-opted them.

Solomon intensified this trend by transforming the ruling class from a military elite to a more complex military-bureaucratic-religious one, introducing bureaucratic administrative forms as vehicles for centralizing power in the country. Both did what they did, however, within the purview and under the gaze of prophetic counterparts who were able to maintain some constitutional limitations on the exercise of kingly power if not on the increase in its scope. Indeed, there is good reason to believe that the prophets were not initially opposed to the centralization of power under the first two Davidic monarchs, seeing the new centralization as a way to better implement God's law in the nation as a whole.

However, when Rehoboam attempted to further extend and intensify the actions of his father and grandfather and impose burdens on the Israelite public that were not only taxing but visibly arbitrary as well, the major prophetic leadership deserted him and fostered a revolution that led to the division of the kingdom into two. While this division brought about an important change on one level, on another it did not mark a full constitutional revolution because even under David and Solomon, the northern tribes and Judah (which had virtually absorbed the tribe of Simeon by that time) had been separate groupings that accepted the rule of David and his son in separate actions. The refusal of

the northern tribes to accept Rehoboam, then, was an act fully conso-
nant with the Israelite constitution as they understood it.

What the division did inaugurate was the development of two different ways of integrating the monarchy into the constitutional framework
of Israel. In the southern kingdom, where the Davidic dynasty continued to rule, the tension between the kings and prophets was usually
resolved in favor of the king, even to the point where specific monarchs
temporarily suppressed the prophetic schools, though at no point was
the tension eliminated. The maintenance of the dynastic principle in-
sured this result in a way that was not possible in the northern kingdom,
where the succession itself was founded upon an opposition to dynastic
rule and a desire to restore the tradition of charismatic leadership.

In the north, the prophets were sufficiently strong to prevent the en-
trenchment of any particular dynasty and, indeed, the prophetic role
became one of supporting or rejecting particular candidates for the kingship (by extending or refusing them God's charisma) and thereby encouraging dynastic changes. Consequently, kingship in the northern tribes
meant, in no small degree, a restoration of the principles and practices
of the tribal federation, with the kings far more limited in power than
their southern counterparts and the older institutions of the tribal federation stronger in their governing role. At the same time, a national ruling
elite did emerge that was tied to the monarchy, even if its composition
changed with the dynastic changes that took place in the north.

The active role of the prophets is attested to in the biblical account,
that reveals far more prophetic activity in the northern kingdom than in
the southern, whether the activity of such political leaders as Elijah or
the more limited kind of protest prophecy of Amos and Hosea. It is
characteristic of the situation that the leading prophet in this constitutional epoch to appear in the southern kingdom was Isaiah, a relative of
the king and a member of the ruling elite, whose background as a courtier stands in sharp contrast to that of Amos and Hosea, not to mention
Elijah himself.[6]

With the destruction of the northern kingdom in 722 B.C.E., the second constitutional epoch came to an end and the third began. The southern kingdom stood alone as the single politically independent entity of
the Jewish people and, indeed, extended its sway over part of the north
and many of its people. It is fair to say that the real meaning of the
destruction of the northern kingdom was not the dispersion of the people
as recorded in the legends of the "ten lost tribes" so much as the destruc-

tion of the ten tribes as political entities.[7] Subsequent Jewish tradition, which sees the restoration of the tribes as a major element in the coming of the messianic age, confirms this.[8]

The architects of the extended kingdom of Judah were King Hezekiah and the prophet Isaiah. Hezekiah was the most important king between Solomon and Josiah, principally because he had the opportunity to reunite the Jewish people and did so, reinstituting the Passover pilgrimage to Jerusalem and extending Judean control over territories of the northern kingdom. In doing all this he was supported by Isaiah, who raised prophecy to a new level in Judah.[9]

Still, elimination of the northern kingdom had the consequence of greatly weakening the role of the prophets as defenders of the traditional constitution in the south, a tendency that was further strengthened by the elimination of the federal institutions that had survived in the north as additional constitutional bulwarks. In the south, where the tribes had already merged into the single polity of Judah, the old federal traditions were preserved only in the local arena. Consequently, the century between the destruction of the northern kingdom and the ascension of King Josiah was marked by the greatest violations of the traditional constitution ever to occur in the biblical period. These violations led to a major constitutional reform under Josiah, whereby the limitations on the monarchy, which the prophets had tried to sustain, were, in effect, brought together in the form of a more clearly written constitution (the Book of Deuteronomy) that successfully changed the power of relationships in the country, at least partly because the kingship itself ceased to be a reality shortly thereafter.[10]

The Josianic reform centered on the introduction of the Book of Deuteronomy as the basic constitutional document of a reconstituted and more limited kingship. The king was further limited by the loss of Israelite independence shortly after Josiah's death. The reduction of the Davidic rule to vassal status in the Babylonian empire at the beginning of the sixth century B.C.E., led, ultimately, to the disappearance of the throne itself in a restored Judea early in the fifth century.

The Babylonian Exile

The Babylonian exile did not put an immediate end to the Davidide regime. Rather, the royal family was transferred to Babylon where they "ate at the king's table," that is to say, were kept more or less under house arrest but retained their titles and status without power. So, too, did the priestly families continue to be recognized as Kohanim and, perhaps most important of all, the prophets continued to prophesize and even gained in influence.

Thus, when Cyrus the Great conquered the Babylonian empire and gave the Jews the right of return in 537 B.C.E., members of the royal and priestly families led the way back to Jerusalem, where they rebuilt the Temple. The descendants of the House of David who returned to Judea were sent as Persian satraps, while the priests of the House of Zaddok were appointed by the Jews themselves. At least two prophets, Haggai and Zachariah, emerged in restored Judea. At first, the representatives of the three *ketarim* were co-equal in Jewish eyes. The Jewish nationalist movement sought the greatest degree of national autonomy or independence—political where possible, cultural in any case—through Zerubavel. Then Shaltiel, the Davidide satrap; Joshua ben Jehozadak the priest, and Haggai the Prophet led an abortive attempt to regain a greater measure of political autonomy than Persia was willing to grant (Hag. 1:3). Zerubavel seems to have been removed; at any rate he disappears. It was at that point that the Jews of Yahud (the Persian name for Judea) began to build up the office of high priest, not because of a sudden theocratic turn but to maintain as much autonomy as possible where political autonomy was limited. Thus, the allegiance of the people was transferred to their own appointees, who, even if they had to be ratified by the Persian government, were appointed under the Mosaic constitution. And thus the regime persisted under Persian sovereignty for three more generations until the days of Ezra and Nehemiah.

By the end of the third constitutional epoch, the monarchy had disappeared as a viable institution, though hope for its restoration became part of Israel's messianic dream. The mysterious disturbances surrounding the last scion of the House of David in the period immediately following the restoration under Cyrus, marked the closing of the monarchic chapter in biblical history (and, except for the Hasmonean interlude, in Jewish history as a whole).[11]

The necessity to develop new modes of group survival in exile enhanced the importance of the Torah as a written constitution and as the principal source of authority in Israel. Consequently, in this third epoch, the Torah became the ascendant political authority in the Israelite polity, with the heirs of the prophets turning their attention to expounding its principles and elucidating its promises for future political success rather than being solely responsible for the maintenance of the constitution.

Conclusion

These biblical paradigms and case studies are intrinsically important for what they tell us about the deeper structure of the biblical text. They are at least equally important for their influence on subsequent political thought and behavior in the Western world.[12] These are the paradigms and case studies that surface time and again in the literature of politics in the West to serve as the meat of political analysis. Prior to the age of empirical political research, they represent the closest thing to data used by students of and commentators on political affairs. In that context, the theory and practice of covenant naturally attracted attention as a vehicle for polity building, constitution making, and governance. Through the Bible, then, what was once a mere technical arrangement was transformed into a means for constituting new communities, and thereby, a seminal political idea, one that has had a signal influence on the history of human liberty.

Notes

1. See, for example, Martin A. Cohen, "The Role of the Shilohnite Priesthood in the United Monarchy of Ancient Israel," in *Hebrew Union College Annual, Vol. 36: Josephus's Antiquities of the Jews* (Cincinnati: Hebrew Union College, 1965); Abravanel's commentary on Deuteronomy and Samuel; Martin Buber, *Kingship of God* (New York: Harper and Row, 1967); and Yehezkel Kaufmann, "The Monarchy," in *The Religion of Israel* (Chicago: University of Chicago Press, 1960), 262-70. While Elijah has traditionally been considered an anti-monarchist, the biblical portrayal of him shows him to have a more complex position, supporting Ahab as king but seeking to keep the monarchy tied to the Torah as mediated through the prophets. The reference here is to the tradition rather than to the more complex reality.
2. Benjamin Offenheimer, *Early Prophecy in Israel* (Jerusalem: Magnes Press, 1973); J. Muilenberg, "The 'Office' of the Prophet in Ancient Israel," in *The Bible in Modern Scholarship*, ed. J. P. Hyatt (1966), 79-97; M. Galston, "Philosopher-King vs. Prophet," *Israel Oriental Studies* 8 (1978): 204-18; Roland de Vaux, *Jerusalem and the Prophets* (Cincinnati: Hebrew Union College Press, 1965); S. Talmon, "Kingship and Ideology of the State," in *The World History of the Jewish People*, vol. 4, part 2 (Jerusalem, 1979), 3-26.
3. A. Alt, "The Monarchy in the Kingdoms of Israel and Judah," in A. Alt, *Essays on Old Testament History and Religion* (1951), English translation (Oxford: Ba-

sil Blackwell and Mott, 1966), 239–59; A. Malamat, "Organs of Statecraft in the Israelite Monarchy," *Biblical Archeologist* 28, no. 2 (1956): 34–50; Roland de Vaux, "The Administration of the Kingdom," in *Ancient Israel*, vol. 1 (New York: McGraw Hill, 1965), 133–42; B. Halpern, *The Constitution of the Monarchy in Israel* (Cambridge: Harvard Semitic Monographs, no. 25, 1981); Y. Kaufmann, "The Monarchy," *The Religion of Israel* (New York: Schocken, 1972), 262–70.

4. Halpern, *Constitution of the Monarchy in Israel*; W. O. E. Oesterley and Theodore Henry Robinson, *History of Israel* (Oxford: Clarendon Press, 1932).

5. Daniel J. Elazar and Stuart A. Cohen, "Epoch IV: *Brit ha-Melukhah* (The Federal Monarchy)," in *The Jewish Polity* (Bloomington: Indiana University Press, 1985).

6. Norman K. Gottwald, *All the Kingdoms of the Earth* (New York: Harper and Row, 1964).

7. John Bright, *A History of Israel* (Philadelphia: Westminster Press, 1960), chap. 7, pp. 249–87; W. F. Albright, "Tribal Rule and Charismatic Leaders," *The Biblical Period from Abraham to Ezra* (New York: Harper Torchbooks, 1968), chap. 7, pp. 67–74; Martin Noth, *The History of Israel* (New York: Harper and Row, 1958), part 3, section 1, pp. 253–99; Oesterley and Robinson, *History of Israel*.

8. Martin Cohen, "The Role of the Shilonite Priesthood in the United Monarchy of Ancient Israel," 59–98; B. Porten, *Archives from the Jews of Elephantine* (Berkeley, 1968).

9. John Bright, "The Monarchy: Crisis and Downfall," in Bright, *A History of Israel*.

10. E. W. Nicholson, *Deuteronomy and Tradition* (Oxford: Basil Blackwell and Mott, 1967); G. von Rad, *Studies in Deuteronomy*, English translation (London: SCM Press, 1953); H. H. Rowley, "The Early Prophecies of Jeremiah in Their Setting," reprinted in *Men of God* (London: Thomas Nelson and Sons, 1963), 133–68; Oesterley and Robinson, *History of Israel*.

11. John Bright, "Tragedy and Beyond: The Exilic and Postexilic Periods," in Bright, *A History of Israel*, 76–94; Leo Schwarz, *Great Ages and Ideas*, pp. 341–401.

12. Cf. Harold Fisch, *Jerusalem and Albion* (New York: Schocken Books, 1964) for an examination of the modern secularization of the covenant idea and John F. A. Taylor, *The Masks of Society, An Inquiry into the Covenants of Civilization* (New York: Appleton-Century-Crofts, 1966) for a contemporary American covenantal perspective. While this article seeks to expound and even shift our understanding of the covenant idea to include and emphasize its political dimension, it also uses theological terminology throughout because the Jewish political tradition of necessity has a philosophic base. Political theology has declined in importance in the West in recent generations; hence, the usages may be somewhat unfamiliar to the reader, but it is nonetheless an old element in political science and legitimate in every respect.

17

Covenant as Judgment, Law, and Government

We have seen how the biblical understanding of covenant has at least three dimensions involving judgment, law, and governance. Each of these dimensions is further explicated in the biblical and other classic Jewish texts. The Psalms, in particular, can be read as an explication of the biblical-cum-Jewish theory of covenant relationships, while the Prophets can be read as an explication of the biblical-cum-Jewish understanding of covenant as judgment. This is not to say that each of those sources is uni-dimensional. All of the dimensions appear in both. Nor that they are the sole sources, only that each emphasizes one in a way more concentrated than in any other single source. Hence, they bear closer examination from this perspective to understand the full range of covenant as forming idea and a way of life.

The true political test of the covenantal system is in governance itself. Thus, the way in which the Israelites actually governed themselves is of critical importance. While our knowledge is limited in that sphere, what we do know suggests a system of communal democracy rooted in federal republicanism.

The Prophets: Covenant and Judgment

Biblical emphasis on covenant and covenantal relationships is not based upon rosy expectations of humanity. Quite to the contrary, the Bible can be read not only as a record of God's efforts to bring humanity to a better state through covenant, but as the record of the consequences of human covenant violations. Human weakness in this regard is reflected in the Torah itself, and in connection with Moses, the greatest of the prophets. Indeed, Joshua is about the only one of the "historical" books of the Bible in which there is only one explicit covenant violation recorded—that of Achan, taking unauthorized spoils of war, an individual violation rather than a national one and of relatively petty dimensions.

In all the other books there are constant references to explicit national violations of the covenant. The Book of Judges, for example, which begins by reaffirming the covenant (2:1-5), continues to repeatedly refer to covenant violations that become so great that the book ends with the issue of the survival of the twelve-tribe system on center stage. This is continued by 1 Samuel, which focuses on covenant violations of individual leaders, beginning with the Shilohnite priesthood, continuing with Samuel's own sons, and concluding with Saul. Judges is paralleled by 2 Samuel, 1 and 2 Kings, and Chronicles in relating the regular violation of the covenant, either by the nation or by its leaders. Needless to say, the Prophetic books emphasize covenant violations and their consequences, first and foremost, as a central motif (e.g., Isa. 24:5; Jer. 22:8-9 and 23:20-26; Ezek. 44:5-7; Hos. 6:6-7 and 7:1; Mal. 2:10-14).

It has been suggested that the prophets even presented their critiques of Israelite society in the form of covenant lawsuits.[1] Thus, Hermann Gunkel and Joachim Degrich suggest that many of the prophetic oracles are presented as lawsuits, following one or another of the following outlines:

1. A description of the scene of judgment
2. The speech of the plaintiff
   A. Heaven and earth are appointed judges
   B. Summons through the defendant or the judges
3. An address in the second person through the defendant
4. Accusation in question form through the defendant
5. Refutation of the defendant's possible arguments
6. Specific indictment
   A. A description of the scene of judgment
   B. The speech by the judge
      i. Address to the defendant
      ii. Reproach (based on the accusation)
      iii. Statement (if the accused has no defense)
7. Pronouncement of guilt
8. Sentence (in second or third person)

If this is indeed the case, then the prophets help to round out the covenantal system by suggesting that it has a negative dynamic as well, that is to say, it provides a framework for bringing charges against *Adat Bnei Yisrael* for violating the terms of the covenant, and this is one of the major tasks of God's messengers, the prophets.

In the biblical presentation of the prophets, they function within a system. They are part of the political system of Israel and later Israel and Judah. The system of government in biblical Israel involved what we call today checks and balances. The prophets arise when one particular set of checks and balances disappears because the premonarchic tribal federation is transformed. After the new constitutional order is introduced, the prophets arise within the new regime for a political purpose, as checks against the kings (not so much against the priests, as the theologians suggest, but against kings). Their other role is primarily that of calling people to hearken to God's commandments. In neither role do they exercise power in the conventional sense, yet they are at times powerful.

There is also a constant problem of true and false prophets. One of the tests of a true prophet is whether the prophet both recognizes the king, that is to say, the political authority, and critiques it according to certain constitutional principles. A self-proclaimed prophet who apologizes for the king is a false prophet, but critiquing the monarchy as such is also rejected. The encounter between Elijah and Ahab is the classic expression of this. Elijah, the preeminent indigenous prophet of the northern kingdom, was involved in what rapidly became a life or death struggle with Ahab, the king of Israel whose foreign wife Jezebel led him into evil ways. Elijah had prophesized and actively worked for the destruction of Ahab's house, yet when the two met by chance on the road, each gave the other his due recognition as legitimate office bearers (1 Kings 18–21). If prophecy is detached from the system, it becomes crazy enthusiasm, a kind of unrestrained power to undermine necessary civil order. Unrestrained power is unacceptable even among prophets.

In sum, one of the greatest contributions of biblical thought is this principle that covenant places humans and their institutions under judgment. Its moral base establishes the standards that humans must maintain and for which they will be judged, while its contractual dimension commits the partners to submit to judgment on the part of the other in terms of the covenantal moral imperative. The prophets of Israel were the human instruments of Divine judgment. Hence, just as the Torah sets out the history and terms of Israel's covenant with God, the Prophetic books record the history and consequence of Israel's efforts to live up to that covenant, and the judgment of their failures to do so, culminating in the destruction of the first Jewish commonwealth. If the prophets are human instruments of Divine judgment, then the nations, according to the Bible, are human instruments of Divine retribution.

The privilege of being a covenantal partner of God does indeed indicate chosenness, although a major part of that chosenness is choosing to be under God's judgment in a special way. It should be noted in that connection that the Bible never describes Israel as the chosen people, but as a people who have a special task. *Segula,* the word used, essentially means vocation, that is, the Jews are the people who have a special vocation as a result of their partnership with God. Indeed, the biblical account suggests that the choosing is mutual.

This becomes even more apparent in the course of Jewish history. Whereas the prophetic books reflect God's judgment of Israel, the postbiblical period often includes accounts of Israel's judgment of God. This is a recurrent theme in postbiblical Jewish theology, that in allowing His covenant partners to suffer so intensely and for so long at a time when they are striving to piously follow His ways, God fails to live up to His commitments under the covenant and hence can be brought to judgment. The modern most famous expression of this in Jewish folklore is the hassidic Rebbe, Yitzhak of Berditchev, calling God to judgment, in an obverse of the prophetic lawsuit, summoning God to give an accounting for His mistreatment of the faithful of Israel. Either way, the fact that covenant implies or requires judgment is basic to the idea itself. This not only denudes the possible *hubris* implied in covenantal relationships of reality, but creates more demanding standards for those bound by covenant.

At the same time, just as the Bible insists on judgment, it makes possible *teshuva* or return in the sense of repentance. The issue of *teshuva* is, in a sense, the final piece of the puzzle of covenantal politics, offering humans a chance to repair their ways through a return to those of God. This is one of the most profound aspects of biblical-covenantal teaching, which, while evident throughout Scripture, reaches its full flowering in post-biblical times.[2]

What must not be forgotten, however, is that the prophets are presented as functioning within a political system. They were not the ancient Israelite equivalent of itinerant evangelicals, although they have often been presented as such by modern commentators primarily interested in their spiritual message. That may have been a role reserved to the folk prophets, the *bnai haneviim* (sons of, or schools of, the prophets) referred to periodically in the Bible, implicitly as being on a lower level than the great spokesmen for God. Almost all of the great biblical prophets who have captured the human imagination over the ages were conscious of being bearers of God's message to kings, rulers, and power elites within the framework of the *edah* and its covenant with God.

David's effort to co-opt Nathan and the other prophets and the mutual acknowledgment of Elijah and Ahab reflect this. Isaiah, often considered the greatest of the literary prophets, prophesied almost entirely within the royal court and, indeed, was a relative of the royal family. His messages show an exceptional sense of realpolitik along with an uncompromising sense of justice and morality. Jeremiah is the prophet of the covenantal system engaged in trying to save Judah from itself, particularly in connection with the foreign policy of its kings. Ezekiel devotes much of his prophecy to presenting a design for the restored tribal federation of the messianic era.

Ezekiel's comprehensive vision of the Israelites' restoration to their land and the coming of the messianic era gave us his understanding of the utopian Israelite commonwealth of the future. He is a biblical messenger in the fullest sense of the term, bringing a message of comfort and hope from God that combines fabulous visions, detailed concern with the ritual minutia of animal sacrifices, and a great utopian scheme for world peace within an appropriate governmental framework, especially for Israel. Penetrating the book of Ezekiel has been a task that has absorbed traditional biblical commentators and modern biblical critics alike over the centuries, yet much remains obscure.[3] For our purposes, however, Ezekiel's message is clear enough.

Ezekiel introduces his vision for the future through an immediate one that calls him to prophecy, followed by an extensive statement of God's charges against Israel that led to their exile. In the latter he restates the failure in every domain of the tripartite division of power: "Calamity shall come upon calamity and rumor shall be upon rumor, and they shall seek [in vain] a vision of the prophet and instruction shall perish from the priest and counsel from the elders. The king shall mourn; the *nasi* shall be clothed with desolation" (7:26-27). He concludes: "I will do unto them after their way and according to their desserts will I judge them and they shall know that I am the Lord."

Only in chapter 11 (v. 14ff.) does Ezekiel begin to talk about the ingathering of Israel and their redemption. In his second and third visions, however (beginning in chapter 8), he does make reference to the continuation of Israelite political institutions in Babylonia, at the same time giving instruction to the Israelite elders as to how the people should adjust to exile so as to preserve their Jewishness. Without attempting to impose too much system on the prophet's words, this is the essence of the second part of the book.

In chapter 16, the prophet paints Israel as a beautiful woman abandoned as a child and subsequently rescued through God's covenant, who then played the harlot with God until God punished her; and now God will reestablish his covenant as an everlasting one once Israel repents. In this and subsequent chapters, Ezekiel emphasizes God's intention to return Israel to *masoret ha-brit* (the bond of the covenant, 20:37). The term *masoret*, whose original meaning as bond is appropriately covenantal, soon came to mean tradition, a meaning it carries to this day. Thus, in biblical terminology and thought, tradition, that set of human artifacts often considered to be the most organic, that is to say, developed without deliberate effort by the human behavior over the passage of time, is basically covenantal, growing out of an initial covenantal bond.

The visions of destruction continue for the first thirty-six chapters of the book. Then in chapter 37 Ezekiel has his vision of the dry bones and the resurrection of the House of Israel and all twelve tribes who will be reunited (37:22). The united nation will be led by a *nasi* from the House of David. Ezekiel is constrained to recognize the Davidides' claim to the *keter malkhut* but he explicitly defines their status as leaders elevated by God and the people. The Temple will be rebuilt as God's sanctuary and dwelling place, and God will make a *brit shalom—brit olam* (an everlasting covenant of peace) with Israel. This, in turn, will lead to the great world war of Gog and Magog, which will open the door to the final redemption.

Ezekiel then has a vision of the rebuilt Temple with its construction and measurements specified to the utmost detail (chaps. 40–42). This in turn leads to the restoration of the priests, the Levites, and the sacrifices. The restoration of the national sanctuary will make it possible for the redivision of the land by lot into each family's inheritance (45:1), with portions set aside to support the priests, the Levites, and public purposes including the *nesiim* according to their tribes. The prophecy then turns to the latter (45:9ff.), who are commanded to eliminate senseless violence and robbery (*hamas v'shod*) and to do justice and righteousness (*tzedek u'mishpat*). With the restoration of the *nesiim* and the *am haaretz* (45:16), the national council, their authority to bring certain sacrifices is also restored, thus relegitimating their direct communication with God. At the same time *nesiim* are forbidden to take the people's assigned portions of land.

Ezekiel's next task is to delineate the territories to be included within the borders of the land of the twelve tribes, where they are to be divided among the families. Within that territory the land is to be divided "according to the tribes of Israel" (28:21). While Ezekiel makes it clear that national unity comes first, the nation is a nation of tribes and the tribes must be restored along with the nation. For Ezekiel, however, mere announcements are not sufficient. In his comprehensive scheme he divides the land among the tribes by allocating specific portions to each, divided in such a way that the priests and Levites are in the middle. The tribal division concludes the book of Ezekiel, the climax, as it were, of his vision of the restoration of the House of Israel.

In his article "The Design and Themes of Ezekiel's Program of Restoration,"[4] Professor Moshe Greenberg states, "Biblical tradition regards Moses as the mediator of Israel's divine constitution, the Torah; it recognizes no other legislator excepting Ezekiel."[5] Greenberg goes on to account for this as a result of the similar position of the Jews exiled to Babylonia and the Jews ending their exile in Egypt but still in the wilderness. Greenberg points out that Ezekiel ties his program of restoration through which his constitutional theory is expressed to his covenantal approach, theologically, ideologically, and politically, beginning with the description of how Israel's "heart of stone" has been replaced by a "heart of flesh" (Ezek. 36:26) that would now assure that the conditions of God's covenant would be met. In the prologue to his program, Ezekiel indicates how he views the Temple as having failed to prevent Israel's departure from God's covenant and how in the program of reconstruction more is needed.

Ezekiel's program has three parts: one, the restoration of an improved Temple in which God's spirit can dwell, new rules governing access to the Temple and activity in it, and the apportionment of the land among the people. All of this can be found in chapters 40–48 of the Book of Ezekiel, the first part encompassing 40:1–43:12, the second 44:1–46:24, and the third 47:13–48:35. The order of introduction of bearers of the three *ketarim* is significant. The *keter torah* in the person of the prophet is identified with the improved Temple; the *keter kehunah* in connection with priests and Levites, and the *keter malkhut* in connection with the *nasi,* his family, and his court are provided for in connection with part 2. The enterings and leavings of the people through their tribes are the focus of part 3.

Each part is designed to represent an improvement over the original Torah. The result is a plan for an improved tribal federation within the original boundaries of the land, approximately as specified in Numbers 34:2-12, excluding the Israelite conquests subsequent to that. Tribal allotments are also redesigned as "latitudinal strips across the breadth of the land." Each tribe is to receive an equal share of the land and each is to make a contribution that will include segments of the cis-Jordan coast, the foothills (shefela), the mountains, and the Jordan valley to assure equality on more than a size basis. Each tribe will contribute part of its allocation to provide a national territory, in the midst of which would be a central city to be the seat of the government. The Temple, however, would be located among the lands of the priests; rather than concentrating all national institutions in Jerusalem, there would be a separation of Temple and civil government with priestly lands around the Temple and the whole national strip uniting the country with God. Apparently Ezekiel only treats those aspects of previous Israelite society that he feels were in need of correction, presupposing the rest.

In the last analysis Ezekiel's program remained a utopian concept only. The return from Babylonia and the founding of the Second Commonwealth took place on an entirely different basis and we have no evidence that the returnees even made reference to Ezekiel's program. For one thing, the tribes were not restored since the province of Yahud remained just that, a small Persian province in part of the territory of Eretz Israel. It had no independent chief magistrate other than the Persian governor who, it is true, was at times a Jew but whose authority flowed rather deliberately from the Persian crown. The rebuilt Temple did not become a center of prophecy; that disappeared from Israel's midst in the earliest stages of the return, though it did become the seat of *keter torah,* as well as the *keter kehunah,* in the form of the *anshei knesset hagedolah.* In that sense there is some parallel to what Ezekiel proposed, but we have no knowledge as to whether Ezekiel had any influence on that happening or whether it was just natural for the Temple to become the seat of government, at least in principle, for all three *ketarim.* Jerusalem not only remained the single capital of the province but the size of

Yahud was such that it became almost a city-state, which, indeed, is what the Hellenists later tried to convert it into.

The prophets' political message was to return to the great days of the *edah* when it was faithful to God and his Torah in every way or, after the destruction of the First Commonwealth, a message of hope that the *edah* would be restored under the Divine covenant. Thus, the prophets were friends of constitutional government as much as they were messengers of God. Prophecy detached from that sense of responsibility becomes irresponsible, and, to the extent that the prophets are detached, they would be exercising unrestrained power, which is never presented as good in the biblical scheme of things. Their responsibility is to hold those who exercise power constitutionally to the terms of Israel's covenant and constitution.

Both the psalmists and the prophets were concerned with false covenantal talk as much as with dynamics of the covenantal system. Covenant is a powerful legitimizer. In covenantal societies, once something is associated with the covenant, there is a tendency to act as if coercion or any other means can be used to achieve goals, whereas both psalmist and prophet emphasized the confrontation between the necessity to use power to achieve good or great ends and the pain that is associated with the use of power. Covenantal theory must of necessity deal with both. There is always the tragic element in life that just cannot be avoided without the awareness of this tragic dimension.

The covenantal process also runs the risk of turning into a Faustian bargain, a covenant with the devil, or making vices out of one's virtues through overemphasizing one's own virtuousness at the expense of reality. Power gone mad is a reflection of the former, part of the tragic dimension in life. Muddle-headed reformism has a tendency to make vices out of virtues by carrying them to inappropriate extremes. Precisely because covenant is such a powerful, such a seminal concept it also must be used carefully and with a certain humility so that even those who claim the protection of the covenant understand that they will be judged by its terms as well.

Ordinary Covenants: The Permeation of the Moral Order

The Bible makes as much of ordinary covenants as of the great ones, undoubtedly to teach us that the moral order must permeate all of life. When the Patriarchs secure their water supply, they make ordinary covenants with their neighbors. David and Jonathan bind their friendship through an ordinary covenant. Marriage is an ordinary covenant, one in which the covenantal dimension is extremely important because, of all human relationships, the marriage bond is the least enforceable without the moral commitment. What is characteristic of all these ordinary covenants is the moral commitment involved in preserving the relationship that is established. That relationship is not simply a contract for mutual convenience. Both parties to it make the moral commitment that places them under judgment as to whether or not they keep their part of the bargain. Ordinary covenants enable people to do even simple things by guaranteeing them through the moral bond.

Ordinary covenants help us understand the biblical view of the public-private relationship. Although the Bible does not use these terms explicitly, it does describe such relationships. Central to them is the idea of stewardship, the principle that humans are God's stewards in this world and bear the responsibility of stewardship.

In some situations stewardship is collective or public and at other times it is private. Thus, the land of Israel is one land, an integral whole, but is divided into tribal areas and family plots. Every family gets its inheritance, which no public authority can touch. A family is responsible for its inheritance forever. Even if alienated, it is to be restored in the jubilee year.

Even a king cannot tamper with that inheritance. If he does, he is denounced. When King Ahab coveted Naboth's vineyard, Jezebel, his foreign queen, conspired to condemn heirless Naboth to death for blasphemy so that the property would revert to the crown. For this Ahab was denounced by Elijah and condemned to a violent death while the queen was condemned to have her body thrown to the dogs by Divine intervention.[8] Thus, humans hold the world in trust for God, with some of its goods held in trust for the community, others for the family and the individual. All come under the terms of stewardship, yet without confusing stewardship with collectivism.

Covenants in International Relations

Among the most ordinary covenants are those regulating international relations. The Bible presents paradigmatic covenants with *ba'alei brit;* that is, for international relations. There are at least fifteen references to international covenants in the Bible, which can be classified in three categories: treaties of alliance, peace treaties among equals (which also establish boundaries), and vassal treaties. As we have seen, Abraham, Isaac, and Jacob are each presented as covenanting with their neighbors.

The Bible specifies that alliances between Israel and the peoples of Canaan are forbidden (e.g., Exod. 23:32, 34:12; Deut. 7:2; Judg. 2:2). The Israelite covenant of peace and alliance with the Gibeonites (Josh. 9) is initiated by the Gibeonites as an agreement among unequals with the initiators subordinate. So, too, is the covenant of subordination, which the people of Jabesh Gilead propose to Nahash the Amonite (1 Sam. 11:1). Similarly, Ezekiel describes a covenant of subordination (of Judah to Babylonia) in 17:12-20.

The covenant of alliance between Israel and Tyre (the Phoenicians) initiated in the days of Solomon and Hiram (1 Kings 5:26) was an alliance of equals. The later violation of this alliance is referred to by Amos as one of the sins of Tyre (1:9). The covenant between Ben Haddad, king of Aram, and Baasa, king of Israel, is portrayed as a peace treaty open to unilateral revocation if a better offer comes along (1 Kings 15 and 2 Chron. 16). A similar peace treaty also involving Ben Haddad is described in 1 Kings 20:26-34 after he surrenders to Ahab, king of Israel. Hosea describes a peace treaty between Ephraim (Israel) and Assyria (2:2). The moral basis of even these clearly political covenants is highlighted in the biblical account of Asa, the king of Judah's attempt to bribe Ben Haddad to break his treaty of peace with Israel and Ezekiel's criticism of the Judean king's violation of their treaty with Babylonia.

The final paradigm is not an actual covenant but the embodiment of the prophetic vision of a covenant of nations which would represent the final triumph of God's kingdom on earth. It is expressed in Zechariah 11:10: "And I took my staff Graciousness, and cut it asunder, 'that I might break My covenant which I had made with all the peoples.'"

Notes

1. Herbert B. Huffmon, "The Covenant Lawsuit in the Prophets," *Journal of Biblical Literature* 78 (December 1959): 285-95.
2. See Leo Strauss, "Progress or Return," and Robert A. Licht, "Communal Democracy, Modernity and the Jewish Political Tradition," *Jewish Political Studies Review* 5 (1993).
3. Works on Ezekiel include Keith William Carley, *Ezekiel Among the Prophets: A Study of Ezekiel's Place in Prophetic Tradition* (London: SCM Press, 1975); Pe-

ter Campbell Craigie, *Ezekiel* (Philadelphia: Westminster Press, 1983); Walter Eichrodt, *Ezekiel: A Commentary* (London: SCM Press, 1970).

4. Moshe Greenberg, "The Design and Themes of Ezekiel's Program of Restoration," *Interpretation,* 38 (April 1984): 181-208.

5. Ibid., 183.

6. This incident teaches us something of the possibilities of *teshuva.* When they have heard his punishment he tore his clothes and put on sackcloth and fasted (1 Kings 27), thereby diverting the evil decree as to when his dynasty would come to an end until his son's time, and he, in turn, was allowed a warrior's death.

7. J. Bright, "The Monarchy: Crisis and Downfall," in *A History of Israel* (Philadelphia: Westminster Press, 1960).

8. Roland de Vaux, *Ancient Israel,* 2 vols. (New York: McGraw Hill, 1965).

18

Covenant Applied:
Israelite Political Organization

By and large, our knowledge of the forms of Israelite political organization is limited. The Bible offers the only available account of the subject, although it can be supplemented by limited archaeological evidence and documents from other West Asian polities of the biblical era. We are assisted by the biblical discussion of political institutions in the context of its larger purposes and our increased understanding of the political institutions of the ancient Near East in general.

Three arenas of political organization are to be noted: local, tribal, and national, each of which underwent transformation through the various constitutional epochs. Local institutions had their origins in the familial structure developed before the first national constitution when the Israelites were semi-nomads. The various *mishpahot* (clans) formed by the combination of households (*bet ab*) formed the tribal substructure in those times. After Israelite settlement of Canaan during the first constitutional period, the clans settled down in discrete villages or townships (a more accurate term) and the relationship among those households was transformed into one that was linked with the particular locality of their settlement. Final human authority for each tribe and clan was located in an assembly of all males for ordinary decisions and all—men, women, and children—for major constitutional decisions such as covenanting. These assemblies were convened as necessary.

The clans were governed on a daily basis by elders (*zekenim*), no doubt consisting of the heads of their several households. After the conquest, these became local councils known as *Sha'arei Ha'ir* (the Gates of the City), referring to the location within the Israelite township at which they met to conduct their business. These local councils seem to have persisted throughout the biblical period and, with some changes, into the post-biblical period as well. We must assume that these local councils handled whatever governmental functions were conducted locally, combining within them such legislative, executive, and judicial functions as were exercised at the various periods of their existence. It is possible that the judicial functions were shared with locally based priests from time to time. These local councils adjudicated disputes, regulated markets, spoke in the name of the township on local affairs and in conjunction with tribal and national bodies. While they were apparently selected by consensus, they were responsible to the township assembly, known in the Bible as *yotzei ha'ir* (those who go out from the city), consisting variously of all local inhabitants on constitutional matters or the military-age males constituting the local militia on others.

Tribal political institutions also grew out of the familial structures of the pre-settlement period. During the first constitutional epoch, the tribes were entrusted with the major governmental responsibilities of the nation, with the linkages among them being essentially confederal in practice. Tribal government was apparently vested in a council of elders representing the various families and clans within each tribe. Specific members of the council of elders or others co-opted for the purpose were given special responsibilities of an executive character, while policy-making and adjudicating functions remained in the hands of the tribal council. It is unclear whether tribes were led by *nesi'im* (singular, *nasi*, erroneously translated as "prince" in many English versions of the Bible, and actually meaning "he who is raised up" or selected to represent; a reasonable English equivalent is magistrate), or whether such *nesi'im* were simply selected to represent the tribes in national activities. During this first period, reference is also made to *sarim* (singular, *sar*, or officer) and *alufim* (singular, *aluf*, leader of a thousand), both military titles used to describe commanders of tribal levies.

During this period, the tribes also took on a territorial basis so that in the course of a few generations, the very term *shevet* acquired strong territorial connotations. The land as divided into tribal segments was further subdivided into private and tribal parcels with cultivated lands passing into family ownership and pasture lands remaining the common property of the tribe.

During the second constitutional epoch, the governmental role of the tribes was substantially reduced as the role of national authorities was strengthened. In the southern kingdom, the virtual merger of the tribes of Judah and Simeon (and perhaps Benjamin, though it seems to have preserved more of its identity and institutions) led to the emergence of a single council of elders, which became, in effect, the popular organ of the state; it shared power with the king in ways not quite clear from the information we have on hand. In the northern kingdom, where central authority remained weak, the tribal councils apparently continued to function and exercise substantial control over tribal affairs. Constitutionally, their powers remained relatively uncircumscribed by the fact of kingship, though particular kings exercised great power over them by virtue of their power position in the kingdom as a whole. These tribal councils disappeared with the fall of the northern kingdom.[1]

The elimination of separate tribal governments with the fall of the northern kingdom ended the federal structure of the biblical polity, though it did not eliminate the use of federal principles in the organization of power in that polity. In the third constitutional epoch, tribal institutions as such were no longer in evidence, though the tribal council survived as the popular body (the Am HaAretz) of the Kingdom of Judah, in the pattern that had already emerged during the previous constitutional epoch. The pattern was carried over into the fourth constitutional epoch when the council became the dominant political institution in the country as the *Anshei Knesset HaGedolah*.

The greatest changes in political forms in the biblical period took place on the national plane. These changes have already been described above. Examining them more directly, we find that in the first constitutional epoch national institutions were rudimentary, consisting primarily of leaders exercising authority nationwide or over several tribes, with small entourages of assistants responsible to them, plus councils and commissions constituted for particular purposes. A rudimentary corps of officials existed in the form of the *shoterim*, who were responsible for implementation of the decisions of the national leadership. In addition to the charismatic leaders, the high priest (and perhaps lesser priests in the period of the Judges) also exercised authority in certain fields, apparently sharing certain powers with the charismatic leadership, particularly where certain impartiality among the tribes was required.

It is unclear as to whether there was a continuing national assembly during the first constitutional epoch or whether ad hoc assemblies of tribal elders functioned in lieu of such a body when the occasion arose. Beyond that, the biblical account portrays the constitution of special commissions for special purposes on the basis of one representative per tribe, such as the commission of the twelve spies to scout out Canaan prior to its conquest, the commission that carried the Ark of the Covenant across the Jordan when the invasion commenced, and the commission established to work with Joshua and Elazar, the high priest, to allocate the land among the tribes after the conquest was completed. Smaller commissions, comprising representatives of more than two but less than the full number of tribes, appear to have functioned during the period of the Judges to assist them from time to time. Thus, national government, in the first constitutional epoch, emphasized joint action on the part of the tribes for very limited purposes.

During the second constitutional epoch, separate, autonomous, and continuing national institutions emerged, centered around the king. The first of these were military and related to the development of a military command structure. This command structure gradually gained civil responsibilities as well and was strengthened by the addition of strictly civil components based on the priesthood and non-Israelite elements.

During the reign of Solomon, a civil bureaucracy was created and the country was divided into administrative districts, which were probably coordinated with the tribal governments over most of the country but in the south, at least, superseded them. While the thrust of this new national structure was primarily to undertake national executive and judicial functions in a political system where legislation in the modern sense was unknown, it essentially preempted the powers of authoritative decision making to itself in all matters that the king deemed to be of national importance, except where he was constitutionally or politically restrained from doing so by effective local institutions or prophetic actions.

These national institutions reached the high point of their strength in the third constitutional epoch and then disappeared in the catastrophe that destroyed the First Commonwealth. Their reemergence in the fourth constitutional epoch was in a substantially different guise, since the kingship could no longer serve as their focal point. Apparently, the scribes staffed the reconstituted national administrative structure functioning within the boundaries of the Torah.

The Exercise of Political Functions

Very little is known about the exercise of political functions in the biblical period. Modern conceptions of limited or unlimited government are not easily applied to a period in which the role of the extended family was extraordinarily strong in fields later to become governmental responsibilities, and the connections between the political and the cultic aspects of life were inseparable. It is clear that the Israelite government was not intended to be one that penetrated into all aspects of life. At the same time, the notion of government limited to the exercise of political powers also would have been foreign to the ancient Israelites. Political and cultic authority were so intertwined as to be inseparable even for analytic purposes. The community felt free to regulate the economy in numerous ways and the state undertook economic development tasks, but government-sponsored social services were essentially nonexistent.[6]

Israelite government pursued a limited but active role in the affairs of society, a role whose level depended upon the needs of the time. It is very likely that local authorities exercised some control over local economic conditions, if only to regulate competition and markets. By the same token, after the rise of the kingship and the development of the commercial dimension of Israel's economy, the national government pursued clearly mercantilistic policies designed to promote commerce through joint governmental-private ventures, which tended to favor the ruling elite.[7] It was during this period that the national government took responsibility for providing a proper infrastructure in the way of roads and security protection for the fostering of commerce. In the domain of religion, it seems that there was general agreement that government had a responsibility to foster proper observance of cultic forms. This was true regardless of whether the cultic forms were those of Israel's God or foreign gods, with the struggle being between parties that wished to direct government effort one way or another.

While the Bible makes provision for public activity in the realm of education and the social services, there is no particular indication that this public activity must be governmental in any way, and it is unclear as to whether government played any role in this realm.[2] Even less is known about the way in which political interests were articulated and aggregated in the biblical period. Was there voting? What does the Bible mean when it says the entire people would gather together to affirm or ratify particular decisions? How were elders chosen? How did one enter the ruling elite in the second and third constitutional epochs? These are questions that remain substantially unanswered.

The Bible does describe various covenant affirmation ceremonies in which the people or their representatives would reaffirm a covenantal relationship with God and a particular constitution or leader. These invariably occurred at points of constitutional crisis when it could not be assumed that a popular consensus persisted from the previous period. These covenantal acts are politically intriguing but their descriptions in the biblical accounts are not very revealing, so that we can only speculate regarding their relationship to the larger political system and processes of ancient Israel.

Fundamental Principles of Government and Politics

It may fairly be said that the fundamental principles animating government and politics in ancient Israel were theocratic, federal, and republican. The theocratic principle underlies all of Israel's political institutions. God is conceived to be directly involved in the governance of *Adat Bnai Yisrael*. During the first constitutional epoch, He is accepted as the king or great governor of the nation. Under the two constitutional periods in which the kingship existed, He was conceived to have, in effect, delegated that direct role to kings. Finally, in the fourth constitutional epoch, He was viewed as having resumed that role, though in ways that were at once better institutionalized and more obscure than in the first period.

This theocratic principle had two immediate consequences in shaping the Israelite conception of politics. In the first place, politics or the governance of the state was not an end in itself in the Israelite scheme of things, but rather a useful way of serving Divine purposes. This meant that the state did not exist as an end in itself. Indeed, Israelite political thought does not conceive of the state as a reified entity. There was no Israelite equivalent of the Greek *polis*, that is to say, the city whose value as a political entity exists independently of its inhabitants. There is no generic term for state in the Bible, only terms for different regimes with *kahal* or *mamlakhah* coming closest to being used generically. *Medinah*, the contemporary Hebrew term for state, is used in Scripture to describe territories with juridical status and a measure of autonomy but without political independence. Even *Adat Bnai Yisrael*, important as it was in the fulfillment of God's plan, was conceived to be a kind of partnership of Israelites and not an entity that existed independently of its people. Political institutions were viewed not as serving the state but as serving this partnership that united the people with each other through their common linkage with God.

At the same time, politics was important because the establishment of the Holy Commonwealth, later to be called God's Kingdom on Earth in some quarters, was a primary goal of the Israelite nation, a goal mandated by God. Thus, the character of Israelite political institutions was constantly judged in the Bible in terms of their success in fostering the development of the Holy Commonwealth. The very institution of the kingship became an issue because it involved the abandonment of God's direct rule over the people and thus was viewed by many as a departure from the path leading toward the Holy Commonwealth. Subsequent to the introduction of kingly rule, particular dynasties were judged in terms of their faithfulness to God's will in this connection. Thus, the disappearance of the ten tribes as political entities is lamented as a break in the right order of things that must be mended if the Holy Commonwealth is to be achieved.

The biblical concern with political matters is so pervasive within its moral framework that references to such matters can be found in virtually every book and range from discussion of the origins of imperialism to the nature of statesmanship, aside from its major concern with the government of Israel. Thus, biblical thought is, on the one hand, highly political and, on the other, very clear in its subordination of the political to higher goals.

The Bible clearly relates the formation of the political institutions of Israel to the Sinai experience, whether in the form of the Book of the Covenant, which is the basis of the first constitution of the Israelite federation, or in connection with Moses's following the advice of his father-in-law to establish a national administrative and judicial structure, which is presented as taking place at the same time, though without the same Divine character attached to it. The Bible is quite clear in indicating that no particular form of government is mandated by God, though some forms receive Divine sanction and others do not.

The theopolitical aspects of this great covenant were reaffirmed at subsequent points in the history of the Israelites, invariably at times when constitutional change had taken place. Thus, the reaffirmation of the covenant under Joshua marked the point where the political institutions of Israel had to be adapted to permanent settlement in Eretz Israel. Similarly, David was made king by covenant, indeed, by two separate covenants, one with the elders of Judah and the second with the elders of Judah and Israel. Covenant ceremonies were held at various times during the history of the kingship when the institution itself was in jeopardy. Finally, the institution of the Josianic reforms and the Deuteronomic constitution involved a major covenant renewal ceremony. The initiation of the fourth constitutional epoch involved another major covenant renewal ceremony with Ezra reading the Torah before the community at Sukkot to obtain their consent to it in the approved constitutional manner.

The covenant not only forms the basis for political organization in Israel but does even more than that. Israel becomes, in effect, a partnership held together by covenantal or federal ties that link the people to each other through their tribes and also link them to God. These federal principles became so ingrained in Israelite political thought that, ever since, Jewish communities have been conceived as partnerships and have been organized through articles of agreement that are in themselves small covenants.

At first, these federal principles were translated into a federal system of government. Even when the Israelites abandoned the tribal confederacy as a form of government, they were careful to retain federal structural elements under the king and would have continued to do so by all accounts except for the conquest of the northern kingdom. Although this federal structure disappeared at the end of the second constitutional epoch because of objective conditions rather than for any internal reasons, the federal principles remained to animate the formally unitary structure that replaced it. At the same time, the federal structure of the earlier age was enshrined in the prophetic literature as a messianic goal. The various biblical descriptions of the ideal commonwealth all emphasize the federal structure as a major element within it.

Republicanism is the third political principle of biblical Israel. Understood in its broadest sense, republicanism reflects the view that the political order is a public thing (*res publica*), that is to say, not the private preserve of any single ruler, family, or ruling elite but the property of all of its citizens, and that political power should be organized so as to reflect this fact. Republican government involves a limitation on the powers of those given authority and some provision for the representation of public concerns as a matter of right in the formulation and execution of public policy. All these conditions prevailed in biblical Israel except during periods when individual kings essentially usurped powers and were considered to be usurpers by the biblical account.

So republican was ancient Israel that even the institution of kingship, limited as it was, persisted for less than half of the biblical period (the precise length of time depending upon the way in which the biblical period is calculated). The Bible does not mandate kingship but makes its institution a matter of public choice and, in any case, clearly provides for constitutional limitations on the king, who is never the sovereign. The prophets, indeed, refrained from referring to kings as kings (*melakhim*), but rather referred to them as *negidim*, God's high commissioners, or, in the case of Ezekiel, as *nesi'im*, God's elected ones.[3] This is a reflection of an antimonarchical tradition that persisted among the prophetic schools during the entire period of the kings, leading in the end to something of a dualism in Jewish political thought whereby the traditional role of Elijah became associated with a kind of prophetic republicanism, with or without a king as a national leader of limited scope in the messianic age.[4]

Similarly, it seems that certain republican institutions were preserved through the period of kingship and emerged as more powerful institutions once that period had come to an end. These institutions embodied principles of shared power that were never relinquished. Out of these three principles there emerges a picture of the ideal commonwealth as embodied in biblical political thought. Two principal descriptions of this ideal commonwealth have been canonized, with a third description that emphasizes political structure and organization less while portraying the kind of life and society that the commonwealth will create. The two descriptions are to be found in the Book of Joshua and in the prophecies of Ezekiel.

The Book of Joshua, an idealized version of the conquest and settlement of Canaan by the Israelites, can properly be viewed as an expression of what the ideal Israelite polity should be, describing as it does in some detail what the polity was conceived to have been at the time of Joshua, that is to say, at the time of its greatest achievements in Canaan. If this biblical utopia looks to a great past situation for its inspiration, Ezekiel's utopia (chaps. 36–48) looks to a great future situation; yet the description that emerges is quite similar to that found in the Book of Joshua. It embodies the theo-political aspirations of the exiles in Babylonia and explicitly foresees the restoration of the covenantal polity in its full multi-tribal form. Finally, Isaiah's messianic vision implicitly assumes conditions such as those described in Joshua and Ezekiel.

Characteristic of these utopian accounts are the three principles described above and the separation of the three *ketarim*. In all three, the theocratic principle is fundamental. Politics becomes a means for achieving and maintaining the Holy Commonwealth. God is sovereign and exercises His sovereignty more or less directly, mediated only through His servants who act as national leaders and the traditional institutions of the people. Those institutions are federal and republican in character, with the federation of tribes at their base and the popular institutions growing out of that federation the major instrumentalities of governance alongside of God, His chief minister, and supporting staff.

Much later, after the demise of the monarchy, Jewish tradition was to make a big thing of the permanency of the Davidic line, partly to legitimize the principal institutions of Jewish autonomy under the Romans and Parthians and partly because the full impact of monarchic rule was delayed until the messianic age so that it was a safe rallying point for the expression of national aspirations. According to the Bible, however, God himself strips the Davidides of all but one tribe (Judah) as their inheritance (1 Kings 11:9–13) explicitly because of Solomon's violation of the covenant and constitution (11:11), leaving the one for David's sake. Moreover, when the monarchy disappears after the Persian restoration of the Jews to their land, it does so without a single lament in the text. Indeed, the Bible does not even mention the matter; there are only vague hints of what happened in the Books of Haggai and Zechariah.

This ideal biblical commonwealth, reflected in the idealization of the realities of political life in ancient Israel, became a major force in the political thought of the Western world, shaping the ideals and animating the visions of most Western thrusts toward republicanism. Echoes and expansion of that vision permeated Western political thought after the rise of Christianity, just as they continued to permeate Jewish political thought after the Bible itself was canonized and the biblical period came to its conclusion.

Closing the Covenantal Circle

The removal of the last of the Davidides from the political scene ended the third constitutional epoch and led to the inauguration of a second historical period, known as the Second Commonwealth, and a fourth constitutional epoch, which brought with it the restoration of a fully republican government. At the beginning of the epoch, the Jewish people were divided among three concentrations: the Persian province of Yahud, or Judea—a small territory around Jerusalem in Eretz Israel; a major concentration in the Persian Empire from Mesopotamia eastward into Iran; and Egypt's Nile Valley. Biblical history concentrates on the Judean community as the continuation of Jewish independence, although, in fact, as the Bible itself indicates, Yahud was only an autonomous Persian province. While there are only a few sources on the subject, it appears that the Jewish communities in the diaspora also had substantial autonomy.[5]

While the proximate restoration of Jewish self-government in Yahud (Judea) late in the sixth century B.C.E., on a home rule basis within the Persian empire, did not even approach that messianic vision, its political dimension was ultimately based on a popular renewal of the covenant in the days of Ezra and Nehemiah when the people assembled on Succoth (440 B.C.E.) to hear the Torah and to assent to its authority, as graphically portrayed in the Bible (Neh. 8–10). As at Sinai, the Succoth covenant set the framework for the renewed Jewish polity while the details of the regime were developed subsequently within it. Overall, the regime seems to have been a noncentralized union of families and community congregations within the framework of the Torah and the developing oral law, whose local and national institutions and leaders were extremely powerful within their respective spheres. While the twelve tribes, as such, no longer existed as separate entities, the governing body of Yahud was the Anshei Knesset haGedolah (Men of the Great Assembly) whose 120 members symbolically represented 12 "congregations" of 10 (the minimum quorum in Jewish law), one for each of the tribes.[6]

Significantly, the biblical account of the inauguration of this fourth constitutional epoch features the repromulgation by Ezra and Nehemiah of the Torah as Israel's constitution by popular demand in a special ceremony. Thus, the Bible presents the covenantal process as having come full circle. At Sinai, God initiated the covenant, which, among other things, launched the first constitutional period in Jewish history. After three epochs, that period came to an end and a new period was inaugurated by the Jewish people in Jerusalem initiating the renewal of the covenant with God.[7]

Characteristic of this fourth constitutional epoch was rule by the *Anshei Knesset HaGedolah*, a council that shared power with the high priest and the *soferim* (scribes). Thus, the separation of powers system inaugurated in the previous constitutional period was maintained. The *Anshei Knesset HaGedolah* represented the *keter malkhut*. The term *knesset* itself was a Hebrew adaptation of the Aramaic *kenishtah*, which means *Edah*. The high priest continued to represent the *keter kehunah* and the *soferim* inherited the mantle of the *keter Torah*. Indeed, it was during this epoch that the three *ketarim* become known as such.[8]

What happened within this separation of powers system was a shift in power, with first the *soferim* and then the high priest becoming the principal leaders of the people. While the biblical canon was not yet completed in this epoch, after the Bible recounts the history of the reconstitution under Ezra and Nehemiah, the period itself drops out of the Bible's purview except for the two accounts of events in the diaspora in the Scroll of Esther and the Book of Daniel.

The founding of the Anshei Knesset HaGedolah represents a political revolution because it represents the revival of the *edah* on a representative basis after the Jews became a scattered people. Undoubtedly the use of the term *knesset* here was deliberate. Thus, the establishment of the Anshe Knesset HaGedolah transformed the *edah*'s governing institutions permanently from those of the original Mosaic regime when, in principle, all members of the *edah* assembled for constitutional and other vital decisions, to one in which a representative assembly meets in place of the entire population. The transition point can be seen at the Succot renewal of the covenant described in Ezra and Nehemiah when the representatives of the *edah* in Eretz Israel assemble for the last time as a group, renew the covenant, hear the reading of the Torah, and, in effect, pass authority to the Anshe Knesset Hagedolah as its representative body.

Ezra and Nehemiah are the heroes of the restoration. Ezra, the heir to the prophets, became the head of the *keter torah*, which came to rest in the hands of the *soferim*. Nehemiah, a Jew empowered by both the foreign suzerain and his own people, reformed the *keter malkhut*. They reconstitute the Israelite polity on a fully republican basis without so much as a word of apology to the Davidic line or anyone else. Their republic, in which God is restored as undisputed king, with constitutionally more faithful human agents, becomes the source and generator of the normative Jewish law and tradition that we know today as Judaism.

It is their reconstitution, the last recounted in the Bible, that remained in place as the basis for Jewish existence for 200 years.

The new regime rested upon two covenants that were made during the tenure of Ezra and Nehemiah. The first was a renewal of the covenant of peoplehood, which involved the removal of foreign wives and children and the cutting of familial ties with their non-Jewish neighbors. The second involved the reacceptance of the Torah as the national constitution. The parallel with Sinai is obvious and is so recognized in Jewish tradition. But there is a new dimension here; both covenants are initiated by the people, not even by their leaders, who only serve as catalysts in both cases. In the first case, Ezra denounces intermarriage, prays and weeps (Ezra 9), but it is the people who suggest a covenant to put away their foreign wives and children (10:2-4) and who do the job (10:9-17). In the second case, the people gather at the Temple of their own accord and ask Ezra to read the teachings of Moses (*Torat Moshe*) before them (Neh. 7:73-8:2). They press the process through to its conclusion, a formal covenant signed and sealed (10:1-29). Thus, the Bible comes full circle, beginning with God's unilateral quasi-covenant with Adam, proceeding through the God-initiated but humanly negotiated and accepted covenants in the wilderness, and concluding with the human-initiated renewal of those covenants in Jerusalem.

A generalized look at the biblical view of the progression of generations shows that progression as following a four-step process: At the beginning of the generation there is a founding, that is to say, the establishment of the framework—structural, institutional, cultural, and procedural—for the organization and the behavior of political society. While the founding period may work well enough according to the principles established within it, it is succeeded by a period of backsliding during which the people fall away from those founding principles and then suffer some kind of catastrophe—invasion, serious drought, a plague, or whatever—which reawakens them and brings them to remorse. This, in turn, leads them to return (teshuva) and reform. Thus, the overall pattern of the generation is founding—backsliding—reawakening and remorse—return and reform.

This pattern repeats itself in every generation until in the tenth generation the political order founded at the beginning of the period ten generations earlier for one reason or another is no longer suitable or reformable per se, so a new founding must take place. That is, the reform must be so extensive that it leads to a refounding. Thus, Noah was a major figure in the tenth generation after Adam and the Flood was the first step in the refounding of the human race. Then, Abraham was in the tenth generation after Noah, coming in the wake of the Tower of Babel. He was entrusted by God with a refounding, the founding of a new people from his seed who were to begin another chapter in human history. David came in the tenth generation after the Exodus when Moses refounded the Jewish people and its polity that settled in the land of Israel and developed the regime and society of Judges. David replaced that regime with a somewhat different one. In sum, there is a mini-cycle in each generation that is part of a macro-cycle that comes after nine generations and begins again in the tenth.

Notes

1. J. Bright, "Israel Under the Monarchy: The Period of Self-Determination," in *A History of Israel* (Philadelphia: Westminster Press, 1960).
2. Roland de Vaux, *Ancient Israel* (New York: McGraw Hill, 1965), especially vol. 1, *Social Institutions.*
3. Moshe Greenberg, *Ezekiel 1–20,* a new translation with introduction and commentary (Garden City, NY: Doubleday, 1983); Moshe Greenberg, "Ezekiel—XV," in *The Anchor Bible* (Garden City, NY: Doubleday, 1983), v. 22, p. 388; Moshe Greenberg and Charles Cutler Torrey, *Pseudo-Ezekiel and the Original Prophecy* (New York: Ktav, 1970); Yehezkel Kaufmann, *The Religion of Israel from its Beginnings to the Babylonian Exile,* translated and abridged by Moshe Greenberg (Chicago: University of Chicago Press, 1960), 426–46.
4. Martin Cohen, "The Role of the Shilohnite Priesthood in the United Monarchy of Ancient Israel," in *Hebrew Union College Annual, Vol. 36: Josephus's Antiquities of the Jews* (Cincinnati: Hebrew Union College, 1965); William Lee Holladay, *Isaiah, Scroll of a Prophetic Heritage* (Grand Rapids, MI: W.B. Eermans, 1978); Yehezkel Kaufmann, *The Religion of Israel from its Beginnings to the Babylonian Exile,* part 3, chap. 12, pp. 378–94 for Isaiah and part 3, chap. 13, pp. 426–46 for Ezekiel; Robert H. Pfeiffer, *Introduction to the Old Testament* (New York: Harper, 1948), part 4, "The Latter Prophets," I, The Book of Isaiah, pp. 415–81; Gil, III, pp. 518–65.
5. Z. Falk, "The Temple Scroll and the Codification of Jewish Law," *Jewish Law Annual* 2 (1979): 33–44; Leo Schwarz, *Great Ages and Ideas, Jewish History* (New York: Holt, Reinhart, and Winston, 1960); Elazar and Cohen, *The Jewish Polity,* Epoch 6; Solomon Zeitlin, *The Rise and Fall of the Judean State,* vol. 1 (Philadelphia: Jewish Publication Society, 1962).
6. See Aaron Schreiber, *Jewish Law and Decision-Making* (Philadelphia: Temple University Press, 1982), 237–39.
7. E. Bickerman, *From Ezra to the Last of the Maccabees* (New York: Schocken, 1962); J. Bright, "The Formative Period of Judaism," in *A History of Israel*; M.

Snaith, "Nehemiah," in *Palestinian Parties and Politics that Shaped the Old Testament* (New York, 1971), 126-47.
8. See Elazar and Cohen, *The Jewish Polity,* Epoch 6.

Part V

The Postbiblical Tradition

19

Talmudic Constitutionalism

There are those contemporary scholars who make a major effort to show that Judaism is a post-biblical phenomenon, that, in effect, a major rupture occurred between biblical religion and what later became normative Judaism. Some scholars place that rupture at the time of Ezra and Nehemiah, others at the beginning of the Christian era. A major part of their argument rests upon the conceptual behavioral shifts from the biblical to the post-biblical eras. Biblical religion is portrayed as one where land, state, and cult were dominant, while rabbinic Judaism is portrayed as emphasizing Torah, *halakhah,* and exile.

The overall problematics of this approach need to be addressed elsewhere. Here, however, we have seen that with all the great adaptations necessary from era to era, the basic thrust of biblical covenantalism remained, only that it was institutionalized in a new way appropriate to the new age. This is a decisive continuity, one that raises serious questions about the whole proposition. Understanding that continuity advances our understanding of the impact of the covenant tradition on Jewish life from ancient times to the present. While this volume concentrates on the Bible and its teachings, it would not be complete if it did not examine the post-biblical continuation of the Jewish political tradition as well.

The Talmud: Covenant as Torah and Halakhah

In addition to the Pentateuch, the Talmud, that massive collection of dialogues explicating the laws and teachings of the Torah, can be read as an explication of the Jewish understanding of covenant as law, both constitutional and ordinary. The Talmud, the great codex of Jewish law and lore that provides the basis for normative Judaism, was the great product of the three immediately post-biblical epochs. It consists of two parts: the *Mishnah,* essentially a collection of legal glosses and elaborations on the *Torah,* which were organized in the middle of the second century of the common era and completed as a code at the end of that century, and the *Gemarah,* an extensive commentary on the *Mishnah,* which was completed in the middle of the fifth century of the common era. The Talmud reflects several dimensions of the complexity of Jewish life at the time.

The effort at codification embodied in the Mishnah was successful in shifting the normative Jewish way from overtly political concerns to a concern for legal details in every circumstance, but the Mishnah's effort to provide a code was limited and premature. Every sentence in that very spare work cried out for interpretation and, in the process of supplying that interpretation, the Gemarah reopened the discussion. Together the two parts of the Talmud established the classically Jewish combination of fixed rules capable of wide-ranging interpretation, endowing the Jewish people with a living constitution in the covenantal spirit, in which dialogue was built into the rules themselves.

A first and even continued readings of the Talmud as a record of debates suggests a compendium based upon free association rather than even a prismatic work. That is a mistaken impression. Moving from issue to issue through association is the essence of its style. Nevertheless, its point of departure is a framework that is itself prismatic and then associative. The Talmud carries prismatic thinking to its outermost limits. Nevertheless, I would suggest that there is still a basic structure to the six *sedarim,* (orders) into which the Mishnah and thus the whole Talmud is divided, that reflects a fully reasonable scheme for ordering the human relationship with the universe about us and gives the Talmud a constitutional framework, one that is quite consistent with the overall tenor of the Jewish constitutional tradition. The six *sedarim* were established in the second century C.E. by Rabbi Akiva for the Mishnah.

The first, *Zeraim* (seeds or sowing), deals with the ordering of space and its uses. Each *seder* is divided into *mesikhtot.* Masekhet *Berakhot* (blessings or sanctifications) is the first in Seder *Zeraim.* It deals with the religious consecration of life and provides a kind of a religio-theoretical framework for what follows. *Moed* (appointed times) is the second *seder.* It deals with the ordering of time and its sanctification. The third *seder* is *Nashim* (women), which deals with the family as a sanctified order. *Nezikin* (damages) is the fourth. It deals with the ordering of community and polity. Its first three *mesikhtot* deal with problems of property, damages, and similar matters of civil law, and the fourth, *Sanhedrin,* deals with matters of governance and the administration of justice. Seder *Kodashim* (holy things), the fifth, deals with the ritual order. The final Seder, *Toharot* (purifications), deals with the corruptions of the first five and the means for their purification.

The organization of the *Mishnah* is one of the landmarks that closed the epoch initiated by the Hasmonean revolution, and the completion of the *Gemarah* closed the epoch immediately following that.[1] The Talmud in both its parts emphasizes the minutae of holiness on a daily, indeed hourly, basis, as the way to be a good Jew. In this writer's opinion, this was a deliberately political act designed to wean Jews away from futile conspiracies to revolt against Rome, which, after two major revolts (the Great Revolt 66–70 and the Bar Kochba uprising 132–135 C.E.) in Eretz Israel, a disastrous one in the diaspora (115–117 C.E.), and who knows how many smaller ones, threatened to destroy the Jewish people. In other words, rather than encourage or even allow the cutting edge of the Jewish people to pursue politically futile and self-destructive military efforts, Jews were encouraged, even commanded, to concentrate on the minutiae of everyday life, which took so much psychic energy that they did not have time or strength for overt political activities.

The Pharisees, who championed this constitutional reinterpretation, succeeded because of the change in objective conditions, whereas their rivals, the Sadducees and the Essenes, lost their power bases in the wake of the failed Jewish revolts, leaving the field open to them. Sadducean Judaism was rooted in Temple and state and when both were destroyed, so, too, were the underpinnings of Jewish expression in that way. Despite their rejection of those formal institutions in favor of self-contained holy communities of their own, the Essenes needed the state to protect their communities and could not survive its fall. Even so, it took the Pharisees generations to secure their victory.[2]

Formally, the Torah remained in force as a constitution, but, where necessary, its provisions were substantially reinterpreted by the Anshei Knesset HaGedolah and the Tanaim, the Sages of the Mishnah, who laid the foundations for a Judaism along *halakhic* lines. Their development of the *halakhah* through the *Torah she be'al peh,* or oral law, which they claimed as being equally Sinaitic in origin as the original Torah, the written law, was an outstanding achievement of constitutional reform. It was undertaken in the spirit of ancient constitutionalism and, indeed, because of the objective conditions of the loss of Jewish political independence, focused even more on holiness than the original.[3] Even so, much of the Torah-as-constitution remains very close in its application to what it originally was, even today, for observant Jews.

The sages of the Talmud also make clear the covenantal basis of the Jewish people and how the fact that their ancestors consented to the covenant at Sinai binds them yet also requires them to constantly reaffirm their own consent:

> "To enter into a covenant of the Lord your God, which the Lord your God is concluding with you this day, with its sanctions" (Deut. 29:11). Three times did the Holy One Blessed be He cut a covenant as they went out of Egypt. Once as they stood before Mt. Sinai, once in Horeb, and once here. Why did the Holy One Blessed be He cut a covenant with them here? He did so because the covenant that He made with them at Sinai had been nullified by saying "These are the Gods..." Therefore, he returned and made another covenant with them in Horeb and set before them a curse for those who would go back on His words. (Midrash Tanhuma, Nitzavim 3, on Deut. 29:11)

This Midrash clearly suggests that the people had the ability to nullify agreements, even with God. Hence, penalties had to be added to discourage them from doing so. The very idea that God had to go through the covenant-making process three times in order to make it stick suggests that consent cannot be passive in the Jewish political tradition but must be recurring for each individual Jew in each generation.

This is reflected explicitly in the order of the liturgy, as pointed out by Yehoshua ben Korkha in connection with the section of the Jewish liturgy referred to as *Kriat Shma*, Judaism's main oath of allegiance repeated thrice daily by every pious Jew to reflect the acceptance of God's sovereignty and covenant.

> Rabbi Yehoshua ben Korkha: "Why does the section 'Hear O Israel' (Deut. 6:4-9) proceed, 'And it shall come to pass if you shall hearken...' (Deut. 11:13-21)? So that a man shall first receive upon himself the yoke of the Kingdom of Heaven and afterwards receive upon himself the yoke of commandments." (Mishnah Berakhot 2:2)

The heart of the Jewish liturgy, which was initially formulated by those sages, involves renewing consent to the covenant three times daily so that there will be no misunderstandings in the matter. There is no reliance on tacit consent here, but on ritual public reaffirmation on the most frequent possible basis. In their system, the polity exists as a consequence of that initial consent and dissolves when that consent dissolves.

There is a stream in Jewish tradition often cited today that suggests that the acceptance of the covenant at Sinai was not a voluntary act. According to it, God owned the Jewish people as slaves because liberating them from Egypt was simply transferring the powers of masterhood from the Egyptians to God and, at Sinai, as the famous Midrash has it, He held the mountain over the Jewish people and said: "Consent or I will bury you under the mountain."[4] But the balance seems to tip by far toward the view presented in Mekhilta 2:207 (see also in TB Sota 37b, Hagiga 6a, and Z'vahim 115b), which projects a clearly and fully voluntary acceptance, with each individual acting separately, even though part of the collective: "'And all of the people answered together...' (Exod. 19:8). They did not give this answer with hypocrisy. Nor did they get it one from the other, but all of them made up their minds alike, and said: 'All that the Lord has spoken, we will do...'" (Exod. 19:8).

While some of the sages suggest an alternative understanding of the covenant, that is to say, as a unilateral expression of God's grace, the normative understanding of the sages was that the covenant was indeed reciprocal.[5] As Freeman says, "Realization of the covenant was dependent on the participation of the community. But so reciprocal was the relationship, that the reality of the community was dependent on its participation in the covenant."[6] This meant that socialization of the individual into the covenant community was based upon his active participation in that community (Mekhilta 2:230).

Bringing Covenanting into the Liturgy

While the literature of those sages is informed by covenantal thought, the actual term *brit* was used by them far less than in the Bible itself. It has four meanings in rabbinic literature: (1) circumcision (*brit mila*), clearly a technical usage; (2) to indicate a Jew (*ben brit*) in contrast to a non-Jew, which follows in the biblical usage; (3) to refer to the written Torah as distinct from the oral Torah, in other words, to identify the written Torah as both constitution and covenant; and (4) to express the truth of a particular statement, in other words, the fulfillment of a promise as in an oath. In usage, however, the Talmudic sages emphasized the word *hesed* rather than the word *brit*. From a covenantal perspective, then, one might reasonably conclude that the Bible lays down the basic structure of covenant while the Talmud focuses on its dynamics.

Torah as Covenant

In order to fully legitimize the oral law that they developed, the rabbis had to claim that it, too, was Divine, that is to say, that it was part of the Divine communication of the founding covenant of *Adat B'nai Yisrael*.

> Rabbi Levi bar Hama said in the name of Rabbi Shimon ben Levi: What does the passage, "And I will give to you the stone tablets and the Torah and the commandments which I wrote to teach them" (Exod. 24:2) [mean]? Tablets: these are the Ten Commandments. Torah: this is the Pentateuch. Commandments: this is the Mishnah. What I wrote: these are the prophets and writings. To teach them: this is the Talmud to teach you that all were given to Moses from Sinai. (Talmud Bavli Berakhot 5a; see also Megillah 19b in the name of Rabbi Hiya bar Aba in the name of Rabbi Yohanan)

> The laws (*hukim*: these are the interpretations) *midrashot*; the judgements (*mishpatim*): these are the laws (*dinim*). The Torah teaches that two Torahs were given to Israel, one written and one oral. Rabbi Akiba asked: Did Israel have but two Torahs, were not may Torahs given to Israel, (e.g.) "this is the Torah of the whole burnt offering," "this is the Torah of the meal offering," "this is the Torah of the guilt offering," "this is the Torah of the peace sacrifice," "this is the Torah in the case of the death of a person in an enclosed place." "Which the Lord gave between Him and the people of Israel": Moses merited being the agent between Israel and their Father in Heaven. On Mount Sinai by the hand of Moses' teaches that the Torah, its laws (*halakhah*) and details (*dikduk*) and explanations (*perush*) were by the hand of Moses at Sinai. (Sifra 112b in Lev. 16:46)[7]

The transformation by the sages of *brit* into Torah reflects the sages' commitment to the Torah as constitution. Using an American analogy, it was not sufficient to concentrate on the Declaration of Independence, however important it is as the foundation stone. Rather, with the adoption of the Constitution, attention was turned to it for concrete guidance in political life. Since the sages sought to provide guidance for the Jewish people in every aspect of life, Torah was the category most important to them, but they understood it in the sense of the product of the covenant.

> Covenant means Torah, as it is said: "But for my covenant of day and night" (Jer. 33:25) (Talmud Bavli Shabbat 33a)

Great is circumcision, since, without it heaven and earth would not endure, as it is written: "But for my covenant of day and night." This conflicts with Rabbi Eleazar who said: "Great is the Torah, since without it heaven and earth would not endure, as it is written, 'But for my covenant of day and night'" (Talmud Bavli Nedarim 32a)[8]

The Bible suggests that the world was established through covenant, giving covenant cosmic significance. The sages, the Talmud, and Midrash give the Torah cosmic significance, indicating that the world exists only by virtue of the Torah, which holds heaven and earth as well as the fabric of society together. Another way in which the sages' view of covenant was made clear states that when the angels wanted to stop God from giving the Torah to mankind, God pointed out to them that the Torah would be given to men because humans had freedom of choice.

The Pharisaic Revolution

The Talmud rapidly became the filter through which Jews interpreted the Bible, since it provided the legal basis for Jewish life in all its facets. Hence, at first reading the relative absence of political focus in the Talmud seems to be especially strange or peculiar, particularly in light of the extensive political dimension of the Bible. A good student of the Talmud, like Sherlock Holmes who was concerned about the dog that did not bark, would raise the question about the relative silence of the Talmud on matters political. The answer to that question tells us a great deal about the political vicissitudes of the Jewish people and how they affected the Jewish political tradition, including its covenantal dimension.

A closer look reveals that the Talmud includes much about matters political, generally subsumed under legal and ritual frameworks, apparently seeking to downplay their separate political dimension. Disastrous revolts against Rome nearly destroyed the Jewish people between 66 and 135 C.E. and threatened to engulf Jewish life for at least a generation before 66 and for almost a century after 135. That period encompassed three major revolts. The first, in Judea, led to the destruction of the Temple and the last remnants of the Jewish polity as constituted by the Hasmoneans. The second (115–117 C.E.) took place essentially in the Hellenistic diaspora and led to the destruction of the major Jewish communities of that diaspora, particularly in Egypt, Cyrenaica, and Cyprus, thereby drastically altering Jewish life in the diaspora. The third (132–135

C.E.) also took place in Judea under the ill-starred leadership of Simon Bar Kosiba (Kokhba) and brought about the final destruction of Judea as the center of Jewish life until our own times. Conventional histories, however, claim that the Jews were dispersed from their land after the destruction of the Temple in 70 C.E. In fact, Jewish life recovered within a generation and flourished throughout the land. Even after 135, when Jewish life in Judea was effectively ended, the Jewish center in the Galilee remained the primary focus of world Jewry and a major concentration of Jews until the fifth century. Only after that can it be said that the Jews were truly exiled from the land, more a result of the rise of Christianity than of Imperial Roman oppression.

The sages of the Talmud, then, were confronted with a situation in which the Jews' political aspirations exceeded their political power, leading to a series of revolts whose consequences brought disaster upon them. The Jewish sages correctly assessed that any further such activity in the political realm beyond the simple maintenance of self-government could signal the end of the Jewish people as an effective body. Hence, they sought to turn the political drives of the Jews into other—religious and legalistic—channels.

In fact, the Pharisaic sages had initiated that effort even earlier, at the time of the Hasmonean kings when they saw that the direction of Jewish political involvement moved against the spirit of Jewish religion and toward involved conquests, which led to compromises with the heathens conquered, absorption of Roman-Hellenistic ways, tendencies toward emphasizing militarism over the ways of peace, and, once again, kingship like all the nations, with all the elements of degradation and degeneration that monarchy as a system of government brought in its wake. Thus, by the middle of the previous epoch there was already a strong tendency in the Pharisee camp to move Jews from political to religious and legal concerns. Still, the Pharisees themselves retained a large place for political concerns until the end of that epoch and its disastrous outcome. Afterward there appears to have been overwhelming support in their ranks for this transformation.

Thus, Jews removed themselves from active consideration of matters political for a very political reason, namely, to try to insure their survival as a minority in a hostile world in which they could not exercise political power commensurate with their political aspirations. In the long view of history this was a very successful technique. What it means is that the Talmud is as overtly apolitical as the Bible is overtly political.

Not that there are not important political materials in the Talmud; indeed there are. After all, the sages themselves sought to maintain Jewish self-government and internal autonomy to the greatest possible extent and obviously had to deal with legal and political questions that arose in connection with the autonomous Jewish communities. Moreover, faithful as it is to the Jewish tradition, the Talmud could not simply eliminate Jewish political concerns, but had to project those concerns into a future messianic age, which it did by addressing itself to the character of the polity when that age would arrive, thereby providing us with a Pharisaic political utopia.

Covenantal Concepts in the Talmud

One result of this was that covenantal concepts must be sought out in the Talmud, although covenant remains the foundation of Talmudic doctrine.[9] Its importance is particularly manifest in the parallel literature of the Talmudic period, for example, in the liturgy that acquired its content at that time, one that it preserves to this day. Perhaps the highest expression of this is to be found in the service for Rosh Hashanah, the Jewish New Year, which in Talmudic times was transformed into a day for acknowledging God's sovereignty over the universe and His covenantal relationship with the Jewish people and all humanity, which brought all under God's judgment annually.

The climax of the Rosh Hashanah service deals precisely with this theme in an explicitly covenantal context. God is depicted as judging states and individuals alike. (Those terms are used explicitly in the prayer.) By reciting a series of biblical verses linked together in poetic fashion, the congregation acknowledges God's sovereignty, the fact that He remembers His covenant and responds to the needs of humanity because of those covenants, and that He is particularly committed to His covenant with Israel as it was cut at Sinai. This latter theme becomes the focus of the climax of the Yom Kippur (Day of Atonement) service, the holiest service of the holiest day of the Jewish calendar, when God is repeatedly called upon to remember His covenant at Sinai and demonstrate His *hesed* (loving covenant obligation) toward His covenant partners, despite the fact that they have sinned.

While these themes are most pronounced in the High Holy Day liturgy, as noted above they recur in the daily prayer services of the Jewish people, precisely in those elements that date from Talmudic times. The language is covenantal and even federal, with the central idea being that God's faithful are bound together as *agudah ahat,* one compound body, utilizing the Hebrew term for a federated association.

The Talmud continues this theme in an eminently practical way, in its discussion of the ideal Jewish polity of the messianic era, which it sees as a reconstitution of the tribal federation under a limited constitutional monarch. As in the Talmud as a whole, the discussions of the subject are barely theoretical. Rather, they emphasize practical matters such as the rights of members of one tribe when they come under the jurisdiction of another, full faith and credit among units of the federation, or the powers of eminent domain that the tribes can exercise within the local communities out of which they are compounded. When all these discussions are brought together, we have a Talmudic program for a federal polity, one of the oldest federal plans extant, all rooted, of course, in the original covenant idea.[10]

The Talmudic Polity

What emerged was an aristocratic republicanism in which instead of a hereditary aristocracy there was an aristocracy of the learned, open and accessible to all. This, indeed, was the great foundation of the sages' claim to authority. On the one hand, with the demise of the hereditary priesthood as a factor in Jewish public affairs, the sages insisted that all Jews truly become what the Torah commanded them to be, namely, a kingdom of priests and a holy nation, and that they do so by fulfilling what the sages claimed was the covenant obligation of learning, which would in turn internalize God's authority within each of them. The most learned would become the leaders of the people, able to express authoritatively God's will through constitutional interpretation of the covenant texts on the basis of the oral Torah.

Thus, teachers acquired a role in the governance of the polity—indeed what they claimed was the principal role, although, in fact, the *keter malkhut* was shortly thereafter revived by Rabbi Judah, the most learned scholar of his generation, who became known as *Nasi*. He claimed descent from King David, further legitimizing his control of the *keter malkhut*. Although the office he established became hereditary, its incumbents were expected to be learned sages as well as bearers of the Davidic heritage, thereby sealing the new regime.

The solution of the sages of the Talmud to the problem of God's authority in the world differed radically from the system developed in Christianity. Christian theologians viewed the covenant as unilateral, a matter of God's grace, to explain why God would relate to an imperfect humanity. Through His graciousness, God entered history to save an otherwise doomed mankind. God became a paternal authority figure who took responsibility for a world of humans unable to take responsibility of their own. All they had to do was properly acknowledge Him to be saved. Politics was rejected as inevitably corrupting; the very political process was immoral and tainted:

> The solution of the Jewish sages who formulated their system at the same time as the Church fathers, was to see the covenant as a matter of reciprocity, making God the ultimate authority [but] completely dependent on his constituency. Everyone was to know the rules and all, including God, were to be dependent upon observing them. If promises were broken, the consequences were cruel indeed. The polity was dissolved and the authority became to all intents and purposes insignificant because He no longer had anyone to rule. Humans were no more perfectible but, since each individual shared in governance, they at least could strive to be more perfectible by fulfilling their covenant obligations. Responsibility rather than being concentrated in one paternal extra-worldly father figure was widely distributed among all members of the holy community. Only when that widely shared responsibility was fully realized would redemption come in fulfillment of the covenant agreement.[11]

This approach not only persists among Jews to this day but would surface in Reformed Protestantism in the sixteenth and seventeenth centuries where it would compete with the normative Christian doctrine of covenant-as-grace.

Covenant as a Value Concept

Not surprisingly, the rabbinic understanding of covenant emphasizes reciprocity; in matters political, reciprocity between ruler and ruled. Indeed, it has been argued that this understanding of covenantal reciprocity represents a fruition in rabbinic sources beyond its biblical, especially prophetic, expression.

In fact, since rabbinic thought is organic in the sense that it avoids the abstract definition of concepts but rather allows different definitions of the same concept to emerge out of the interaction between concepts, the reciprocal dimension is especially important. In rabbinic thought one idea has no meaning outside of its relation to others. The idea changes its nuances as it relates to other ideas or concepts. In contrast, definition of concepts involves setting limits in a spatial sense whereas rabbinic religious thought, like other experiences of God, is essentially temporal, especially since in Jewish thought it revolves around the spatially unbounded character of God's relationship to His people in history.

In the last analysis, the concepts are like living organisms that can only survive with proper nourishment under proper environmental conditions. Max Kadushin, who has done the major work in systematically analyzing rabbinic thinking, put it as follows:

> All the organic concepts...are integrated with one another and inextricably interweave with each other. The organic concept possesses its own individuality and cannot be inferred from any other concept... and individuality of organic concepts and process of the integration of the organic complex of a whole are not separable, in other words, the *wholeness* of this organic complex and the *particularity* of the individual organic concept are mutually interdependent.[12]

Rabbinic thinking follows in the tradition of the prismatic thought of the Bible, but in infinitely more complex ways. This system of thought is the ultimate in antihierarchical thinking. As Kadushin said, "They cannot be made parts of a nicely articulated logical system or arranged in a hierarchical order."[13]

The concepts developed by the sages present the values of the community and through those values distinguish the community from all other historic groups. Hence, Kadushin refers to them as "value concepts," which he defines as

> rabbinic terms...[which] are noun forms, but they have a different character than other types of terms or concepts...in relation to matters which are not objects, qualities, or relations in sensory experience. Their function is to endow situations or events with significance. These value concepts are related to each other not logically but organismically. This means that the value concepts are not deduced from one another and that they cannot be placed in a logical order. Instead the coherence or relatedness of the value concepts is such that they interweave dynamically.[14]

For the sages, the Bible becomes the repository of community values and their understanding of covenant flows out of this organic model. Since their thought is based upon the principle of Divine communication via self-revelation, theirs is a political theology not a political philosophy, which is limited to what is accessible to the unassisted human mind. Covenantal thought begins in political theology. For those to whom the Bible is not a Divine communication, it is the first major work of political theology. For those who accept that the Bible is a Divine communication, the Jewish sages who began to build the system of rabbinic Judaism on biblical foundations from the time of Ezra, in the fifth century before the Common Era, were political theologians. In that sense, Ezra can be considered the first political theologian.

Value concepts around which the Talmud is built all have their roots in covenant. Take, for example, the concept of *yishuv ha'aretz* (the settlement of the earth, a key talmudic concept in both the Mishnah and the Gemarah, which refers to actions necessary for the proper development of the Land of Israel and, by extension, the world, the task God assigned to Adam and Noah). This concept shapes economic life, agriculture, and urban planning (Baba Kama 80b; Mishnah Bava Batra 2:5; see also commentaries of Rashi and Rambam on Baba Kama). For example, it can be very specific such as the prohibition of using grape vines or olive trees, which are agriculturally protected for the Temple sacrifices (Mishnah Tamid 2:3).

Its obverse is the value concept *bal tashhit,* which consists of negative prohibitions that would interfere with *yishuv ha'aretz.* Its basis is in the Torah's prohibition against wanton destruction in military campaigns. The Talmud broadens the concept to civil and peaceful conditions (Baba Kama 91b; Shabbat 129a). The provision is applied to trees (Baba Kama 91b), food (Shabbat 140b), clothing (Kedushin 32a), furniture (Shabbat 129a), and water (Yuvamot 11b), namely, all objects of potential benefit to man. The Sifrei, a mishnaic commentary on the Torah that supplements the Talmud, includes prohibitions on indirect destruction, for example, cutting off the water supply from trees (Sefrei Devarim 20:19). This concept is later supported by Maimonides (Hilhot Melahim 6:8). The prohibition of *bal tashhit* may well apply also to the destruction of a species (see the discussion of the relation between Noah and the raven in Sanhedrin 108b; also Ramban's commentary to Deut. 22:6).

These value concepts are extended to the world through that of *yishuv olam* (settlement of the world) and *tikkun olam* (the repair of the world). Both relate especially to social behavior and the development of human society. They are derived as commandments by the Talmud from Isaiah 45:18 and are matters of considerable attention in the Talmud to the point of authorizing courts to interfere with personal rights to protect the environment under certain conditions (summed up in the Shulkhan Arukh, Hoshen Mishpat 175:26). The application of these to all peoples is presented in the value concept *mipnei darkhai shalom* (because of the ways of peace [among people]), a covenantal concept using a covenantal word.

We do not know why the sages limited their use of the term. Freeman suggests that because the early Christians appropriated the term covenant for their new faith, the sages emphasized the term Torah to suggest that the covenant with Israel was everlasting but belonged only to those who studied and lived according to the teachings of Torah. There are any number of places where Torah and *brit* are equated in the rabbinic literature; Rabbi Elazar said: "If it were not for the Torah, heaven and earth would not be established, as it is said: 'Without My covenant day and night, the laws of heaven and earth I would not place'" (Jer. 33:25 as quoted in Talmud Bavli Pesahim 68b).[15]

As a value concept, this covenant/Torah relationship marks the reciprocity of the relationship between God and Israel. It is a reciprocity between God and people in which the individual integrity of each person (*haver* in the sages' vocabulary, a new covenantal term meaning covenant partner) is preserved. "Rabbi Shimon Ben Yehuda of Kfar Akko said in the name of Rabbi Shimon: 'There is not a single commandment written in the Torah in connection with which 48 times 603,550 [the number of people who left Egypt] covenants were not made'" (T.B. *Sota* 1 37b).

The value concept best reflecting this sense of reciprocity is *gemilut hasadim*, which can be translated "reciprocal acts of covenant love." As the sages interpreted *gemilut hassadim*, it was most explicitly applied to acts that went beyond the letter of the law, such as burying and attending to the funeral needs of a dead person, an act that he could not possibly repay. The Siddur, the Jewish prayerbook, lists *gemilut hasadim* as one of the primary *mitzvot*, one of those acts that has no limit in this world but for which the reward is in the world to come.

To give another example in the Talmud Bavli, Tractate Baba Metzia, second chapter (Ailu Mitziot) there is a reference to Rabbi Jonathan's statement that Jerusalem was destroyed because the courts did not judge according to the law of the Torah but according to the law of the Magi, meaning that if they had judged according to the law of the Torah they would have judged not only by the letter of the law but by its spirit (*lifnim meshurat hadin*), i.e., applying *hesed* to *brit* rather than allowing *brit* to stand alone.

Whatever the limits on the use of the word *brit*, rabbinic literature frequently uses the word *hesed*, always in the sense of acts in conformity with the covenant between man and God.[16] That the sages understood the relationship between the two is illustrated by the famous Midrash from Deuteronomy Rabbah 3:9.[17] From a larger covenantal perspective, this suggests that the Bible lays down the basic covenantal structure of the Jewish people and the universe while the Talmud focuses on its dynamics.

The sages were also fond of linking the terms *hesed* and *rahamim*. *Hesed,* which refers in their sense to covenant love, is paralleled by *rahamim,* from the Hebrew word for womb, *rehem,* which means family or parental love, in other words, the two forms of love that link kinship and consent to family and the larger society. This theme, first struck in Isaiah 1 (2:19), was of crucial importance for the sages of the Talmud.

Holy Community

Building on the concepts of the *edah,* the sages emphasized the *kahal kadosh* (holy community), established by covenant as the Jewish equivalent of the Greek *polis* and the Roman *imperium*.[18] Government and rule in the eyes of the sages of the Talmud is based upon mutual independence of authority and community, linked by communication and commentary. Every member of the community participates in studying the holy texts and applying them to life. By doing so he participates in God's holy commonwealth.[19] Governing involves communication from the authority to the community, which must hearken or respond; the hearkening completes the act of governing.

At the same time, in the *kahal kadosh* it is expected that the governed will progressively know more of the will of the authority as they study the texts. Hence, they become their own authority. Indeed, the ultimate goal is for each person to govern himself within the framework of Torah scholarship by relating to the agreement that binds him to God and by sharing the experience of that relationship with others who also participate in the endeavor. The system that emerged, the system of Talmud study and observance of the commandments, which the sages derived from the Torah, became the basis of a portable commonwealth, rooted on just this kind of polity.

In building this system the sages who created the basis of the Talmud, the Mishnah (which itself means the repetition of the teaching, i.e., Torah) were responding to the great first and second century C.E. crisis in Eretz Israel. The crisis led to a breakdown of the old political order based upon state and temple, and required the construction of a new order in which normal political sovereignty would not be necessary for Jewish corporate survival, without giving up hope for restoration of political independence, yet without encouraging false hopes, which would lead to suicidal acts of rebellion against the powerful Roman Empire. Since there was no external means to maintain authority on a coercive basis, it was necessary to reconstruct the Jewish people so that every Jew would internalize authority through the study of Torah. Once internalized, a state would not be needed to enforce authoritative decisions and adherence to its commandments.

The rabbis developed a conception of God studying along with His people, while at the same time closing the doors to Divine revelation by insisting that decisions on matters of Jewish law did not come from heaven but were made by the majority of the Sanhedrin. The fulfillment of the covenant in their eyes lay in the autonomy of the duly constituted institutions of the Jewish polity to interpret the Divine teaching that had become both the constitution of the Jewish people and their code. The sages advanced the claim that they were the direct heirs of the Sinai tradition and that the interpretations of the written Torah that they developed, which they called the oral Torah, were authoritative in all cases. While recognizing the principle of separation of powers among the three domains of kingship, priesthood, and Torah, the effective demise of the first two and their new control over the domain of Torah, gave them the dominant position.

The Talmudic Regime

After the closing of the Talmud at the end of the fifth century, the Jewish people had a new regime to serve them in their exile and dispersion. For our purposes this regime can be seen to have had two dimensions. One was the *halakhic* dimension, involving the application of Jewish law to every aspect of Jewish life through the new prism of the Gemarah. The second consisted of the development and periodic renewal of the intellectual foundations of the new regime through the various devices of systematic (or prismatic) thought used by the Jewish people: Midrashim, commentaries on specific texts, and, beginning in the ninth century, systematic works treating the themes known among the nations as theology and philosophy.

The first found concrete expression in the lives of the people and written expression in the *responsa* (Hebrew: *she'elot v'teshuvot*) of *halakhic* authorities and in the codes that attempted to make a path through the "sea of the Talmud" by stating simply and systematically the principles and requirements of *halakhah*. The *responsa* were part and parcel of the governance structure of the Jewish communities wherever they were. Indeed, for many years the dispersed Jewish people was held together primarily by the exchange of *halakhic* questions and answers, which helped them retain a common constitutional framework based upon shared case law. The developments described in chapter 19 are rooted in that case law. Indeed, much of our documentation of those developments is found in the preserved *responsa* of which there are several thousand volumes extant.[20]

This case law system, which goes back more than a millennium and a half, is a fully living tradition that continues to be the basis for *halakhic* decision making today. Those authorities who issued *responsa* became known as *posekim* (*halakhic* decisors). Obviously falling within the *keter torah*, they became the decisive constitutional authorities between the closing of the Talmud and the rise of modern Zionism. Great chains of *posekim* developed over the generations, continuing the work of various "schools" of constitutional interpretation.[21] These *posekim* dealt with the entire range of *halakhah*, with both civil and ritual matters and everything in between. Until modern emancipation cost the Jews their autonomy in such matters, approximately 80 percent of the *responsa* issued were devoted to civil matters, and only 20 percent to those matters more narrowly defined by moderns as "religious." This continued to be true among Jews in Arab lands until the dissolution of their communities after the establishment of the state of Israel.

Notes

1. See Adin Steinsaltz, *The Essential Talmud* (New York: Bantam, 1977) and Herman Stroouk, *Guide to the Talmud.*
2. On the Pharisaic shift, see Daniel J. Elazar and Stuart Cohen, *The Jewish Polity* (Bloomington: Indiana University Press, 1985), Epochs 7 and 8; Louis Finkelstein, *The Pharisees: Their Origin and Their Philosophy* (Cambridge, MA: Harvard University Press, 1929); George Foote Moore, *Judaism in the First Centuries of*

the Christian Era, the Age of the Tannaim (Cambridge, MA: Harvard University Press, 1958); Jacob Neusner, *From Politics to Piety; the Emergence of Pharisaic Judaism* (Englewood-Cliffs, NJ: Prentice-Hall, 1973).

3. On the *halakhic* reinterpretation of the Torah, see Elazar and Cohen, *The Jewish Polity,* Epoch 6; Salo Baron, *A Social and Religious History of the Jews,* vol. 6 (Philadelphia: Jewish Publication Society, 1952).

4. Shabbat 88a.

5. Gerald J. Blidstein, "In the Shadow of the Mountain: Consent and Coercion at Sinai," *Jewish Political Studies Review* 4, no. 1 (Spring 1992): 41–53.

6. Gordon Freeman, *The Heavenly Kingdom: Aspects of Political Thought in the Talmud and Midrash* (Lanham: University Press of America and Jerusalem: Jerusalem Center for Public Affairs, 1986).

7. See also Toseftah Hala 1:1; Talmud Yerushalmi Peah V, 21; Talmud Bavli Pesahim 38b; Gittin 60b; Sotah 37b; Berakhot 59a. Used in the biblical sense, usually in connection with *halakhah,* see Talmud Bavli Rosh Hashanah 17a; Gittin 66b; Sifra Ahare 8:10; B'hukotai 1,2:5. In reference to biblical quotation, see Sifra Nedavah 14b.

8. Babylonian Talmud Pesahim 68b, in a parallel text, quotes Rabbi Eliezer in place of Rabbi Elazar. There is some indication for parallel usage already in biblical literature in Daniel 9:11. Also, 2 Kings 28:8, 11 and 23:2, the "Book of Torah" and "Book of Covenant" are used in parallel. See K. Baltzer, *The Covenant Formulary in the Old Testament, Jewish and Early Christian Writings,* trans. D. Green (Philadelphia: Fortress Press, 1971), especially p. 59, note 115 for other examples.

9. See Gordon Freeman, "The Rabbinic Understanding of Covenant as a Political Idea," in *Kinship and Consent,* ed. Daniel J. Elazar (Ramat Gan: Turtledove, 1981).

10. The Talmudic vision must be culled from the pages of the *Babylonian Talmud.*

11. Freeman.

12. Max Kadushin, *Organic Thinking: A Study in Rabbinic Thought* (New York: Jewish Theological Seminary, 1938), 184.

13. Max Kadushin, *The Rabbinic Mind,* 2d ed. (New York: Blaidsel Publishing Company, 1965), 47.

14. Max Kadushin, *Worship and Ethics: A Study in Rabbinic Judaism* (Evanston: Northwestern University Press, 1964), vii.

15. See also T.B. Shabbat 88a, Avoda Zara 3a and Ruth Rabba 1.

16. Jacob Neusner, *A Life of Rabban Yohanan Ben Zakkai* (Leiden: E.J. Brill, 1962), 143.

17. Cf. Song of Songs Rabbah 5:3 and Exodus Rabbah 29:3.

18. Cf. Leo Baeck, *This People Israel* (Philadelphia: Jewish Publication Society, 1965) for a similar conception applied to community building.

19. Cf. R. Trevors Herford, *The Pharisees* (Boston: Beacon Press, 1962), 141ff.

20. These *responsa* are being collected at both the Hebrew University of Jerusalem and at Bar-Ilan University and organized for easier use today. Bar-Ilan is computerizing all of them and already has several thousand volumes in the computer where the material contained can be retrieved by a key word system.

21. Cf. *Etz HaHaim.*

20

Medieval Covenant Theory

The Beginnings of Systematic Jewish Political Thought

Even as the Talmud was being developed, Jews living in the world needed to try to penetrate and convey the truths of Judaism in a more intellectual form, at the very least to reach those Jews influenced by the larger environment in which they found themselves, including many of "the best and the brightest." In truth, systematic Jewish political thought goes back to Hellenistic times, the first Jewish encounter with another civilization that specifically fostered systematic use of intellectual power. Philo and Josephus were the first to attempt to explain the political ideas of the Bible in Greek philosophic or Roman legal-historical terms.[1] While they had a very important influence on Christianity, they were virtually forgotten within Judaism. Their major impact on later generations was to distort the covenantal foundations of the Jewish people through their efforts to "translate" Jewish ideas into Greco-Roman frameworks. The impact in this regard cannot be overestimated. It persists to this day, having penetrated into the very heart of modern Judaism.

It was only after the completion of the Talmud that the chain of systematic Jewish thought emerged. The intellectual expression of medieval Jews was manifested through five frameworks. Most visible were the works of systematic thought beginning with Saadia Gaon and Isaac Israeli at the turn of the ninth century, which appealed to students of philosophy and were recognized by them but which had little impact beyond those circles. These works were written in the forms and styles appropriate to one or another school of medieval philosophy or theology, and, accordingly, were the least likely to overtly deal with covenantal themes that were generally absent from both. While, of necessity, those who understand the covenantal basis of the entire Jewish system will find covenantal elements embedded in those works, the effort to reach those whose thoughts were structured along the quite different philosophical or theological lines of the period generally prevented covenantal themes from visibly emerging.[2]

Even more popular at the time were Kabbalistic works. Theosophical Kabbalism was very attractive in the Middle Ages, when many of the very best Jewish minds were deeply committed to Kabbalah and their thought consequently deeply rooted within its framework. The fantastic elements of Kabbalistic thought led to a rejection of Kabbalah in the modern epoch and its rediscovery only in the twentieth century, particularly after World War II. While more open conceptually to covenantal ideas, the spiritual and apolitical direction of most Kabbalistic thought transformed covenantal ideas originally political in character in metaphysical directions. While it has its moments, it, too, is not a primary source for our exploration.[3]

A third category and perhaps the most widely used, albeit not necessarily for speculative purposes, was that of the commentaries, principally on the Bible but also on the Talmud. Biblical commentaries in particular are rich in political thought and of necessity deal extensively with covenant. Such a major figure of Jewish political thought as Don Isaac Abravanel (1437–1508) chose the biblical commentary as his principal medium for such political expression. Ramban (Nachmanides, 1194–1270) and a long line of less well-known figures also found a medium of political expression through traditional textual commentary on classic Jewish texts. From Rashi in the eleventh century to Meir Leibush (Malbim) in the nineteenth, many now standard Bible commentaries paid due attention to matters political from covenantal grounding.[4] These, too, have not been systematically explored for our purposes.

A fourth source consists of systematic halakhic works. Among these is Maimonides's (1135–1204) *Mishneh Torah,* the most systematic of *halakhic* codes, grounded in a worldview presented in its pages along with the *halakhot* themselves. These systematic works were essentially expositions of or commentaries on the Torah-as-constitution, so perforce had to relate to its covenantal basis, sometimes in so many words and sometimes through constitutional interpretation. They also had to relate to the division of domains and other institutional manifestations of a covenantal polity. Because they used more authentic Jewish terminology than the first two categories, which either followed the terminology

of the philosophers or invented a terminology of their own, their covenantal ideas are more easily accessible. For example, many have commented on the differences between the Maimonides of the *Guide of the
Perplexed* and the Maimonides of the *Mishneh Torah* or the *Commentary on the Mishnah*. Because of their differing audiences and context,
the first was written more in the language of the philosophers and the
second more in the language of Jewish tradition.[5]

Finally, there were the responsa themselves. Although not written to
present systematic theory, they can be used as sources to determine what
constituted the ideational systems upon which their writers relied. This
is particularly true of the responsa of the great medieval Jewish consti-
tutionalists who appeared to reconstruct *halakhah* to accommodate regime change in the century and a half from the mid-eleventh to early
thirteenth centuries when the constitutional foundations for the medieval *kehillah* developed in this manner.[6] Such figures as the Maharam of
Rothenberg (c.1215-1293), R. Shlomo ben Aderet (Rashba, c.1235-
c.1310), R. Asher ben Yehiel (Rosh), and others deliberately set about to
create a new constitutional basis for Jewish self-government, responsive to the conditions that brought the Jews of Europe, Sephardic and
Ashkenazic, to live in separated small communities rather than united in
larger territories. Even lesser figures frequently addressed questions of
governance in their responsa, which can be analyzed to reveal a theory
of political organization, power and public policy. In these in particular,
much turned on the use of covenantally loaded terminology, with many
issues turning on the degree of consent involved in establishing a particular institution.[7]

This is a vast literature, much of it still unpublished and more
unanalyzed. Most analyzed are the major speculative works in the philosophic mode; least analyzed are the responsa. Except for the first category and, to some extent, the biblical commentaries, most of what has
been analyzed has been analyzed by specialists in each period following
the popular theories of what to look for; hence, it is particularly difficult
to draw conclusions about this literature or the epochs it covers without
substantial reanalysis.

This chapter does not pretend to even begin such analysis. Here we
merely seek to outline a few of the possibilities among the leading Jewish speculative thinkers who flourished between the ninth and the sixteenth centuries. In a sense, it is the beginning of an agenda of research,

one that will require the substantial effort of many scholars. In view of the great expertise in the field, this writer makes no pretense as to be able to be the one who will undertake that exploration. Nor is this volume the place in which to do so. I would only like to suggest some lines along which such an inquiry might be undertaken.

Saadia Gaon

The beginnings of the chain of medieval Jewish thought are to be found in the works of Saadia Gaon (Saadia ben Joseph, 882–942 C.E.), the principal leader of the *keter torah* of world Jewry in his lifetime. Born in Egypt, he reached his eminence in Babylonia where he was head of the leading yeshiva (at Sura) and, as his title indicates, the principal counterpoint to the Resh Galuta, the head of the *keter malkhut*. Thus, he straddled both strands of Talmudic development, serving as a communal leader and *posek* (he may have been the first to systematically issue responsa), and also as a systematic thinker whose major work, *Sefer HaEmunot v'HaDeot* (*The Book of Beliefs and Opinions*), laid the foundations for systematic Jewish thought within the rabbinic tradition.

Saadia's understanding of matters political was undoubtedly tempered by his own political struggles with David ben Zakkai, the Resh Galuta of his time, and after he became Gaon of the Yeshiva at Sura, with his counterparts at the Yeshiva of Pumbedita. If not the first *posek* in the post-Talmudic chain of *posekim*, he was certainly one of the founders of the system. Indeed, his most important *halakhic* works cover issues of Jewish civil law, although he wrote extensively on ritual matters as well. His books of *halakhic* decisions were organized logically and systematically; hence, they constituted a revolution in *halakhic* literature.

Saadia's systematic thought rested on his understanding that Jews were Jews by virtue of the Torah, in other words, on a covenantal-constitutional basis. Here, too, his major work served as the foundation for subsequent systematic Jewish thought. The purpose of the book was to provide a rational underpinning for that constitution in both its written and oral facets. In the manner of systematic Jewish thought, it was more of a polemic designed to justify Jewish belief and practice than a philosophic inquiry attempting to know the unknown. His work was phrased in the language of the philosophic theology of the Muslim thinkers of his day, the Mu'tazilites. Hence, the covenantal aspects of his theology are obscured by the use of a different language. They are more pronounced in his *halakhic* works and, perhaps not surprisingly, in his grammatical ones where he perforce uses a covenantal terminology.[8]

Moses Maimonides

Moses ben Maimon, Maimonides or Rambam, is generally acknowledged as the greatest Jewish speculative thinker. He is even claimed by the philosophers as a philosopher by virtue of his *Guide of the Perplexed,* which seems to offer the possibility of interpretation as a work of philosophy, one that does not start with prior acknowledgement of the existence of God, the starting point for all truly philosophic thought.[9] In his *Milot Hahigayon* (Tractate on Logic), chapter 14, Maimonides makes the point that the function of the Torah is emphatically political, an issue on which he elaborates in *The Guide of the Perplexed,* a book devoted to "the governance of the city."[10] Strauss argues that Maimonides "suggests that the function of revealed religion is emphatically political."[11]

Be that as it may, our concern with Maimonides is, of course, with whether there are or are not covenantal dimensions to his thought. Obviously, in the theological sense there must be, with the Sinai covenant occupying the premier place in his thought. Expectedly, that covenant has a strong political dimension for Maimonides, whose political concern and understanding were very well developed within the tradition. All this is clearly expressed in the *Mishneh Torah,* Maimonides's great code of Jewish law through which he attempted to provide a comprehensive guide for Jewish life, embracing the entire Torah as interpreted by rabbinic tradition and restated by him. The *Mishnah Torah* does not particularly emphasize covenantal features but cannot avoid questions of covenantalism.

Maimonides's presentation of both the best regime as he understands the Torah and his discussion of how to organize Jewish life in the diaspora that he knew together demonstrate how clearly he is in the mainstream of the Jewish political tradition, even where one disagrees with him on particular matters, such as his emphasis on the necessity for a king when the Jewish state is restored. He begins with the *kahal,* the assembled people (of Israel), as the foundation of proper government and treats the division of authority and power among the three *ketarim* as a Divine requirement and anticipates the restoration of the *ketarim* following a fairly literal reading of the Torah, with priests, kings from the Davidic line, and prophets restored to their respective places.

The latter are of particular interest to Maimonides. While he insists on the restoration of kingship, he restricts the king to a very limited role, principally as military leader defending Israel against its enemies. He sees the Sanhedrin as the continuing body of Torah interpretation and judgment dating back to the time of Moses, but in general and more especially in the *Guide of the Perplexed*, he looks to the *navi* (prophet) to play the major role in governance. Students of Maimonidean thought have emphasized the degree to which the *navi* is Maimonides's parallel to the Platonic philosopher-king. Indeed, as Leo Strauss has persuasively argued, Maimonides does seem to be more of a Platonist than an Aristotelian.[12] But his emphasis on the role of the prophet should also be read as an effort to provide a meta-*halakhic* voice for the *keter torah* with Moses the *eved adonai* as his model. The *navi* occupies an ambiguous role in this respect. Clearly anchored within the *halakhah*, he is also God's messenger above it, far more than merely the best *halakhic* interpreter of his generation; he is not a "rabbi." We can detect a certain Islamic influence in this as well by making the *navi* the direct instrument of God, and more, the wise statesman.

It seems to be a feature of non-kabbalistic medieval Jewish speculative thought to revive the role of the prophet in order to partially escape the limits of *halakhah*. Maimonides is the apotheosis of this phenomenon. Maimonides goes furthest to naturalize prophecy and as such his views are rejected by others including Don Isaac Abravanel, the other leading figure in medieval Jewish political thought.

The implicit division of the *keter torah* into *halakhah* and prophecy with both existing side-by-side essentially reverses the Tannaitic view that the sages who formulated the *halakhah* had replaced the prophecy. Through the category of prophecy, the medieval speculative thinkers tried to do for *keter torah* what had from the first been done with *keter malkhut*, namely, the development of the *mishpat hamelukhah* as a category derived from the Torah and supplemental to *halakhah*. In both cases this may reflect the necessity to respond to political reality, whereby ideal categories must be supplemented by more realistic ones.

Maimonides, who was deeply involved in questions of governance throughout his life, both within the Jewish community and through his closeness to the foreign suzerein whom he served, also pays attention to *mishpat hamelukhah* as a category. Indeed he gave traditional Judaism its prevailing understanding of the relationship between *halakhah* and *mishpat hamelukhah*. Certainly, he understood the realities of exercising power by virtue of his experience. This is reflected especially well in his responsa where he deals with the specifics of real problems.

Judah Halevi

Judah Halevi stands in great contrast to Maimonides in just about every respect, emphasizing and justifying what Maimonides tries to explain away, holding fast to those signs of divinity that Maimonides prefers to pass over.[13] His great work, *The Kuzari,* is permeated with covenantal language and spirit, politically and theologically. In Judah Halevi, covenantal terminology is used systematically and consistently as part of the political language of his argument on behalf of the superiority of Judaism over Christianity, Islam, and classical philosophy. Thus, the exemplars of Judaism are known as the *haver* and the *hasid,* with the latter term being used to describe the ideal political leader, one who is expert in managing his polity, similar to Maimonides's *navi*.

> The *hasid* is the man who is in charge of his polity and who gives to all its residents their lawful needs in right measure. He deals with all of them justly, favoring no one of them, and giving none of them more than what is due him. Consequently at the time he needs them, they all *hearken* [my emphasis] to him and hurry to respond to his call to carry out all that he commands and be careful to avoid all that he has forbidden to them.

In other words, the *hasid* as ruler first supplies the material needs of his nation, then establishes just laws to govern the polity. Only after that is he in a position to invite sacrifices on the part of the nation.

This description of the *hasid* is provided by the *haver* (best translated as partner), the term that Judah Halevi uses for his Jewish protagonist, which is itself covenantal. According to the author, the term comes from the covenant that God cut with his people through which all *hit-habru,* that is to say, formed a partnership (*Kuzari,* chap. 2, par. 34):

> We have a *hit-havrut* [partnership] in connection with God based on those commandments which God established through covenant between us and Him, like the covenant of circumcision, of which it is said [in the Torah] "My covenant" and like the Sabbath of which it is said "it is a sign between Me and between you for the generations" and in addition the covenant with the fathers and the covenant of the Torah that God made [literally, cut] with us.

Continuing the dialogue, the Kuzari (the King of Khazaria) asks, "I ask, is that the task of the *hasid* and not the ruler?" (The author has him assume that the task of the *hasid* is to deal only with spiritual matters while the ruler deals only with material ones, i.e., the two swords theory of medieval Christianity.) The *haver* answers, "The *hasid* is the ruler," meaning that only he who deals with spiritual matters is worthy of dealing with material ones. There is no separation between the spiritual and the material nor any contradiction between them. "And he is the man who is worthy of rule because if he stood at the head of the polity he would deal with it justly, just as he acts justly with his body and his soul."

In the beginning of his discussion, the *haver* uses the term *medinah* or polity generically. When the Kuzari king turns the questioning to Israel specifically, the *haver* turns to specific terminology, referring to Israel as the *edah,* explaining that the *edah* is the polity in which the *shekhina* (Divine presence) dwells, observes its behavior, and rewards or punishes it accordingly; the polity established by God's covenant and organized by Moshe Rabbeinu (Moses, our teacher) at Sinai.

Moreover, since the *edah* assists the *hasid* in his efforts to reach higher levels of *hasidut,* he is dependent upon them for spiritual advancement. This ties the leader to his *edah* and he cannot function apart from it. The Kuzari brings Moses at Sinai as the classic example of this (chap. 4, par. 11):

> He (Moses) brought the entire people to stand before Mt. Sinai so that they would see with their own eyes, each person according to his ability, the light that he (Moses) saw, after which he called to the seventy elders and they too saw God, as it is written, they saw the God of Israel. Subsequently he again brought together the seventy elders and delegated to them from the light of the prophecy until they reached his level...and all the prophets are witnesses to Moses, may he rest in peace, and called upon the people to observe the Torah of Moses.

The Kuzari continues to describe how the political leader is connected in two ways: in one, to the entire nation, with each person according to his ability; and in the second, to the chosen of the nation as represented by the seventy elders. Thus, the prophet at times prophesied in the name of the people and at times in the name of their chosen officials. In both capacities the leader functions as the *nasi.* To demonstrate this, Halevi brings examples from the relationship between King David and God.

Don Isaac Abravanel

Don Isaac Abravanel was the last great civil leader of Spanish Jewry on the Iberian Peninsula. He served three foreign suzereins in senior positions, in Portugal, Spain, and, after 1492, in Italy. In each case he also was a recognized leader of the local Jewish community.[14]

Abravanel combined deep piety with deep political understanding. Having experienced the corruptions and weaknesses of monarchs in three kingdoms, he concluded from bitter experience that kingship, even when restrained, was folly. Therefore, he aligned himself with the anti-monarchist position in the Jewish political tradition, emphasizing the need to restore the classic Mosaic regime rather than its Davidic modification. His ideal regime was an aristocratic republic based on his understanding of the original biblical model. Since the basis for his prescriptions are inevitably in the Torah, he too, inevitably, emphasizes the covenantal foundations of his political thought.

Students of Jewish political thought have as a matter of course juxtaposed Maimonides and Abravanel, and with reason. Maimonides seems to be the ultimate monarchist in postbiblical Jewish tradition, while Abravanel is the ultimate republican. His experience with the capriciousness of monarchs made him a decisive partisan of the original Mosaic federal republic, which he understood to be an aristocratic republic very similar to that of the Venice of his time. The contrast between the two and its limits is instructive. Abravanel shines through the ages as the most comprehensive and systematic medieval defender of aristocratic republicanism in the Jewish world, while even Maimonides's king has very limited powers. In other words, if Abravanel supports the first classic regime of the Bible, Maimonides supports the second, but in its early Davidic form, not as it later evolved.

Others to Consider

Covenant themes are less resonant in the works of Joseph Albo. He accepts the covenantal foundations of Judaism and the Jewish people as a matter of course. It could hardly be otherwise. But he does not build directly upon those foundations in the construction of their systems in any special way.[15]

It should be noted that, while substantial advances have been made in studying the political dimensions of medieval Jewish thought in recent decades, this issue has not been properly explored. It remains a major item on the research agenda for exploring the covenant tradition.

Other Jewish speculative thinkers whose covenantal thought is apparent include Nachmanides (Ramban—R. Moshe ben Nachman), Gersonides (Ralbag—R. Levy ben Gershon), R. Moses Girondi, and R. Hasdai Crescas. Characteristic of all of them is the same combination of speculative thought, public leadership, and active participation in the constitutional process as *posekim*.[16]

Look at the sequence of events chronologically. Maimonides died in 1204. Nachmanides, the founder of the major school of Spanish kabbalists and a chief figure in the leadership of the Jewish community of the Kingdom of Aragon, was born in 1194 and died in 1270 after having been forced to leave Spain several years earlier as a result of his victory in one of the Jewish-Christian dialogues of the time. His major disciple was Rabbi Solomon ben Aderet (Rashba—1235-1310) who inherited Nachamides position as the head of the circle of Kabbalists and as a community leader. He, in turn, was succeeded by Rabbi Nissim of Gerona (RAN—1310-1375). Maimonides, Rashba, and Rabbi Nissim, in writing about community matters, used the term *tikkun hamedinah* (the repair or correction of the polity) and its variant *tikkun medini* (political correction/repair) in their responsa, enabling communal leaders within the *keter malkhut* to take steps not otherwise authorized by the Torah but that fitted the needs of the time. Maimonides, indeed, used both the traditional biblically originated phrase *mishpat hamelekh* (the law of the king) or its variant *mishpat hamelukhah* (the law of the kingdom) and *tikkun hamedinah* or *tikkun medini* more of less interchangeably. Both can be defined as a certain field of activity separated from the law of the Torah and justified within the category *hora'at sha'ah* (the dictates of the times).

The shift to the newer term was medieval, although its roots can be found in the usage of *medinah* for something akin to a province, that is to say, an autonomous political entity but part of a larger political body as in the Persian empire as described in the Scroll of Esther. The Talmud uses the phrase *medinah u'mikdash* (roughly, state and temple) to describe the political beliefs of the Sadducees in their conflict with the Pharisees. It was introduced into Jewish political thought as the equivalent of the Greek *polis* in the eleventh century in part because of the Arabic word *madina,* the Arabic equivalent of the same term, otherwise meaning city. Maimonides talked about the two concerns of philosophy, *tikkun hanefesh* (correction/repair of the soul) and *tikkun haguf* (correction/repair of the body), and referred to political philosophy as addressed to the latter category.

Crescas, for example, was the chief rabbi of Aragon during the very difficult period of the anti-Jewish pogroms of 1391. As such he was very much involved in representing the Jewish community before the king of Aragon to seek his intervention and assistance against the pogromists. More than that, he was a close advisor to the king in more normal times. In his capacity, he prepared a draft constitution for the Jewish community of Saragossa in the mid-1390s and presented it for ratification to the general assembly of the community.[17]

What is common to all of the foregoing speculative thinkers plus most of the others who illuminated medieval Jewry is that they were personally involved in public affairs, in holding positions of responsibility. Saadia, Rambam, and Abravanel were the principal leaders of their communities, Saadia from within the *keter torah,* Rambam principally within the *keter torah* but with responsibilities of the *keter malkhut* as well, and Abravanel from the *keter malkhut.* Saadia and Rambam were *posekim* who issued many *halakhic* rulings. All four wrote biblical commentaries or commentaries on the biblical text. Thus, it is accurate to say that the most notable Jewish "philosophers" spanned the range of Jewish political life and thought in their personas.

Kabbalah and Covenant

The hardest case for demonstrating that the presence, not to speak of the pervasiveness, of covenantal modes in Jewish tradition is that of Kabbalah. The relationship of Jewish mysticism and covenant is the missing piece of premodern Jewish tradition. Thanks to the last seventy years of research by Gershom Scholom and his students, we now understand how fully normative Kabbalah was within Jewish life from the Talmudic era until Jews were engulfed by modernization.[18]

It is in the nature of mysticism to seek organic rather than covenantal relationships in the universe and Kabbalah is no different. At the same time, Jewish mysticism is less concerned with the individual's binding to God than with understanding the mysteries of the Torah and the universe. Still, because of its mystical character, there is no aspect of Judaism that is less political than Kabbalah. Less political, however, does not mean not at all political. Quite to the contrary, classic Kabbalistic models, including the ten *Sephirot,* recognize *malkhut* and the exercise of power as integral to the universe as much as the seeking after unity with God. God himself exercises power (in Kabbalistic terms, *gevurah*) as part of the Divine scheme of things, although in the system of Sephirot, which Kabbalists use to account for the connection between God and our world, *malkhut,* human governance, is the farthest removed from the *Ein Sof,* the pure Godhead. Nonetheless, it is an integral part of the system.

It is to the Kabbalistic system of Sephirot, the emanations from the *Ein Sof* (the unlimited Godhead) that progressively concretized the utterly spiritual character of God into the predominantly material world of our reality, that we must look in our quest. What is characteristic of the ten Sephirot is their combination of separation and linkage and the way they balance one another, both longitudinally and laterally. Even without searching Kabbalistic texts for use of covenantal terminology, a person with a covenantal perspective will find echoes of that perspective in *torat hasephirot* (the teachings about the emanations)—as this writer did at the very beginning of his pursuit of covenant in Jewish tradition, at the time when he was engaged in the study of Kabbalah as well. Covenant, after all, as we have seen, is a matter of separation and linkage, of balancing separate centers of power, which each of the Sephirot are, and with bridging between what are separately unbridgable phenomena such as God and man.

Beyond those covenantal foundations that lie at the very foundations of Kabbalah as a teaching, there is another aspect of Kabbalah developed much later in the sixteenth century by Rabbi Isaac Luria, *HaAri HaKadosh* (Ari is an acronym for his name, that also means "lion," and *kadosh* means "holy"), the greatest figure in late medieval Kabbalah, whose teachings, known in English as the Lurianic Kabbalah, became the foundations of the most practical manifestations of Jewish mysticism in this world. Lurianic Kabbalah influenced much of contemporary Sephardic Kabbalism, as reflected in the *Shulhan Aruch,* the last of the great *halakhic* codes that has come to be recognized as authoritative throughout the *halakhic* world and remains so, and Hasidism, the pietistic mystical movement that has continued as a strong presence in Judaism to this day.[19]

Luria (1534–1572), who spent the most important years of his life in sixteenth-century Safed, then the intellectual center of the Jewish world, developed the doctrine of *tzimtzum* (contraction), which attempted to explain how a material world could be created where God is all spirit and all-pervasive in his universe and how evil could enter a world of God's creation. Lurianic doctrine has it that in order to create the material world God first had to contract himself to leave space for it. Then, in the process of creation of the material world, whose material character is analogous to that of a clay pot or vessel, the inflow of God's spirit was too great for the vessels to contain. Hence, they broke, and in the breaking generated evil. The humans who resulted from that creation are touched by this evil, but are also responsible for the reassembly of the vessels to make them whole again, which is how the Ari understood or reinterpreted an old Talmudic concept of *Tikkun Olam* (the repair or reformation of the universe).

This doctrine was developed by Luria at the same time that, at the other end of the then-known West, Reformed Protestant, especially Puritan, theology developed an analogous doctrine of God's contraction and return to the world through his covenants with humanity. Just as the Puritans built their new network of covenants on their original scriptural predecessors, so, too, did the Ari, in perfect piety, see the Torah as the link between God and man necessary to teach the ways of *Tikkun Olam,* augmented, or at the very least understood, through the perspective of his doctrine. Those who took this task upon themselves were hassidim in the traditional sense of fulfilling the *brit* through *hesed.* It is no surprise, then, that the mass movement that grew out of Lurianic Kabbalah two centuries later was named by its founders *Hassidut,* that is to say, the expression of *hesed* by human Hassidim in pursuit of the Divine.

Just as the Ari taught at the time of the Puritans, albeit 2,500 miles to the east of them, so, too, did *Hassidut* arise in the middle and later part of the eighteenth century, at the same time as Methodism in England and the new United States. Both were pietistic responses to the increasing intellectualism and elitism of Judaism and Puritanism respectively. As in the case of the Methodists, the religion of the Hassidim, with its mystical emphasis on *dvekut,* which can be understood as the merging of the human soul with God, and the system of *tzaddikim* or rebbis that grew up after the movement's founding generation, whereby individual personalities became the sole connection for individual pietists and God, overrode all of the auxiliary precautions of the covenantal system. Soon it not only ceased to be covenantal but became its hierarchical antithesis. Still, in its origins the Hassidic movement represented another effort to find human expression for the covenant idea.[20]

This is, at most, a first word about Kabbalah and covenant. Much study needs to be undertaken before a further word can be given. Yet it seems that, even in that sphere of Jewish organic mysticism, covenant was not absent.

Conclusion

As we have consistently seen throughout this book, the hardest cases in which to find manifestations of covenant are in the realm of speculative thought, most influenced by other systems, whether philosophical or mystical. Nevertheless, even a cursory survey of Jewish speculative thought shows that the fundamental character and pervasiveness of the covenant idea is manifest in every facit of the Jewish experience. One of the reasons that this has not been much noted by contemporary students of Jewish civilization is because the modern explorations of both forms of Jewish speculative thought were begun under conditions of the overall late modern depreciation of covenantal in favor of organic or hierarchical thinking. Thus, original covenantal dimensions need to be recovered, at the very least through reanalysis and in many cases through original exploration.

Notes

1. On Philo, see Hans Lewy, ed., *Three Jewish Philosophers* (New York: Atheneum, 1969), 7–112; Harry Austryn Wolfson, *Philo: Foundations of Religious Philosophy in Judaism* (Cambridge, MA: Harvard University Press, 1947).

    For writings by Josephus, see *The Jewish War*, trans. G. A. Williamson (Harmondsworth: Penguin, 1980); *The Jewish Antiquities*, trans. H. St. J. Thackeray, Loeb Classical Library (Cambridge, MA: Harvard University Press, 1934); *Jerusalem and Rome: The Writings of Josephus* (New York: Meridian, 1960); and for his complete works, see *Complete Works*, translated by William Whiston (Grand Rapids: Kregel Publications, 1960). For a recent collection of essays dealing with Josephus's thought, see Louis H. Feldman and Gohei Hata, ed., *Josephus, Judaism and Christianity* (Detroit: Wayne State University Press, 1987).

2. See, for example, Isaac Husik, *A History of Jewish Philosophy* (Jewish Publication Society) for a list of Jewish "philosophers" from the ninth to the fifteenth centuries and a very conventional analysis of their thought. Julius Guttmann, *Philosophies of Judaism*, trans. David W. Silverman (Philadelphia: Jewish Publication Society, 1964) is the standard work from the covenantal viewpoint in use today.

   Leo Strauss emphasized the hidden commitment to philosophy of the "greats" among these men. See his *Persecution and the Art of Writing* (Glencoe, IL: Free Press, 1952); his introduction to Moses Maimonides, *Guide for the Perplexed*, trans. Shlomo Pines (Chicago: University of Chicago Press, 1963); and his *Essays in Platonic Political Philosophy*, ed. Thomas Pangle (Chicago: University of Chicago Press, 1983). See also Leo Strauss and Joseph Cropsey, eds., *History of Political Philosophy*, 3d ed. (Chicago: Rand McNally, 1987), esp. the chapters on Maimonides and Albo.
3. On the more theosophical dimensions of Kabbalah, see Gershom Scholem, *Major Trends in Jewish Mysticism* (Jerusalem: Schocken Publishing House, 1941); Louis Ginzberg, *On Jewish Law and Lore* (New York: Atheneum, 1970). For a sampling of Kabbalistic writing, see *The Zohar* (London: Soncino, 1934, reprinted in 1973).
4. On a history of biblical commentary, see *Encyclopedia Judaica*, vol. 4, pp. 890–915. While some of the classic commentators have been "translated" into English, most of the translations are highly interpretive to conform with the orthodoxies of the translators; hence, recourse must be made to the Hebrew originals either through such classic collections as *Mikraot Gedolot* or through more recent separately published compilations of the commentaries of individual commentators, such as Rashi, Ramban, Abravanel, and Malbim.
5. The principal systematic works are R. Isaac Alfasi, *Sefer HaHalakhot* (Jerusalem: Magnes Press, 1969); R. Moshe ben Maimon, *Mishneh Torah: The Code of Maimonides* (New Haven, CT: Yale University Press, 1949–1971); R. Joseph Caro, *Shulhan Arukh* (New York: Jewish Publication Society, 1959). For a discussion of Caro, see R. J. Zwi Werblowsky, *Joseph Karo: Lawyer and Mystic* (Philadelphia: Jewish Publication Society, 1980).
6. Cf. Menahem Elon, *The Principles of Jewish Law* (Jerusalem: Encyclopedia Judaica, 1975); Daniel J. Elazar and Stuart Cohen, *The Jewish Polity* (Bloomington: Indiana University Press, 1985), Epoch 11, pp. 160–77.
7. Cf. Elon, *The Principles of Jewish Law*; and Elazar and Cohen, *The Jewish Polity*.
8. On Saadia Gaon, see *Encyclopedia Judaica*, vol. 14, pp. 543–54.
9. Leo Strauss is perhaps the strongest proponent of this view. See his *Persecution and the Art of Writing*, and his introduction to the Pines English translation of Maimonides, *Guide for the Perplexed*.
10. Leo Strauss, "Maimonides' Statement on Political Science," Proceedings of the American Academy for Jewish Research, New York, 1952–1959, vol. 21–23, p. 117.
11. Ibid., 119.
12. Leo Strauss, *The Rebirth of Classical Political Rationalism*, ed. Thomas Pangle (Chicago: University of Chicago Press, 1989).
13. Judah Halevi, *The Kuzari: An Argument for the Faith of Israel* (New York: Schocken, 1971).
14. Isaac Abravanel, *Commentatio in Testamentum Patriarchae Jacobi in Latinam Translata Linguam* (Hafniae: Rothe, 1734), *Principles of Faith* (Rutherford, NJ:

Fairleigh Dickinson University Press, 1982); Ben-Zion Netanyahu, *Don Isaac Abravanel: Statesman and Philosopher* (Philadelphia: Jewish Publication Society, 1972); Leo Strauss, *On Abravanel's Philosophical Tendency and Political Teaching* (Cambridge: Cambridge University Press, 1937).

15. For Albo, see *Sefer HaIkkarim,* trans. Isaac Husik (Philadelphia: Jewish Publication Society, 1930). See also the chapter on Albo in Strauss and Cropsey, *History of Political Philosophy.*

16. For Gerundi, see Gerald J. Blidstein, "'Ideal' and 'Real' in Classical Jewish Political Theory," *Jewish Political Studies Review* 2, nos. 1 and 2 (Spring 1990). For Nachmanides, see Rabbi Moses Nachmanides, *Explorations in His Religious and Literary Virtuosity,* ed. Isadore Twersky (Cambridge, MA: Harvard University Press, 1983). For Gersonides, see Judah David Bleich, *Providence in Late Medieval Jewish Philosophy* (Ann Arbor: University Microfilms International, 1980). For Crescas and translations from his *Light of the Lord,* see Warren Zev Harvey, *Crescas' Critique of the Acquired Intellect* (Ann Arbor: University Microfilms International, 1976).

17. Yitzhak Baer, *A History of the Jews in Spain,* vol. 2 (Philadelphia: Jewish Publication Society, 1966), 126–30.

18. See, for example, Gershom Scholem, *Major Trends in Jewish Mysticism* (Jerusalem: Keter, 1974), *On the Kabbalah and its Symbolism,* trans. Ralph Manheim (New York: Schocken, 1965), and *Origins of the Kabbalah,* ed. Zwi Werblowsky, trans. Allan Arkush (Philadelphia: Jewish Publication Society, 1987); Moshe Idel, *Kabbalah: New Perspectives* (New Haven, CT: Yale University Press, 1988), *Studies in Ecstatic Kabbalah* (Albany: SUNY Press, 1988); Isaiah Tishby, *The Wisdom of the Zohar,* 3 vols., trans. David Goldstein (Oxford: Oxford University Press, 1989); Joseph Dan, ed. *The Early Kabbalah* (New York: Paulist Press, 1986), and *Jewish Mysticism and Jewish Ethics* (Seattle: University of Washington Press, 1985); Louis Ginzberg, *On Jewish Law and Lore* (New York: Atheneum, 1970).

19. On Lurianic Kabbalah, see Isaac Tishbi, *Torat Hara: Haklipah b'Kabbalat HaAri* (1942); S. A. Horodezky, *Torat Hakabbalah shel Rebbi Yitzhak Ashkenazi v'Rebbi Haim Vital* (1947); Levi I. Krakovsky, *Kabbalah: The Light of Redemption* (Jerusalem: Yeshivat Kol Yehuda, 1970).

20. On Hasidism, see Solomon Schechter, *Studies in Judaism,* vol. 1 (New York: Meridian Books, 1958), 1-45; Gershom Scholem, *Major Trends in Jewish Mysticism* (Jerusalem: Schocken Publishing House, 1941); I. Halperin, *Origin and Meaning of Hassidism* (1960); H. M. Rabinowicz, *Guide to Hassidism* (1960), and *The World of Hassidism* (London: Valentine, Mitchell, 1970); Samuel H. Dresner, *The Zaddik* (London: Abelard-Schumen, 1960).

21

Covenant and Polity in the Premodern Jewish Historical Experience

In the past two decades, there has been a significant rediscovery of the covenantal basis of Judaism in most if not all contemporary Jewish intellectual circles and the literature dealing with covenant and its implications has grown accordingly.[1] The thrust of this literature has been theological in character and not improperly so. Yet, as we have seen, covenant is as much a political as a theological phenomenon in its original biblical form. So it continues to be in the Jewish political tradition.

From a spiritual perspective, it can be said that, in "Jewish tradition, the ties of covenant are the concretization of the relationship of dialogue, which, when addressed to God, makes humans holy and, when addressed to one's peers, makes people human." As the Bible itself makes clear, the covenantal bonds transform such a mystical union into a real political order, one that Jewish tradition understands as being like Jacob's ladder, with its feet on the ground and its top reaching up to heaven. The Hebrew expression for that political order is *malkhut shamayim*, the kingdom of heaven. The compound is, in itself, covenantal. The two words not only form a unity affirming God's sovereignty and the human need to respond to it but reflect a certain recognition of tension between *malkhut* (kingdom or rule), with its power, and *shamayim* (heaven or God), with its emphasis on justice.[2] The polity, then, reflects the tension between the organization and management of power, on one hand, and the definition and pursuit of justice, on the other.

The Epochs of Jewish Constitutional History

Ultimately the concrete political embodiment of the covenant model takes two forms: (1) the union of families or individuals to form bodies politic and (2) the federation of bodies politic to form even more complex political systems. Jewish constitutional history embraces manifestations of both forms. Figure 21.1 delineates the fourteen constitutional epochs in Jewish history and the covenant or constitutional change that inaugurated each. What follows is a brief survey of those manifestations within the Jewish body politic over space and time and then a survey of the ways in which the covenant idea has been applied through the Jewish political tradition.

It should be understood from the first that the covenant has consistently manifested itself on three levels: the intellectual, the cultural, and the operational. All three are treated here without necessarily distinguishing between them in so many words at every turn. The reader should be prepared to recognize these three levels and make the requisite distinctions.

The biblical covenants not only transformed a *goy* into an *am* but the *am* became an *edah*. The term literally implies an assembly that meets at regular times or frequently. Even in the earliest period it became the Hebrew equivalent of "commonwealth" or "republic" (in the original sense of *res publica*—a public thing—rather than the private preserve of any person), with strong democratic overtones. The idea of the Jewish people as an *edah* actually described the regime prior to the introduction of the monarchy.[3] In this respect it parallels (and historically precedes) similar usages of *Landesgemeinde* in Switzerland and town meeting in the United States. What is crucial is that it continued to be used to describe the Jewish body politic in every period down to the present. Only in contemporary Israeli colloquial usage has the term lost its authentic meaning to become a sociological expression intentionally devoid of political content.

The documentary literature of every age is full of the classic usage. Moreover, the *edah* was invariably defined as including all adult males as participants in fundamental decision making. At the very least, the *edah* as a whole was responsible for actions of a constitutional character, whether electing kings in ancient Israel, constituting the Council of the Four Lands in medieval Poland, or forming communities in medieval Spain. The *edah* offered a variety of adaptations of covenantal principles, with a new one for each new era of Jewish political adjustment. A high point was reached in the Jewish communities of the Middle Ages. The congregational form itself, the *kahal* or *kehillah,* is a subsidiary

FIGURE 21.1
Constitutional Referents and Principal Regimes of the Jewish Polity

Period	Dates BCE	Constitution	Founding Events	Climactic Events	Culminating Events
1. Ha-avot (The Forefathers)	c. 1850–1570	Abraham's Covenant	Abraham leaves Haran	Jacob becomes Israel	Descent to Egypt
2. Ayout Mizrayim (Egyptian Bondage)	c. 1570–1280	Patriarchal covenant as reaffirmed	Settlement in Goshen	Egyptian slavery	Exodus
3. Adat Bnei Yisrael (The Congregation of Israelites)	c. 1280–1004	Mosaic Torah	Sinai	Gideon rejects kingship	David accepted as king
4. Brit Hamelukhah (The Covenant of Kingship)	1004–721	Covenants of Kingship	David's kingship	Division of kingdom	Destruction of Israel
5. Malkhut Yehuda (The Kingdom of Judah)	721–440	Deuteronomy	Judean rule consolidated	Josianic reform	Abortive restoration of monarchy
6. Knesset Hagedolah (The Great Assembly)	440–145	Ezra/Nehemiah Covenant	Ezra restoration	Shift to Hellenistic world	Hasmonean revolt
7. Hever Hayehudim (The Jewish Commonwealth)	145 B.C.E–140 C.E.	Oral Tradition (Torah)	Hasmonean kingship	Destruction of Temple	Bar Kochba Rebellion
8. Sanhedren Ve-nesi'ut (The Sanhedrin and Patriarchate)	C.E. 140–429	Mishnah	Organization of Mishnah/Renewal of Exilarchate	Christian ascendancy established anti-Jewish policy	End of Patriarchate
9. Yeshivot Ve-rashei Hagolah (The Yeshivot & Exilarch)	429–748	Gemara	Completion of Gemara	Jews come under Islam	Reunification of Jews under Islamic rule
10. Yeshivot Ve-geonim (The Yeshivot & the Geonim)	749–1038	Talmud & Codes	Geonim and first codes	Last Israel-Babylonian controversy	End of Gaonate
11. Hakehillot (The Communities)	1038–1348	Sefer HaHalakhot	Passage of hegemony to Europe	Kabbalah in Spain. Re-establishment of Jewish settlement in Jerusalem	Black Death massacres
12. Vaadei Kehillot (Community Federations)	1348–1948	Arba'ah Turim	Polish Jewry's charters. Council of Aragonese community	Spanish expulsion and aftermath	Sabbatean movement
13. Hitagduyot (Voluntary Associations)	1648–1948	Shulhan Arukh	Rise of Modernism	Emancipation	The Holocaust
14. Medinah Ve-am (State and People)	1948–	?	Establishment of Israel	?	?

product of the linkage of the covenant and the *edah*.[4] Ten male Jews, heads of families, come together to form a *kahal* by covenanting among themselves to create a local framework (within the larger framework of the Torah) for the conduct of their religious, social, and political life. Even the terminology of congregational organization reflects its covenantal orientation. Among Sephardic communities, for example, the articles of agreement establishing congregations are known as *askamot*, a term that has an explicitly covenantal derivation and significance. Thus the term *kahal*, well-nigh used synonymously with *edah* in the Bible, became the terminological subsidiary of *edah*—the *edah* in its constituted local dimension.

Postbiblical Covenantal Institutions

We have already suggested that Jewish communities and polities, congregations and federations all reflect the covenant idea in operation. Figure 21.2 summarizes the principal forms of organization that have predominated within the Jewish people since the Exodus and their particular internal character. The overwhelming majority of them were created by covenant and many were federal. Even the ones that were not, were essentially unions compounded out of local communities and/or congregations.

Of the eleven general patterns of communal organization shown in the figure, only one, the Babylonian-Near Eastern diaspora, came close to being organized on a hierarchical basis, and it was modified by an internal reform movement of revolutionary proportions. Only two others, the southern kingdom of Judah after the division of the tribes and contemporary Israel, were centralized arrangements imposed upon an earlier covenantal base in such a way as to formally supersede but not eliminate it. In all the rest, the covenantal framework was carried through from first to last, either directly or in one permutation or another.

In addition, the small congregations and *hevrot* (associations), which represented the first step beyond the family as an organizational unit, reflect the same covenantal base. Traditionally, the Jewish people has consisted of families rather than individuals bound together by covenant, thereby accommodating the realms of both kinship and consent.

By the time of the Alexandrian conquest of Judea, the high priest had become the leading figure in the Jewish polity. This arrangement was quite suitable to Alexander and his heirs. High priests were common in

FIGURE 21.2
The Jewish Edah and Its Principal Regimes

Locale and Regime	Political System
Eretz Israel (Palestine)	
Adat Bnei Yisrael (13th–10th centuries B.C.E.)	Federation of tribes
Mamlekhet Yisrael	Monarchy overlaying federation of tribes
Mamlekhet Yehudah (10th–5th centuries B.C.E.)	Monarchy overlaying union of local communities
Knesset HaGedolah (5th–2nd centuries B.C.E.)	Union of local community-congregations governed by General Assembly comprised of representative Torah authorities and local notables
Patriarchate (2nd–5th centuries C.E.)	Patriarch and Sanhedrin (Assembly of Torah authorities) govern ethnic community within Roman empire with local home rule
Contemporary Israel (1948–)	Centralized parliamentary state superimposed on on network of cooperative associations
Diaspora	
Hellenistic and Roman Empires—Politeuma	Loose league of diaspora communities (each the product of a local compact) and Israel
Babylonian-Near Eastern Exilarchate/Gaonate	Centralized ethnic polity with powers shared by Exilarch and Yeshivot (Assemblies of Torah authorities)
Spanish and Rhenish Communities	Communities organized locally by compact which occasionally federated with one another on a regional basis
Eastern European Lands	Federated *(Vaad Arba Aratzot)* unless prevented from doing so by the non-Jewish authories
Near Eastern-North African Lands	Individual congregation-communities linked locally through confederations or leagues
Modern Diaspora	Federations of congregations, camps and/or funcational agencies

the other provinces of the empire and even their having political power did not disturb Hellenistic notions of imperial solidarity. Various members of the House of Zaddok were drawn into the political vortex, taking sides in the struggle between Seleucids and Ptolemies.

With the coming of Hellenism, incumbency in the office of high priest began to turn over as the political fortunes of the incumbents shifted. The office became further detached from its roots in the traditional constitution to the point where it ceased to be filled by Jewish appointment according to the terms of Jewish law subject to imperial ratification. Instead, the imperial authorities in Damascus or Alexandria made the appointments directly. At that point power began to shift to the representatives of the *keter torah*—the *zugot* or pairs who constituted the scholarly leadership of the *keter*.

With the high priest now a tool of foreign interests and no longer a center for the preservation of Jewish autonomy, power passed to other priests who maintained their office according to the Torah. Thus, the Maccabean revolt, led by the priestly family of Hasmoneans, has as one of its dimensions the restoration of the *keter kehunah* into Jewish hands. What began initially as no more than an attempt to return to the old autonomy of a Jewish-appointed high priesthood by replacing the corrupted House of Zadok became a full-scale revolt whereby the House of Mattathias took both the priesthood and the *keter malkhut* as Judea became fully independent again.

The Hasmonean error was in combining the two *ketarim* in one leader. For this as much as for their more concrete excesses as rulers they were roundly criticized and opposed by the officers of the *keter torah*, especially the Pharisee party. With all the Jewish parties appealing to foreign rulers for support, foreign intervention put an end to Judean political independence after no more than three generations. The Romans under Pompey intervened in 63 B.C.E. to make Judea a protectorate and its rulers puppets. The Romans separated the offices of kingship and priesthood, keeping control over both. The Jews, in turn, operationally abandoned both of them and turned to the *keter torah*, by now embodied in the Pharisee-dominated Sanhedrin, seeking a new center of Jewish self-rule and a leader in the struggle for autonomy. Thus, the rise of the Sanhedrin in the first century B.C.E. was brought about by Roman intervention.

During the Second Commonwealth, necessity required the Jews to develop four variants of the covenanted community.[5] Most visible was the Hasmonean state, a polity established by the covenant between Simon, the first Hasmonean *nasi*, and the people of Israel, which became the basis of the Hasmonean regime, not only for the eighty years of its independent existence, but at least through the death of Agrippa I, 100 years later. Agrippa, the last of the Hasmonean kings to recognize those covenantal bonds, attempted to renew that covenant under Roman protection during the years 41 and 44 of the Common Era.

The second was the covenanted community of the *perushim*, (Pharisees) who, as their name indicates, separated themselves from the general community of Jews in Judea to refine and purify Judaism through the development of the complex system of laws and *mitzvot*, which together became *halakhic* Judaism, formulated in new covenantal terms by the sages (cf. chap. 16).

The third form was developed by the covenanted communities of the desert, of which the Qumran community is the best known. The Essenes and their partners sought to separate themselves physically as well as sociologically from the community by founding small covenanted communities in the desert for the remnant of true Jews, "sanctuaries of purity" for "those who entered the new covenant in the land of Damascus." Theirs were fellowship communities based upon rigid manuals of discipline.

Finally, there was the *politeuma*, the quasi-independent community within the Hellenistic *polis* of the diaspora, created by covenant among the Jews of a particular city whose powers were affirmed by compact with the host *polis*, to grant the Jews substantial autonomy without necessarily denying them a role in the *polis* as a whole.

Of these four forms of covenanted community, two, the Hasmonean state and the desert fellowships, could not survive the destruction of the Temple. The Hasmonean state rested on Saduccean Judaism, which required state and temple as the central elements in the structure of Jewish life. When both disappeared, so did they. The desert communities, even though they rejected the trappings of a Jewish state, needed its protection in order to survive. Once that protection was removed, they were left open and vulnerable and were apparently finally destroyed in the Bar Kochba rebellion (132–135 C.E.).

The diaspora *politeuma* was destroyed in its original form as a result of the diaspora uprisings against Roman rule during the time of Emperor Trajan (115–117 C.E.). Driven by a combination of local anti-Semitism and a false sense of self-confidence, these communities revolted and were destroyed, requiring Jewish autonomy to be reconstituted in the diaspora on a different basis. In the end, only the Pharisees survived and over the course of the next two centuries, their Judaism was to become normative. What is important is to recognize that all four were branches from the same root, that is to say, each developed the Jewish idea of covenant and its tradition in concrete, practical ways that provided for self-government.

The Succoth covenant in the days of Ezra and Nehemiah was the last of the biblical covenants. The regime it produced survived until the time of the Hasmoneans. In 145 B.C.E., it was supplemented by an additional covenant between "the priests, the people, the heads of the nation, and the elders of the land" on the one hand, and Simon the Maccabean on the other, whom they designated as "high priest, commander-in-chief and *nasi*"—restoring the classic term—which was embodied in a document given in full in 1 Maccabees 14:25-49:

> On the eighteenth of Elul in the year one hundred and seventy-two, which is the third year of Simon the great high priest, in Asaramel, in the grand assembly of priests and people, leaders of the nation and elders of the country, we were notified as follows:

> "When there was frequent fighting in the country, Simon, son of Mattathias, a scion of the line of Joarib, and his brothers courted danger and withstood the enemies of their nation to safeguard the integrity of their sanctuary and the Law, and so brought their nation great glory (14:28-29)."

> "The people saw Simon's faith and the glory he had resolved to win for his nation; they made him their leader and high priest because of all these achievements of his and the justice and faithfulness he had maintained toward his own nation, and because he sought every means to enhance the honor of his people. In his day and under his guidance they succeeded in rooting out the pagans from their country, including those in the City of David in Jerusalem, who had converted it into a citadel for their own use from which they would sally out to defile the surroundings of the sanctuary and violate its sacred character. He settled Jewish soldiers in it and fortified it as a protection for the country and city, and heightened the walls of Jerusalem. In consequence of this, King Demetrius confirmed him in the high-priestly office, made him one of his Friends and advanced him to high honors; he had heard that the Romans named the Jews friends, allies and brothers, and that they had given Simon's ambassadors an honorable reception; and further, that the Jews and the priests had agreed that Simon should be their perpetual leader and high priest until a trustworthy prophet should arise; he was also to be their commissioner and to be responsible for the sanctuary and for the appointment of officials to supervise the fabric, to administer the country, and to control the arsenal and fortresses; he was to take charge of the sanctuary, and everyone had to obey him; all official documents in the country were to be drawn up in his name; he was to assume the purple and wear golden ornaments. No member of the public or the priesthood was to be allowed to set aside any one of these articles or contest his decisions, or convene a meeting anywhere in the country without his leave, or assume the purple or wear the golden brooch. Anyone contravening or rejecting any of these articles was to be liable at law. All the people consented to grant Simon the right to act on these decisions. And Simon accepted and consented to assume the high-priestly office and to act as military commissioner and ethnarch of the Jews and their priests, and to preside over all."

> They ordered that this decree should be inscribed on bronze tablets and set up in the Temple precinct in a prominent place, and that copies should be deposited in the treasury, and made available to Simon and his sons. (14:35-49)

Even those later Hasmonean rulers who referred to themselves as kings in Greek, cautiously continued to refer to themselves as high priests and *nesiim* in Hebrew, as attested by their coins and documents.

In both cases, these political covenants confirmed the inauguration of new constitutional epochs for the Jewish people. Characteristic of the first was the abjuration of monarchic leadership in favor of what has been termed theocracy but is better characterized as a nomocracy in which powers of government were shared by priests, *soferim* ("secretaries" as in Secretary of State), and an assembly of family heads and notables. In the second epoch, a strong executive leader was added to the structure of the regime.

In the immediate postbiblical period, Jewish political thought took two directions that had a vital impact on later generations' view of the covenant idea. Under Hellenistic influences, an attempt was made to reconcile the biblical and philosophical worldviews by recasting the history of ancient Israel and the political teaching of the Bible in Greek modes. Philo and Josephus are the two most prominent exemplars of this effort. The effort was made to satisfy Jews who had come under Hellenistic influences and to explain Judaism to the non-Jewish world that engulfed it. This tended to substantially reduce the emphasis on the covenant idea, which was not indigenous to Greek thought, in Jewish intellectual circles. It had a lasting influence on our understanding of the Jewish political tradition, precisely because it filtered that tradition through a very powerful and compelling non-Jewish filter.[6] Nevertheless, the continued utilization of the principle shows through in the descriptions of actual political behavior from that period, as in the case of the elevation of Simon and his Hasmonean heirs to leadership.

New Institutions—New Covenants

The epoch initiated by the Hasmonean revolution reached a climax in the destruction of the Second Temple (70 C.E.) and came to an end after the failure of the Bar Kokhba rebellion. Subsequently, such institutions of national authority as the Jews were able to maintain (e.g., the Patriarchate in Israel and the Exilarchate in Babylonia) were formally instituted by the foreign powers holding dominion over them as much as by the Jews and existed at the sufferance of those powers. Nevertheless, the Jewish people were recognized as a nation in exile, entitled to live under their own laws and, hence, to maintain their own political institutions within the framework of the host polity. One of the struggles of the two millennia following the loss of Jewish political sovereignty in their own land involved the Jews' effort to infuse their own consensual-covenantal dimension into institutions that were designed to rule them hierarchically precisely because they were forced upon them by foreign powers seeking to keep control over them.[7]

The Babylonian case (along with that of modern France) represents the hard case in the scheme. The fact that the Talmud was developed in Babylonia under the conditions that prevailed requires us to consider the implications of that case. What is significant about it is the way in which Jews succeeded in reintroducing the familiar and by then traditional framework through various internal devices. Thus, the Talmud discusses appointments to the district courts, which were made by the Exilarch in consultation with the appropriate *Yeshivah* (Assembly of Torah authorities) and how the Jewish communities insisted on parallel local appointees as well as local veto powers over the Exilarch's appointees after they appeared on the local scene: "When he (the Exilarch-appointed judge) reaches his destination (a particular community), he chooses two of the important men of the town to sit with him."

This problem is reflected in the Chronicle of Rabbi Nathan, which describes how the community acted to assume a role in the appointment of the Exilarch, a position that was actually hereditary: "When he is appointed, if the mind of the community has agreed to appoint him, the two heads of the Yeshivot met with their students and all the heads of the congregation and the elders appoint." In this way the dual principles of consent and power sharing were at least formally maintained.[8]

In the interim, however, the Jews had developed a device through which to maintain their own autonomy and in a covenantal manner, namely, the local house of congregation or assembly, in Hebrew, *bet knesset*, which is generally known by its Greek name, "synagogue." The congregation (in Hebrew, *kahal*) with its *bet knesset* or synagogue became a crucial vehicle for Jewish self-expression precisely because it was based upon authentic Jewish political principles and was eminently suited to the wide variety of conditions under which Jews found themselves in their dispersion. As an institution, a congregation could be established anywhere, wherever ten Jewish males came together. Thoroughly portable, it could adapt itself to particular geo-historical conditions to provide the Jews with whatever degree of self-government they were allowed and had the strength to maintain. Thus, in the land of Israel and later in the small Jewish settlements of the medieval diaspora it was usually synonymous with the local community, where it was given the Hebrew name *kahal* or *kehillah,* while in the great Hellenistic cities, and later in the great cities of Europe and America, it was perhaps one of several synagogues, sometimes linked within a larger communal framework on a federal or confederal basis and sometimes independent for all intents and purposes.

The *bet knesset* emerged during the Babylonian exile, in the sixth century B.C.E., as a partial substitute for the lost Judean polity. It was brought back to Judea by the returnees, from whence it spread to the entire Jewish world, becoming the instrument for establishing an organized Jewish community wherever the dispersed people found themselves. Under Jewish law, any ten males of the age of thirteen or beyond can constitute themselves into a *kahal* whose seat is the *bet knesset,* which, in the absence of any more comprehensive authority, has the power to enact ordinances and exercise judicial powers within the framework of the Torah.

Every congregation by its very nature came into existence through a pact or covenant between its founders, which was extended to those who subsequently became joined to it. Although there is some dispute in the halakhic literature with regard to the precise legal implications of this, in effect every local Jewish community, as a congregation, was considered to be a kind of partnership based upon a common contractual obligation within the framework of the overall Jewish constitution, namely, the Torah. In the Sephardic world, these compacts came to be called *askamot,* perhaps best translated as articles of agreement. The flexibility of this form led to a variety of arrangements depending on local circumstances. In some communities, the entire community was organized as a single congregation with the appropriate governing bodies usually divided along functional lines. On the other extreme, the community as a whole consisted of a loose league of many independent congregations, each of which represented a particular religious point of view or socioeconomic distinction.

Thus, the Jews invented what may be the ultimate covenantal instrument of constitutional design: portable; flexible in its membership, scope and powers; modular; based on public consent. It is no wonder that this instrument was later adopted by Protestant Christians at the time of the

Reformation and influenced institutional design throughout the mono-theistic world.

From the time of the organization of the *Mishnah* in the mid-second century C.E. until the middle of the eleventh century, the vast majority of world Jewry lived in communities that functioned within larger *edah*-wide frameworks, which were also covenantal in character, at first centered in Eretz Israel and then in Babylonia. In the first, power was divided between the *Nasi* and the Sanhedrin and in the second between the *Resh Galuta* (literally, Head of the Exile) and the two principal *Yeshivot* (*ye-shiva* = *knesset* = assembly).

Both ended up as classical manifestations of the *ketaric* division into domains, although both developed from quite different starting points. In Eretz Israel, after the destruction of the Temple, the priesthood lost whatever power in the *keter kehunah* that remained in its hands and the chance for national leadership in the *keter malkhut* also disappeared. *Keter torah* was the only domain that was able to survive in its full sense. According to the Talmud, Rabban Yochanan ben Zakkai, the foremost sage of the time, had himself smuggled out of Jerusalem in the latter stages of the Great Revolt and secured from the Romans the right to open an academy in Yavneh out of which there developed the Pharisaic-led Sanhedrin of the last generation of the first century of the common era.

Within that academy there was a power struggle between Pharisaic representatives of the priestly families and scholars drawn from the ranks of the rest of Israel. The latter won, preventing the extension of special privileges or status to the former other than in very formalistic ways (e.g., administering the priestly blessing during prayer in the Beit Knesset). In the two generations following the Bar Kochba revolt, the Sanhedrin, that is, the *keter torah*, had well-nigh exclusive powers within the Jewish community of Eretz Israel, with national leadership provided by the *nasi*, an office developed jointly by the Jews and the Romans and occupied by a member of the leading family in the Sanhedrin. At the end of the second century of the common era, however, the *nasi* and his office, with Roman assistance, had become sufficiently separated from the Sanhedrin to become the expression of the *keter malkhut*, while leadership of the Sanhedrin passed to the *av beit din* (literally, the head of the court), who served in a role somewhat analogous to speaker of the house).

In Babylonia the process was just the reverse. The office of Resh Galuta was established first by the foreign suzerein with the support of the Jewish community. Hereditary and also claiming descent from David, the Resh Galuta briefly exercised essentially absolute power over the Jewish population of the Parthian empire. However, within generations two major yeshivot had developed and claimed for themselves the right to interpret the Torah and to bind the Resh Galuta by their interpretations. A power struggle ensued, which ended with a power-sharing agreement whereby the strong institutions that emerged within the *keter torah* were reorganized by the empire. The Resh Galuta remained as head of the *keter malkhut* while the two yeshivot became strong institutional embodiments of the *keter torah,* sharing power with him.

The establishment of the great Babylonian *Yeshivot* and the struggle between the leaders of those academies and the Exilarch is reflected in *Bereshith Rabbah,* the Midrashic commentary on the Book of Genesis, in its comments on the biblical verse (Gen. 49:10): "The scepter shall not depart from Judah, nor the ruler's staff from between his legs." According to the Midrash, "The scepter" is interpreted as the Exilarchs in Babylon, who rule the people, Israel, with the stick, while "the ruler's staff" represents the patriarchs of the family of Rav, who teach the Torah to the populace in the land of Israel.

Another explanation of the verse is offered:

> The scepter is the Messiah, son of David (*Mashiach ben David*), who will rule over the kingdom, that is to say, Rome, with a stick. And the ruler's staff are those who teach *Halakhah* to Israel.
>
> Even after the Messiah comes, there will have to be a separation of powers, for even the Messiah is not to be trusted with all the powers alone. Even if he can rule over Rome, there still must be the great Sanhedrin to teach *Halakhah* to Israel.[9]

Even the *keter kehunah* had something of a revival, though strictly on the local plane, through the emergence of the *hazan* (governor) and other officiants of the bet knesset. Thus, the tripartite division was restored because the Jewish people could not function comprehensively without it.

In the fourth century C.E., the Roman Empire became officially Christian and divided into two. The Eastern Empire, ruled from Byzantium, applied extraordinarily oppressive measures to the Jewish community of Eretz Israel. Consequently, this community diminished in size and importance until, by the end of the fifth century, the principal leadership role in world Jewry had shifted to the Jewish community of Babylonia, which lived under better conditions.

After the rise of Islam in the seventh century, and the Arab conquest of western Asia, North Africa, and the Iberian Peninsula, well over 90 percent of the Jews came within a common imperial regime where they lived under their own authorities, consisting of the Resh Galuta and yeshivot of Babylonia. That situation persisted for several centuries but began to become unraveled by the end of the tenth century as parts of the Arab empire seceded, de facto or de jure. At the same time, Jews began to move north of the Alps in pursuit of economic opportunity or security in small but significant numbers and to organize themselves into separate, small, local communities.

The Kehillah: A Covenantal Partnership

By the middle of the eleventh century, changes in world conditions shifted the balance of power within the Jewish world to Europe where no such overarching institutions were able to take root because of the fragmented character of European political organization.

The associational model that emerged from this enforced localism was the congregational form that became the basis for the entire web of Jewish communal organization in the European diaspora. As Jews found themselves in new locales, they utilized the power provided them by the Talmud to organize themselves into authoritative communities through covenants. This is reflected in *Sefer HaShtarot* (The Book of Contracts) compiled in eleventh-century Aragon by R. Judah HaBarceloni as the classic collection of model laws for the governance of the Jewish people in the Middle Ages. *Sefer HaShtarot* includes, inter alia, a model charter for establishing a congregation-community, whose preamble (an excellent example of the style of covenant documents essentially unchanged since the first ancient Near Eastern vassal covenants) is worth quoting in full:

We, the elders and leaders of the community of -x-, due to our many sins we have declined and become fewer and weaker, and until only few have been left of many, like a single tree at the mountaintop, and the people of our community have been left with no head or *nasi*, or head justice or leader, so that they are like sheep without a shepherd and some of our community go about improperly clothed and some speak obscenely and some mix with the gentiles and eat their bread and become like them, so that only in the Jewish name, are they at all different. We have seen and discussed the matter and we agreed in assembly of the entire community, and we all, great and small alike, have gone on to establish this charter in this community.

The model charter continues to describe how the community, by this action, establishes its right to enact ordinances, establish institutions, levy and collect taxes, in short, carry on all the functions of a municipal government.[10]

The principles of community enunciated in the foregoing document are clear. In order for the actions of a community to be legally binding in Jewish law, it had to be duly constituted by its potential members, preferably through a constituent assembly and a constitutional document. They must be able to say that "we have met together as the elders," that "we have discussed the matter," that "we have agreed in assembly of the entire community" (recall the descriptions of covenanting in the Bible). If these patterns were not followed, the action would not be valid.

In those cases where communities created intercommunity confederations, as in northern France and the Rhineland, the Council of the Communities of Aragon, and the Council of the Four Lands in Poland, such covenants were used to restore the second stage of federal organization within the overall constitutional framework.[11] Within communities, individual *hevrot* (associations, from *haver*, comrade or partner) were similarly organized as partnerships on a subcommunal basis, usually with some functional orientation.[12] This trend, which became prominent after 1348, reached its apotheosis in the Council of the Four Lands (1568-1764), the federation of Jewish communities in Poland.

The great questions of power and authority in the medieval Jewish community were for the most part based upon differences of opinion regarding the implications of this covenantal base. So, for example, questions of the apportionment of taxation or the reduction of air rights (so important in densely populated medieval towns) were often related to the issue as to whether or not the community was a partnership, and if so, what were the rights of the partners. In essence, the partnership issue was important in all questions of whether decisions could be made by majority vote or required unanimity.[13] Thus, Rashba (R. Shlomo ben Aderet), who, along with Rabbi Meir of Rothenberg, established the constitutional and jurisprudential basis for the medieval Jewish community, responded to a question from the Jewish community of Lerida in fourteenth-century Spain as follows:

> In all matters of the community, no one part of the community is permitted to do so as they please, unless the entire community consents. For the community are as partners in all communal responsibilities and in all communal appointments, such as tax collectors, unless there exist men who have been appointed to deal with communal affairs; those who are called by our sages the seven *tuvei ha'ir*. In most places, nowadays, the important men of the community direct the affairs of the community in consultation and agreement. In general, it is assumed that the individual avoids his own opinion, but if some of the community, even from among those who are not great in wisdom, object, their objection stands. This is certainly so, where the objection is made by some of the men who are normally those to be consulted.

This was qualified in a further response to the Jews of Saragossa:

> The customs of different locales differ in these matters, for there are places where all matters are handled by their elders and advisors, and there are places where even the council can do nothing without the consent of the entire congregation in which there is found the agreement of all, and there are places which appoint for themselves a group of men whose direction they will follow for a given period of time in all matters related to the group.

This is the kind of debate that can only occur in a covenant-created setting where what is at stake is the definition of how much autonomy each partner maintains. The resolution of this issue (and there are opinions on both sides) is less important for our purposes here than the fact that it was an issue at all, that the discussion was not whether there should be rule by one or by the few or by the many, but whether in a system in which the many were assumed to rule, how they were to arrive at their decisions. The fact that many communities did become oligarchies and a few even fell under autocratic domination is significant and deserves exploration in its own right as well as in relationship to the theory, but the theory also reflected real circumstances, perhaps more so than any of the other forms. We know this because we find records of the debate, not in the esoteric writings of learned men and abstract thinkers but in the responsa (legal opinions) of the great sages of those generations, who were forced to adjudicate real disputes.[14]

These questions took on special importance in cases involving the admission of new members to the community, particularly people who wanted to move in from outside in situations where the non-Jewish ruling power made living conditions particularly difficult for the existing Jewish residents.[15] In short, the greater part of Jewish public law in the medieval period had to do with interpreting the meaning of pacts and the rights and obligations of those who came to be party to them, so much so that several historians of the period have correctly suggested that Jewish thought on these matters follows along the same lines as that of Hobbes, Locke, and other seventeenth-century social compact theorists. Without minimizing the differences between the secularizing elements of the latter and the piety associated with the former, it is important to recall that both schools flowed from a common source.[16]

The eminent Israeli scholar and jurist Menachem Elon, who has pioneered in the study of Hebrew law, has claimed that as a result of the changed circumstances in which the Jews of Europe found themselves there was a veritable constitutional revolution in Jewish public law in the twelfth and early thirteenth centuries resting on covenantal principles. Drawing upon the biblical and Talmudic bases, the foremost rabbinical authorities of the time constructed through their *responsa* a constitutional law that enabled the Jewish people to preserve their autonomy through these *kehillot*, but ground their authority and powers within a *halakhic* framework. To do so it was necessary to draw upon the covenantal tradition going back to the Bible itself, to the point where *responsa* dealing with these matters often went straight back to the biblical text for authoritative citation.[17]

Covenant Ceremonies

One group of Jews has maintained a formal annual covenant renewal ceremony throughout the ages. These are the Jews of Ethiopia who have a fall holiday, falling in the Hebrew month of Heshvan (October-November), known as the Festival of the Oath. Every year all of the Jews of Ethiopia, men, women, and children from all the villages, come together on the summit of a high hill in the Gondar region, led by their priests who read appropriate chapters from the Torah before the assembled multitude, accompanied by moral preaching regarding relations between man and God and man and man, after which all swear their loyalty to the Torah and to each other as a community. The Ethiopian Jews consider this ceremony as a continuation of the covenant renewal of Ezra and Nehemiah.[18]

Less exotic Jews have their covenant renewal ceremonies built into the ordinary flow of Jewish practice. At their most prosaic, the three daily services, which every Jew is commanded to perform, devote a major part of the liturgy to reaffirming acceptance of the covenant.[19] Sabbaths, holidays, and festivals all have added elements of covenant reaffirmation culminating in the Additional (*mussaf*) Service on Rosh Hashanah, the Jewish New Year, which consists in essence of a massive covenant renewal ceremony based upon the three basic elements of covenanting—*malkhuyot*, the proclamation of God's sovereignty; *zichronot*, the remembrance of the covenant; and *shofrot*, the proclamation of covenant loyalty.

Traditionally at least since the days of Ezra, every seven years there is a formal national ceremony of covenant reaffirmation known as *hakhel*, or assembling (from *kahal*). This *hakhel* takes place during the interim days of Sukkot at the end of the sabbatical year when the whole people is to gather in Jerusalem in the presence of king, prophets, and priests— the three *ketarim*—with each playing a role in a common covenant renewal ceremony. The king as the head of the civil authority is to read from the Torah in the presence of prophet, priests, and people, who are to answer "amen," that is to say, to reaffirm their covenantal commitment. In modern Israel this ceremony has been revived with the president of the state reading the Torah in the presence of the chief rabbis and the people in approximation of the classic assembly.

Notes

1. See, for example, Arnold Jacob Wolf, ed., *Rediscovering Judaism* (Chicago: Quadrangle Books, 1965), which includes essays by several of the principal North American exponents of this covenant theology, and Jakob J. Petuchowski, *Ever Since Sinai* (Milwaukee: B. Arbit Books, 1979). Martin Buber emphasizes the covenant in all of his works. Rabbi J. D. Soloveichik, among others, refers to two separate covenants, of fate and faith, in "Lonely Man of Faith," *Tradition* 14, no. 3 (Summer 1974). Since he takes the covenant and basis of Jewish peoplehood seriously, his discussion deserved particular notice even if it is only tangentially political in orientation. See also Harold Fisch, *Jerusalem and Albion* (New York: Schocken Books, 1964) for an examination of the modern secularization of the covenant idea and John F. A. Taylor, *The Masks of Society, an Inquiry into the Covenants of Civilization* (New York: Appleton-Century-Crofts, 1966) for a contemporary American covenantal perspective. While this article seeks to expound and even shift our understanding of the covenant idea to include and emphasize its political dimension, it also uses theological terminology throughout because

the Jewish political tradition of necessity has a philosophic base. Political theology has declined in importance in the West in recent generations; hence, the usages may be somewhat unfamiliar to the reader, but it is nonetheless an old element in political science and legitimate in every respect.

2. I am indebted to Ella Belfer for drawing my attention to this combination/contradiction. See Ella Belfer, *Am Israel u-Malkhut Shamayim—Iyunim baMusag heTheokratia haYehudit* (The People of Israel and the Kingdom of Heaven—Studies in Jewish Theocracy) (Ramat Gan: Bar-Ilan University, Dept. of Political Studies, Covenant Working Paper No. 11), also presented to World Congress of Jewish Studies, 1977.

3. Moshe Weinfeld, "From God's Edah to the Chosen Dynasty: The Transition from the Tribal Federation to the Monarchy," in *Kinship and Consent, the Jewish Political Tradition and Its Contemporary Manifestations*, ed. Daniel J. Elazar (Ramat Gan: Turtledove Publishing, 1981). See also Daniel J. Elazar, "Kinship and Consent in the Jewish Community: Patterns of Continuity in Jewish Communal Life," *Tradition* 14, no. 4 (Fall 1974): 63–79.

4. Leo Baeck, *This People Israel: The Meaning of Jewish Existence* (Philadelphia: Jewish Publication Society of America, 1964).

5. Cf. Salo W. Baron, *The Jewish Community: Its History and Structure to the American Revolution*, 3 vols. (Philadelphia: Jewish Publication Society, 1942), esp. chaps. 2-3; Victor Tcherikover, *Hellenistic Civilization and the Jews* (Philadelphia: Jewish Publication Society, 1959); and Solomon Zeitlin, *The Rise and Fall of the Judean State: A Political, Social and Religious History of the Second Commonwealth*, 3 vols. (Philadelphia: Jewish Publication Society, 1968).

6. Cf. Flavius Josephus, *The Jewish War*, trans. G. A. Williamson (Harmondsworth: Penguin, 1980); *The Antiquities of the Jews*, especially "The Polity Settled by Moses," trans. H.St.J. Thackeray, Loeb Classical Library (Cambridge, MA: Harvard University Press, 1934); *Jerusalem and Rome: The Writings of Josephus* (New York: Meridian Books, 1960).

The best and most accessible English translations of Philo of Alexandria's writings are found in *Three Jewish Philosophers*, ed. Hans Lewy (New York: Atheneum, 1969). The complete edition of Philo's works in Greek with English translation has been published in the Loeb Classical Series, trans. F. H. Colson and G. H. Whitaker (Boston: Harvard University Press, 1929-1962).

For the best single work on Philo, see Harry Austryn Wolfson, *Philo: Foundations of Religious Philosophy in Judaism, Christianity and Islam*, 2 vols. (Cambridge, MA: Harvard University Press, 1947).

7. For a description of those efforts see Michael Avi-Yonah, *The Jews of Palestine, a Political History from the Bar Kokhba War to the Arab Conquest* (New York: Schocken Books, 1976).

8. For a study of power relationships in Babylonian Jewry, see Jacob Neusner, *There They Sat Down* (Nashville and New York: Abingdon Press, 1972).

9. *Bereshith Rabbah.*

10. Judah HaBarceloni, *Sefer HaShtarot.*

11. Louis Finkelstein, *Jewish Self-Government in the Middle Ages* (New York: Philip Feldheim, 1964); Daniel J. Elazar and Stuart Cohen, *The Jewish Polity* (Bloomington: Indiana University Press, 1985), Epoch 11.

12. Salo W. Baron, *The Jewish Community*, 3 vols. (Philadelphia: Jewish Publication Society, 1938-1942).

13. Menachem Elon, "Authority and Power in the Jewish Community" in Elazar, ed., *Kinship and Consent*; Irving A. Agus, *Urban Civilization in Pre-Crusade Europe*, 2 vols. (New York: Yeshiva University Press, 1968), 2 vols.; and Isadore Epstein, *Studies in the Communal Life of the Jews of Spain* (New York: Herman Press, 1968). This writer follows Elon in the view that, more often than not, majority rule was the accepted standard, a position entirely consistent with the covenant principle. The more important point is that either position supports the thesis advanced here.

14. Thus, the Workshop in the Covenant Idea and the Jewish Political Tradition, in cooperation with the Responsa Project at Bar-Ilan University, has systematically identified hundreds of practical applications of the word *brit* in the selected responsa presently stored in the project's computer. They are now being classified and analyzed.

15. Gerald Blidstein, "Individual and Community in the Middle Ages: Halakhic Theory," in Elazar, ed., *Kinship and Consent*; and *Notes on Hefker Bet-Din in Talmudic and Medieval Law* (Jerusalem: Center for Jewish Community Studies, 1975).

16. Blidstein "Individual and Community" and *Notes on Hefker*. Elon, "Authority and Power"; Agus, *Urban Civilization*; Epstein, *Studies in the Communal Life*.

17. Menachem Elon, *The Principles of Jewish Law* (Jerusalem: Encyclopedia Judaica, 1975).

18. See A. Z. Escholi, *Sefer HaFalashim Yehudai Habash Tarbutam u'Masoroteihem* (Jerusalem: Reuven Maas, 1943) and Yael Kahana, *Achim Shchorim: Haim B'Kerev HaFalashim* (Tel Aviv: Am Oved, 1977).

19. Cf. Gordon Freeman, *The Politics of Prayer* (Philadelphia: Center for Jewish Community Studies, 1977), Covenant Workshop Paper CW5.

22

The Covenant Tradition in Modernity

Modern Adaptations

With the breakdown of the medieval community, diaspora Jewry had to reorganize itself once again. As the Jewish people ceased to be regarded in the West as a nation among the nations, their polity ceased to be a state within a state. The reorganization was partly forced upon the Jews by the governing authorities of the new nation-states that emerged in the seventeenth century and subsequently, and partly followed internal Jewish initiatives seeking to adjust to the situation. It resulted in the creation of quasi-voluntary communities in the sense that Jews could now choose to cease to be Jews but, if they chose to remain within the Jewish fold, they had to be members of a Jewish community.

Perhaps more surprisingly, we can also trace one stream of the Jewish political tradition that was outside the traditional *halakhic* and Jewish framework and went into the modern epoch. Baruch Spinoza was both a catalyst and a bridge for this phenomenon. Spinoza was the first modern secular Jew as well as one of the most important architects of modernity. He himself rejected and was rejected by the Jewish community of Amsterdam but his cultural roots were Jewish and even though he saw himself as becoming a fully modern man rooted in European, even European Christian, culture, he remained what he was, well-educated in the Bible and its traditional commentaries, a man who could enter into a debate with Maimonides (through his works of course) and advocate an alternative political vision (thereby, incidentally, adding another confirmation to the essentially political character of Maimonides' thought and reaffirming its importance as part of the Western philosophic tradition).

Spinoza is regarded as the founder of modern biblical criticism, which he developed for his own political purposes but that led others down an important scholarly path. His *Tractatus Theologicus Politicus* was not only his most important political work that laid the foundations for his political teaching, but an important study of the ancient Jewish polity and its political tradition in its own right. It seems Spinoza did not care at all about retaining any Jewish ties and he wrote in order to reach the dominant Christian majority, but Jews seeking to leave the ghetto seized upon his philosophy as the key to their own European future.

Not only did Spinoza's thought lie at the basis of the worldview of every Jewish assimilationist, no matter how he or she wished to assimilate, but it also formed the basis for the leading streams in Jewish thought that tried to reconstruct Judaism on a modern basis, beginning with Moses Mendelssohn himself who found in Spinoza the modern foundations of his Jewish thought, and continuing through the other figures including Moses Hess, a strong Spinozist and one of the fathers of modern Zionism who based his thinking on Spinoza's suggestion that the Jewish political tradition was only valid in a Jewish state and that if a Jewish state should ever be reconstituted, it could be revived. Hess proposed doing just that.

Spinoza's influence continues on to our own day where Israeli professor Yirmiyahu Yovel has tried to base a new secular Israeli Judaism on Spinoza's thought. While not every Jewish thinker cites Spinoza, his influence on them all is apparent whether mentioned by name or not. While many if not most of his heirs lost the sense of the Jewish political tradition that Spinoza had, his work remains accessible to all to rediscover that tradition, at least substantial parts of it.

The fact that Spinoza's modern political thought provided the foundation for modern democracy is not incidental either. Spinoza's democracy was secular and was based at least in part on an attack on the theo-political bases of earlier traditions, including Jewish tradition (indeed, he used Jewish tradition as a target because it was easy to do and did not bring him into direct confrontation with the Christian world). The result was a kind of secularized version of that tradition in the same way that Hobbes, Locke, and their successors were to provide a secularized version of the Reformed Protestant reinterpretation of that tradition. Hobbes, indeed, was the single greatest philosophic influence on Spinoza, who cites him frequently. Because Spinoza, like Hobbes and Locke, had to attack the existing worldview to advance their own, this is often overlooked by subsequent students of their works, but in fact they represent as much a continuity as a discontinuity in that tradition.

In the end, even traditional rabbis who wanted to absorb elements of modernism into traditional frameworks were attracted to Spinoza who, whether he intended to or not, gave them a way to reinterpret the Jewish political tradition in modern democratic terms without doing it any serious injustice. Thus Spinoza provided a bridge across which the tradition could be stretched.

Spinoza scholars generally agree that what Spinoza wanted was the total assimilation of the Jews into Western European culture. What came out in the end may have come out in contradiction to his hopes but it was both very real and very important nonetheless. Indeed, the founders of modern Israel led by Ben-Gurion himself were keen followers of Spinoza and many, including Ben-Gurion, said so explicitly.

In nineteenth-century Eastern Europe, the *shtetl* became the archetypical covenantal community. Since the Russian authorities in particular made every effort to destroy the formal institutions of Jewish self-government, Jews were forced to retreat into the sociological community more than at any other time in their history. In their classic study of the *shtetl, Life is With People,* Zborowski and Herzog describe the *shtetl* as the covenanted community par excellence.

Perhaps ironically, as the Jewish community in the Russian empire lost its political autonomy, the *shtetl*, its principal form of settlement, became from a sociological perspective even more completely the covenanted community.[1]

At the other end of Europe, German Jewry, which had passed through the process of emancipation and no longer lived in self-contained communities, was positing the congregation as the continuation of the covenanted community.[2] Legally, these communities were religious associations organized on a membership basis in keeping with the associational or contractual character of modern liberal society. In the Germanies and the other Central European countries under Germanic influence, local communities were further federated into countrywide bodies.

In France, a centralistic pattern common to modern French society was imposed upon the Jewish community as well, while the Jewries of Great Britain were united in a union of congregations just as the United Kingdom was a union of countries. In short, there was an even greater tendency than in previous epochs for the local Jewish community to take on the organizational characteristics of its host environment, at least in externals. In this case, however, the organizational forms of modern society served to strengthen the contractual character of the communities more often than not. Whatever the formal framework, the associative and increasingly voluntary character of the community maintained the by now traditionally Jewish covenantal base in the forefront, even if the community itself functioned on a reduced basis.[3]

Replacing the local covenantal communities in Eastern Europe at the end of the nineteenth century were new mass-oriented political movements, Zionist or revolutionary in orientation. The Jewish Workers Bund, established in the Russian empire in 1897 to advance socialism among the Jews of that empire and the world, is a secular example of the persistence of covenant in the Jewish political tradition. This group of secularized Jews, many if not most of whom had abandoned traditional Jewish religion to devote their messianic fervor to what they believed was a more worldly form of redemption, still permeated their movement with covenantal structures and symbols. The very term *Bund,* meaning covenant or federation, says it all. In addition, their hymn, written by S. Ansky, famed author of *The Dybbuk,* was called Der Shvua, or the oath. The organization had a federated structure based upon a secularized version of the covenanting of all members with one another to work together to achieve their utopian socialist dream.

The indigenous Bund was wiped out in the USSR in the early 1920s. While the Bolsheviks claimed they were opposing Jewish separatism, given their willingness to tolerate and even encourage the self-expression of other Soviet peoples, one might assume that the real reason was that the form that Jewish self-expression took was covenantal, ergo, free, and that assaulted the very foundations of the totalitarian state and society that the Bolsheviks were trying to build.

In the New World, the voluntary character of the Jewish community was total from the very first. Even where Jews were not fully admitted into the larger society, nowhere in the New World were they required to be members of a Jewish community. While kinship propelled them toward membership, affiliation came only on the basis of active consent. As a result, Jewish institutions were built on an entirely voluntary or associative basis. The initial affiliation of Jews was voluntary and the subsequent linkage among Jewish organizations was even more so.

The Jewish response to New World conditions was to adapt the covenant principle through federative arrangements, generally without any conscious awareness that they were continuing the Jewish political tradition. In the United States, the Jews developed federations of Jewish social service agencies, on the one hand, and federations of congregations on the other.[4] In Canada, they developed the Canadian Jewish Congress, a countrywide federation of local communities compounded out of community relations and Zionist bodies.[5] In Latin America, country-of-origin groups formed their own communities, which, over time, confederated with one another to create citywide or countrywide bodies for limited purposes.[6] Whatever the particular form, characteristic of the whole was the covenantal relationship and the institutional structures and processes that flowed from it.

Perhaps the last of the great traditional political commentators to focus on the covenantal political tradition in his commentary was Meir Leibush (Malbim), who wrote in Romania in the late nineteenth century. His commentary has been added to the canon of biblical commentaries in the tradition of the great medieval Bible commentators. Malbim deviates from the thrust of the post-medieval Eastern European biblical commentators who did not look at the Bible in all its facets by including its political dimensions and devoting substantial sections of his commentary to discussing matters political and thereby building a political teaching. Malbim left us with an extensive political teaching that can be culled from his commentaries without difficulty. In that respect, he was in the tradition of Abravanel and Nachmanides.

Rabbi Haim Herschensohn (born in Eretz Israel in 1856 and died in Hoboken, New Jersey in 1930) was a growing boy in Malbim's time; his writing was done a generation after Malbim's death. He was the first of the Eastern European-style rabbis to seek to trace out the Jewish political tradition, especially its covenantal dimensions, in a more modern way through systematic and thematic organization, not as commentaries on the Bible and other traditional works. The first, *Eleh Divrei HaBrit* (These are the Words of the Covenant), was written at the time of World War I in response to Woodrow Wilson's Fourteen Points and the establishment of the League of Nations. Inspired by Wilsonian covenantalism, Herschensohn produced four volumes. In them he found a biblical basis for Wilsonian ideas and presented that basis comprehensively in a traditional Jewish manner.

Several years later, Herschensohn produced *Malkhi Bakodesh* (My Holy Kingdom), a six volume work developed in response to the letter that the British Foreign Secretary, Arthur James Balfour wrote to Lord Rothschild indicating that "His Majesty's government views with favor the establishment of the Jewish national home in Palestine." It became known as the Balfour Declaration and was the foundation stone of international recognition of the legitimacy of the Zionist effort in the land of Israel. Herschensohn saw a Jewish state in the offing and sought to ground it in the Jewish tradition. So he turned to traditional sources to provide a comprehensive view of what that state should be like, dealing with such difficult questions as women's suffrage, as well as more conventional ones such as governmental organization, all within a *halakhically* legitimate framework.

Herschensohn's work was as extraordinary as it was neglected at the time, but it has since been reviewed by Professor Eliezer Schweid, one of Israel's leading thinkers, who analyzed it in a book *Democracy and Halakhah*,[7] as well as by this writer. Herschensohn himself had long since been driven out of the land of Israel by the ultra orthodox precursors of today's anti-Zionist rejectionists who refused to recognize the Jewish state. The political tradition that he exemplified was to continue in the new world, after taking several twists. His daughter, Tamar, married Rabbi David deSola Pool, the rabbi of Shearith Israel in New York, the oldest synagogue in North America, and their son, Ithiel, became a noted political scientist whose own works were among the leading products of the field in the post-World War II years. Herschensohn's works were among the last to devote very substantial attention to the Jewish political tradition in its traditional format and his emphasis on covenant is very important. At the very intersection of the end of traditional Jewish society and the rebirth of Israel as a modern Jewish state, he gives us a summary of that tradition in all of its covenantal-political dimensions as a summary and a starting point.

The real influence of the covenantal tradition on modern Jewry was far less direct, but culture and circumstance combined to make it no less real. Jews coming to the United States and rapidly acculturating into American society discovered, to their immense pleasure, that American society was founded on the covenantal tradition brought to British North America by the Puritans and others, which, in turn, derived from the Reformed Protestant understanding of the Bible. The more they acculturated, the more American Jews identified with that tradition in one way or another, sensing that it legitimized them as Americans.

More important, the nonhierarchical, egalitarian thrust of American society had its impact on the Jews, reinforcing their own nonhierarchical, egalitarian culture. Efforts to build Jewish institutions on organic principles acquired in Europe were found to be inapplicable; for example, efforts to establish religious authority along those lines through a chief rabbinate failed almost before they began. Efforts to force Jewish involvement and commitment based upon a monopolistic structure may have made a bit more headway for a short time if they were sufficiently democratic in their organization. But they, too, failed often as a result of other Jews using the U.S. Constitution to protect their competitive rights.

On the other hand, Jewish welfare federations, now known as Jewish community federations, were organized as federations of separate charitable eleemosynary and educational institutions and conquered the communities. At first, their leaders had problems with identifying the institutions as Jewish in an overt way that could be identified as religious, but when it became apparent to them, after the 1960s, that those institutions would only survive through an appropriate identification with Jewish ideas, they explicitly embraced covenantal ideas and covenantal terminology. These were especially prominent leadership development,[8] and campaigns to raise funds for Israel through their instrument, the United Jewish Appeal, whose slogans involve keeping the covenant in one form or another, meaning the sense of bonds and obligations between Jews wherever they might be.[9]

What took place in the United States was replicated to a greater or lesser extent in Jewish communities in other countries of the modern world.[10] This writer has described this in connection with the Jewish political tradition elsewhere. The situation in modern Israel is somewhat more complex. The first two generations of pioneers in Israel, including the pre-Zionist settlers who came after 1840 and the Zionist settlers of the period from 1880 to 1900, applied traditional principles of Jewish communal organization and hence were covenantal to the core, implicitly and overtly. The more radical socialists who began coming after 1904 saw state building as following along European statist lines and society building as following along socialist ones. Thus, they denigrated overt use of traditional forms, though, in fact, their culture led them to use many of those forms in their efforts, albeit under other names.

As I have discussed elsewhere, in *Israel, Building a New Society,*[11] Israel has been the site of a conflict between traditional Jewish political culture in modern form and European statist and socialist imports since then. The latter have given external form to the polity while the former are strongly manifested within that form. Thus, Jewish political culture has continued to be covenantal down to the present, even if at times the formal institutions of that culture have followed other models more accepted in those times.

Contemporary Israel

To no small extent, the reconstituted Jewish polity in Israel also reflects a continuation of the covenant tradition, although, after 1948, a state of the nineteenth-century European model was superimposed on what started as a continuation of older Jewish practice along new lines.[12] The beginnings of modern Jewish resettlement in the land followed the patterns of Jewish "colonization," which had apparently existed since the earliest days of the diaspora, adapted to local circumstances. That is to say, individual Jewish householders banded together to establish pioneering societies to accomplish specific or general tasks, whether the construction of new neighborhoods outside the walls of Jerusalem, or the establishment of agricultural settlements, or the organization of cooperative enterprises. In doing so, they covenanted or compacted together by drawing up articles of agreement reminiscent of those establishing medieval communities or modern congregations, which served as both covenants and constitutions for their enterprises. In many cases, these documents literally were called covenants by those responsible for them.[13]

Parallel to these developments in the land of Israel proper, Zionist societies were organized abroad on the same basis, as pioneering nuclei, as fundraising instrumentalities, or political action groups, finally coming together as the World Zionist Organization, which began as a federation of local or countrywide Zionist societies and rapidly became a federation of ideological-political movements. The Zionist experience is a classic example of the Jewish use of federative arrangements. Zionism as a whole quickly came to represent the common messianic movement at the cutting edge of modern Jewry. However, in the Jewish fashion, agreement as to a general messianic vision was accompanied by sharp disagreement as to the precise character of the goals to be achieved, which led in turn to the development of movements within the Zionist framework that were not only highly competitive on one level but essentially hostile to one another since they represented sharply different approaches to solving the Jewish and human problems to which Zionism was directed. Nevertheless, the movements quickly came to recognize the necessity for common action in order to advance both the common and specific elements in their respective goals.

The solution was a federation based upon inter- and cross-movement compacts for the sharing of power within the overall Zionist organization, and the division of resources within it. The coalition politics was based on the party key or proportional representation with each movement counted according to the support it received in Zionist elections. This became characteristic of the World Zionist Organization and, later, the state of Israel as the principal manifestations of this federative arrangement, the building blocks for all Zionist endeavors.

Parallel to the federation of parties, the Yishuv (the Hebrew term for the organized Jewish community in British Mandatory Palestine) in Israel constructed federations of settlements and institutions (for example, the Histadrut), which together comprised the "state on the way" of the interwar period.[14] In the process, movements developed that offered their members a comprehensive environment, providing them with educational facilities, social services, sports and recreational opportunities, and even military units. The end result was a system of consociational self-government. Its "pillars" were three grand political "camps": labor, civil, and religious, each embracing its own shifting congeries of political parties.[15]

The network of charters and compacts from both provided a constitutional basis for the rebuilding of the land, which culminated in the Declaration of Independence proclaiming the new state of Israel. The content of the Declaration, known in Hebrew as the Scroll of Independence, is, in itself, of constitutional significance in the traditional way, that is to say, as a founding covenant that sets forth the fundamental principles of the polity and the guidelines within which a constitution can be developed and a regime established without specifying either.[16] Israelis frequently recur to the Declaration in public debates on first principles and their application (e.g., civil rights, the Jewishness of the state) and Israel's

Supreme Court has recognized the constitutional status of at least part of the document.

While the Zionist pioneers relied upon Jewish political tradition, implicitly at least, in nation building, when it came to state building, they turned to the European models they knew, superimposing upon the network of compacts and charters a centralized and highly bureaucratic model of parliamentary democracy. In this respect at least, it is ironic that the communal structure of the diaspora remains closer to the Jewish political tradition than the new Jewish state. The end result was not a replacement of a covenantal orientation with a bureaucratic one but a great dysfunctionality between the formal structure and the ways of doing public business rooted in Jewish political culture.

The transfer of functions from the parties to the state transformed the former from comprehensive movements—states within a state-in-the-making—into competitors for the rewards that only the state could offer. This led to a network of compacts for the division of those rewards to limit competition and give each party its due share. Interparty compacts also survived in the various electoral blocks formed and reformed in the years since 1948 and in governmental coalition making. The latter actually rest upon signed documents hammered out among the partners.

The formal federative framework, as such, continued to persist only in the rural areas through the sectorial and territorial settlement federations such as the several kibbutz and moshav movements and the regional councils. There the gap between structure and practice has been much smaller, with notable results. In sum, where pre-state developments have survived, so too have federative arrangements. Where they have been replaced by post-1948 modes of organization or where such modes of organization have been instituted and have become dominant, only echoes of covenantal arrangements are to be found, by and large in the semi-formal substructure that has grown up within the centralized state to make the latter work.

Buber: Zionist Covenantal Thought

Out of Zionism there emerged at least one covenantal thinker who gained worldwide renown and whose thought had a universal impact—Martin Buber. Buber, like Herzl, came from an assimilated German Jewish family. He became enthralled with Hassidic Jewry, which he encountered through his grandfather, less for their outward style than for the covenantal teachings implicit in Hassidic tales. As part of his return to Judaism, Buber became a Zionist, subsequently settling in Eretz Israel where he was one of the first generation of professors at the Hebrew University. In the world he is best known for his theory of "I-Thou" versus "I-It" relationships and all that flowed from it, a clearly covenantal position.

Buber in his persona represented a felicitous convergence of time, place, and sensibility that brought him to give expression to all of the critical dimensions of covenant in Western civilization: its biblical foundations; its meaning for Jews, particularly the religious and social meaning it gave to the Zionist enterprise; its role in bringing about rapprochement between Jews and Christians, for whom he sought a covenant of reconciliation; for purposes of political and social justice; and as the basis for defining the universal relationship of humankind. The foundations of Buber's thought are to be found in his commentaries on the Hebrew Scriptures. While he deals with most facets of biblical polity and society, he is particularly concerned with kings and prophets, that is to say, the juxtaposition of civil and Divine rule.[17]

The culmination of Buber's work on the subject is his book *Kingship of God*.[18] Its title is taken from the traditional Jewish value concept used to describe the ideal polity, *malkhut shamayim*. There he presents what Bernard Susser has described as his anarcho-federalistic view of the holy commonwealth.[19] *Kingship of God* is basically a discussion of the tribal federation in the historical epoch that began with the Exodus and in Sinai and ended with the institution of kingship through Saul and David, as the classic Jewish polity because of its anarcho-federalistic character, that is to say, its existence as a quasi-voluntary league of individuals, families, and tribes that functioned through a minimum of coercion and a maximum of consent. This classic polity was founded on the classic biblical covenants, covenants that, according to Buber, were violated with the introduction of human kingship.

Buber applied this same model in his contemporary political theory, the culminating work of which was *Paths in Utopia*, his description of the kibbutz as the successful demonstration and, hence, proof that utopian socialism could work and that people need not turn to Marxian socialism and its offshoots with the coerciveness and terror that develop in their wake.[20] At the beginning of *Paths in Utopia*, Buber describes the ideal polity by quoting the definition first provided by the sixteenth-century Reformed Protestant political philosopher, Johannes Althusius: the bridge between medieval and modern federalism, the polity is a *consociatio consociationum,* a consociation of consociations or, in our terms, a federal association compounded of federal associations. He saw the kibbutz as the best model of the primary federal association out of which larger federal associations could be compounded.

Each of those federal associations was, for Buber, ideally to rest on appropriate I-Thou relationships, his universal and meta-political message. Thus, Buber closed the circle, beginning with his restoration of the covenantal meaning of Scripture, carrying it through to form a prescription for contemporary human political and social life whose prime exemplar he hoped would be the reconstituted Jewish commonwealth in the Land of Israel. Unlike many other philosophers but much in keeping with Jewish tradition, Buber put his life on the line in his effort to achieve this. In doing so he was personally disappointed by his confrontation with a much harsher reality than he envisaged when he began his thought in the salad days of the late nineteenth century and, for that matter, he disappointed others who were more prepared to adjust to those harsh realities. But his work stands as a twentieth-century landmark in covenantal thinking. In a sense he, more than anyone, revived systematic covenantal political thought in our times.

The New Covenant Theology and Its Political Implications

After World War II, there was a revival of the influence of the covenant idea in the diaspora after 150 years of emancipationist thought, which led in other directions. The revival began in the United States with the emergence of a school of covenant theologians in the late 1950s. While their concerns were theological and sociological and not political in the usual sense of the term, they stimulated people concerned with the Jewish community as a polity to reexamine the Jewish covenantal tradition.[21] No doubt the reestablishment of a Jewish state in Eretz Israel was a factor in this since issues of linkage between Israeli and diaspora Jews had become permanent items on the Jewish agenda, which could be resolved only by finding a formula that would recognize the mutual obligations of Jews wherever they were, but within a voluntary context in keeping with contemporary expectations.

The one Jewish thinker to explore the covenantal implications of this was Mordecai M. Kaplan, the most distinguished twentieth-century American Jewish thinker and perhaps second in the world only to Buber. In his book, *A New Zionism,* he proposed the actual development and signing of a new covenant of Jewish peoplehood by all Jews throughout the world as a means to reform the Jewish people in the wake of the Holocaust and the reestablishment of an independent Jewish state. While his idea remained entirely in the realm of the theoretical, the thrust of his thinking prefigured the direction of Jewish thought over the next decades.[22]

Approximately a decade after the emergence of this new covenant theology came the Six-Day War, which generated a new enthusiasm among Jews everywhere for unity in the face of the apparent indifference or hostility of the non-Jewish world. It also stimulated the development of an ideology of mutual covenantal obligation as the basis for revived Jewish organizational structure within each country of Jewish residence and worldwide through a number of common instrumentalities that were reorganized to reflect this new ideology in concrete organizational terms. While covenantal language has been used more extensively in the diaspora than in Israel, it is not absent in the Jewish state.[23]

The founders of the revived covenant theology were existentialists seeking a new postmodern and post-Holocaust understanding of Judaism after Nazism had finally demonstrated for them the inadequacy of philosophic rationality as an explanation of human behavior, of the kind espoused by the last great nineteenth-century German Jewish philosopher, Hermann Cohen, who also denigrated Jewish peoplehood as part of his pan-German outlook. But theirs was a *Jewish* existentialism, collective rather than individualistic. As Eugene Borowitz, who rapidly became the leader of the school, put it,

> The covenant was, of course, made not with an individual but with a folk.... The covenant exists between God and the people of Israel. Hence, utilizing the term brings peoplehood, in its full ethnic dimension, to the center of our Judaism, indicating that our Jewishness is not auxiliary but essential to our existence.

Significantly, covenantal theology was also a reaction against the religious naturalism espoused by Mordecai M. Kaplan, which denied the independent existence of a transcendent living God. Concerned as it was with *mitzvah*, what Jews are commanded by God to be and do, in Borowitz's words, "the term covenant, by contrast, pointed up the two-sidedness of Jewishness and, as against Kaplan, indicated that God was to have at least equal status in our Judaism, even as, against Cohen, the people of Israel was recognized as his partner."

At the same time, most of the covenant theologians, especially Borowitz, were religious liberals who wanted to go beyond the limits of traditional Judaism. For them, to quote Borowitz again, "the term covenant...gave man a greater role in the creation of Jewish law than either Rosensweig or Heschel seem prepared to grant and so delineated our greater appreciation of man's autonomy under the law." For Borowitz, one of the great virtues of this new theology was that it provided a proper language for Judaism, what he referred to as "covenant-talk."

The covenant theologians emphasized the covenant dialectic, which linked God and the people Israel, rejecting an overemphasis on human rationality or human subjugation. Thus, for Borowitz, "God-Israel is the primal term of Judaism...God-Israel alone is classic Jewish faith—covenant." While covenant can strengthen the Jewishness of Jews, through the covenant with the sons of Noah it also linked Jews with all of humankind to prevent excessive ethnocentrism. From this perception of covenant flows the *mitzvah* of Jews' involvement in the great political and social issues of our time. "Our responsibility to God under the covenant is to do our duty as best we can determine it."[24]

Notes

1. Cf. M. Zborowski and E. Herzog, *Life is With People* (New York: Schocken Books, 1952) for a discussion of the *shtetl* as the covenanted community.
2. Cf. Leo Baeck, *This People Israel: The Meaning of Jewish Existence* (New York: Holt, Rinehart and Winston, 1964.
3. Daniel J. Elazar, "The Reconstitution of Jewish Communities in the Postwar Period," *Jewish Journal of Sociology* 11, no. 2 (December 1969): 187–226.
4. Daniel J. Elazar, *Community and Polity: The Organizational Dynamics of American Jewry* (Philadelphia: Jewish Publication Society, 1976).
5. Moshe Davis, "Centres of Jewry in the Western Hemisphere: A Comparative Approach," reprinted in *Five Lectures Delivered at the Third World Congress for Jewish Studies in Jerusalem* (Jerusalem: Hebrew University Institute for Contemporary Jewry, 1964). See also the other lectures reprinted in that pamphlet.
6. Ibid.
7. Eliezer Schweid, *Democracy and Halakha* (Lanham, MD: Jerusalem Center for Public Affairs and University Press of America, 1994).
8. Jonathan Woocher, *Sacred Survival* (Bloomington: Indiana University Press, 1986).

9. I have described this phenomenon in *Community and Polity: The Organization Dynamics of the American Jewish*, 2d ed. Community (Philadelphia: Jewish Publication Society, 1994.

10. Daniel J. Elazar, *People and Polity* (Detroit: Wayne State University Press, 1990).

11. Daniel J. Elazar, *Israel: Building a New Society* (Bloomington: Indiana University Press, 1986).

12. See Emile Marmorstein, *Heaven at Bay* (London: Oxford University Press, 1969); Daniel J. Elazar, *Israel: From Ideological to Territorial Democracy* (New York: General Learning Press, 1970); Eliezer Don-Yehiya, *The Secularization, Negation and Integration of Perceptions and Concepts of Traditional Judaism in Labor Zionism* (Hebrew, Bar-Ilan University, Covenant Workshop Paper No. 14, 1980).

13. For example, Petach Tikvah, Rishon le-Tziyyon, Rehovot. Many of these documents have been assembled in the archives of the Jerusalem Center for Public Affairs.

14. S. N. Eisenstadt describes this process in *Israeli Society* (New York: Basic Books, 1967).

15. Cf. Arend Lipjart, *Consociational Democracy*; Horowitz and Lissak; Daniel J. Elazar, *Israel: Building a New Society* (Bloomington: Indiana University Press, 1986).

16. Horace M. Kallen has examined the ideological implications of the scroll in this way in *Utopians at Bay* (New York: Theodore Herzl Foundation, 1958), 15-19. For a discussion of the scroll's quasi-constitutional character, see Amnon Rubinstein's work in Hebrew, *The Constitutional Law of the State of Israel* (Jerusalem and Tel-Aviv: Schocken, 1969), chap. 1.

17. Martin Buber, *On the Bible: Eighteen Studies* (New York: Schocken Books, 1982).

18. Martin Buber, *Kingship of God*, 3d ed., trans. Richard Scheimann (New York: Harper and Row, 1973).

19. Bernard Susser, "The Anarcho-Federalism of Martin Buber," *Publius* 9, no. 4: 103-16.

20. Martin Buber, *Paths in Utopia*, trans. R. F. C. Hull (London: Routledge and K. Paul, 1949).

21. See note 1 of chap. 21.

22. Mordecai M. Kaplan, *A New Zionism* (New York: Theodor Herzl Foundation, 1955).

23. Eugene B. Borowitz, *Commentary* (July 1961) and "Covenant Theologies—Another Look," *Worldview* (March 1973): 21-27; Daniel J. Elazar, *People and Polity: The Organizational Dynamics of World Jewry* (Detroit: Wayne State University Press, 1989).

24. "Crisis, Community and the Jewish Theology," *Commentary:* 36-42.

23

The Covenant Idea and the Jewish Political Tradition: A Summary Statement

An Aristocratic Federal Republic

The Jewish people are clearly republican in their orientation; they have a partnership that is based on the principle that the community is a *res publica*, a public thing, not the private preserve of any person or group, whose leaders are drawn from and are penultimately responsible to the people. Ultimately, all are responsible to God; but penultimately, for matters of this world, leaders are responsible to the people in some way. In fact, much of the internal political history of the Jewish people revolves around the balancing of power among those who are seen as representatives of God's will and those whose authority stems from the people. This fundamental division of powers is crucial to any Jewish polity and is even reflected in modern Israel in the deference shown those recognized as representatives of normative Judaism, which goes beyond the demands of coalition politics.

The Jewish community is republican but it is republican in an aristocratic as much as in a democratic way. It must be carefully noted that, although the Jewish community has generally attempted to be democratic in its involvement of the people (and all the people—men, women, and children) in covenants crucial to its formation and governance, it was not meant to be simply democratic, in the sense that we talk about any person being eligible for formal leadership simply by virtue of some kind of public selection. It also seeks to embody the aristocratic ideal because leadership in the Jewish community was and is invariably invested in those able to claim legitimacy on the basis of some authoritative source that stands external to the members of the community, per se. Ideally, the source of authority of the communal leadership is God.

According to tradition, it is He who determines what the earthly forms of legitimacy will be, through His covenant with the people and its expression in the Torah. After the days of the judges, God Himself no longer directly anointed leaders. Consequently, even when Jews were God-fearing, they did not expect God to anoint their leaders, but they did recognize their ultimate responsibility to Him.

This apparent rejection of simple democracy in favor of a kind of aristocratic federal republicanism is perhaps difficult to appreciate in a democratic era that increasingly equates true democracy with its Jacobin version. Nevertheless, Jews came to the conclusion that the maintenance of the special purpose of the Jewish people necessitated such a stance. While all power must be subject to checks by the people, ultimately the nature of the community is also determined by something higher than the people, there is a vision that stands above the simple counting of heads.

In practice, this has not always prevented the development of rabbinic oligarchies supported by claims to Divine favor or oligarchies of moneyed leaders capable of providing for the needs of diaspora communities comprising a barely tolerated minority in powerful Christian or Islamic societies, but most of the time it has created a framework for power-sharing that has prevented autocracy, even in the most autocratic periods of world history. Indeed, the Jews have no history of dictatorship or autocratic rule. The only cases of autocracy (beyond what may have happened in occasional small communities) in Jewish history are those of usurpations by legitimate rulers—Athaliah in ancient Judah and Herod in Hasmonean times, both of whom were resisted and rejected by the Jewish people.[1]

Every covenantal system true to its fundamental principles emphasizes the sharing of power and authority among institutions and offices rather than its concentration. The Jewish polity is no different. In every arena of Jewish political organization, authority and power are distributed among several reshuyot (authorities). From the time of the foundation of the edah in Sinai, these reshuyot have been clustered into three sets of authoritative combinations, each with its own direct source of Divine authority. This unique tripartite division of authority allows the Jewish polity to encompass far more than the narrow functions of contemporary political systems, to include means of governance usually identified with tribal societies and voluntary associations as well as conventional states. Through the three ketarim, the multifaceted character of the Jewish people finds political as well as religious expression in a way that constitutionalizes power sharing. Each *keter* has a permanent share in the governance of the *edah* through institutions and offices that are empowered by it.

What distinguishes the division of authority among the *ketarim* from conventional separation of powers systems is that the *ketarim* address themselves principally to the source, character, and purpose of authority, and only secondarily to issues of function (e.g., executive, legislative, judicial). Those functions are usually shared by two or more of the *ketarim*. From time to time, the institutions that embody each interchange or acquire a share in more than one domain as a consequence of certain historical circumstances but the basic tripartite division constantly reasserts itself. At its best, the *edah* had fully articulated and functioning institutions in each of the three *ketarim* that combined the various elements of political and religious activity as appropriate to it. Moreover, as the institutions of one *keter* changed, those of the others changed or adapted themselves accordingly.[2]

The Covenant Idea in Jewish Political Thought

Classical Jewish sources do not clearly separate political and other teachings. Indeed, the methodological problem of uncovering the Jewish political tradition from within those sources is deserving of extensive treatment in its own right. By and large, standard exegetical techniques (the Midrashic method) serve to identify the political ideas contained in those texts and relate them to one another so as to uncover a systematic teaching.

A very useful starting point for understanding the Jewish political tradition is the language of political discourse among Jews, the recurring basic terminology that creates the conceptual and perceptual framework for considering and dealing with public affairs. In Kadushin's terms, the exploration of this dimension of Jewish tradition is possible through the identification and explication of *value concepts*, in this case terms and phrases bearing political content.[3]

The Bible is rich in political terminology, as any close reading of the text in context reveals. Indeed it remains the prime source of Hebrew political terms, many of which have been transmitted with minimum change in meaning over the millennia. The terminology as such and in context has substantial implications for understanding the sources of the

Jewish political tradition and deserves full treatment on its own. Among those terms and phrases are several that are of special importance because they give and continue to give meaning to fundamental political relationships and the regimes they shape. In essence, they are the Hebrew equivalents of the classic political terminology of ancient Greek and Latin. The classic character of this political terminology can be illustrated through the device of the "mapping sentence" as devised by Louis Guttman as the basis for hypothecation in social research.[4]

The classic Jewish political worldview can be summarized in the following way. The family of tribes descended from Abraham, Isaac, and Jacob that God raised up to be a nation (*goy*) became the Jewish people (*Am Yisrael*) through its covenant (*brit*) with God, which, in turn, laid the basis for the establishment of a Jewish commonwealth (*edah*) under Divine sovereignty (*malkhut shamayim*) and hence bound by the Divine constitutional teaching (*Torah*). The *am* so created must live as a community of equals (*kahal*) under the rule of law (*hukah, hok*), which applies to every citizen (*ezrah*), defined as a partner to the covenant (*ben-brit*). Every citizen is linked to his neighbor (*rea*) by covenant obligation (*hesed*). Within these parameters there is wide latitude in choosing the form of government or regime as long as the proper relationships between the various parties referred to above are preserved. That, in turn, requires a system of shared authorities (*reshuyot*), what today would be termed *checks and balances*. These *reshuyot* are combined under three authoritative categories (*ketarim*): the authority of Torah (*Keter Torah*), the authority of civil governance (*Keter Malkhut*), and the authority of the priesthood (*Keter Kehunah*), each of which plays a role in the government of the *edah* through a system of shared powers. At any given time, different religious and political camps (*mahanot*) and parties (*miflagot*) within those camps compete for control of the governing institutions of the *edah*. Moreover, since the full achievement of its religio-political goals requires redemption (*geulah*), the Jewish political worldview is messianic in orientation, looking toward a better future rather than a golden past.

Man, Government, and Politics

From the Jewish perspective, humans are partners with the Sovereign of the Universe (*Ribbon HaOlam*) in the development and governance of this world, which partnership is established by covenant (*brit*). Humans have both good and evil inclinations (*yetzer hatov* and *yetzer hara*). Because they have inclinations to evil, they require laws to guide them. Because they are more good than bad, their behavior can be improved by proper institutions (especially good laws). At the same time, people, when unrestrained, are capable of utilizing government and politics for the institutionalization of their evil inclinations, thereby greatly increasing their capability to do evil.

Government and, concomitantly, politics are necessary parts of human existence in every case but, necessary and important as they are, government and politics are merely tools for the achievement of more sacred goals and not ends in themselves. Politics is a universal and serious human activity but only as a means to achieve holy purposes. Since politics are part and parcel of the way of man (*derekh ha'adam*), it is a mixture of the petty as well as the grand. Its importance must be recognized but always with a certain ambivalence given its propensities to serve unwarranted ambition. In the last analysis, however, full achievement of the goals of political activity is dependent upon God's intervention to redeem (*geulah*) humanity. Hence, it is necessary to look to a better future in the messianic age (*yemot hamashiah*).

Law and Justice

Law, in the sense of the Divine constitutional teaching (*Torah*), provides the foundation of human polity. Divine law is comprehensive and immutable but properly constituted human agency has been granted broad powers of interpretation. This strong commitment to constitutionalism and the rule of law tends to elevate judges to a position of special authority within the body politic. In its most narrow application, this commitment tends to encourage hairsplitting legalism. On the other hand, it can be coupled with an equally strong operational commitment to the idea that every individual must ultimately decide for himself to what extent the law applies in his case, a kind of rule of law by repeated acts of consent. In certain ways, law is understood as a norm to be attained as much as a fixed rule or boundary.

Justice is intimately associated with Divine law but the association extends beyond a simple 1:1 relationship to involve practical considerations of covenant obligation (*hesed*) and mercy (*rahamim*). This often leads to a paradoxical condition whereby legal support for doing justice exacts the strongest penalties for unjust acts, penalties that are rarely if ever applied on grounds of tempering justice with mercy.

Political Authority and Obligation

The universe and all its parts is under Divine sovereignty (*malkhut shamayim*) and hence all human institutions possess only delegated authority and powers. That is the essence of Jewish theocracy. In fact, the good political order is a complex of interlocking authorities whose legitimacy is derived from the covenant-established partnership between God and man.[5] In some cases, the former elects and the latter ratifies, and in others the process is reversed, but in every one the two sides of the partnership are somehow represented. This can lead to power sharing at its best or, in extreme manifestations, to near-anarchy. Part of the theocratic character of the Jewish political tradition is reflected in a constant tension between the Divine (*shamayim* or *theo*) and rule (*malkhut* or *cratos*), which must be reconciled by federal or covenantal linkage.[6]

The basis for political authority is invariably covenantal, and political obligation flows from that covenantal base.[7] Covenanting makes Divine sovereignty concrete and human self-government possible in this world but if the former is removed it can lead to the institutionalized expression of Faustian ambition on the part of humans.[8]

The Polity

Polities (*kibbutzim mediniim*) are extensions of the covenantal relationship, constituted consensually by compact, as partnerships or meta-partnerships of their constituents. There is no "state" in the Jewish political tradition in the sense of a reified political entity complete in and of itself. The contemporary Hebrew term for state, *medinah,* refers to a political unit with its own jurisdiction (*din*) within a larger entity, or a province. While the term is used for state today, its classical echoes still remind us that polity would be a better translation. The latter term offers wider and narrower expressions of meaning consistent with the Hebrew original—wider in that all entities with their own political-legal jurisdiction are polities (cf. the Arabic *medinah* meaning city) and narrower in that no polity exists apart from its component elements nor does it possess absolute sovereignty. Both dimensions are vital elements in the Jewish political tradition. In fact, the Jewish political tradition does not recognize state sovereignty in the modern sense of absolute independence. No state—a human institution—can be sovereign. Classically, only God is sovereign and He entrusts the exercise of His sovereign powers to the people as a whole, mediated through His Torah-as-constitution as provided through His covenant with Israel.[9]

The Jewish people (*Am Yisrael*) is a polity of equals, a commonwealth (*edah*), with all that implies for the organization and conduct of Jewish political affairs.[10] While no single form of political organization is mandated by Jewish law or tradition, any form chosen must embody this basic republican (*res publica*, a public thing) principle.[11] Jewish regimes have not always been democratic republics; because of the emphasis on the Divine role, they have aristocratic tendencies that often have degenerated into oligarchic patterns of rule. But with very few exceptions, they have not been autocratic in character. The republican foundations of the Jewish political tradition have prevented that.

A proper Jewish polity is one that embodies a proper set of political relationships rather than any particular structure or regime.[12] This emphasis on relationships is particularly relevant to a covenantal polity and helps reinforce Jewish republicanism but it can also lead to ignoring structures unless confronted by extreme difficulties with them.

The Jewish people as an *edah* takes as its point of departure a strong commitment to bargaining as the basic mode of political decision making. In its best sense, this leads to negotiated cooperation based upon covenant obligation; in its worst, to willingness to subject everything to haggling without regard to norms or accepted procedures.[13]

Political Responsibility

The basis of Jewish political responsibility rests upon the collective self-perception that the Jews are a special people, that they are shaped by their combined religio-political character, which, in a certain sense, transcends time and space, although always focused on the land of Israel as the only place where complete Jewish individual and collective self-fulfillment is possible. At best, this has facilitated the maintenance of the unity and survival of a people in exile for millennia and dispersed throughout the world. It has also led to periodic attempts to deny the political dimension of Jewishness.[14]

Responsible policy-making rests upon the collective self-perception that the Jewish people share as a perpetually small minority, usually isolated from the larger world when their own basic interests are involved, which must develop and pursue survival strategies accordingly. This set of perceptions encourages a wide variety of strategies, both accommodationist and hostile, integrationist and isolationist.[15] Each of these elements recurs in one form or another in every period of Jewish history and, in fact, the changing modes of their expression can be used to identify and demarcate the various epochs of Jewish history from a political perspective.[16]

The covenant idea can be seen to be significant in shaping at least five themes of Jewish political thought: (1) man's stewardship on earth; (2) the special role of Israel among the nations in God's scheme for redemption; (3) the appropriate political regime for the Jewish people; (4) the Jewish conception of the polity as such; and (5) the ideal polity of the messianic age and the political character of the age itself.

The Jewish worldview suggests that man and God are partners in the management of the world. This partnership began when God delegated to Adam the right to name the creatures. Adam, however, is entirely dependent upon God's good will. With Noah, the partnership is regularized through a covenant that is interpreted by the sages as having a political component in the requirement to establish courts of justice, or government, in the world. The Talmudic discussion of the seven Noahide *mitzvot* is very revealing in that it suggests that six of the seven *mitzvot* were already demanded of Adam, but in effect, the sages teach us, they were not put together into a coherent doctrine based upon a formalized relationship between man and God until God covenanted with Noah.[17] Of course, the stewardship question goes beyond that and can be explored in several directions, involving such concepts as *tikun olam* (the repair, or reform, of the world, a central Talmudic value concept), but the basis of man's relationship remains rooted in the covenant-created partnership.

The special role of Israel among the nations was established by the covenants with Abraham and at Sinai. Through the latter, God assumes direct responsibility for governing His people, a major aspect of their special position as a people set apart (made holy) for exemplary purposes. By and large, this issue is treated by contemporary Jewish thinkers as a theological problem. Yet Moses and the prophets treated it as a political problem first and foremost and there are even echoes of its political character in the Talmud, despite the very real efforts on the part of the Jewish leadership in those centuries to deemphasize the strictly political dimension of Jewish life in an effort to adjust to the new conditions of exile and relative powerlessness. How does one deal with the problem of "entangling alliances" that were such anathema to the prophets, or sharing the land with another people, so strongly opposed in the *Humash* and the Book of Joshua, except from a perspective that emphasizes the resolution of the political problems involved as a necessary precondition to the attainment of theological goals.

At least as early as the Jews' encounter with Hellenism, the issue of Israel's special role became closely entwined with the question of whether the Jewish people existed simply by virtue of kinship, or common descent, or also by virtue of consent, an argument that has carried over into our own times. For those who believed the former, a Jew was set apart from all other men by virtue of his very biology and, even if he strayed, was more open to redemption than any non-Jew because of an inherited "Divine spark." This seems to have been the view of Judah HaLevi, the Maharal of Prague, and the late Rabbi Abraham Isaac Kook, among others.

On the other hand, there were those who argued that consent was at least as important as kinship, if not more so; that every Jew had to accept the covenant to be truly part of Israel. This seems to have been the view of Philo, Saadia Gaon, and Maimonides, among others. Philo discusses the admission of proselytes on equal terms with those born Jews into the Jewish polity and suggests that the basis of that polity is not common descent but the common heritage of the Torah, that is, common consenting to the commandments of the Torah. Thus, in *De Specialibus Legibus,* Philo says, "The native born Jews obtain the approval of God not because they are members of the God loving polity from birth but because they were not false to the nobility of their birth," while the proselytes obtain God's approval "because they have thought fit to make the passage to piety" (*Spec.* 1,9,51). Philo terms such relationships as "kinships of greater dignity and sanctity" (*Spec.* 1,58,317).

The latter view is that of the most modern Jewish theologians and thinkers, reinforced by the realities of the open society and the general commitment of the moderns to voluntarism. On the other hand, the former view remains strongly that of groups like the Habad (Lubavitch) Hassidim, which helps explain why, on the one hand, they pursue every Jew with equal vigor and, on the other, have a negative attitude toward conversions to Judaism. In fact, the Talmud suggests that it is the covenant between God and Israel that makes "All Israel responsible for one another." In the larger context, this seems to represent a synthesis between kinship and consent. Certainly the Hebrew term for responsible used in the passage, *arevim,* has strong contractual connotations.

The Appropriate Regime

Some have explained the original covenantal ceremony of animal sacrifice and the rite of male circumcision, as well as such biblical examples as that of Exodus 24:6–8, where Moses takes the blood of the sacrificed oxen and sprinkles half of it against the alter and half on the people at Sinai, as efforts to bridge the gap between kinship and consent. That is to say, to give acts of consent a dimension of kinship by uniting them by blood. While this may have been true in the very earliest history of Israelite religion, it was subsequently deemphasized, replaced by Torah, the legally binding teaching, by tradition dictated to Moses by God at Sinai, which becomes the new binding element as the B'nai Yisrael became b'nai brit. Torah replaces blood to create a *hever,* a confederation of tribes or families. The Torah, as much as blood, gives life. As is stated in Deuteronomy 30:15,19:

> See, I have set before thee this day, life and good and death and evil, and that I command thee this day to love the Lord thy God, to walk in His ways, to keep His commandments and His statutes and His ordinances; then thou shalt live and multiply...I call heaven and earth to witness against you this day that I have set before thee life and death, the blessing and the curse; therefore choose life, that thou mayest life, thou and thy seed.

Thus, covenant is identified with marriage, a kind of kinship established by consenting partners. In rabbinic literature the brit is normatively presented as a marriage of God with the people, Israel, whose product is the Torah. Marriage is frequently referred to as a brit, especially in *halakhic* literature. Preliminary evidence suggests that the most frequent usage of the term *brit* in medieval *responsa* is in connection with marriage. Marriage between two individuals establishes a new community that is based on the paradigmatic community, namely, the marriage of God and Israel, and makes possible the continuity of the covenant through procreation. To "be fruitful and multiply" is a covenantal command going back to God's implicit covenant with Adam and specific covenant with Noah. In that way the chain of generations is established which makes possible community, which must be an intergenerational affair.

The discussion of the appropriate political regime for the Jewish people has been linked with the covenant idea from the first, as illustrated by *Parashat Yithro,* the Torah portion dealing with Jethro and the establishment of the Mosaic polity and with the giving of the Ten Commandments. As that *parashah* indicates, while the covenant establishes the constitutional grounding of the Jewish people, it does not establish any particular form of government. The Torah itself presents two options, a nomocratic tribal federation ruled by God and led by prophets and judges or one under the leadership of kings and priests. These two options—the first based upon a highly noncentralized regime of locally rooted leaders and the second based upon a court with a bureaucratic structure— with some variations, remain the principal choices before the Jewish people throughout the biblical period, and may even be seen as prototypes of the choices confronting the Jews as a polity ever since. Subsequently, other variations of those options were developed and instituted through various local compacts (or by outside powers where the Jews were unable to determine their own forms of government).

The struggle between the two options is generally couched in covenantal terms, namely: what were the demands of the original covenant at Sinai that established God's direct rule over His people and did God modify those demands by His covenant with David and his house? This debate is one of the great debates in Jewish political thought, manifested in the Talmud (which, as we have suggested, attempts to bring about a synthesis of the two, to be achieved in the messianic age), in the medieval world (for example, Maimonides, who emphasizes that a constitutional monarchy is obligatory, versus Abravanel, who suggests that republicanism is the preferred form of government and monarchy a reflection of a lapse in Jewish virtue), and down through modern times (for example, Chaim Herschenson's *Malkhi BaKodesh* and Martin Buber's *Kingship of God*).[18] It has also operated on an immediate level in matters regarding the forms of governance, the organization of authority, and the distribution of powers within particular Jewish communities. The responsa literature is replete with references to these two options and seeks to apply them to local situations.[19]

If the Jewish sources do not mandate a particular form of government, they do have a great deal to say about what component elements are necessary for the construction of a good regime. These include both institutions and processes involving such things as the separation of powers and responsibilities, expectations of standards of behavior of political officeholders, and requirements for what moderns refer to as the protection of individual rights, or, more correctly, obligations and the rights gained through them. In short, an appropriate political structure within the covenantal framework is one that secures both the position of the Torah in the Jewish polity and the liberties (in the classic sense) of the Jewish people.

The lack of emphasis on a particular governmental form is a reflection of the emphasis of the covenantal approach on particular kinds of political relationship: between governors and governed, between components of the polity (or between polities), between God and man. Covenants, after all, are designed to establish relationships, which are then given form rather than establishing forms that are, in turn, are given content. This emphasis on relationship has been a distinguishing characteristic of the Jewish political tradition from the first and helps explain why a variety of regimes have proven acceptable to the interpreters of Jewish tradition and also why some forms of regime are simply unacceptable, no matter what.

Covenant and Tensions in the Tradition

Every polity is built around certain basic tensions, which play a major role in giving it form and in defining its continuing concerns as a polity. Those tensions come on the scene in the course of the very founding of the polity in the first place and are, in all likelihood, inherent in the tensions that necessarily result from the founding synthesis. Every generation must grapple with these tensions and work out some *modus vivendi* to manage them so that they are not so exacerbated as to cause the dissolution of the polity in question. At the same time, the tensions are never completely resolved as long as the polity exists. In fact they can be resolved only upon the demise of the polity. Thus, part of the dynamic of every polity is its particular set of tensions and the interaction that occurs between them.

The principal tensions within the Jewish polity are derived from or closely related to the covenant idea. One such tension revolves around the problem of reconciling Divine and popular authority. On the one hand, God is the sovereign of the Jewish people and His authority is ultimate and unchallengeable. On the other, for day-to-day matters and even for matters of interpreting Jewish law, authority is vested in humans and, for many such matters, in human majorities. For example, in ancient times, the powers of legal interpretation were entrusted to the Sanhedrin as the ultimate human agency for interpreting the law, and, according to the famous *Midrash* on Achnai's oven, their decisions are by majority rule even when God Himself gives a sign as to the rightness of the minority view. The covenant is perhaps the principal bridge between the two authoritative forces, since it is through the covenant that God has invested human institutions with authoritative roles. Moreover, it is through the various subcovenants that humans have organized their institutions to exercise those roles.

Closely tied in with the question of the appropriate political regime for the Jewish people is the appropriate conception of the polity. Here the covenant idea plays an especially important role. If the Jewish political tradition conveys a clear sense of the existence of polities and their importance, it does not, in its authentic form, have any conception of the state in the modern sense of the term. The word *medinah* appears in the Bible (as do almost all the words that we now take for granted as part of the Jewish language of politics), where it is used to describe a territorial unit possessing its own political or administrative institutions but clearly not an independent one, in other words, an administrative district (as the usage in Kings) or a province (as used in Esther). The Bible does not discuss sovereign states because, according to the Bible and the Jewish political tradition generally, sovereignty rests only in heaven. All powers possessed by humans are subsidiary ones, delegated by the Almighty to the people or their representatives as variously defined.

In the Jewish political tradition, polities come in all forms—peoples, nations, cities, tribes, kingdoms, empires, and so on in the biblical period and, by extension, modern states as well—and none is considered to be *the* generic form, although the Bible seems to suggest that peoples are generic in some way. As time went on and the Jews experienced a wider variety of political systems, this principle became refined with a new dimension added, namely, that a good polity is in some ways a partnership of its members. This was a natural outgrowth of the covenant idea.

The elimination of the problem of human sovereignty and the absence of any generic form of polity helped reinforce a strong predisposition in Jewish political thought toward the view that all government is a matter of delegated powers. The term *reshut,* which first appears in the Talmud, probably comes closest to encapsulating this concept, reflecting as it does an authority whose powers have been granted by another source. The principle of *reshut* has been institutionalized in Jewish liturgy and ritual as a sign of the equal sharing of God's covenant-granted authority among all Jews. Thus, in the *Siddur,* the hosts of heaven grant *reshut* to one another to praise God and the leader of the *birkat hamazon* (blessing after the meal) requests *reshut* from his peers (literally stated, his teachers, with the implication that those present are more knowledgeable than he) to lead them in the prayer.

We have already suggested that the principle of *reshut* is politically operationalized through *reshuyot.* Among other things, this makes possible overlapping political jurisdictions and structures, each with its own powers or competences, a phenomenon that we already encounter in biblical times as a feature of Jewish governments and that has been a continuing reality of Jewish political life ever since. This theoretical perspective was further reinforced by the long diaspora experience of the Jews, where, in effect, the Jews had obligations to more than one polity simultaneously.

Finally, Jewish political thought has concerned itself with the messianic age and the ideal polity that is to come into existence with the coming of the messiah. Jewish tradition is rather clear on this point. The messianic age will be the age of the realization of God's kingdom upon this earth with all the political implications contained in that phrase. Consequently, a political order will be necessary, but of course it will be the ideal political order. By and large, Jewish equivalents of utopias are directed toward discussion of the messianic polity. Both Isaiah and Ezekiel bring their versions of that polity, and Talmudic and post-Talmudic literature has other such visions.[20] In almost every case, they involve the fulfillment of God's covenant with Israel and the restoration of the tribal federation. All other aspects flow from those two starting points.

The sophistication of the covenant idea in Jewish political thought is perhaps best revealed in the relationship between *brit* and *hesed*. *Brit* represents the structural manifestation of the covenant idea, while *hesed* is its dynamic component. If a *brit* creates a partnership, then *hesed* is what makes the partnership work.[21]

Through the combination, Jewish tradition interprets one's covenantal obligations broadly rather than narrowly, the broader the better. Thus, *hassidim* have traditionally been those who have defined as their obligations vis-à-vis God and their fellow men to include a dimension above and beyond that which is normally required. Jewish history has known three *hassidic* movements identified by that name: the *hassidim* of the Second Temple, those of medieval Ashkenaz, and those who emerged in eighteenth-century Eastern Europe. Each was a unique movement in many ways, but what was common to them all was this "above and beyond the call" commitment. They accepted a more broadly construed obligation than that which Israel's covenant with God ordinarily demanded. In essence, they were attempting to fulfill in their own lives the Talmudic dictum that *lifnim meshurat hadin din hu,* going beyond the law is the law. A *brit* without *hesed* is indeed a narrow thing and, according to Jewish tradition, God Himself provides the model of the extension of *hesed* by maintaining His relationship with Israel despite the Jews' repeated violations of the terms of the covenant. That is the finest example of taking the extra step.

Jewish Political Culture and Behavior

The precisely proper combination of *brit* and *hesed* is left to theoretical speculation and the end of days. In the interim, however, the concepts have entered the political culture of the Jewish people to exercise a pronounced, if partial and necessarily flawed, influence on a regular basis. Even in the absence of systematic studies, a reasoned assessment of the evidence can lead us to a certain understanding of the matter. So, for example, as befits a people who see themselves as partners of the Almighty, Jews are not prone to relate to each other (or to others) hierarchically. Quite to the contrary, even the authority of particular leaders is accepted voluntarily on the basis of equality.

For most Jews, not even the religious leadership is able to form a permanent elite. Every Jew feels free to recognize his own authoritative interpreters of the Torah. Acceptance of authority in other spheres may involve the recognition of sociological realities, for example, that in a voluntaristic community the wealthy will have more power since they contribute a larger share of the budget, but does not endow the leadership with any special status per se. The status exists by consent of the community in both cases.

Melvin Urofsky describes Louis Dembitz Brandeis's reaction to his first serious encounter with still-unassimilated Eastern European Jewish immigrants to the United States as the mediator of the great New York garment workers' stroke of 1910:[22]

> While going through the lofts, he heard numerous quarrels between workers and their bosses, and was amazed that they treated each other more like equals than as inferiors and superiors. In one argument an employee shouted at the owner, "Ihr darft sich shemen! Past dos far a Yid?" ("You should be ashamed! Is this worthy of a Jew?"), while another time a machine operator lectured his employer with a quotation from Isaiah: "It is you who have devoured the vineyard, the spoil of the poor is in your houses. What do you mean by crushing My people, by grinding the face of the poor? says the Lord God of hosts."

Brandeis's experience is matched in Israel (or any other Jewish environment) everyday. Jews do not "obey orders." They can be brought to act in a certain way either on the basis of understanding or trade-offs, but not on the basis of commands. Even in the military framework, where there is no problem of obeying immediate commands, the Israeli army has found that it must first inculcate understanding so that it can succeed in commanding. This, indeed, has been Israeli military doctrine from the first. Behaviorally, this manifests itself in a Jewish conception of leadership, which involves leaders actually going first, what in the Israeli army is known as the *"aharai"* or "follow me" principle. It is no accident that the Israeli army gains its greatest strength following this principle, just as on a very different level the most influential Jewish leaders in the United States are the big contributors to the annual campaigns who are the only American Jewish leaders who lead by going first and setting the pace.

The operation of this principle can be seen throughout Jewish history. Successful leaders were those who accepted the heavier burdens in whatever direction they desired to lead, else they had no significant influence. It is highly significant that classical Hebrew uses *shamoa* (hearken), a term that embraces hearing before acting and implicitly involves the principle of consent. That is to say, an individual—as befits a partner to God's covenant whose integrity and autonomy are established—hears, considers, and decides. He cannot be ordered to do something, but must consent to it. Even "Har kaGigit," the *Midrash* that stands in greatest conflict with the covenant idea, the one describing Israel's acceptance of the Sinai covenant only after God held a mountain over them, still reflects this perspective. According to that *Midrash,* God put Israel in a most untenable position, forcing them to consent, but they still had to consent. He did not simply force them to obey, and that is probably the most extreme example (and by no means to be taken as the mainstream view) of a master-servant relationship in classical Jewish thought. Thus, a kind of partnership attitude is a basic datum of Jewish existence. Anyone who attempts to lead, govern, or even work with Jews comes up against it every day in every way.

The covenantal solution to the problems of Jewish unity can also be seen as cultural and behavioral manifestations of *brit ve'hesed.* Jewish political thought and culture are characterized by a strong messianic dimension, again as part of the sense that man works in partnership with God to reconstruct or redeem the world. An equally pronounced element in Jewish political culture and behavior has been the conceptualization of the messianic task in a different way, creating a kind of pluralism within Jewish life that manifests itself in the division of Jewry into various movements or camps. It seems that a camp comes into existence when its adherents compact among themselves, implicitly or explicitly, to follow a certain form of Jewish discipline, in effect becoming congregations or covenantal societies within the overall framework of the Jewish people. So it was with the Pharisees and Essenes in the days of the Second Temple, so it is with the contemporary Orthodox, Hassidic, Conservative, Reform, Reconstructionist, Liberal, and Progressive religious movements, and so it has been with the Zionist parties.

The relationship among camps has been more problematic. Either some linkage has been achieved among them on a federative basis or there has been hostility even to the point of civil war. In the days of the Second Temple, the latter condition prevailed with disastrous consequences for the Jewish people. Since then, there have been moments when a similar result seemed to be in the offing, as in the struggle between Karaites and Rabbanites and later between the Orthodox and the

Reformers, but the diaspora situation of the Jewish people in effect prevented them from such suicidal behavior.

Twentieth-century Jewry, with all its problems, has implicitly (if not always happily) recognized that the camps are inevitable as long as Jews are free to pursue their respective messianic visions, but has also recognized the necessity for national unity. Thus, in both Israel and the United States, in particular, federative arrangements have been applied to create sufficient unity to undertake common action to protect common interests or advance common goals without interfering with the basic integrity of the camps themselves. Obviously, this involves a continuing process and has left certain continuing problems as well, not the least of which is one inherent in the pursuit of any messianic vision, namely, that there is a limit to the ability of one camp to tolerate another, particularly when they involve grossly contradictory visions and ways of life.

In this respect, twentieth-century Jewry has managed to devise methods that flow out of the Jewish political tradition, even if unawares (one of the best indicators of the existence of a Jewish political culture is that such things can happen unawares), that have more or less satisfactorily dealt with a major flashpoint in Jewish life, one that has brought Jews great grief in the past. Thus, the self-restraint of the overwhelming majority of the various Jewish camps of our times can be looked upon as a signal accomplishment, even if it leads to a certain amount of impatience on the part of those who see their particular messianic vision somehow compromised by the acceptance of various status quo arrangements.

Contractual behavior, if one may so term it, which seems to be endemic to Jewish political culture, is manifested through the series of partnerships that comprise the Jewish community, each of which combines the fundamental autonomy of its members within a bargaining relationship. We have already suggested that leadership under such circumstances has to take on a different character. So, too, decision making becomes principally a matter of negotiation among equals.

At various times in Jewish history, these partnerships have included such phenomena as *haverim behevruta* in the study of the Talmud, the kinds of partnerships that S. D. Goitein describes as coming in place of employer-employee relationships in the Egypt of the *Geniza*, and the *bait shitufi* (cooperative residential building of contemporary Israel).[23] It is likely that every society has some kinds of cooperative relationships within it, so that the discovery of such relationships is not definitive, per se. It is the prevalence and salience of such relationships that count. In that regard, the Jewish people represent one of those societies that stand out in their utilization of partnership devices, all of which also have their roots in the covenant idea.

Political life in Jewish communities and polities has usually involved the following factors:

1. The initial consent of the members to the community's authority and to the authoritative structures and processes of governance within it;
2. A commitment toward participation in communal affairs on the part of a relatively substantial percentage of the citizenry;
3. The utilization of various forms of representation (usually premodern, and only recently modern ones) where direct participation was not feasible; and
4. A system of dispersed decision making with different tasks assigned to different bodies often involving the same individuals wearing many different hats, moving from body to body in their leadership capacities. It is within this framework that links between the covenant idea and the practice of governance in Jewish polities can be made.

It is obvious from the Jewish experience that the sweep of the covenant idea is broad indeed. Nevertheless, to suggest that the covenant idea informs a political tradition is not to suggest that it answers all questions, any more than the idea of natural law does in the tradition it informs. What it does do is set the parameters of the debate.

Precisely because of its breadth, the concept requires as much specification as possible. Perhaps the best way to emphasize its specificity is by indicating what would be inconsistent with covenantal relationships, in other words, what is not covenanted. We can begin by excluding the relationship between master and slave (in any form, including political slavery). In that sense, any relationship that denies the fundamental freedom of any of the parties to it is not covenantal—in relation to polities, non-republican.[24] Significantly, the Jewish experience decisively rejects both slavery and autocracy as not befitting a civilized people. Their political history is transformed by the exodus from Egyptian bondage and the inauguration of the Jews as a people and *edah,* a republic, at Sinai.

The Biblical-Covenantal Approach to Political Morality

It has been noted that, according to the Bible, God orders the world through covenant, which includes the principle of consent, yet the world is divided into nations organically, on the basis of kinship. Either way, the world order is based on the existence of real distinctions between God and humans, between men and women, between nations, and so forth. Some of those distinctions are natural; others are established through covenants. The preservation of proper distinctions is part of moral behavior. Finally, political life is essential since the goal of the Bible is the development of the holy commonwealth. Nevertheless, political life has two faces: that of power and that of justice.

The implications for achieving these underlying principles is that the future of the world lies in building a community of nations linked by covenant, not a universal homogenized mass society. Proper relations within and between nations must be established by covenant. Within that framework, however, there are three kinds of nations or peoples. The most favored are those formed by covenant, whose people are *b'nai brit* either through the Noahide or the Sinai covenant. Relations both within and between these nations are based upon *hesed*, which is essentially unlimited.

There is a second order of nations and peoples, those who are more or less neutral. They are not formed by covenant but it is possible to develop links with them through treaty covenants whose partners are *ba'alei brit*. The relations among them and especially between them and covenanted nations are determined by the terms of each specific covenant as agreed to by the parties, as long as they are not in contradiction with Divine teaching.

Finally, there are nations and peoples that are so sinful and depraved that they are outside of all covenants. Normal rules do not apply to them and establishing covenants with them, even treaty covenants, much less showing *hesed* toward them, is a sin. The most one does is to preserve the peace with them for reasons of prudence.

Good politics is the pursuit of justice but within a context that recognizes the role of power and authority. In that respect, the Bible is both anti-anarchy and anti-authoritarian. Its principles are federalist, republican, and constitutional. The *edah*, that is to say, the people organized into a body politic, is essential for the good life. Radical individualism is a deviation. At least for Jews, that good life can only be gained through the Torah, a constitutional document, transcendentally established, yet modified through human interpretation in different epochs. No part of it is every abolished but parts are ignored or transcended. The Bible offers a series of case studies of political morality based upon these underlying principles and their implications.

Within the context of this morality, it is not surprising that the Jewish people is committed to its survival as a people and the building of a Jewish state in Eretz Israel. Both the people and the state are necessary for Jewish and human salvation and redemption and for the bringing of the messianic era, just as all individuals, families, and peoples should be in their own lands for the messianic era to arrive. These national goals do not come in conflict with the covenantal peace of the messianic era but rather are necessary conditions for the achievement of that peace.

More immediately, Jews are committed to political involvement and activism wherever they are, prior to the messianic era but in the effort to achieve the coming of the Messiah. The Bible advocates prudent messianism, but once released, messianism has a difficult time staying within the bounds of prudence. Hence, just as one of the great strengths of Jewish political culture is the Jews' commitment to involvement and activism wherever they are, one of its great weaknesses is that this commitment is often translated into the pursuit of imprudent messianic policies. The biblical case studies try to encourage Jews to avoid extremist, unrealistic positions, to combine messianic ends and sober expectations, which is not an easy task.

The covenantal approach offers a major vehicle for trying to maintain a proper balance between sobriety and prudence on the one hand, zealous messianism on the other. Indeed, the Jewish worldview sees the universe as intrinsically dynamic. This worldview reached its fullest expression in *kabbalah* (Jewish mysticism), which was long the norm in Jewish thought—indeed, until it was replaced in the twentieth century by dynamic psychology, which preserves many of the same elements. In Kabbalistic terms, evil was defined as an excessive and unbalanced application of some otherwise vital and good principle. Kabbalistic thought with its system of *sefirot* or emanations is in fact based upon pairings, what may be termed in covenantal language as: covenants between opposite principles so as to create the necessary balance between them even while recognizing the worth and importance of each.

A fuller exploration of Jewish political thought would involve an examination of concepts and behavior as reflected in classic texts and in the history of the Jewish people. It would explore the Jewish language of politics and major figures, both thinkers and actors, who gave—and give—expression to the Jewish political tradition. That task is beyond the scope of this book. Here, it is only possible to suggest that every aspect of that tradition is informed by the concept and reality of covenant.

Notes

1. Daniel J. Elazar and Stuart A. Cohen, *The Jewish Polity: Jewish Political Organization from Biblical Times to the Present* (Bloomington: Indiana University Press, 1985).
2. Stuart A. Cohen, *The Concept of the Three Ketarim* (Ramat Gan: Workshop in the Covenant Idea and the Jewish Political Tradition, 1982).
3. Max Kadushin offers an excellent exposition of Jewish modes of thought in *The Rabbinic Mind*, 2d ed. (New York: Blaidsell Publishing Co., 1965), and *Organic Thinking: A Study in Rabbinic Thought* (New York: Jewish Theological Seminary, 1938).
4. Louis Guttman, "An Additive Metric from All the Principal Components of a Perfect Scale," *British Journal of Statistical Psychology* 8, part 1.
5. Adin Steinsaltz elaborated on these arrangements in a series of still unpublished lectures delivered at the Van Leer Institute in Jerusalem during 1974–1975. See also Daniel J. Elazar, "Government in Biblical Israel," *Tradition* (Spring-Summer 1973), and "The Kehillah: From Its Beginnings to the End of the Modern Epoch," in *Comparative Jewish Politics: Public Life in Israel and the Diaspora*, ed. Sam Lehman-Wilzig and Bernard Susser (Ramat Gan: Bar-Ilan University Press, 1981); Elon, "Power and Authority," in *Kinship and Consent*, ed. Daniel J. Elazar (Ramat Gan: Turtledove, 1981).
6. Belfer, in Elazar, ed., *Kinship and Consent.*
7. Daniel J. Elazar, "The Covenant as the Basis," in Elazar, ed., *Kinship and Consent,*; Ilan Grielsammer, *Notes on the Concept of Brit* (Ramat-Gan: Bar-Ilan Department of Political Studies, Covenant Working Paper No. 4, 1977); Gordon M. Freeman, "The Rabbinic Understanding of the Covenant as a Political Idea," in Elazar, ed., *Kinship and Consent.*
8. Harold Fisch, *Jerusalem and Albion* (New York: Schocken Books, 1964), and *Covenant with the Devil* (Ramat-Gan: Bar-Ilan Department of Political Studies, Covenant Working Paper No. 9, 1978).
9. Buber, in Elazar, ed., *Kinship and Consent*; Emanuel Rackman, *One Man's Judaism* (New York: Philosophical Library, 1970); Eliezer Schweid, "The Attitude Toward the State in Modern Jewish Thought Before Zionism," in Elazar, *Kinship and Consent.*
10. Robert Gordis, "Democratic Origins in Ancient Israel—the Biblical Edah," *Alexander Marx Jubilee Volume* (New York: Jewish Theological Seminary, 1950); Moshe Weinfeld.
11. Leo Baeck, *This People Israel* (Philadelphia: Jewish Publication Society, 1965); Elazar, "Government in Biblical Israel."
12. I am indebted to Gordon Freeman for clarifying this point and its significance.
13. Norman Snaith, "The Covenant Love of God," in *The Distinctive Ideas of the Old Testament* (New York: Schocken Books, 1964), chap. 5.
14. Jacob Katz, *Out of the Ghetto* (Cambridge, MA: Harvard University Press, 1973); Michael A. Meyer, *The Origins of the Modern Jew* (Detroit: Wayne State University Press, 1967); Stuart A. Cohen, "The Conquest of a Community? The Zionists and the Board of Deputies in 1917," *Jewish Journal of Sociology* 19, no. 2 (1977); Michael Selzer, *The Wineskin and the Wizard. The Problem of Jewish Power in the Context of East European Jewish History* (New York: Macmillan, 1970); Emile Marmorstein, *Heaven at Bay* (London: Oxford University Press, 1969).

15. Cf. Ismar Schorsch, *On the History of the Political Judgment of the Jew* (New York: Leo Baeck Institute, 1976).

16. See Daniel J. Elazar, *The Constitutional Periodization of Jewish History* (Jerusalem: Center for Jewish Community Studies, 1980).

17. See Saul Berman, "Noahide Laws," in *Encyclopedia Judaica* 12:1189-91 for a good summary and references to the relevant texts.

18. See Gordon Freeman, "Rabbinic Understanding of the Covenant," in Elazar, ed., *Kinship and Consent*; also Chaim Herschenson, *Malchi Bakodesh,* 6 vols. (Hoboken, NJ: 1923-1938); and Buber, *Kingship of God* (New York: Harper and Row, 1956).

19. See the material of the Responsa Literature Information Storage and Retrieval of the Institute for Data Retrieval of Bar-Ilan University, and the files of the Covenant Workshop.

20. See, for example, Stephen Schwarszchild, "A Note on the Nature of the Ideal Society—a Rabbinic Study," in *Jubilee Volume Dedicated to Curt C. Silberman,* ed. Herbert A. Strauss and Hanns G. Reissner (New York: American Federation of Jews From Central Europe, 1969).

21. Nelson Glueck documents this in his *Hesed in the Bible* (Cincinnati: Hebrew Union College Press, 1967) without attempting to make the point.

22. Melvin I. Urofsky, "On Louis D. Brandeis," *Midstream* (January 1975): 42-58.

23. S. D. Goitein, *The Community, Vol. 2: A Mediterranean Society* (Berkeley and Los Angeles: University of California Press, 1971); and Harry Viteles, *A History of the Cooperative Movement in Israel,* 7 vols. (London: Vallentine Mitchell, 1966).

24. There are those—anarchists, for example—who argue that any political association that rests on the possibility of coercion cannot be covenantal. This writer clearly rejects that position. A state association can be fully covenantal if it is internally constituted on the right principles, that is, if it is compounded of free citizens and is linked with other state associations in a federal manner.

Index